WITHDRAWN & Baja

4th Edition

by Valerie Hamilton

WILEY

John Wiley & Sons, Inc.

Since her first venture into La Baja more than twenty years ago—two late-night hours in Tijuana, with predictable consequences—**Valerie Hamilton** has refined her travel tastes considerably. Down the peninsula and through the years, she's traded tequila shots for chocolata clams and that wet t-shirt for a full wetsuit, but she still hasn't found anything that beats a great fish taco. A news journalist and author of 17 travel guides to Mexico, the US, and Italy, she lives in Mexico City.

Published by:
JOHN WILEY & SONS, INC.
111 River St.
Hoboken, NJ 07030-5774

ISBN 978-1-118-08604-9 (paper); ISBN 978-1-118-16275-0 (ebk); ISBN 978-1-118-16274-3 (ebk); ISBN 978-1-118-16273-6 (ebk)

Editor: Melinda Quintero with Jamie Ehrlich
Production Editor: Katie Robinson
Cartographer: Andrew Dolan
Photo Editor: Richard Fox
Production by Wiley Indianapolis Composition Services
Front Cover Photo: An aerial view of the rocks and the sea, Cabo San Lucas ©Image Source / Getty Images.
Back Cover Photo: Cyclist riding on a dirt road in Sierra de la Laguna, Baja California Sur ©Marcos Ferro / Aurora / Getty Images.

For information on our other products and services or to obtain technical support, please contact our Customer Care Department within the U.S. at 877/762-2974, outside the U.S. at 317/572-3993 or fax 317/572-4002.

Wiley also publishes its books in a variety of electronic formats. Some content that appears in print may not be available in electronic formats.

CONTENTS

8 PLANNING YOUR TRIP TO LOS CABOS & BAJA 179

9 SURVIVAL SPANISH 199

Index 208

LIST OF MAPS

HOW TO CONTACT US

In researching this book, we discovered many wonderful places—hotels, restaurants, shops, and more. We're sure you'll find others. Please tell us about them, so we can share the information with your fellow travelers in upcoming editions. If you were disappointed with a recommendation, we'd love to know that, too. Please write to:

Frommer's Los Cabos & Baja, 4th Edition
John Wiley & Sons, Inc. • 111 River St. • Hoboken, NJ 07030-5774
frommersfeedback@wiley.com

ADVISORY & DISCLAIMER

Travel information can change quickly and unexpectedly, and we strongly advise you to confirm important details locally before traveling, including information on visas, health and safety, traffic and transport, accommodations, shopping, and eating out. We also encourage you to stay alert while traveling and to remain aware of your surroundings. Avoid civil disturbances, and keep a close eye on cameras, purses, wallets, and other valuables.

While we have endeavored to ensure that the information contained within this guide is accurate and up-to-date at the time of publication, we make no representations or warranties with respect to the accuracy or completeness of the contents of this work and specifically disclaim all warranties, including without limitation warranties of fitness for a particular purpose. We accept no responsibility or liability for any inaccuracy or errors or omissions, or for any inconvenience, loss, damage, costs, or expenses of any nature whatsoever incurred or suffered by anyone as a result of any advice or information contained in this guide.

The inclusion of a company, organization, or website in this guide as a service provider and/or potential source of further information does not mean that we endorse them or the information they provide. Be aware that information provided through some websites may be unreliable and can change without notice. Neither the publisher nor author shall be liable for any damages arising herefrom.

FROMMER'S STAR RATINGS, ICONS & ABBREVIATIONS

Every hotel, restaurant, and attraction listing in this guide has been ranked for quality, value, service, amenities, and special features using a **star-rating system.** In country, state, and regional guides, we also rate towns and regions to help you narrow down your choices and budget your time accordingly. Hotels and restaurants are rated on a scale of zero (recommended) to three stars (exceptional). Attractions, shopping, nightlife, towns, and regions are rated according to the following scale: zero stars (recommended), one star (highly recommended), two stars (very highly recommended), and three stars (must-see).

In addition to the star-rating system, we also use **eight feature icons** that point you to the great deals, in-the-know advice, and unique experiences that separate travelers from tourists. Throughout the book, look for:

special finds—those places only insiders know about

fun facts—details that make travelers more informed and their trips more fun

kids—best bets for kids and advice for the whole family

special moments—those experiences that memories are made of

overrated—places or experiences not worth your time or money

insider tips—great ways to save time and money

great values—where to get the best deals

warning—traveler's advisories are usually in effect

The following abbreviations are used for credit cards:

| AE | American Express | DISC | Discover | V | Visa |
| DC | Diners Club | MC | MasterCard | | |

TRAVEL RESOURCES AT FROMMERS.COM

Frommer's travel resources don't end with this guide. Frommer's website, www.frommers.com, has travel information on more than 4,000 destinations. We update features regularly, giving you access to the most current trip-planning information and the best airfare, lodging, and car-rental bargains. You can also listen to podcasts, connect with other Frommers.com members through our active-reader forums, share your travel photos, read blogs from guidebook editors and fellow travelers, and much more.

THE BEST OF LOS CABOS & BAJA

Seen from the air, Baja California is a remote and forbidding place. Hulking mountains jut spiky peaks high into the sky, casting shadows on canyons tinted blue-green with copper and pink with iron ore. Dry arroyos are scrubbed with cacti and untouched by all but the very barest of roads. The landscape pushes up through the sea like a knife, and you know the tiny whitecaps you see from the air are, close up, crashing surf. You could be at the edge of the earth—the tip of the peninsula is called Land's End for a reason. The landscape seems alien, unknowable.

But as you draw closer, details of life begin to take shape. A dirt road traces a vertiginous cliff, fishing boats cut wake through blue water, glittering lights come up as the sky goes red in an eternity of spectacular sunsets. Forests of palm cast shadows over an oasis, seabirds circle and dive, and suddenly the wilderness gives way to a mission, a town, a city, a name. This wild and foreign place is, face-to-face, full of life—a life that despite all of Mexico's challenges, goes on.

Baja California is Mexico's most paradoxical region, a twisting peninsula of superlatives like driest, highest, richest, least-populated, and most-visited that defy one easy definition. It's Mexico, of course, but it's also the original California. It's a desert, with forests and oases; it's 4,828km (3,000 miles) of coast that is actually mostly high mountains. It's a million-tourist magnet that's mostly unpopulated, and it's a celebrated highway that leads, finally, to Land's End. It's the energy of all these contradictions that fuels Baja's distinctive culture and brings outsiders back, year after year.

To really know this place can take several lifetimes, and plenty of dedicated travelers and foreign residents have devoted theirs to just that. But its delights are so many and so diverse that to fall in love with *la Baja* is a matter of moments—the moments when your feet hit the sand through clear, turquoise water; when you're toasting the valley and the sunset with a glass of Baja chardonnay; when you first look a gray whale straight in the eye. Of all Baja's pleasures, the greatest is discovery.

To discover your own Baja moments, read on.

THE most UNFORGETTABLE TRAVEL EXPERIENCES

- **Feria de San José:** Those nostalgic for the traveling carnivals of old will find just the sensory overload they've been missing in the litigious U.S. For a full week at the end of March, the carnival comes to downtown San José del Cabo in celebration of San José Day. With it come endless booths of spicy food and full-service bars, rickety rides, housewares hawkers, shooting and dart games you're never supposed to win, live *banda* music, a Palenque tent with organized cockfights, and even a house of mirrors. See p. 30.

- **Carnaval in La Paz:** Baja's best Carnaval (or Mardi Gras) party is in La Paz, where round-the-clock revelries take place just prior to Lent. The oceanfront *malecón* is the site of most of the festivities as this generally tranquil town swings into party mode. See p. 30.

- **Arts Festival in Todos Santos:** Although Todos Santos has a creative, artistic ambience at any time of year, it reaches a peak each February during the annual Arts Festival. Held since the early 1990s, the festival continues to grow in popularity and content. See p. 105.

- **Surfing in Cerritos:** It's always summer at Baja's favorite surfing beach. This crescent of sand has a special vibe, and whether you're riding the waves or sipping a beer and watching the surfers against the sunset, you'll feel it. See p. 110.

- **Cave Paintings of Central Baja:** Primitive rock paintings on the walls of caves in Central Baja are the only examples of this type of art on the North American continent. Their origin remains a mystery, and researchers say they could date back as far as 10,000 years, created during the Prehistoric Age. The colorful, mystical murals are impressive regardless of who created them and when. And the journey to reach them is an adventure in itself. See "Baja's Cave Paintings: A Window in Time" on p. 135.

- **Whale-Watching in Magdalena Bay:** Few sights are as awe-inspiring as watching whales in their natural habitat, and few places in the world can offer as complete an experience as Mexico's Baja peninsula, especially in Magdalena Bay in the El Vizcaíno Biosphere Reserve. The various protected bays and lagoons in this area on the Pacific coast are the preferred winter waters for migrating gray whales as they journey south to mate and give birth to their calves. See chapter 6.

- **Bullfights in Tijuana:** No matter what your opinion of bullfighting may be, the pastime is an undeniable part of the sporting culture of Mexico, drawing from its Spanish heritage. Considered among the best venues for watching this sport in North America, Tijuana's Plaza de Toros features top matadors in their contests against bulls. See p. 153.

- **Harvest Festival in the Valle de Guadalupe:** Mexico's wine country comes alive in true fiesta style each year, from late August to early September, during this annual wine festival. The celebrations combine wine tastings with parties, concerts, blessings of the grapes, and other events. See p. 174.

Palm Springs
Oceanside
CALIFORNIA
Salton Sea
Colorado
PHOENIX
Mesa
Gila R.
SAN DIEGO
TIJUANA
Tecate
Mexicali
Yuma
ARIZONA
Rosarito
San Luis
Río Colorado
Ensenada
N.P. Constitución
de 1857
Gran Desierto
de Altar
TUCSON
Sierra de Juárez
N.P. Sierra de
San Pedro Mártir
San Felipe
Puerto
Peñasco
S.O.N.O.R.A.N DESERT
U.S.A.
MEXICO
Heroica
Nogales
Agua
Prieta
C. San Quintín
S. San Pedro Mártir
Caborca
BAJA
CALIFORNIA
Gulf
I. Ángel de
la Guarda
SONORA
Hermosillo
I. Tiburón
I. Cedros
Bahía de
Sebastián
Vizcaíno
Guerrero
Negro
California
Pta. Eugenia
L. Ojo
de Liebre
Sierra de la Giganta
Guaymas
Ciudad
Obregón
Santa Rosalía
Mulegé
Navojoa
BAJA
CALIFORNIA
SUR
Loreto
I. Carmen
PACIFIC
Ciudad Constitución
C. San Lázaro
I. San José
Bahía de La Paz
I. Espíritu Santo
OCEAN
I. Sta. Margarita
La Paz
I. Cerralvo
S. de la Laguna
Todos Santos
Cabo San Lucas
San
José del
Cabo

0   100 mi
0   100 km

THE best BEACH VACATIONS

- **Los Cabos Corridor:** Dramatic rock formations and crashing waves mix with wide stretches of soft sand and rolling surf breaks here. Some of Mexico's most luxurious resorts, verdant golf greens, and crowd-free surf breaks are along this coastal stretch. Start at Playa Palmilla in San José del Cabo and work your way down to the famed Playa del Amor at Land's End in Cabo San Lucas. Some beaches here are more suitable for contemplation than for swimming, which isn't all bad. See chapter 4.

- **La Paz:** Some of Baja's best Caribbean–blue beaches are just a short drive from this sleepy, pleasant provincial city, the capital of Baja California Sur. Soak up the day-time sun and the nighttime atmosphere: Stylish restaurants, jazz bars, and a bustling bayside promenade are all great places to show off your tan. See chapter 5.

- **Cerritos Beach:** Surfing, swimming, Pacific sunsets, and killer pizza—Cerritos has it all, wrapped up in one California–perfect crescent of sand. Watch professionals trick-ride one of Mexico's favorite waves, or rent a board and catch it yourself. When things get too hot, the swimming beach will cool you off, as will a beer at Cerritos's central-casting surfside bar. See p. 109.

- **Loreto:** Once the center of the Jesuit mission movement in Baja, Loreto is both a town of historical interest as well as a naturalist's dream. Offshore islands provide abundant opportunities for kayaking, snorkeling, diving, and exploring, and the beaches to the south of town are downright dreamy. If you tire of the big blue, plenty of inland explorations are nearby as well. See chapter 6.

- **Rosarito to Ensenada:** Northern Baja's beach towns may be primarily known for attracting a rowdy party crowd on weekends, but regardless of whether you're here for the revelry, you'll also find this stretch of coast ideal for great surfing and dramatic diving. See chapter 7.

THE best MUSEUMS

- **Museo de Antropología, La Paz:** If you can't make it to see the actual cave paint-ings of Central Baja, this museum has large, although faded, photographs of them along with a number of exhibits concerning the geology and history of Baja Cali-fornia. See p. 98.

- **Museo de las Misiones, Loreto:** The missionaries who came to Baja in the 17th through 19th centuries did more than work on converting the local populations to Christianity. This museum features a complete collection of historical and anthro-pological exhibits pertaining to the Baja peninsula, and includes the zoological studies and scientific writings of the friars. It also documents the contribution of these missions to the demise of indigenous cultures. See p. 125.

- **Museo Regional de Historía, Mulegé:** It's not so much the museum that fasci-nates us; it's more the fact that it was once a state penitentiary that allowed its inmates to leave during the day—on the condition they return at dusk! Believe it or not, under the prison's honor-system, escape attempts were rare. The museum details the operation of this unique entity and the history of Mulegé. See p. 136.

- **Museo de las Californias, Tijuana:** Located inside the Centro Cultural Tijuana, this permanent collection of artifacts from pre-Hispanic through modern times displays the gamut of Baja California's historical and cultural influences, leaving visitors with a better understanding of this complex society. See p. 152.

○ **Museo Histórico Comunitario:** Northern Baja's wine country was originally settled by Russian immigrants who were granted political asylum by Mexico in the early 1900s. This small museum pays tribute to these pioneers and the wine industry they founded. See p. 174.

THE best OUTDOOR ADVENTURES

○ **Sportfishing in Los Cabos:** You're as likely to reel in the big one here as anywhere in the world, where bringing in a 45-kilogram (100-lb.) marlin is considered routine. The Sea of Cortez has an abundance of fighting fish, and easy access to the Pacific provides opportunities for stellar sportfishing in all seasons. Among your likely catches are sailfish, wahoo, tuna, and the famed marlin, in black, blue, and striped varieties. See chapter 4.

○ **Golf in Los Cabos:** Los Cabos has evolved as one of the world's top golf destinations. It currently has more than a dozen courses open for golfers or in the works. The destination master plan calls for a total of 207 holes of play, challenging golfers at all levels. And Cabo's reliable weather means you can enjoy the championship design, quality, and exquisite desert-and-sea scenery of these courses year-round. See chapter 4.

○ **Surfing the Baja Coastline:** Southern Baja guarantees premium waves and worry-free beach camping year-round, while Northern Baja has the perfect combination of perpetual right-breaking waves and cheap places to stay, not to mention the legendary Killers Break at Todos Santos Island. See chapters 5 and 7.

○ **Swimming with Sea Lions:** The rocky shores of the Sea of Cortez all the way from Cabo to Loreto are home to sea lions, whose playful, curious babies swim over, around, and sometimes right up to swimmers, snorkelers, and divers—it's like being inside an aquarium. See chapter 5.

○ **Freediving & Spearfishing off La Paz:** Gliding beneath the water on a deep breath alone—without a heavy scuba tank or bubbles—is as liberating as it gets. And, if above-surface fishing bores you, a deep breath is the first step to your handpicked catch. Test your spear-gun shot underwater against the sea's pelagic predators. Tour companies offer freediving and spearfishing instruction; and in the reefs surrounding La Paz, you never know what may swim by. See chapter 5.

○ **Kayaking the Islands off Loreto:** The offshore islands and inlets surrounding Loreto are a kayaker's paradise, and numerous outfitters are equipped to take you on day trips or overnight kayak excursions. Especially popular is exploring Isla del Carmen, a mostly inaccessible private island just offshore. See chapter 6.

○ **Exploring the Caves in Central Baja:** The goal of a trip to these caves is to see the mysterious cave paintings that potentially date back to the Prehistoric Age, but the journey to the caves is an adventure in itself. Treks can be moderate to difficult. They'll take you through the canyons, crossing streams, and up challenging climbs. In many protected areas, access is allowed only with an authorized guide. The caves are in the San Francisco de la Sierra and Santa Marta mountains in Central Baja. See chapter 6.

○ **Hiking the National Parks of Northern Baja:** In Northern Baja, several national parks provide ample opportunities for hiking, camping, climbing, and other explorations. The Parque Nacional Constitución de 1857, a 5,000-hectare (12,350-acre) preserve, averages 1,200m (3,936 ft.) in altitude, and, contrary to what you may expect in Mexico, it has a large lake in an alpine setting. If you make it there in the winter, you might even catch some snow. In the Parque Nacional Sierra San Pedro Mártir, you'll find the Picacho del Diablo (Devil's Peak), a mountain with a summit at 3,095m (10,152 ft.) from which you can see both oceans and an immense stretch of land. See chapter 7.

THE best PLACES TO GET AWAY FROM IT ALL

o **Cabo Pulmo, East Cape:** It's only a 37km (60-mile) drive from the Los Cabos airport to Cabo Pulmo, yet if the mounded Sierra de La Laguna peaks weren't a dead giveaway for Baja, you could be in the South Pacific. In the shade of a *palapa*-roofed bungalow fronting the Sea of Cortez, you won't care where you are—you just won't want to leave. The coral reef itself is a sight to behold, but the real attraction is the flourishing sea life in this protected marine park. Extensive hiking/mountain-biking trails loop through the mountains, for those who prefer the peace of the desert. See chapter 5.

o **Rancho Pescadero:** The perfect getaway, this "different kind of dude ranch" nestled against the Pacific dunes in Pescadero is its own universe. Swim, surf, or just walk the miles of deserted beach; when you get back, there's a glass of wine, and no hassles, waiting on the sunset terrace for you. See p. 111.

o **Camping Near Loreto:** The beautiful succession of tranquil coves and beaches bordering Loreto makes for a few great places to set up camp. You can kayak the coast, explore the desert, hike a hill, or just hold court on the sand. See chapter 6.

o **Rancho La Puerta:** This pioneering resort spa opened its doors in 1940, and in the decades since, it has earned a reputation for staying at the cutting edge of health and wellness. It's a relaxing and pristine place to get away from it all, and its holistic mind-body-spirit philosophy ensures that you leave in better shape than when you arrived. See p. 170.

o **Valle de Guadalupe:** Mexico's wine country bears little resemblance to the tourism-oriented wineries of Northern California. Here you'll find plenty of peace and quiet in the midst of acres of vineyards. A couple of small inns welcome visitors who want to stop and smell the grapes—or vintages produced here. And, its eclectic history makes exploring the area a treat. See chapter 7.

THE best SHOPPING

Some tips on bargaining: Although haggling over prices in markets is expected and part of the fun, don't try to browbeat the vendor or bad-mouth the goods. Mexicans are almost pathologically polite, and vendors won't bargain with people they consider disrespectful unless they are desperate to make a sale. In the resort areas of Baja, unless it's an open-air market, the prices in stores are fixed, so bargaining is not an option. (Nevertheless, it never hurts to ask.) For best results, be insistent but friendly.

o **Boutique Finds in San José:** As San José del Cabo becomes increasingly gentrified, so does its shopping experience. In Southern Baja, the best boutiques and shops offering clothing, jewelry, and decorative items for the home are found within the lovely colonial buildings in this tree-lined town. See p. 54.

- **Homemade Candy in San Bartolo:** The unassuming stand at the curve in Hwy. 1, between La Paz and Los Cabos, is home to delectable macaroons made of *cajeta* (caramel made from goat's milk) and rough-hewn coconut thick and fresh from the grove in the valley below. Buy it by the truckload, if you can. Fresh fig jam and *cajeta* caramels are other worthy reasons to stop. See p. 90.

- **Ibarra's Pottery, La Paz:** Not only can you shop for hand-painted tiles, tableware, and decorative pottery here, but you can also watch it being made. Each piece on sale in this popular shop is individually made. See p. 99.

- **Art in Todos Santos:** Whether it's oil on canvas, pottery, or weavings, you'll find very high-quality original works of art in this cultural community. The annual Arts Festival, held every February, brings an even greater selection of works to choose from. See p. 105.

- **Tecolote Books, Todos Santos:** Baja's best English-language bookstore is a tiny storefront on Todos Santos' main drag, but it's a treasure-trove of offbeat fiction, hard-to-find Mexican esoterica, and excellent advice. See p. 105.

- **Pasaje Rodríguez, Tijuana:** This made-over tourist alley is Tijuana's newest arts district, chockablock with funky furniture, antiques, photography, and Tijuana's best outsider art. By shopping here, you're a part of Tijuana's rebirth. See p. 151.

- **Carved Furniture in Rosarito:** Rosarito Beach's Bulevar Benito Juárez has become known for its selection of shops featuring ornately carved wooden furniture. Comparing the offerings has become easy, with so many options in one central location. See p. 158.

THE hottest NIGHTLIFE

Although, as expected, Cabo San Lucas is home to much of Baja's nightlife, that resort city isn't the only place to have a good time after dark. Along the northern Pacific coast, beachside dance floors with live bands and extended happy hours in seaside bars dominate the nightlife. Here are some of our favorite hot spots:

- **Passion, Cabo San Lucas:** The most consistently cool of Cabo's nightclubs, Passion is the hunting grounds of the young and the sexy. Champagne cocktails, low lighting, and Cabo's best DJs keep it spinning as late as you can go. See p. 83.

- **Locals Bars in Loreto:** In Loreto, "nightlife" starts well before sundown. A couple draft beers at Del Borracho, which closes at sunset, will jump-start the afternoon. Then, roll into Augie's Bar & Bait Shop around 4pm, take a seat at the bar, and wait for the rowdy barrage of friendly expats to join you for half-priced drinks till 7pm. Chances are, you'll make a few friends and end up coming back for more the next day. See chapter 6.

- **Calle 6 in Tijuana:** The tourists are gone and the hipsters are back at Tijuana's coolest nightspots, an arty collection of cantinas, clubs, and even a retro diner packed into 5 short blocks. See chapter 7.

- **Beach Bars in Rosarito & Ensenada:** It doesn't have to be spring break in Rosarito or Ensenada to find a similar let-loose party atmosphere here. The favored spot is Papas & Beer, which has a location in both of these beach towns. And both regularly draw a young and spirited crowd for endless-summer–style fun and potential love matches. See chapter 7.

THE most LUXURIOUS HOTELS

o **Las Ventanas al Paraíso** (Los Cabos Corridor; www.lasventanas.com): Super-stylish and ultra-elite, Las Ventanas is a fantasy of whitewashed chic and desert sunsets. Pamper yourself at private pools, on rooftop terraces, and inside one of Baja's best spas. See p. 63.

o **One&Only Palmilla** (Los Cabos Corridor; www.oneandonlypalmilla.com): The most luxurious hotel in Los Cabos is one of the best in Latin America, a magical cliff-side oasis of palm gardens, ocean views, private beach coves, and exquisitely graceful service. See p. 63.

o **Posada de las Flores** (Loreto; www.posadadelasflores.com): The best of old-world style and modern comforts meet in this historic building on Loreto's main square. A rooftop pool, top-notch linens, and detailed service are matched by location, charm, and ambience. See p. 126.

o **Casa Natalie** (Ensenada; www.hotelcasanatalie.com): Quiet and comfort are the marks of this modern boutique resort. Neutral colors contrast the blue of the ocean, cozy nooks await peace seekers, the rooms are some of the best in Baja, and an overall atmosphere of unpretentious luxury ensures a divine experience. See p. 166.

THE best BUDGET INNS

o **Cabo Inn** (Cabo San Lucas; www.caboinnhotel.com): This former bordello is the best budget inn in the area. Rooms are small but extra clean and invitingly deco-rated, amenities are generous, and the owners/managers are friendly and helpful. Ideally located close to town and near the marina, the inn caters to sportfishers. See p. 79.

o **Hotel Mediterrane** (La Paz; www.hotelmed.com): This stylish, economical inn mixes Mediterranean decor with Mexican charm. The location near the *malecón* means you're close to everything, and the on-site Trattoria La Pazta restaurant is one of La Paz's best. See p. 100.

o **La Damiana Inn** (Loreto; www.ladamianainn.com): This charming inn, crafted from a century-old family home, is a cozy, well-appointed hideaway perfect for couples, families, and solo travelers alike. The friendly service can't be topped. See p. 127.

o **Hotel Hacienda Mulegé** (Mulegé; ✆ 615/153-0021): Right in the heart of Mulegé, this former 18th-century hacienda is a comfortable and value-priced place to stay, complete with a small shaded pool and popular bar. See p. 137.

THE best UNIQUE INNS

o **Casa Natalia** (San José del Cabo; www.casanatalia.com): This renovated historic home, now a masterfully crafted inn, is an oasis of palms, waterfalls, and flowers set against the desert landscape. The restaurant is the hottest in town. See p. 55.

o **Bungalows** (Cabo San Lucas; www.cabobungalows.com): Wonderful private suites with terra-cotta tiles, hand-painted sinks, and breezes off the bay make this inn a retreat, a world away from the tourist bustle of Cabo 5 blocks downhill—plus, it's got the best breakfast in town. See p. 78.

- **Hotel California** (Todos Santos; www.hotelcaliforniabaja.com): The Hotel California is the hippest sleep in Todos Santos. Jewel-tone rooms and a profusion of candles and eclectic accents make this a study in creative style. Although you can check out anytime you like, chances are you won't want to after being lured in by the inviting pool area and the popular La Coronela Restaurant and Bar. See p. 106.
- **La Villa del Valle** (Valle de Guadalupe; www.lavilladelvalle.com): Lavender fields flanking the property, a chef-ready garden vibrant with herbs, and this six-room country inn make for an idyllic stay in the heart of Baja's wine region. Come for dinner and stay for the night. See p. 176.

THE best DINING EXPERIENCES

In this section, best doesn't necessarily mean most luxurious. Although some of the restaurants listed here are fancy affairs, others are simple places to get fine, authentic Mexican cuisine.

- **El Chilar** (San José del Cabo; ✆ **624/142-2544**): In a small dining room in a cozy former private home, the low-key ambience is a smokescreen for high-style food with a playful attitude, and one of the peninsula's best selections of tequila to keep the party going. See p. 58.
- **Mi Cocina** (San José del Cabo; www.casanatalia.com/dining.htm): Is it the creative menu, the captivating garden setting, or the hibiscus-infused martinis? Whatever the reason, Mi Cocina, at Casa Natalia, is one of the best dining experiences in Los Cabos. See p. 58.
- **Café Corazón** (La Paz; ✆ **612/128-8985**): This fun, sunny place in a historic downtown courtyard has La Paz's best vibes, and an inventive, well-priced menu that plays on traditional Mexican flavors while feeling completely, and delightfully, new. See p. 101.
- **Café Santa Fe** (Todos Santos; ✆ **612/145-0340**): Excellent northern Italian cuisine prepared in the exhibition kitchen of this gracious cafe has drawn people to Todos Santos over the past decade. Enjoying lunch here in the flower-filled courtyard is a particularly wonderful way to pass an afternoon. See p. 108.
- **Ristorante Tre Galline** (Todos Santos; ✆ **612/145-0274**): The most authentic Northern Italian country cooking anywhere will have you seeing stars. Handmade everything from pasta to bresaola and cheeses imported from Italy are as old-world as it comes. See p. 108.
- **Napoli Pizzeria** (Pescadero): This ordinary-looking roadside taco shack isn't a taco shack at all—it's a wood-oven pizzeria, serving Baja's best crispy, Italian-style pizza. See p. 112.
- **La Picazón** (Loreto; ✆ **613/109-5078**): Between the cacti and the sea at the end of a half-hour of dirt-road driving is this beachside gem, Loreto's favorite place to watch the sun go down over a plate of fresh-caught fish. Bring your boat and make a day of it. See p. 128.

- **Mision 19** (Tijuana; © 664/634-2493): One of the most important and exciting restaurants in Mexico is just a stone's throw from the border, taking advantage of markets and growers from San Diego to the Valle de Guadalupe for its inventive locavore menus and top-notch cocktails. See p. 155.

- **Manzanilla** (Ensenada; © 646/175-7073): Arguably the leader of the Baja Med culinary revolution, bad-boy chef Benito Molina breaks the rules every day. His flagship is one of Mexico's very best, where local meets creative meets out of this world. See p. 168.

- **Laja** (Valle de Guadalupe; www.lajamexico.com): This lovely adobe-and-stone sustainable gourmet restaurant has become a reason in and of itself to visit Mexico's wine country. A daily fixed menu of four to eight courses draws daily crowds, and consistently wins accolades. See p. 177.

LOS CABOS & BAJA IN DEPTH

Baja California is a place of complementary contrasts: hot desert and cool ocean, manicured golf greens and craggy mountains, glistening resorts and frontier land. Baja is part of Mexico—and yet it is not. Attached to the mainland United States and separated from the rest of Mexico by the Sea of Cortez (also called the Gulf of California), the Baja peninsula is longer than Italy, stretching approximately 1,220km (758 miles) from Mexico's northernmost city of Tijuana to Cabo San Lucas at its southern tip. Volcanic uplifting created the craggy desertscape you see today. Whole forests of cardoon cactus, spiky elephant trees, and spindly ocotillo bushes populate the raw, untamed landscape.

Culturally and geographically, Baja is set apart from mainland Mexico, and it remained isolated for many years. As such, it lays claim to a striking and peculiar blend of Mexican and American cultures that can't be found anywhere else in Mexico. However, tourism has left its mark over the length of Baja, especially its southern third, where golf, fishing, diving, and whale-watching abound. For early travelers in the '50s and '60s, great sportfishing was the first draw to Los Cabos, and it remains a lure today, although golf may have overtaken it as the principal attraction. Once accessible only by water, Baja attracted a hearty community of cruisers, fishermen, divers, and adventurers, starting in the late 1940s. By the early 1980s, the Mexican government realized the potential of Los Cabos and invested in new highways, airport facilities, golf courses, and modern marine facilities. Expanded air traffic and the opening of the Carretera Transpeninsular, or Transpeninsular Highway, in 1973 paved the way for the area's spectacular growth.

Most travelers to the area will be drawn to Baja's cobalt-blue waters and desert landscapes, but the place has a deeper attraction too: the vast and mysterious interior of the peninsula and the strength of character it requires to survive and thrive there.

LOS CABOS & BAJA TODAY

The Baja peninsula's physical separation has helped contribute to the sense of cultural separation from the rest of its homeland. Although as in the rest of Mexico, there's a deep sense of national pride, in Baja there is also a close sense of kinship with its neighbor to the north—the U.S. state of California, which, of course, was once part of Mexico itself.

Today, many travelers to Baja say this region feels more like an extension of Southern California than it does Mexico. This is especially true in the Los Cabos area, at the southern tip of Baja (ironically, the farthest point from Southern California on the peninsula), where a large and growing expatriate community of Americans and Canadians has taken up residence. There, English is as common as Spanish, and dollars are interchangeable with pesos. Expats have a lower profile in mid-Baja and the North, which maintain their mostly rural Mexican identity.

But Baja has its own unique cultural identity too. It was and remains a rough and rugged place, and has been, through the years, as much a home to pirates, outlaws, and adventurers as to anyone. To survive here has always been a challenge, and the generations who've faced it look on their accomplishment with a justifiable pride.

While most of the peninsula remains thankfully distant from Mexico's ongoing drug war, Baja has suffered a major drop in tourism, its main source of income, from bad press related to the violence elsewhere in the country. The economic downturn in the U.S. hasn't helped either, as tourists have either turned to cheaper destinations or stayed home altogether. Tijuana and its immediate surroundings are struggling to preserve a tenuous peace, while law enforcement fights to maintain the gains of the last years. And in the rest of the peninsula, small communities are trying to balance the temptations of tourism and real-estate development with preserving the laid-back lifestyle and natural splendor that drew so many people here in the first place.

But signs indicate they're on the right track. The violence at the Mexico–U.S. border has never spread into Baja, and even Tijuana is a safer place to live than it was just a few years ago. While tourism at the border remains down 18% in the last four years, visits to the rest of Baja are up. Hotels that slashed prices in the last lean years are seeing the rewards, and at least some of the newest development projects show a sensitivity to environment and place that, if not a victory for preservationists, can be seen as a truce.

Baja's Culture & People

Because Baja's geography created a natural barrier to growth for so many years, many of Baja's inhabitants are transplants from the north or from other parts of Mexico, most a mix of foreign and indigenous ancestry. In addition to the European settlers, who included sea-weary sailors and English pirates who jumped ship, the early pioneers of Baja included Chinese immigrants brought here to work, a colony of Russian refugees granted political asylum who came to the Valle de Guadalupe, and French miners who settled in Santa Rosalía. Their descendants have greatly contributed to the come-one-come-all spirit of Baja.

However, there remains a sense of separatism to this culture, and as such, you may not find the bursting cultural pride of other parts of Mexico. What you will often encounter, though, is an eagerness by locals to share the natural treasures of Baja— the unique desert flora, the rich underwater life, or even basic survival skills in this challenging terrain. Most of Baja's long-term residents are deeply respectful of the surrounding nature and, especially in the middle and southern reaches, grateful for its bountiful seafood, available work, and sunny weather.

Religion, Myth & Folklore

Today's Mexico is predominantly Roman Catholic, a religion introduced by the Spaniards during the Conquest. But it's not necessarily the religion the Spaniards brought with them. Throughout Mexico, the Catholic faith has been entwined and influenced

There is nothing more doleful than a lit-tle cantina. In the first place it is inhab-ited by people who haven't any money to buy a drink. They stand about waiting for a miracle that never happens: the angel with golden wings who settles on the bar and orders drinks for everyone. This never happens, but how are the sad handsome young men to know it never will happen? And suppose it did happen and they were somewhere else? And so they lean against the wall; and when the sun is high they sit down against the wall. Now and then they go away into the brush for a while, and they go to their little homes for meals. But that is an impatient time, for the golden angel might arrive. Their faith is not strong, but it is permanent.

—John Steinbeck's take on Cabo San Lucas in *The Log from the Sea of Cortez* (1951)

by Mexico's pre-Hispanic belief systems, creating a hybrid religion whose tenets owe as much to the conquered ancestors as to the *conquistadores*. Modern scholars have less information about Baja's original inhabitants than they do about populations in mainland Mexico, and their original belief systems remain as yet unstudied.

We do know that many of Baja's people today have their own regional versions of popular Mexican myths. For example, the Baja version of the tale of **La Llorona (The Weeping Woman)** tells of a young woman who loves to party so much that she throws her demanding children in a river so she can enjoy her fiestas. When she finally reaches the afterlife, she's sentenced to an eternity of wandering riverbeds in search of her children and weeping for all to hear.

Although the Catholic Church has no well-established saints in Baja California, residents do look to their own unofficial folk saint **Juan Soldado** for help and guid-ance. Juan Castillo Morales was a peasant farmer from Oaxaca who moved north to be a soldier in the Mexican army and was later put to death for the rape and murder of a young girl in 1938. His followers—many of them undocumented migrants—believe he was falsely accused and now look to him for help and guidance before crossing the border. The Catholic Church does not recognize the young soldier saint, but that doesn't stop believers from paying their respects. Thousands visit his grave in Tijuana's Panteón Número Uno cemetery to recite the phrase *"Juan Soldado, ayú-dame a cruzar"* ("Soldier John, help me across.").

LOOKING BACK AT LOS CABOS & BAJA
Pre-Hispanic Baja (12,000 B.C.–16th C.)

The earliest Mexicans were Stone Age hunter-gatherers from the north, descendants of a race that had probably crossed the Bering Strait and reached North America around 12,000 B.C. They arrived in what is now Mexico by 10,000 B.C. It is likely that Baja was inhabited by human populations well before mainland Mexico, as Baja was the logical termination point for the coastal migration route followed by Asian groups crossing the Bering Strait. The **San Dieguito** culture migrated south into Baja some-where between 7000 and 5000 B.C. Sometime between 5200 and 1500 B.C., in what

Mexico

UNITED STATES

Tijuana
Mexicali
Ensenada
BAJA
CALIFORNIA
NORTE
Puerto
Penasco
San
Quintin
Nogales
Ciudad
Juárez
SONORA
Hermosillo
CHIHUAHUA
Chihuahua
Ojinaga
Isla
Cedros
Guerrero
Negro
Guaymas
Ciudad
Obregón
Cuauhtémoc
COAHUILA
Santa
Rosalía
Delicias
Jiménez
Monclova
Mulegé
Hidalgo
del Parral
BAJA
CALIFORNIA
SUR
Loreto
Los
Mochis
SINALOA
Torreón
Saltillo
La Paz
Culiacán
DURANGO
Todos Santos
San José
del Cabo
Mazatlán
Durango
Fresnillo
Cabo San Lucas
ZACATECAS
Zacatecas
San
Luis
Potosí
Tuxpan
AGUASCALIENTES
San Blas
Tepic
Aguascalientes
Islas
Marias
NAYARIT
León
Puerto Vallarta
Guadalajara
Guanajuato
GUANA-
JUATO
JALISCO
Lake Chapala
Morelia
Barra de Navidad
Uruapan
Pátzcuaro
Manzanillo
Colima
MICHOACAN
COLIMA
Lázaro
Cárdenas
Zihuatanejo
& Ixtapa

Gulf of California

*PACIFIC
OCEAN*

0   150 mi

0   150 km

UNITED STATES

Piedras Negras

Nuevo Laredo

85
D

Monterrey

Matamoros

NUEVO
LEÓN

180

85

Gulf of Mexico

TAMAULIPAS

Ciudad Victoria

Ciudad Mante

Tampico

Río Lagartos

Isla Mujeres

SAN LUIS
POTOSÍ

Progreso

Valladolid

Cancún

San Miguel
de Allende

Celestún

Tuxpan

Mérida

180
D

Playa del
Carmen

Cozumel

QUERÉTARO

Poza Rica

YUCATÁN

HIDALGO

Papantla

Querétaro

Pachuca

180

Campeche

180

QUINTANA
ROO

*Punta
Allen*

Mexico City

Xalapa

*Bay of
Campeche*

CAMPECHE

Bacalar

Toluca

TLAXCALA

Tlaxcala

Veracruz

261

*Majahual
Peninsula*

Cuernavaca

186

Chetumal

MORELOS

PUEBLA

Orizaba

Catemaco

TABASCO

Escárcega

Taxco

95

Tehuacán

VERACRUZ

Villahermosa

186

BELIZE

*Caribbean
Sea*

GUERRERO

190
D

175

Coatzacoalcos

Palenque

Oaxaca

186

Tuxtla
Gutiérrez

San Cristóbal
de las Casas

Acapulco

200

OAXACA

CHIAPAS

Comitán

GUATEMALA

Puerto Escondido

Salina
Cruz

Puerto
Ángel

Huatulco

200

HONDURAS

*Gulf of
Tehuantepec*

Tapachula

EL
SALVADOR

CORTEZ, MOCTEZUMA & THE spanish conquest

In 1517, the first Spaniards arrived in what is today known as Mexico and skirmished with Maya Indians off the Caribbean coast of the Yucatán peninsula. A shipwreck left several Spaniards stranded as prisoners of the Maya. Another Spanish expedition, under **Hernán Cortez,** landed on Cozumel in February 1519. The coastal Maya were happy to tell Cortez about the gold and riches of the Aztec empire in central Mexico. Disobeying all orders from his superior, the governor of Cuba, Cortez promptly sailed into the Gulf of Mexico and landed at what is now Veracruz.

Cortez arrived when the Aztec empire was at the height of its wealth and power. **Moctezuma II** ruled over the central and southern highlands and extracted tribute from lowland peoples. His greatest temples were plated with gold and encrusted with the blood of sacrificial captives. A fool, a mystic, and something of a coward, Moctezuma dithered in Tenochtitlán, sending messengers with gifts and suggestions that Cortez leave. Meanwhile, Cortez blustered and negotiated his way into the highlands, cloaking his intentions. Moctezuma, terrified by the Spaniard's military tactics and technology, was convinced that Cortez was the god Quetzalcóatl making his long-awaited return. By the time he arrived in the Aztec capital, Cortez had accumulated 6,000 indigenous allies who resented

paying tribute to the Aztec. In November 1519, he took Moctezuma hostage in an effort to leverage control of the empire.

In the middle of Cortez's manipulations, another Spanish expedition arrived with orders to end Cortez's unauthorized mission. Cortez hastened back to the coast, routed the rival force, and persuaded the vanquished to join him on his return to Tenochtitlán. The capital had erupted in his absence, and the Aztec chased his garrison out of the city. Moctezuma was killed during the attack—whether by the Aztec or the Spaniards is not clear. For a year and a half, Cortez laid siege to Tenochtitlán, aided by rival Indians and a devastating smallpox epidemic. When the Aztec capital fell, all of central Mexico lay at the conquerors' feet, vastly expanding the Spanish empire. The king legitimized Cortez's victorious pirate expedition after the fact and ordered the forced conversion to Christianity of the new colony, to be called New Spain. By 1540, New Spain included possessions from Vancouver to Panama. In the centuries that followed, Franciscan and Augustinian friars converted millions of Indians to Christianity, and Spanish lords built huge feudal estates with Indian farmers serving as serfs. Cortez's booty of silver and gold made Spain the wealthiest country in Europe.

is known as the **Archaic period,** they began practicing agriculture and domesticating animals.

Between 1500 B.C. and A.D. 300, the San Dieguito culture either developed into, or was superseded by, the **Yumano** culture, believed to be the creators of the rock paintings and petroglyphs found on the central interior of the peninsula. The Yumanos made use of more sophisticated hunting equipment as well as fishing nets, and also created ceramics. Paintings also indicate a fundamental knowledge of astronomy and depict solstice celebrations. Descendants of this culture were the natives found living here by the Spanish in the 16th century.

The three most populous indigenous groups at the time of the arrival of the Spaniards were the Cochimi and Guaycura of the north and central regions, and the Pericú who dominated the south. All three groups were nomadic hunter-gatherers without permanent means of shelter.

The **Cochimi** were centered near modern-day San Javier and El Rosario and were hunter-gatherers. They spoke a language that is similar to that of the modern Yuman indigenous peoples who still live in parts of California and Arizona. Among their notable practices was *maroma,* in which a piece of meat was tied to a string and systematically consumed and regurgitated by several people until there was nothing left.

The **Guaycura** populated the region around Loreto and Todos Santos and are credited with being the first to create Damiana, a liqueur made from a shrub native to Baja. It's still produced and sold as an aphrodisiac today (it's said to be the secret ingredient in Sammy Hagar's Waborita), although the Guaycura used it only for ceremonial purposes. Modern archaeologists have found milling stones and arrowheads in their burial caves. Their shamans or spiritual leaders usually had a small amount of facial hair and carried wands or spirit sticks.

In the south, the **Pericú** utilized wooden rafts and paddles and had complicated fishing techniques. Their loose political system, based on age, often had female leaders. They practiced both monogamy and polygamy, the latter of which caused a revolt when the Jesuit priests tried to prohibit it. Although the Pericú and Guaycura were neighbors, they didn't appear to speak the same language—literally or figuratively; skirmishes over land control were frequent.

Several smaller indigenous groups existed in the region including the **Monqui,** who may have been the first to greet Spanish explorers near La Paz, and the **Kiliwa, Pai Pai Cocopa,** and **Kumayaay,** who were all centered near modern day Tijuana and Tecate.

Spanish Exploration (16th C.)

In 1532, nearly a decade after he defeated the Aztecs in Mexico's capital, Spanish conquistador **Hernán Cortez** was looking for a new angle. Among the bounty of the defeated Aztec leader Moctezuma were many precious pearls; when Cortez asked of their origins he was told they came "from an island in the west." That fit irresistibly with a legend from the times of Marco Polo about a magical land called Calafia where beautiful women and abundant jewels were available for the taking. Putting two and two together, Cortez sent his cousin, Diego Hurtado de Mendoza, to investigate. Mendoza and his men sailed up from present day Nayarit, but never spotted land.

Cortez persisted and sent another two ships the next year. The first ship, under the charge of Hernán Grijalva, turned back after discovering the Revillagigedo Islands, uninhabited by beautiful women or pearls. The second ship, led by Diego Bercera de Mendoza, fell to mutiny. Bercera and several crew members were killed, and Fortun Ximenez led the survivors to the shore in present day La Paz, where many likely perished in clashes with the indigenous population. The survivors returned to mainland Mexico with tales of black pearls that convinced Cortez he was on the right track.

Cortez led the next mission himself in 1535. He was 50 years old, had two useless fingers on his left hand, a fractured arm from falling off a horse, and a bad leg from falling off a wall in Cuba. But, with a crew of 300 men and 20 women, he made his

The Dividing Line

So what makes Baja California different from Baja California Sur? Other than a slight difference in the size of the shrimp, the two states were originally divided by religious affiliation. During the mission period, the austere Dominicans ran the missions in the North, while the education-focused Jesuits dominated in the south.

way to Santa Cruz, later the modern city of La Paz. And although he never discovered the land of available women, he left his legacy here in the name California: either a corruption of the yearned-for magical land of Calafia, or of the Latin "Cala Fornix," or "cove arch"—for a rock formation he particularly liked. (It's not as sexy as naming it after an island of Amazon women, but the name is closer.)

Although Cortez made at least one trip to mainland Mexico for grain, pigs, and sheep, the small settlement eventually ran out of supplies and had to be abandoned.

Cortez sent out one final expedition in 1539 under the direction of Capt. Francisco de Ulloa, who explored the entire perimeter of the Sea of Cortez, establishing that Baja was not an island, but a peninsula.

The Mission Period (17th–18th C.)

Among the subsequent expeditions sent by the Spanish crown, many included Catholic priests seeking to establish missions for converting the native cultures to Christianity. Padre Juan Maria Salvatierra was the first to succeed in establishing a permanent settlement on the Baja peninsula, when he founded the mission Nuestra Señora de Loreto in 1697, at the site of present-day Loreto. This began the Jesuit Mission period in Baja, which lasted until 1767. In this time, Italian and Spanish priests established 20 missions, covering an area from the southern tip of the peninsula into Central Baja near present-day Cataviña. The mission system worked by offering protection to the natives by the Church and the Spanish crown, in exchange for submitting to religious instruction. That's "protection" in the Mafia sense of protection from the people who were offering them protection: If they resisted, they were generally punished or massacred. If they played along, they were given religious instruction, European–style trade and farm training, and refuge in the mission, which they helped to build.

Unlike their counterparts on the mainland, none of the Jesuit priests operating in Baja ever produced a text recording the indigenous languages. During the mission years, the local populations were decimated by a combination of repeated epidemics of smallpox, syphilis, and measles, as well as lives lost in rebellions, leaving Baja primarily to the new European settlers. The Jesuit missions were followed by missions established by the Franciscans and Dominicans, leading to a more diverse population of European cultures. By the end of the 18th century, the native population in Baja numbered fewer than 5,000.

Highway to Opportunity (20th C.)

The Baja peninsula was for years one of Mexico's least populated regions. With the exception of the stretch of coast between Tijuana and Ensenada, whose lenient liquor laws began attracting spirited travelers from the U.S. during Prohibition, only a few

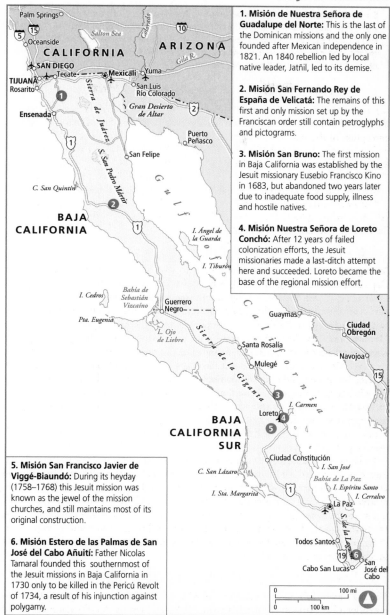

1. Misión de Nuestra Señora de Guadalupe del Norte: This is the last of the Dominican missions and the only one founded after Mexican independence in 1821. An 1840 rebellion led by local native leader, Jatñil, led to its demise.

2. Misión San Fernando Rey de España de Velicatá: The remains of this first and only mission set up by the Franciscan order still contain petroglyphs and pictograms.

3. Misión San Bruno: The first mission in Baja California was established by the Jesuit missionary Eusebio Francisco Kino in 1683, but abandoned two years later due to inadequate food supply, illness and hostile natives.

4. Misión Nuestra Señora de Loreto Conchó: After 12 years of failed colonization efforts, the Jesuit missionaries made a last-ditch attempt here and succeeded. Loreto became the base of the regional mission effort.

5. Misión San Francisco Javier de Viggé-Biaundó: During its heyday (1758–1768) this Jesuit mission was known as the jewel of the mission churches, and still maintains most of its original construction.

6. Misión Estero de las Palmas de San José del Cabo Añuití: Father Nicolas Tamaral founded this southernmost of the Jesuit missions in Baja California in 1730 only to be killed in the Pericú Revolt of 1734, a result of his injunction against polygamy.

hardy souls resided in the central and southern parts of the peninsula working as ranchers or fishermen.

It wasn't until the Carretera Transpeninsular (Hwy. 1) was completed in 1973, connecting Tijuana with Cabo San Lucas, that the peninsula opened up to settlers and travelers. Before the highway, it took 10 days to travel the rugged dirt roads between Tijuana and La Paz (today—at a speed of 80kmph/50 mph, it would take 23 hr.). The population in the southern region exploded, and the area has flourished ever since.

In the last few years, the Mexican tourism crisis, brought on by a triple whammy of the world economic downturn, H1N1 flu, and the Mexican drug war, has prompted some Baja soul-searching. Baja is proudly Mexican, but its own tourism doldrums are a case of guilt by association—the H1N1 flu scare and the drug war have barely touched the peninsula, but tourists are staying away nonetheless. There's talk in tourism circles of rebranding Baja, Mexico, as simply Baja, a stand-alone destination apart from Mexico, but it would be a controversial and, many feel, unpatriotic move. Meanwhile, the real-estate boom that mushroomed here as everywhere else has gone bust too, and with it some of the boom-town attitudes that old-timers lamented were turning the whole peninsula into a Cabo-in-waiting. But if Baja's past is any indication of the future, any major changes will be a long time in coming.

ART & ARCHITECTURE

Pre-Hispanic Forms: Cave Paintings

Pre-Hispanic cultures left a wealth of fantastic painted **murals and cave paintings,** many of which are remarkably well preserved, in the central mountain region concentrated in the San Francisco de la Sierra mountains. Cave drawings in Bahía de los Angeles, San Ignacio, Mulegé, and San Francisco de la Sierra show humans and larger-than-life animals like deer, fish and manta rays, rendered with natural stone and clay pigments. One modern theory suggests that the paintings are an attempt to magically improve hunting conditions; there is also evidence that painters of at least one site, El Vallecito, near Tecate in Northern Baja, used knowledge of astronomy: a human figure is lit up for just a few moments every year on the winter solstice.

Spanish Influence: Missions

Almost every major town in the Baja peninsula has the remains of a **mission** nearby. Many were built in the late 17th century following the arrival of Jesuit friars. Prime examples include the **Misión Nuestra Señora de Loreto,** the first mission in the Californias, started in 1699. The catechization of California by Jesuit missionaries was based here and lasted through the 18th century. **Misión San Francisco Javier** is one of the best-preserved, most spectacularly set missions in Baja—high in a mountain valley beneath volcanic walls. Founded in 1699 by the Jesuit priest Francisco María Píccolo, it was the second mission established in California, completed in 1758. Its walls were constructed with rock from a nearby quarry and its gilded altarpieces were brought in on mules all the way from Tepoztlán, south of Mexico City. It's about 2 hours from Loreto, on a section of the old Camino Real used by Spanish missionaries and explorers. The original building of the **Misión Santa Rosalía de Mulegé,** founded in 1706 by Father Juan de Ugarte and Juan María Basaldúa, was completed in 1766. A fire a few years later destroyed nearly all the

Originally from Guadalajara, **Einar and Jamex De La Torre** (www.delatorrebros.com) have been creating bi-cultural and border-inspired glass work in Ensenada and San Diego since the 1990s. Their larger-than-life pieces are bursting with imagery from both sides of the *frontera:* bleeding hearts, flaming Virgins, skeleton revolutionaries, and frog mariachis matched with Elvis heads and Budweiser bottles. In addition to showing in galleries around the world, their work has been incorporated into the private collections of Cheech Marin, Elton John, and Sandra Cisneros. If you can't find an exhibition while you're in Baja, their website is a trip in itself, straight into the broken heart of border art.

common buildings, and the mission was rebuilt on the site it occupies today, on a bluff overlooking the river.

Arte Moderno

It's easy to miss amid the scary headlines, but **Tijuana** is home to one of Mexico's most vital and important art scenes, charged by the volatile cultural mix of the border. Its graffiti artists splash the city with edgy, accomplished murals; its film and art collectives tweak convention and play with political fire, and its musicians are responsible for hot new styles with fans on both sides of the border. In 2002, *Newsweek* crowned Tijuana one of the world's "top new cultural meccas"; escalating violence since then has only inspired artists more.

The quiet, sunny streets of **San José del Cabo's Art District** are home to at least a dozen galleries and a Thursday evening Art Walk, and nearby **Todos Santos** has matured into a worthy art destination as well. While far from the cutting edge, inventive and colorful painting and sculpture by local artists as well as occasional shows by internationally known talent draw an increasingly sophisticated audience to these two southern towns.

LOS CABOS & BAJA IN POPULAR CULTURE

Since Steinbeck made his first road trip to Baja in 1941, this magical place has inspired artists, writers, and dreamers to record their experiences and create their own visions. Brushing up on your Baja means understanding Mexico and California, too; today's Baja owes its identity to both and the contrasts between them.

Books

For a survey of Mexican history through modern times, *A Short History of Mexico* by **J. Patrick McHenry** provides a complete, yet concise account. For contemporary culture, start with **Octavio Paz**'s classic, *The Labyrinth of Solitude,* which still generates controversy among Mexicans for its warts-and-all profile of the national soul. **Earl Shorris**'s *The Life and Times of Mexico* is a critically acclaimed history of Mexico seen through the lens of traditional Aztec beliefs.

Jorge Ibargüengoitia, one of Mexico's most famous modern writers, died in 1983 but remains popular in Mexico and is available in translation. His novels *Estas Ruinas Que Ves (These Ruins You See)* and *The Dead Girls* (a fictional account of a famous 1970s crime) display deft characterization and a sardonic view of Mexican life.

Juan Rulfo, one of Mexico's most esteemed authors, wrote only three slim books before his death in 1986. His second, *Pedro Páramo,* is Mexico's equivalent of Shakespearean tragedy and has never been out of print since its publication in 1955. The short novel of a son's search for his abusive, tyrannical father is told in competing first- and third-person narration and had a major influence on the magical realism movement. It has been translated twice into English and been made into film several times.

The earlier novels of **Carlos Fuentes,** Mexico's preeminent living writer, are easier to read than more recent works; try *The Death of Artemio Cruz.* **Angeles Mastretta**'s delightful *Arráncame la Vida (Tear Up My Life)* is a well-written novel about a young woman's life in post-revolutionary Puebla. **Laura Esquivel**'s *Like Water for Chocolate* (and the subsequent movie) covers roughly the same period through a lens of magical realism and helped to popularize Mexican food abroad.

Hasta No Verte Jesús Mío by **Elena Poniatowska,** and anything by Pulitzer winner **Luis Alberto Urrea,** offer hard looks at third-world realities.

Guillermo Arriaga, screenwriter for *Amores Perros,* is a brilliant novelist, too. *El Bufalo de la Noche,* about a young man reeling from his best friend's suicide, is available in English. *Retorno 201,* a collection of stories set on the Mexico City street where Arriaga grew up, was published in 2005.

In 1941, **John Steinbeck** joined his marine biologist friend, Ed "Doc" Ricketts, on a journey along the Sea of Cortez. The result was Steinbeck's book, *The Log from the Sea of Cortez;* while technical in spots, this is a must-read for those impassioned by Baja's sea. Ricketts went on to become a minor celebrity after Steinbeck used him as the model for "Doc," a character in his popular novel, *Cannery Row.* Another one of Steinbeck's classic novels, *The Pearl,* tells the story of Kino, a pearl diver from La Paz, who must deal with the consequences of potential sudden wealth.

For a modern account of Steinbeck's experiences, read **Andromeda Romano Lax**'s travel narrative *Searching for Steinbeck's Sea of Cortez: A Makeshift Expedition Along Baja's Desert Coast.* In it, Lax attempts to trace Steinbeck and Ricketts's journey with her husband and young children in tow.

Graham Mackintosh left his home and family in England to walk across Baja, alone. He lived to tell the tale, in *Into a Desert Place.* He repeated the feat, but with company, in *Journey with a Baja Burro. Nearer My Dog to Thee,* and *Marooned with Very Little Beer* continue his Baja-based adventures, which are self-published but available in many Baja bookstores and online at bajadetour.books.officelive.com.

Miraculous Air, a travel memoir by **C. M. Mayo,** takes the reader on a journey through the history, culture, economics, and lifestyle of the entire Baja peninsula.

For a gritty take on Northern Baja, **Kem Nunn**'s excellent "surfer noir" novel *Tijuana Straits* follows a retired surfer who makes a grim discovery while out hunting south of Tijuana.

Baja's ancient history lives in **Harry W. Crosby**'s *The Cave Paintings of Baja California,* a book that delves into the history and mystery of indigenous people long forgotten.

And Baja's modern history gets colorful in **Greg Nieman**'s book, *Baja Legends: The Historic Characters, Events, and Locations That Put Baja California on the Map.*

Markes Johnsen brings Baja's unique geology alive in *Discovering the Geology of Baja California: Six Hikes on the Southern Coast.*

Ann Hazard's *Cooking with Baja Magic Dos,* the sequel to her first cookbook of the same name, can help you re-create some of that Baja cuisine—and Baja magic— at home. And the Hotel California's chef **Dany Lamote** has compiled some of his award-winning tequila recipes in the *Hotel California Tequila* cookbook, available in the hotel gift shop in Todos Santos.

Film

GOLDEN AGE & CLASSICS

Mexico's "Golden Age of Cinema" refers to a period in the 1940s when the country's film studios dropped their attempts at mimicking Hollywood and started producing black-and-white films that were Mexican to the core. The stars of the day are now icons of Mexican culture. **Mario Moreno,** also known as Cantinflas, was the comedic genius that personalized the cultural archetype of *el pelado*—a poor, picaresque, appealingly naughty character looking to get ahead by his wits, and not getting very far at all. His speech is a torrent of free association and digressions and innuendo that gives the comedy a madcap quality. **Dolores del Río** was the Mexican beauty who was later shipped off to Hollywood to fill the role of steamy Latin babe. **Pedro Infante** expressed the ideal of Mexican manhood, and was also Mexico's singing cowboy.

For some takes on old-school Mexico, check out Elia Kazan's 1952 classic, *Viva Zapata!,* written by Baja California fanatic John Steinbeck and starring Marlon Brando as the Mexican revolutionary Emiliano Zapata. Then there's Orson Welles's *Touch of Evil,* about drugs and corruption in Tijuana (preposterously starring Charlton Heston as a Mexican). Or rent the HBO flick *And Starring Pancho Villa as Himself* with Antonio Banderas, a true story about how revolutionaries allowed a Hollywood film company to tape Pancho Villa in actual battle.

THE NEW CINEMA

Since the ignition of Mexico's drug war, Tijuana is experiencing a mini-film boom, as a center for narco-stories both on and off-screen. Most are low-budget

---

Ricky Loves Baja

Known to his beloved fans as Ricky Ricardo, Desi Arnaz, the legendary Cuban band leader and on-screen/off-screen partner to Lucille Ball on the 1950s TV sitcom *I Love Lucy,* had a special fondness for Baja. Arnaz entertained other fast-living Hollywood heartthrobs including Bing Crosby and Clark Gable around his flamenco guitar-shaped swimming pool at a resort on the Sea of Cortez. He may remain, at least in spirit: Several fan sites claim that his ashes were scattered into the sea in front of his home in Rancho Las Cruces, southeast of La Paz, upon his death in 1986.

shoot-'em-uppers; some even feature local drug lords in cameos and their homes as locations. They're available on DVD from Baja Films, **www.bajafilms.com.mx**. In happier times, better films were being made: *Tijuana Makes Me Happy* (2005), directed by Dylan Verrechia, paints a bright and realistic picture of Tijuana. The film aims to break down stereotypes of the city by focusing on the personal stories and struggles of its characters. The film won the Grand Jury Prize in the 2007 Slamdance Film Festival.

Stephen Soderberg's Academy Award–winning *Traffic* (2000), starring Benicio del Toro, includes some powerful scenes focusing on the drug war at the Tijuana border. The documentary *Tijuana Remix* (2002), celebrates the city's culturally unique and idiosyncratic qualities. You can also get a great "tourist guide" online via a short film called *Tijuana es Addiccion* made by local Jacinto Astiazaran.

Alfredo Zacarias's *The Pearl* (2001) is based on John Steinbeck's novel of the same name and stars American actor **Lucas Haas** as Kino the fisherman and Mexican actress **Tere Tarin** as his wife, Juana. No one's going to be winning any awards for this lemon, but fast-forward through the bad Mexican accents and enjoy La Paz's beautiful coastline.

While there aren't very many movies about Baja, a lot have been shot there. The former set for Cameron Crowe's *Titanic* (1997), in Rosarito, has now been turned into a museum called **Xploration** (p. 157). Other recent films shot on location in the state of Baja California include *Tomorrow Never Dies* (1997), *Pearl Harbor* (2001), *Jarhead* (2005), and *Borderland* (2007). Recent movies filmed in Baja California Sur include *Troy* (2004), *The Sisterhood of the Traveling Pants* (2005), and *The Heartbreak Kid* (2007).

Music
MARIACHI & RANCHERA
Mariachi is the music most readily identified with Mexico, and mariachis, with their distinctive costume—big sombreros, waist-length jackets, and tight pants—easily stand out. The music originated from a style of *son* played in the state of Jalisco. It was rearranged to be played with guitars, violins, a string bass, and trumpets. Now you hear it across Mexico and much of the American Southwest.

Ranchera music is closely associated with mariachi music and is performed with the same instruments. It's defined by its expression of national pride, strong individualism, and lots of sentiment, hence its favored status as drinking music. The most famous composer is José Alfredo Jiménez, whose songs many Mexicans know by heart.

NORTEÑA, GRUPERA & BANDA
Norteña owes its origins to *tejano* music, coming out of Texas. Mexicans in south central Texas came in contact with musicians from the immigrant Czech and German communities of the Texas Hill Country and picked up a taste for polkas and the accordion. Gradually the music became popular farther south. *Norteña* music tweaked the polka for many of its popular songs and later borrowed from the *cumbia,* slowing the tempo a bit and adding a strong down beat. It also incorporated a native form of song known as the *corrido,* which is a type of ballad that was popularized during the Mexican revolution (1910–17). *Norteña* became hugely popular in rural northern Mexico through the 1970s and later generated spinoffs, which are known as *grupera* or *banda,* a style of *norteña* from the area of Sinaloa, which replaces the accordion with electric keyboards. **Los Tigres del Norte,** with their catchy melodies

Herb Alpert: Original Tijuana Mix Master

The musical trend of splicing and mixing different genres to create new sounds is not a 21st-century invention. In fact, one of the pioneers of this dubbing technique was **Herb Alpert,** who was inspired to create the sound for his 1962 hit "The Lonely Bull" after watching a bull fight in Tijuana. Alpert utilized an overdubbed trumpet sound as well as actual recordings of the crowd in order to create a unique sound that he believed captured the excitement of the experience. Pepe "Fussible" Mogt, one of the founders of the critically acclaimed **Nortec Collective** has said that Alpert served as a musical influence when he and fellow DJs Bostich, Clorofila, Hiperboreal, and Panoptica began fusing electronic and *norteña* music to form their signature sound.

backed by hopped up accordion and bass guitars, are probably the most famous practitioners of *norteña* music.

BAJA ROCKS

While Sammy Hagar of Van Halen fame became the posterboy for rock in Baja after opening his wildly successful Cabo Wabo bar in Cabo San Lucas, he's not the only rocker who has been influenced by the spirit of the peninsula. Mexican-American rocker **Carlos Santana** got his start in the 1950s playing at bars and clubs in Tijuana and Mexicali. After visiting for a surfing trip with his buddies, **Chris Isaak** went directly to his studio to produce the 1996 album, *Baja Sessions*.

EATING & DRINKING IN LOS CABOS & BAJA

Los Cabos and Baja are full of tourists, and where there are tourists, there are restaurants. And what restaurants: From the lowliest streetside taco stand to the swankiest seaside five-star, you're sure to eat like a king.

Because there are so many short- and long-term expatriates living in Baja, a parallel restaurant culture has grown up beside the preexisting Mexican one. It's easy to tell the difference. "Gringo" places are owned by, run by, or at least targeted to non-Mexicans, and tend to be more expensive, more decorated, and offer a more diverse and often more inventive, although less Mexican–style of cooking. They're also much more likely to tell you where they buy their ingredients, and put more stock in organic or naturally-prepared food. "Local" places are nearly all traditionally Mexican, in cuisine and preparation, with little tweaking of age-old recipes. They're cheaper and, some would argue, more authentic; they're a place to connect with Baja's Mexican culture, and are often mouth-wateringly delicious, but they're not going to blow your socks off with creative cuisine. (The exception to this, as in many things, is Tijuana, where Mexican *alta cocina* is being invented and reinvented by Mexican chefs for cross-border audiences; there are also a few similar places in Ensenada.)

Bridging the gulf, beloved by *bajacalifornianos* of all origins, *taquerías* are Mexican fast-food joints, where everything is made to order and the buzzwords are quick, greasy, and cheap. A *taquería* will serve anywhere from one type of taco to 20, but the basic model is a few slices of spiced cooked meat or vegetables on a tortilla, served on a plastic plate. Taco stands with a building and running water are thought to be more sanitary than those serving their treats on the street, with the added plus that you can wash your hands before you eat. For lunch, the main meal of the day, some restaurants offer a multicourse blue-plate special called **comida corrida** or **menú del día.** This is the least expensive way to get a full meal; look out for these in simple local restaurants, in Baja often with *palapa* straw roofs.

The star of the region is its fresh and varied **seafood.** In many restaurants, *palapas,* and roadside stands throughout the peninsula, the very best meals are, simply, the catch of the day. In areas like La Paz and Loreto, it sometimes seems like everyone has a fishing boat, and the abundance of **marlin, sea bass** *(corvina),* and **skate** *(raya)* from the Pacific and **snapper** *(huachinango),* **parrotfish** *(perico),* and **crab** *(jaiba)* from the Sea of Cortez is itself a reason to visit.

Up and down the coasts in Baja Sur, you'll find small stands selling **almejas,** or clams—a regional delicacy plucked right from the surrounding waters. Depending on where you are, the size and taste of the **almejas** may vary slightly, but the methods of preparation are generally the same. If you order them served raw, you will be presented with a smorgasbord of toppings including lime (squeeze it on the clam before you eat it; if it moves, it's said, it's still alive and safe to eat), Worcestershire sauce, any number of tiny bottles of salsa, and salt. The *relleno,* or stuffed version, has been filled with cheese, butter, ham, jalapeños, and tomatoes, wrapped in tinfoil, and baked in an oven or over an open fire.

Baja's influx of culinary influences is not a recent phenomenon, and by no means limited to North America. According to Edith Jiménez-Smith, the namesake of **Edith's Restaurant** (p. 80) in Cabo San Lucas, Baja's current culinary landscape began to take shape in the late 17th century with the arrival of the Jesuit missionaries. On her website, www.edithscabo.com, she writes: "Spanish missionaries, English pirates, French miners, Italian vintners, Chinese merchants, Japanese fishermen, American mariners, Canadian developers, up to the current tourists . . . all have left, some more and some less, a token of their tastes in food and certain peculiar ways of preparing it." As a result of this cultural mix, you can find Chinese food in La Paz, world-class sushi restaurants along the Cabo San Lucas–San José del Cabo corridor, and dedicated French chefs in Ensenada. Just because there are no beans, rice, or spicy salsa involved, doesn't mean it's not authentic.

In this guide, we've grouped restaurants and other eateries into categories based on price. We're comparing main course prices, or the equivalent cost of a full meal without drinks in places that don't serve main courses. Expect beverage prices to vary accordingly.

A Guide to Restaurant Pricing in Los Cabos & Baja (Main Course Prices, in Pesos)

Very Expensive	200.00 and up
Expensive	150.00–200.00
Moderate	80.00–150.00
Inexpensive	80.00 and below

The Staples

Authentic Mexican food has little to do with its U.S. namesake; it's fresher, more diverse, and healthier, going light on the cheese and the cream. It's based on a few

While ice in Mexico used to be a game of digestive Russian roulette, nowadays nearly everyone buys purified ice to cool their drinks. You can spot machine-made ice for its cylindrical block shape with a hole in the center. You don't need to avoid ice in hotels or restaurants; at market stalls or street vendors, just ask.

traditional ingredients, which haven't changed since before the Spanish touched down: beans, corn, squash, tomatoes, and onions.

Mexican food usually isn't spicy-hot when it arrives at the table (though many dishes have a certain amount of piquancy, and some home cooking can be very spicy, depending on a family's or chef's tastes). Chiles and sauces add heat and flavor after the food is served; you'll never see a table in Mexico without one or both of these condiments. If you're concerned about eating fresh sauces, ask for a bottle.

For more information on Baja's cuisine and menu terminology, see chapter 9.

TORTILLAS Traditionally, Mexican tortillas are made from corn, but in Baja, you'll often find flour tortillas, which consist of lard, wheat flour, salt, and water. When the Spaniards tried to imitate traditional corn tortillas with flour imported from the Old World, the humid conditions in southern and central Mexico ruined the dough. They had more success in hotter, drier conditions in northern states like Sonora, Chihuahua, and Baja California, and over time, their popularity spread north. Today, virtually all the tortillas you'll find in supermarkets north of the border are made of flour. However, the traditional corn tortilla, made from corn that's been cooked in water and lime, then ground into *masa* (a grainy dough), patted and pressed into thin cakes, and cooked on a hot griddle known as a *comal*, remains king in most of Mexico. You can still find corn tortillas in Baja—just ask.

ENCHILADAS The original name for this dish would have been *tortilla enchilada*, which means a tortilla dipped in a chile sauce. In like manner, there's the *entomatada* (tortilla dipped in a tomato sauce) and the *enfrijolada* (in a bean sauce). The enchilada began as a very simple dish: A tortilla is dipped in very hot oil and then into chile sauce (usually with ancho chile), then quickly folded or rolled on a plate and sprinkled with chopped onions and a little *queso cotija* (crumbly white cheese) and served with potatoes and carrots. You can get this basic enchilada in food stands across the country. In restaurants you get the more elaborate enchilada, with different fillings of cheese, chicken, pork, or even seafood, and sometimes prepared as a casserole.

TACOS A taco is anything folded or rolled into a tortilla, and sometimes a double tortilla. The tortilla can be served either soft or fried. A classic taco consists of a bit of grilled, spiced meat on a corn tortilla, served DIY with hot sauce, onions, and cilantro. *Flautas* and quesadillas are species of tacos, too. The taco is Mexico's quintessential fast food, and the taco stand *(taquería)* is ubiquitous all over Baja.

CHILES There are many kinds of hot peppers, and Mexicans call each of them by one name when they're fresh and another when they're dried. Some are blazing hot with little flavor; some are mild but have a rich, complex flavor. They can be pickled, smoked, stuffed, or stewed.

Baja Love Potion	

Where do the spring breakers at Cabo Wabo get that lovin' feeling? As if the sunsets weren't enough, Baja boasts its own native-grown aphrodisiac: **Damiana**, a liqueur made from the leaves and stems of the Damiana plant. Sold in a babe-shaped bottle that drives the point home, Damiana has a sweet, honey-like flavor and can be served straight up or mixed in with a margarita.

Drinks

All over Baja, you'll find shops selling *licuados*—excellent and refreshing juices and smoothies made from every imaginable kind of tropical fruit. *Aguas frescas*—water flavored with hibiscus, melon, tamarind, or lime—are Mexico's answer to soft drinks. If you ask for "agua" and the response is "What kind?," you're in for a treat.

Mexico has a proud and successful **beer**-brewing tradition that goes back to the European immigrants who arrived in the early 1800s. Baja's conventional beers are **Tecate** and **Pacífico,** available everywhere and roughly similar in flavor and quality. But it doesn't stop there. A trip to Tijuana wouldn't be complete without a trip to the **Tijuana Brewery,** where master brewers use techniques picked up in the Czech Republic. In San José del Cabo, microbrew lovers now have a home at **Baja Brewing Company,** a joint run by a group of gringo friends who couldn't face another **Corona.**

Baja's **wine industry** is small but growing, a labor of love for the winegrowers of the Valle de Guadalupe, near Ensenada. Some of the best labels are **Monte Xanic** and **Bibayoff; L.A. Cetto** produces inexpensive, drinkable whites and reds.

Tequila is the heady result of fermenting the hearts of the blue agave plant, a species of agave that grows in and around the area of Tequila, in the state of Jalisco. It's something of a national pastime in Mexico, and Baja is no exception—but beware of the bad stuff, which will leave you feeling awful for days, possibly years to come. The best tequilas are labeled 100% agave, which means that they were made with a set minimum of sugar to prime the fermentation process. These tequilas come in three categories based on how they were stored: *blanco, reposado,* and *añejo. Blanco* is white tequila aged very little, usually in steel vats. *Reposado* (reposed) is aged in wooden casks for between 2 months and a year, and *añejo* (aged) has been stored in oak barrels for at least a year. Leave the José Cuervo to the frat boys and try a **Herradura** or **Cazadores** for a taste of the real thing. ¡*Salud!*

WHEN TO GO

Baja California is one of those rare four-season destinations, offering a different slant on fun in the sun for every month of the year. Prices are highest at Christmas and New Years, lower in the spring, and hit rock-bottom in the summer, the time for killer deals and comparatively empty beaches. Although hurricanes here are rare compared to the Caribbean, September does host a big blow now and then, so figure that into your plans. Air and water temperatures (see below) make a big difference in the kind of active vacations Baja was made for, so think about how you want to spend your time before you book. Winter waters are cold for diving and snorkeling, but cooler winter temperatures are just right for hiking and boating. Summer heat makes swimming a joy, but you'll bake by the pool.

If you're planning to surf, it bears mentioning that the surf switches sides with the seasons, so the waves break on the eastern side of the peninsula in the spring and summer (Mar–Oct) and on the west in the fall and winter (Nov–Mar). The most popular summer breaks start at San José's Playa Acapulquito and extend up the East Cape (p. 85), while the hot spot for winter waves is Cerritos Beach (p. 109), south of Todos Santos.

These days, there's hardly a time when you'll find Los Cabos and Baja overrun, but it's worth keeping a few major festivals in mind. Christmas and New Years are ultra-high season, when hotels and beaches fill up. March is fiesta time, with La Paz's Carnaval and San José del Cabo's Fiesta Patronal. The week leading up to Easter is the time when Mexicans from all over the country head to the beach; partying can be raucous and beaches packed. Mexican Independence Day, September 16, is a party throughout the country, and a fun time to visit cities like La Paz and Tijuana, where celebrations tend to be better-funded.

Weather

Baja may look like a desert, but there's more climatic variation than you might think. The north has a dry Mediterranean climate, with rain and cool nights in winter, and hot, dry summers. The east coast along the Sea of Cortez is much warmer than the Pacific coast summer and winter, and in late winter and early spring can be fantastically windy. The west (Pacific) coast is cool and breezy in winter and warm and breezy in summer, on average 5°C (10°F) cooler than the Sea of Cortez side. The same goes for water temperatures: In winter, it's too cold in the Pacific for anyone but the sea lions, but the Sea of Cortez is usually warmer, with winter averages of 22°C (71°F) and summer of 28°C (82°F).

Average Temperatures

CABO SAN LUCAS

	JAN	FEB	MAR	APR	MAY	JUNE	JULY	AUG	SEPT	OCT	NOV	DEC
Avg. High (°C)	23	25	27	30	31	34	35	35	34	32	28	25
Avg. High (°F)	74	77	81	86	89	94	96	95	94	90	83	77
Avg. Low (°C)	12	12	13	14	16	18	22	23	23	20	17	14
Avg. Low (°F)	54	55	56	58	61	66	73	75	75	68	63	58

LORETO

	JAN	FEB	MAR	APR	MAY	JUNE	JULY	AUG	SEPT	OCT	NOV	DEC
Avg. High (°C)	23	25	26	28	31	34	35	36	35	33	28	24
Avg. High (°F)	74	76	78	83	88	94	96	97	96	91	83	76
Avg. Low (°C)	10	10	11	13	16	21	25	25	24	20	14	12
Avg. Low (°F)	50	50	52	55	61	69	76	77	75	67	58	53

TIJUANA

	JAN	FEB	MAR	APR	MAY	JUNE	JULY	AUG	SEPT	OCT	NOV	DEC
Avg. High (°C)	20	21	20	21	21	23	24	26	26	24	22	21
Avg. High (°F)	68	69	68	70	70	73	76	78	79	76	72	69
Avg. Low (°C)	8	9	10	12	14	16	18	18	18	14	10	7
Avg. Low (°F)	46	48	50	53	57	60	64	65	64	58	50	45

Calendar of Events

For an exhaustive list of events beyond those listed here, check http://events.frommers. com, where you'll find a searchable, up-to-the-minute roster of what's happening in cities all over the world.

Note: Banks, government offices, and many stores close on national holidays.

Día de Año Nuevo (New Year's Day). This national holiday is perhaps the quietest day in all of Mexico. Most people stay home or attend church on the first day of the year. All businesses are closed. In traditional indigenous communities, new tribal leaders are inaugurated with colorful ceremonies rooted in the pre-Hispanic past. January 1.

Día de los Reyes (Three Kings Day). This day commemorates the day the Three Wise Men arrived bearing gifts for the Christ Child. On this day, children receive gifts, much like the traditional Christmas gift-giving in the United States, although Santa Claus has melded with Mexican traditions in Los Cabos. Friends and families gather to share the Rosca de Reyes, a ring-shaped cake. Inside the cake is a small doll representing the Christ Child; whoever receives the doll must host a tamales-and-*atole* party on February 2, or Dos de la Candelaria. January 6.

FEBRUARY

Día de la Candelaria (Candlemas). Music, dances, processions, food, and other festivities lead up to a blessing of seed and candles in a ceremony that mixes pre-Hispanic and European traditions marking the end of winter. Those who attended the Three Kings celebration reunite to share *atole* and tamales at a party hosted by the recipient of the doll found in the Rosca. February 2.

Día de la Constitución (Constitution Day). This national holiday is in honor of the current Mexican constitution, signed in 1917 as a result of the revolutionary war of 1910. It's celebrated through small parades. February 5.

Carnaval. Carnaval takes place over the 3 days before the beginning of Lent. La Paz celebrates with special zeal, and visitors enjoy a festive atmosphere and parades. The 3 days preceding Ash Wednesday.

Miércoles de Ceniza (Ash Wednesday). The start of Lent and time of abstinence, this is a day of reverence nationwide; some towns honor it with folk dancing and fairs.

MARCH

Feria de San José. The end of March brings a weeklong party to downtown San José del Cabo, where carnival rides and games, traditional Mexican food, and jewelry and knickknack vendors fill the streets. San José Day is March 19.

Semana Santa (Holy Week). This week celebrates the last week in the life of Christ from Palm Sunday through Easter Sunday with somber religious processions almost nightly, spoofing of Judas, and reenactments of biblical events, plus food and crafts fairs. Businesses close during this traditional week of Mexican national vacations. If you plan on traveling to or around Mexico during Holy Week, make reservations early. Late March or April.

MAY

El Día del Trabajo (Labor Day). Workers' parades take place countrywide, and everything closes on this national holiday. May 1.

La Paz Foundation, La Paz. This celebration observes the founding of La Paz by Cortez in 1535 and features *artesanía* exhibitions from throughout Southern Baja. May 1 to May 5.

Cinco de Mayo. This holiday commemorates the defeat of the French at the Battle of Puebla. May 5.

JUNE

Día de la Marina (Navy Day). This day is celebrated in all coastal towns, with naval parades and fireworks. June 1.

Corpus Christi. This day, celebrated nationwide, honors the Body of Christ (the Eucharist) with processions, Masses, and food. *Mulitas* (mules), handmade from dried cornhusks and painted, are traditionally sold outside all churches on that day to represent a prayer for fertility. Dates vary, but celebrations take place on the Thursday following "Holy Trinity" Sunday.

AUGUST

Fiestas de la Vendimia (Wine Harvest Festival). Ensenada's food-and-wine festival celebrates the annual harvest, with blessings, seminars, parties, and wine tastings.

Call ☏ **800/44-MEXICO** (800/446-3942) for details and schedule. Mid- to late August.

SEPTEMBER

Día de la Independencia (Independence Day). This national holiday celebrates Mexico's independence from Spain with a day of parades, picnics, and family reunions throughout the country. At 11pm on September 15, the president of Mexico gives the famous independence *grito* (shout) from the National Palace in Mexico City. At least half a million people crowd into the capital's *zócalo* (town square), and the mayor of each town across the country gives the *grito* in front of thousands in his own town square. Those who don't venture into the craziness of their main plaza to celebrate do watch the event on TV. September 15 and 16.

OCTOBER

Festival Fundador. This festival celebrates the founding of the town of Todos Santos in 1723. Streets around the main plaza fill with food, games, and wandering troubadours. October 10 to October 14.

Día de la Raza (Ethnicity Day, or Columbus Day). This day commemorates the fusion of the Spanish and Mexican peoples. October 12.

NOVEMBER

Día de los Muertos (Day of the Dead). This national holiday (Nov 1) actually lasts for 2 days: All Saints' Day—honoring saints and deceased children—and All Souls' Day, honoring deceased adults. Relatives gather at cemeteries countrywide, carrying candles, food, flowers, and colorful decorations, and often spend the night beside graves of loved ones. Weeks before, bakers begin producing bread in the shape of mummies or round loaves decorated with bread "bones." Sugar skulls emblazoned with glitter are sold everywhere. Many days ahead, homes and churches erect altars laden with bread, fruit, flowers, candles, favorite foods, and photographs of saints and of the deceased as a way of remembering them. Traditionally, costumed children walk through the streets both nights carrying mock coffins and pumpkin lanterns, into which they expect money will be dropped. However, in Americanized Los Cabos, costumed kids are out in full force for Halloween rather than on Day of the Dead. November 1 and 2.

Día de la Revolución (Revolution Day). This national holiday commemorates the start of the Mexican revolution in 1910 with parades, speeches, rodeos, and patriotic events. November 20.

DECEMBER

Día de la Virgen de Guadalupe (Feast of the Virgin of Guadalupe). Religious processions, street fairs, dancing, fireworks, and Masses honor Mexico's patroness. It is one of the country's most moving and beautiful displays of traditional culture. The Virgin of Guadalupe, an apparition of the Virgin Mary, appeared to a young man, Juan Diego, in December 1531 on a hill near Mexico City. Her image in a cloth is on display at the Basílica de Guadalupe in Mexico City. It's customary for children to dress up as Juan Diego, wearing mustaches and red bandannas. December 12.

Christmas Posadas. On each of the 9 nights before Christmas, it's customary to reenact Mary and Joseph's search for an inn in which to have the baby Jesus. Door-to-door candlelit processions pass through cities and villages nationwide. Hosted by businesses, community organizations, and even among friends, these take the place of the northern tradition of a Christmas party. December 15 to December 24.

Navidad (Christmas). Mexicans extend this celebration and leave their jobs, often beginning 2 weeks before Christmas and continuing all the way through New Year's. Many businesses close, and resorts and hotels fill. December 23 to December 25.

Víspera de Año Nuevo (New Year's Eve). As in the rest of the world, New Year's Eve in Mexico is celebrated with parties, fireworks, and plenty of noise. However, contrary to U.S. custom, Mexicans celebrate the New Year at home over a traditional dinner with their families and then hit the town after midnight. December 31.

LAY OF THE LAND

It's no wonder the earliest explorers thought Baja was an island: Its jagged mountains rise like a mirage from the endless sea, and its coastline, all 4,800km (2,976 miles) of it, goes on until eternity. But in fact, it's a peninsula, 1,220km (758 miles) long, jutting out from Southern California deep into the Pacific, slicing the Sea of Cortez from the ocean like a finger from a palm. It's skinny, from its widest point—193km (120 miles) at the U.S. border—to its narrowest, 45km (28 miles) of desert between the Bay of La Paz and the Pacific coast. And it's tall: The mountain ranges that run the length of the peninsula soar up from the sea as high as 3,095m (10,152 ft.) at Picacho del Diablo, the menacingly-named Devil's Peak. All this geologic action would speak of diversity, but in fact, more than 65% of Baja is desert, and despite conifer forests in the north and scattered oases in the south, the peninsula is for the most part an arid, rocky, mountainous land.

Natural Life & Protected Areas

Baja has two national parks on land and two in the sea, all considered some of the region's most spectacular places. The 5,000 hectare (12,372 acre) **Parque Nacional Constitución de 1857** (p. 164) is at high altitude within the Sierra de Juárez mountain range, a landscape of diverse pine forests with some trees growing to heights of over 30m (98 ft.), that attracts hikers, climbers, cyclists, and bird-watchers. The area was declared a national park in 1962, and in 1983 it became a part of the country's protected natural areas, offering some protection to the park's population of pumas, golden eagles, coyotes, and bighorn sheep. You can camp in official campsites or rent one of a few simple cabins directly from the park. Two ecotourism ranches, Rodeo del Rey and Los Bandidos, offer rustic rooms in the park as well, along with campsites and related services. An information booth with maps is just past the entry point; a per-vehicle entry charge applies.

The **Parque Nacional Sierra San Pedro Mártir** (p. 164), 210km (130 miles) southeast of Ensenada, is at lower altitude than the Sierra de Juárez, but you're still likely to see snow in the winter—dress warmly! The 72,000 hectares (177,840 acres) of pine forests are home to Mexico's National Astronomical Observatory and to a small population of California condors who've been reintroduced to the wild. Hike 2km (1.2 miles) up to the El Altar viewpoint, at a 2,888m (9,473 ft.) elevation, for a view of both the Pacific Ocean and Sea of Cortez. In the southeast portion of the park is the highest peak in Baja, Picacho del Diablo (Devil's Peak), at an elevation of 3,095m (10,152 ft). It's a popular place for mountain climbing and rappelling. No services are available once you're inside the park, so it's essential to bring your own supplies. Camping areas, restrooms, and forest ranger services are available.

Jacques Cousteau called the Sea of Cortez "the world's aquarium" and "the Galápagos of North America." A visit to its marine parks shows you why: **Cabo Pulmo National Marine Park** (p. 86), 64km (40 miles) east along an unpaved road from the Los Cabos International Airport, is a paradise of 7,111 hectares (17,571 acres) of coral reefs, seamounts, wrecks, warm blue waters, and hundreds of species of fish. Stretching 11km (7 miles) from Bahía Las Barracas in the north to Bahía Los Frailes to the south, this Sea of Cortez haven is open to anyone but fishermen: Snorkeling (which can be done right from the shore), scuba diving, freediving, and kayaking are all fair game. Prepare to see anything from manta rays and giant grouper to sea horses and whale sharks, against a backdrop of bright swaying corals and myriad colorful reef fish. Beach camping is popular on Playa Los Arbolitos, and bungalows are available through Cabo Pulmo Beach Resort or through independent homeowners in this dusty cash-only town.

The deep waters of **Loreto Bay National Marine Park** are the stomping grounds for blue whales, orcas, and dolphins, as well as sea turtles, mantas, and your everyday giant squid. You can explore the park underwater by snorkel or with your scuba diving equipment; from the surface by kayak and sailboat; or skip the wet stuff altogether and simply bask on the beaches of Coronado, Carmen, and Danzante islands, all easy day-trips from Loreto. In summer, Loreto Bay has some of the best sportfishing in Baja.

RESPONSIBLE TRAVEL

With such an overwhelming array of unique natural attractions, development—sometimes overdevelopment—has proven irresistible, to the point where in some parts of Los Cabos and Baja, it's damaging the very natural wonders it's trying to exploit. Take water, for instance, a vital resource and an open question in this desert place. San José del Cabo is blessed with underground aquifers, a reason the Spanish settled there in 1730. Cabo San Lucas is not. For the moment, Cabo shares San José's water supply—but massive tourism growth and more on the way will overwhelm it. Plans for a desalination plant to slake Cabo's thirst sound great, until you ask the question, what happens to the runoff? Developers say the sea is big enough to absorb a little salt; environmentalists say it could have devastating effects. Cabo's not the only place where increased tourism is coming counter to the natural world. If a proposed hotel development project in Cabo Pulmo becomes reality, some worry it could destroy the park's living coral reef.

Concerns about the sea don't end with pollution, though. Several estimates suggest fishing stocks in the Sea of Cortez have declined 90% since the 1960s, much of that since the 1980s when commercial fishing moved in. Commercial longline fishing brings in hundreds of marlin, sailfish, and dorado daily, as well as endangered sharks and mantas. Gill nets catch and drown sea turtles, sea lions, dolphins, and whales. Indiscriminate shrimp trawling pulls in tons of bycatch that's left to die. And there's still a black market in endangered sea turtles, eaten for purported medicinal qualities.

Pressure on the fish means pressure on the fishermen. Traditional fishing communities, where catch is barely above subsistence level, are dying out. Fishing captains who've led tourists to game catch since the 1940s are having a harder time

---

Saving the Sharks

When a permanent ban on shark fishing in Honduras was signed into law in 2010, Peter Wilcox was cheering. The Cabo-based course director at **Manta Scuba** (p. 74) is the founder of the **Shark Legacy Project** (www.shark legacyproject.com), whose research, education, and lobbying work were responsible for the law. Upwards of 70 million sharks are killed worldwide each year for their fins, a billion-dollar industry. But Wilcox and his partners convinced the Honduran government that sharks are more valuable alive, as part of the marine wilderness that draws divers and snorkelers to local tourism. They're hoping to repeat their success in Mexico in the coming years.

earth MOVERS

In researching this guide, we've made an effort to identify businesses that are ahead of the sustainability curve.

HOTELS

El Angel Azul, La Paz (p. 100): A conservation pioneer, using local and humanely produced products in the kitchen, biodegradable soap in the laundry room, low-watt bulbs in the light sockets—all in a 140-year-old building in the city.

Prana del Mar, West Cape (p. 110): Solar energy, gray-water irrigation, organic cotton towels instead of paper, low-flow showers and toilets, and an organic garden make this yoga retreat an earthly paradise.

Villa del Faro, East Cape (p. 88): 100% solar-powered, off the grid and built with sustainable materials, with clotheslines for laundry and xeriscaped grounds.

RESTAURANTS

Flora's Field Kitchen, San José del Cabo (p. 58): It doesn't get more local than this: Everything on your table was produced right there on the organic farm.

Laja, Valle de Guadalupe (p. 177): What doesn't come from their own garden comes from sustainable and humane local production; they're known for their organic wines, too.

Mision 19, Tijuana (p. 155): Cross-border farm-to-table in Baja's first LEED Gold eco-friendly building, with a citrus orchard in the courtyard.

TOUR OPERATORS

Baja Big Fish, Loreto (p. 120): Owner Pam Bolles is a longtime champion of sustainable fisheries, and that includes her own billfishing trips, which are strictly catch-and-release.

Baja Expeditions, Los Cabos (p. 36 and 94): Environmental activism that puts its money where its mouth is: All profits from Conservation Expeditions go directly to local environmental organizations.

Baja Trek, Los Cabos (p. 36): Carbon-neutral tours down the peninsula, in a school bus retrofitted to run on recycled vegetable oil—it's hippie, it's dippy, and it's totally green.

finding fish. The same goes for local businesses, being squeezed out by U.S. and Canadian developers and giant international retail chains. The less people here are able to survive as they have for generations, the more likely they are to leave their communities to look for work elsewhere, accelerating the kind of social decline mainland Mexico knows all too well.

Baja hotel and restaurant operators are just waking up to the challenge of sustainability, and some are responding with gray-water irrigation systems, auto-off air-conditioning, and the use of organically grown vegetables, in addition to the lip-service reuse-your-towel signs that pass for a conscience in the tourism industry. Much more active are many Baja tour operators and guides who take every contact with visitors as an opportunity to educate them about the fragility of this natural environment and the rewards of good stewardship. Low- or no-impact marine and land tours, catch-and-release big game fishing, and wildlife research tourism have become an important part of Baja's tourism landscape.

If you're concerned about the impact of your vacation, consider the following ways to reduce your footprint and preserve Baja for your next visit. Stay at small hotels, whose infrastructure uses less energy and water per head than big resorts. Turn off air-conditioning when you leave your room, or open the window and don't use it at all. Ask where your fish comes from, and try to only eat seafood from small local fishermen or cooperatives. (And when you're at home, buy only fish that's been sustainably harvested—programs from the **Marine Stewardship Council,** www.msc. org, and the Monterey Bay Aquarium's **Seafood Watch,** www.montereybayaquarium. org/cr/seafoodwatch, make it easy.) Skip megastores and patronize local businesses, to help Baja stay Baja.

You can learn more about Baja's environment and the challenges facing it through the following organizations: **Wildcoast** (www.wildcoast.net) is a bilingual environmental action group for the protection of both the Californias; **Pro Peninsula** (www. propeninsula.org), based in San Diego, is focused on Baja; **Eco Alianza Loreto** is working to protect Loreto's National Marine Park, while **Angels of the Estuary** (www.delestero.org) cares for San José's estuary; **Grupo Ecologista de Tijuana** (www.grupoecologista.com) is working for the reforestation of land around the border and a greening of this polluted city. In addition to the resources for Los Cabos and Baja listed above, see frommers.com/planning for more tips on responsible travel.

SPECIAL-INTEREST TOURS
Language Classes & Academic Trips

LANGUAGE LEARNING   As a crossroads of Anglophone and Spanish-speaking cultures, Baja is a great place to study Spanish. La Paz and Ensenada are home to a number of language programs, some of which include homestays and tours. In La Paz, check out **Study Abroad International** (www.studyabroadinternational.com), **Centro de Idiomas, Cultura y Comunicacion** (www.cicclapaz.com), or **Se Habla La Paz** (www.sehablalapaz.com). In Ensenada, **Baja California Language College** (www.bajacal.com) and **Center of Languages** (www.spanishschoolbaja.com) offer full-immersion programs.

PHOTO SAFARIS   **Road Scholar** (© 800/454-5768 in the U.S.; www.road scholar.org) and **Jim Cline** photo tours (© 858/350-1314 in the U.S., or 877/350-1314; www.jimcline.com) organize Baja tours to some of the greatest photo ops, and help photographers make the most of them.

ART TOURS   Several tour companies organize guided tours to the missions and the ancient cave paintings of mid-Baja: **Tour Baja** (© 800/398-6200 and 707/942-4550 in the U.S.; www.tourbaja.com) and **Mulegé Tours** (© 615/153-0232; www. mulegetours.com; at the Las Casitas Hotel in downtown Mulegé). **Baja Outback's** 4-day Mission Trail Expedition (© 624/142-9200; www.bajaoutback.com) combines cave paintings with visits to the missions of Loreto, Mulegé, La Purisima, San Miguel, San José de Comondu, and San Javier. (For more information on the cave paintings, see "Baja's Cave Paintings: A Window in Time" in chapter 6.)

For a look at some of Baja's present-day art, check out the art tours of San José and Todos Santos offered by **Cabo San Lucas Tours** (© 866/348-6286 in the U.S., or 800/822-4577; www.cabosanlucastours.net). **Turista Libre** (http://turistalibre.com) offers idiosyncratic walking and bike tours of Tijuana street art and galleries.

Adventure & Wellness Trips

MOTORCYCLE TOURS **Cabo BMW Rentals,** on Lázaro Cárdenas across from McDonald's in Cabo San Lucas (© **866/241-9899** in the U.S., or 624/143-2640; http://jimster.net/bmw_rentals/index.htm), offers guided and self-guided motorcycle tours around Southern Baja. A good resource for motorcyclists in B.C.S. (Baja California Sur) is the *Cabo Loop Riders Guide,* available for $25 through their website.

OUTDOOR ADVENTURE Baja has as many tours into its natural wonders as there are wonders to explore. Mule treks, Humvee expeditions, ranch living, and beach camping are just a start; check out trips organized by **Baja Expeditions** (© **800/843-6967** or 858/581-3311 in the U.S.; www.bajaex.com), **Tour Baja** (© **800/398-6200** or 707/942-4550 in the U.S.; fax 707/942-8017; www.tourbaja. com), **Natural Habitat Adventures** (© **800/543-8917** or 303/449-3711 in the U.S.; www.nathab.com), **Sea and Land Eco Tours** (© **613/144-7294;** http:// loretoseaandland.com), and **Baja Outback** (www.bajaoutback.com). **Baja Trek** (© **619/937-1546** in the U.S., or 665/391-1682; www.bajatrek.com) organizes carbon-neutral surfing, hiking, and beach tours aboard their retrofitted school bus or in more comfortable vans.

SEA KAYAKING The Sea of Cortez is one of the world's great kayaking locations, with a wealth of offshore islands to explore. Experts and beginners alike are welcome on trips by **Sea Trek** (© **415/488-1000** in the U.S.; fax 415/488-1707; www. seatrekkayak.com), **Mountain Travel Sobek** (© **800/227-2384,** 888/687-6235, or 510/527-8100 in the U.S.; www.mtsobek.com), and **Sea and Land Eco Tours** (© **613/144-7294;** http://loretoseaandland.com). In addition to Sea of Cortez trips, **Sea Kayak Adventures** (© **800/616-1943** or 208/765-3116 in the U.S.; fax 208/765-5254; www.seakayakadventures.com) has the exclusive permit to paddle Magdalena Bay's remote northern waters, and they guarantee gray whale sightings.

SURFING Baja's waves are world-famous, and whether you're a beginner or a veteran, this is a great place to hang ten. **Baja Surf Adventures** (© **800/428-7873** in the U.S.; www.bajasurfadventures.com) organizes trips to Northern, Central, and Southern Baja's Pacific coast; they do surfing lessons too. **Baja Trek** (© **619/937-1546** in the U.S., or 665/391-1682 in Mexico; www.bajatrek.com) organizes low-budget surf tours from its "hostel on wheels" that hit all Baja's major surfing sites. Women only need apply at Milagro Retreats' **Surfari** (© **866/373-4316;** www. milagroretreats.com), a women's surf retreat in Todos Santos.

YOGA Spiritual wellness is a growth industry in Baja, and many yoga centers offer weeklong retreats centered on a daily schedule of yoga and meditative practice, often held at the off-grid **Prana del Mar** on the West Cape. Contact Prana del Mar directly, or go through **Milagros Retreats** (© **866/373-4316;** www.milagro retreats.com).

Food & Wine Trips

All the wineries in Northern Baja offer tours and tastings by appointment or are open to the public. Local hotels can help arrange transportation to visit a few at a time, working in wine tastings, lunch, a cheese tasting and even a horseback ride. Talk to **Casa Natalie** (© **619/246-9772** or 646/174-7373; www.hotelcasanatalie.com) or

Adobe Guadalupe (© 649/631-3098 in the U.S., or 646/155-2094; www.adobe guadalupe.com).

But Northern Baja's foodie destinations are also close enough to the border for a day trip from San Diego. **Baja California Tours** (© 858/454-7166 in the U.S.) offers a day tour of three wineries and lunch in the Guadalupe Valley. The Baja California Lobster Culinary Tour takes in tourist sights in Tijuana and Rosarito, with a lunch of guess what in Puerto Nuevo; contact **Destination Store** (© 866/431-1634 in the U.S.; www.destination-store.com) for details.

Volunteer & Working Trips

A variety of sea turtle conservation organizations offer visitors the chance to participate in nest monitoring and hatchling release in summer, and research and tagging year-round. Check out trips from **Earthwatch** (www.earthwatch.org) and **Baja Expeditions** (www.bajaex.com), as well as summertime activities at **Zoetry Casa del Mar** (p. 62) and **Las Ventanas al Paraíso** (p. 63).

Walking Tours

Discovering Baja's cities and towns from the inside is easier with a local who knows the turf and can open doors. Most of the companies listed under "Adventure & Wellness Trips" (see above) offer day trips from La Paz or Los Cabos. La Paz-based dive operator **Fun Baja** (© 612/106-7148; www.funbaja.com) offers walking tours of San José and Todos Santos, as well as the lesser-known villages of El Triunfo, near La Paz, and Pescadero, near Todos Santos, with offbeat stops like a silver smelter and a strawberry farm. Family-run **Todos Santos Eco Adventures** (© 619/446-6827 in the U.S., or 612/145-0189; www.tosea.net) will take you bird-watching, hiking, or walking along the cliffs and beaches near Todos Santos. **Turista Libre**'s (http://turistalibre.com) offbeat cultural tours of Tijuana include art and architecture walks.

SUGGESTED LOS CABOS & BAJA ITINERARIES

3

Most visitors to Baja never see more of it than a high-energy day trip over the border to Tijuana or a fly-in hedonistic beach week in Los Cabos. But with a little bit of effort, there's much more to discover. Since the Trans-peninsular Highway was completed in 1973, Baja has become one of the great road trip destinations, 1,220km (758 miles) of desert highway cutting across the mountains from ocean to sea and back again. Even without driving the whole thing—27 hours from Tijuana to Cabo—you can spend many happy weeks exploring the vastly different regions here, and a lifetime trying all they have to offer. Name your poison: hiking, biking, colonial history, marine life, adrenaline sports, haute cuisine—it's all here, you just have to go live it.

This is not a place for people who don't like driving—it is California, after all—and the itineraries we list here assume a car. Bus service connects most larger towns, but often, as in the case of Los Cabos, taxi prices can be so steep that you're better off just renting a car if you plan on exploring at all. In areas outside of cities and large towns, a four-wheel-drive vehicle, or one that sits higher up, such as an SUV, are the best bets—it's still a rugged landscape here, and the vast majority of the peninsula's roads are unpaved. But if you're planning to stay on the highway and in town, an ordinary car should be fine.

None of the following itineraries can be called exhaustive explorations of Baja, but neither are they exhausting. Consider them as a sampler of the best of Baja, so that upon a return visit you'll know more about where you'd like to concentrate your time.

THE REGIONS IN BRIEF

BAJA CALIFORNIA SUR   Of the peninsula's three regions, Baja Sur is the most developed for tourism, starting with the fun-loving party town **Cabo San Lucas,** at the southern tip. Great swimming beaches, snorkeling and diving, fishing, and golf are the active draws here, as are hot nightclubs and an American–style good-time vibe. Its nearby fraternal twin, **San José del Cabo,** trades the nightlife and the tequila shots for an arts district, booming restaurant scene, and mission-era historic architecture. Together, the two Cabos make up the lion's share of Baja's tourism receipts.

The **Corridor,** the coastal road that runs between the two, is the gateway to a string of spectacular beaches and coves—some of the peninsula's best. It's no surprise that this is where most of the Cabos's luxury resorts have chosen to build, amid moneyed real-estate developments looking out to the sea. In between, you'll find the world-class golf courses that have made Baja a golfer's favorite vacation spot.

Los Cabos can feel like a southern extension of the United States West Coast, but other areas of Baja Sur are some of the wildest corners of Mexico. The peninsula's **East Cape,** just northeast of San José del Cabo, is a rocky, romantic landscape of beaches, coral reefs, dive sites, hiking paths, and waterfalls, along the coast of the Sea of Cortez. Keep driving north and you'll hit **La Paz,** the capital of Baja Sur, an easygoing maritime port that's a great jumping-off point for adventures on land and sea as well as a pleasant cultural center in its own right.

Along the Pacific coast north of Cabo San Lucas, the **Pacific Side** is one long, wild beach, with world-class surfing and a funky vibe. Just north, the palm oasis of **Todos Santos** draws artistic and epicurean travelers to its galleries and some of the best restaurants in Baja.

MID-BAJA The breathtaking badlands of mid-Baja are about as impassible as it gets, which makes it all the more exciting to get there. **Loreto** is the original capital of the Californias, with Baja's first Spanish mission and a tiny but lovely historic district at the edge of a protected marine reserve bay. The town and its offshore islands are a famed center for dorado and billfish sportfishing, kayaking, snorkeling and diving, as well as the region's best hiking, through desert canyons to ranching regions untouched by development. To the north, **Mulegé** is a palm-filled desert oasis, a favorite of U.S. and Canadian snowbirds and a staging ground for visits to the region's cave paintings. **Santa Rosalía** is an anomaly along the coast: French-style colonial wooden homes and a church designed by Gustav Eiffel are this busy port town's draw.

But between January and March, all this is eclipsed by the most thrilling reason to visit any part of Baja—the annual migration of gray whales to calve in mid-Baja's Pacific lagoons. In **Laguna Ojo de Liebre, Laguna San Ignacio,** and **Bahía de Magdalena,** mother whales coax their newborns right up beside whale-watching *pangas,* in one of the most magical wildlife experiences to be had anywhere.

BAJA CALIFORNIA (NORTE) The state encompassing Northern Baja is officially known as Baja California. Its commercial capital, **Tijuana,** has many dubious distinctions: It's the most-visited, most-maligned, and most-misunderstood city in all of Baja. Booze and drugs, human smuggling and immense factories, the cruelties of the border and the violence of Mexico's drug war are strong influences here, although it's easy for visitors to look the other way. Crime is still a problem for residents, although much less for tourists (see "Safety," p. 194). But the other side of adversity's coin is the creative energy it can generate, and Tijuana is indisputably Baja's cultural capital, with flourishing food, art, and film scenes, burgeoning hipster nightlife that goes way beyond tequila shots, extensive shopping, and a truly international identity. **Rosarito Beach** is Tijuana's resort town, which got a boost after the movie *Titanic* was filmed here (the set is now a movie-themed amusement park). Farther down the Pacific coast is the lovely port town of **Ensenada,** a favorite cruise ship stop known for its prime surfing and sportfishing. The nearby vineyards of Mexico's wine country, in the **Valle de Guadalupe,** are a new and growing attraction, and just north, the border town of **Tecate** is Tijuana's opposite: sleepy, peaceful, home to a famed brewery, some ancient cave paintings, and not much else. Down the road south, **San Felipe** wins the prize as Baja's northernmost resort boomtown.

NORTHERN BAJA IN 6 DAYS

The destinations in this itinerary have taken a huge tourism hit from Mexico's drug war, even though the violence remains removed from tourist areas. But things are looking up: Ensenada and Tijuana are the vanguard of a culinary revolution that's made Northern Baja the new foodie mecca of Mexico. Hipster clubs and edgy galleries are opening in Tijuana, a new tower has opened in the storied Rosarito Beach Hotel, and events like the wine festival in Ensenada continue to draw enthusiastic crowds. One silver lining to the cloud over the border are discounted hotel prices; another is that beaches, once packed, are now peaceful and clean.

This is a driving itinerary, by far the easiest way to get around Northern Baja. Make sure you're properly insured (p. 181), and avoid driving after dark—roads here are fine in daylight but tricky at night. The early part of this journey takes in a few kitschy sites—consider it a sampling of the singular Mexican vision of magical realism—then goes on to some lovely places that will give you an appreciation of the natural beauty and range of experiences available here.

Day 1: Arrive in Tijuana

Tourism here has tanked, thanks to Tijuana's bad-to-worse reputation. But that's engendered a damn-the-torpedos revival in arts and dining that's made Tijuana more interesting than ever. Skip sleazy, so-last-century Avenida Revolución in favor of the upscale Zona Río, for Tijuana's best cultural attractions. Start at the **Centro Cultural Tijuana** (p. 152) for an art exhibit, dance show, historical reenactment or IMAX film, then swing down to **La Querencia** (p. 155) for a new-wave Baja Med lunch. Stop in at **Cava de Vinos L.A. Cetto (L.A. Cetto Winery;** p. 152), for a taste of Baja's wines; alternatively, taste Tijuana's own beer at the **Cerveza Tijuana** brewery (p. 152). Make an evening of cocktails and dinner at **Mision 19** (p. 155), or fuel up on awe-inspiring tacos at **Tacos Salceados** (p. 156), then head out for some cool-kid clubbing at **Calle 6** (p. 151).

Day 2: Rosarito Beach

Just 20 minutes (29km/18 miles) south of Tijuana, this old-fashioned Mexican beach resort is a complete change of scene. Stop for a break at the **Rosarito Beach Hotel** (p. 159), which attracted scores of celebrities and other notables during the later days of Prohibition. Then continue on a few miles south of Rosarito proper to Fox Studios' **Xploration** (p. 157), a cinema-themed museum and entertainment center. When you're finished, head back to Rosarito Beach for the evening, where enjoying a sunset *cerveza* at **Papas & Beer** (p. 161) on the beach is de rigueur.

Days 3 & 4: Exploring Ensenada

Spend the afternoon exploring this classic town to have the next day free for fishing, kayaking, surfing, or a visit to either of the two national parks, the

Suggested Los Cabos & Baja Itineraries

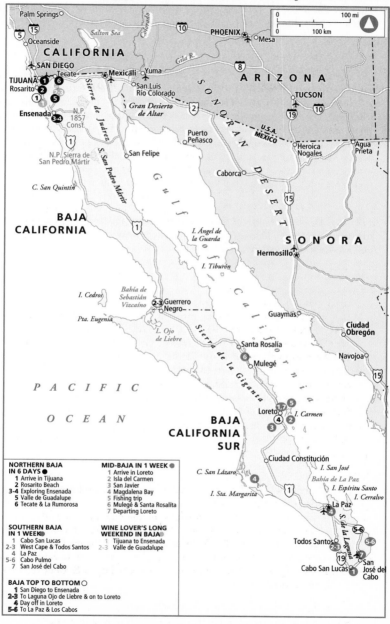

NORTHERN BAJA IN 6 DAYS ●
1 Arrive in Tijuana
2 Rosarito Beach
3-4 Exploring Ensenada
5 Valle de Guadalupe
6 Tecate & La Rumorosa

MID-BAJA IN 1 WEEK ●
1 Arrive in Loreto
2 Isla del Carmen
3 San Javier
4 Magdalena Bay
5 Fishing trip
6 Mulegé & Santa Rosalía
7 Departing Loreto

SOUTHERN BAJA IN 1 WEEK ●
1 Cabo San Lucas
2-3 West Cape & Todos Santos
4 La Paz
5-6 Cabo Pulmo
7 San José del Cabo

WINE LOVER'S LONG WEEKEND IN BAJA ●
1 Tijuana to Ensenada
2-3 Valle de Guadalupe

BAJA TOP TO BOTTOM ○
1 San Diego to Ensenada
2-3 To Laguna Ojo de Liebre & on to Loreto
4 Day off in Loreto
5-6 To La Paz & Los Cabos

Parque Nacional Constitución de 1857 (p. 164) or the **Parque Nacional Sierra San Pedro Mártir** (p. 164). For an unforgettable meal in Ensenada, dine at **Manzanilla** (p. 168)—most say it's one of the best restaurants in Mexico. For a more casual good time, you have your choice of **Hussong's Cantina** (p. 169) or **Papas & Beer** (p. 169), both institutions of the party crowd.

Day 5: Valle de Guadalupe (Mexico's Wine Country)

One day makes for a quick survey of Mexico's wine country. Start with a visit to the **Museo Comunitario del Valle de Guadalupe** (p. 174) and the **Museo Histórico Comunitario** (p. 174), just across the street, for a quick history lesson. Make time for a very special lunch at **Laja** (p. 177), with a lovely drive through the valley thrown in. Then it's tasting time: Take your pick of the boutique **Monte Xanic** (p. 175), **Chateau Camou** (p. 175), and **Mogor Badan** (p. 175), or neighboring **L.A. Cetto** (p. 152) and **Domecq** (p. 175). Turn in at one of many lovely country hotels, like **La Villa del Valle** (p. 176).

Day 6: Tecate & La Rumorosa

Drive up Route 3 through the desert to **Tecate**, perhaps Mexico's most pleasant border town. Spend the day touring the Tecate **brewery** (p. 171), with lunch and a free tasting in its pleasant beer garden. If you're not thirsty, drive 58km (36 miles) to El Vallecito for a look at its **ancient cave paintings** (p. 172). If you've come from the U.S., you'll save time crossing back here; to return to Tijuana, take Route 2 for 35km (22 miles) west.

MID-BAJA IN 1 WEEK

This trip takes you into the heart of Baja and showcases the region's wild, natural beauty. It's an especially appealing trip for those who prefer their travels with a generous dose of activity in the mix.

Day 1: Arrive in Loreto

Upon arrival in Loreto, take the afternoon to explore this small, lovely town and stop in the **Misión Nuestra Señora de Loreto** (p. 124), the first mission established in Baja, dating back to 1699, and in the **Museo de las Misiones**, next door. The town is easy to navigate, with one main road that runs parallel to the waterfront boardwalk. Most attractions are near the central square and old mission, but take the time to walk the cobbled pedestrian-only length of Salvatierra to look at the wooden homes that date back to the 1800s. For your first evening in town, try some local seafood in the garden at **El Papagayo Cantando** (p. 129).

Day 2: Isla del Carmen

You'll need to arrange this trip through one of Loreto's tour companies, but plan on an enchanting day of kayaking, snorkeling, or hiking at Isla del Carmen, the largest of Loreto's offshore islands. Even if your preference is for water-bound activities, it would be a shame to miss a walk or nap on the white-sand beaches of this or Coronado Island. See p. 120.

Day 3: San Javier

Explore mid-Baja's wild interior by visiting the **Misión San Francisco Javier** (p. 124), about 2 hours from Loreto along the old Camino Real dirt road. From here, if you're traveling with an authorized guide, you can stop to visit some of the **cave paintings** (p. 135).

Day 4: Magdalena Bay or Loreto's Islands

Although **Magdalena Bay** is on the opposite side of the peninsula (on the Pacific coast), it's an easy 2-hour drive and, once there, you can board a skiff and spend the day communing with calving gray whales. It's a remarkable sight, one that visitors count among their most thrilling, ever (p. 141). If you're here out of whale season (which runs Jan–Mar), book a trip to whichever of Loreto's off-shore islands you missed on Day 1, stopping at **La Picazón** (p. 128) on the way back for sunset drinks or an early dinner.

Day 5: Fishing Trip

Now that you've settled in, do as the locals do and go fishin'. There's a species for every season, and you're guaranteed to come home with at least a fishing tale or two.

Day 6: Mulegé & Santa Rosalía

Road trip! On the way north, speed past **Mulegé** and go straight 61km (38 miles) to **Santa Rosalía,** so you get there in time for the best offering at the **El Boleo** bakery (p. 140). Thus fortified, walk down the two blocks to Gustave Eiffel's **Iglesia de Santa Barbara** (p. 140), and through the narrow streets lined with French-colonial wooden houses. If you prefer activities to sightseeing and sneakers to dress shoes, you may want to forego Santa Rosalía and concentrate your time in Mulegé instead, where you can visit, with a guide, the series of **cave paintings** in **La Trinidad** (p. 134), a remote ranch 29km (18 miles) west of Mulegé, or at **San Borjitas** (p. 134). Literally an oasis in the desert, Mulegé is a small, run-down town with a large English-speaking community, but beyond the **Misión Santa Rosalía de Mulegé** and the **Museo Regional de Historía** (p. 136 and 136), the town itself doesn't offer much in the way of sightseeing. Time spent here generally revolves around visiting its lovely surrounding beaches. The return trip from Mulegé to Loreto is 137km (85 miles), taking about 1½ hours.

Day 7: Departing Loreto

Use your final day to relax, or, if it's your pleasure, play a round of golf at the **Campo de Golf Loreto** (p. 121) or tennis at the **Loreto Bay Tennis Center** (p. 122). The renowned spa at the **Posada de las Flores** (p. 126) will do the trick, too.

SOUTHERN BAJA IN 1 WEEK: A SAND-IN-YOUR-TOES TOUR

Baja's star attractions are, of course, the twin towns at its tip, San José del Cabo and Cabo San Lucas—but visitors shouldn't miss what lies beyond. This itinerary summarizes the best of Baja Sur's well-traveled and out-of-the-way destinations, and it is tailored to fit Southern Baja's most popular missions: partying, surfing, and soaking up the sun.

Day 1: Cabo San Lucas

Fly in to Los Cabos International for the best range of flights. For a night of luxurious relaxation, book yourself into the top-rated **Esperanza** resort (p. 62). For a night on the town, opt for a hotel in Cabo itself, then hustle to get yourself a seat for Cabo's famous sunsets, on **Playa el Médano** (p. 71) or on a sunset cruise (p. 72). Get into the Mexican spirit with dinner at **La Fonda** (p. 80), and then go out in Cabo, knocking back a few margaritas at **Cabo Wabo Cantina** (p. 83) and hoping for a Sammy Hagar sighting.

Days 2 & 3: West Cape & Todos Santos

After some of **Mama's** (p. 81) famous pancakes, pick up Hwy. 19 and drive up along the crashing Pacific coastline to **Cerritos** (p. 109). Turn off the highway here and follow the dirt road to the surfing beach, where you can take a lesson or just take a chair and watch how the pros do it. **Rancho Pescadero** (p. 111), 8km (5 miles) south in **Pescadero,** is the perfect place to dig in, at the private beach or too-cool pool. **Napoli Pizzeria** (p. 112) is a terrific roadside pizza place on the main road for dinner. The next morning, head up the road to **Todos Santos,** browsing the art galleries and colonial buildings of the historic district, and picking up some beach reading at **Tecolote Books** (p. 105). While away your afternoon snacking in a cafe, or bird-watching on the lagoon at **Posada la Poza** (p. 106). Schedule time to dine at **Tre Galline** (p. 108) for some of the best Italian food outside of Italy.

Day 4: La Paz

Drive an hour up the highway from Todos Santos, and you're in Southern Baja's only real city, a small and vibrant portside capital with excellent restaurants in town and beautiful beaches about a half-hour out. Stroll the *malecón* in the morning, then head out to **Playa Tecolote** for a lobster lunch and a swim in the Sea of Cortez. When evening falls, you're in for a treat: It's hard to get a bad meal in La Paz (we have a selection of very good ones on p. 101).

Days 5 & 6: Cabo Pulmo

It's a gorgeous drive from La Paz, 3 hours south to **Cabo Pulmo,** with plenty of optional stops for refreshments along the way. But to make the most of it, drive straight through: One day is not enough in this out-of-the-way paradise. Grab a mask and snorkel and swim out from the shore to explore the coral reef. Just before dusk, pull into **Playa Los Arbolitos** and take the cliff-side coastal hike to **Playa La Iguana,** where the setting sun adds a warm glow to one of the most beautiful—and private—coves in all of Baja. Sleep tight in one of **Cabo Pulmo Beach Resort'**s (p. 88) bungalows and rise early to hike, bike, or jog the desert trails before spending a day on—or in—the water of this protected marine park.

Day 7: San José del Cabo

Back in civilization, alas. But as civilization goes, **San José** is pretty nice. Poke around the arts district for souvenirs, then cruise down to **Zipper's** beach (p. 52) for a spin on the waves and a burger. As evening falls, take a stroll around the square, and then treat yourself to dinner at **Tequila Restaurant** (p. 58) or **El Chilar** (p. 58). You've, um, earned it?

SPRING BREAK REVISITED: 3 days IN CABO SAN LUCAS

If you're longing for your spring break days, Cabo San Lucas is happy to help. Book a long weekend at the **ME Cabo** resort (p. 77) on Médano Beach and the rest is easy. You remember the spring break schedule, don't you? Sleep as late as you want. Lounge by the **Nikki Beach** pool. Order a late lunch in the sun. Sip margaritas in a pool cabana in the after-noon, then get ready for the main event. Evenings start with a late dinner in San Lucas, drinks at a marina-front bar till 11pm, and dancing in a club till your stilettos can't bear another step (flip-flops are welcome, too). Then back to the resort for low-key partying until first light or straight to bed to rest up for the next day.

A WINE LOVER'S LONG WEEKEND IN BAJA

Admittedly, Mexico is not the first country that comes to mind when thinking of wine, but the emerging wine country in Baja does make for a memorable exploration and a unique and easy trip from Southern California. Take a long weekend and indulge in an exploration of the spirits—and the scenery—here.

Day 1: Tijuana to Ensenada

Cross the border into Mexico and make a stop in Tijuana for a generous sampling of Baja's wines at the **Cava de Vinos L.A. Cetto** (**L.A. Cetto Winery;** p. 152). Cava is big and commercial, but it will give you an introduction to what Mexican wines have traditionally been known for. The cork-covered building is a sight to see in and of itself. When you're finished (and of course you will have designated a driver), have lunch at **La Contra** (p. 168), which crafts its menu to complement wines. Be sure to book a room in advance at **La Villa del Valle** (p. 176) or you can stay in Ensenada, but it's a winding 29km (18-mile) drive.

Days 2 & 3: Valle de Guadalupe

Take a break from drinking and pay a visit to the **Museo Comunitario del Valle de Guadalupe** (p. 174) and the **Museo Histórico Comunitario** (p. 174), for a crash course in the region's history. Then it's back to the bottle. Don't miss smaller, boutique wineries, such as **Adobe Guadalupe, Monte Xanic, Chateau Camou,** or **Mogor Badan,** but the larger, industrial Guadalupe branch of **L.A. Cetto** and **Domecq** put out a gracious welcome too. Be certain to plan a meal (reservations are recommended) at **Laja** (p. 177), or, in summer, at **Silvestre** (p. 177), before heading back. Get more information on all of the above in "The Valle de Guadalupe: Mexico's Wine Country" on p. 172.

BAJA TOP TO BOTTOM: SAN DIEGO TO CABO SAN LUCAS

The mother of all Baja road trips is the ride down iconic Hwy. 1 from start to finish—a must for surfers, seekers, and latter-day Steinbecks. More than a thousand miles of tarmac slice south through desert, mountains, and coast, and once you're on it, you're on it. This trip is for road junkies only. Although you can drive Highway 1 year-round, winter is best, offering less-punishing desert temperatures and a chance to commune with migrating whales. For information on bringing your own car across the border, see "Getting There: By Car" in chapter 8.

Day 1: San Diego to Ensenada

If you're bringing your own car, take I-5 south from **San Diego, California,** and cross the border, where you'll buy Mexican car insurance if you haven't already done so online (p. 181). If you're renting a car, use an office in **Tijuana.** Once through the border, simply follow the signs for Hwy. 1, and you're on your way. The first overnight stop is **Ensenada,** about 1½ hours south, where you'll take in the sea breezes with your fish carpaccio at **Muelle Tres** (p. 168), right on the seaside *malecón.* Tour **Santo Tomás** winery (p. 162) or catch some waves at **San Miguel** (p. 160) before bedding down at **Casa Natalie** (p. 166).

Days 2 & 3: To Laguna Ojo de Liebre & on to Loreto

On day 2 it's 7 hours of road through Baja's surreal desert. Your destination is whale-happy **Laguna Ojo de Liebre** (p. 142) near Guerrero Negro. Spend the night here so that on the morning of day 3, in the January to March gray whale calving season, you'll be ready bright and early for a play date with the gregarious giants. After communing with the whales, drive across the peninsula to the Sea of Cortez and you're halfway to Cabo. Stop in **Santa Rosalía** for a sweet snack at **El Boleo** (p. 140), then keep driving to **Loreto,** where you can relax with a cold microbrew at **1697** (p. 128) or a hot Jacuzzi at **Las Cabañas** (p. 127).

Day 4: Day Off in Loreto

By day 4, you've earned some R & R. After brunch at **Los Mandiles** (p. 128), amble down to the harbor for a trip to **Isla Coronado** (p. 120). In the afternoon, stroll the cobbled streets around Loreto's **historic mission** (p. 124) before taking a taxi out to the pebbly beach at **La Picazón** (p. 128) for a plate of fresh snapper.

Days 5 & 6: To La Paz & Los Cabos

The drive on day 5 cuts right through the copper mountains of the Sierra Giganta on the way to **La Paz,** southern Baja's quirky capital, where you'll spend the day soaking up the sun on **La Concha** (p. 94) beach and the evening soaking up the atmosphere at **Café Corazón** (p. 101). On the morning of day 6, sleep in. From La Paz, Hwy. 1 winds south around rocky cliffs and the occasional oasis, but by the time you stop for sweets in **San Bartolo** (p. 90), it's smooth sailing. You'll hit **San José del Cabo** (p. 47) for lunch at one of old town's excellent restaurants and a few hours strolling the Art District's galleries and shops. Then, the home stretch: The last 29km (18 miles) of Hwy. 1 bring you to **Cabo San Lucas** (p. 67), otherwise known as Land's End. Turn off that engine and go enjoy the sunset—you made it.

LOS CABOS

Los Cabos (the Capes) are not one place but two very different ones, separated by 33km (22 miles) of wild, gorgeous beaches and a roster of luxury resorts. San José del Cabo, known as San José, is the original Cabo, founded in 1730 by Spanish missionaries in a fertile plain uphill from the sea. Cabo San Lucas, known simply as Cabo, is the upstart—up until the 1950s, it was a small fishing village, albeit at the edge of some of the most dramatic coastline in the Americas.

How things have changed. Today, nearly two million people visit Los Cabos every year, and the mission settlement and the fishing village have grown into sophisticated tourist playgrounds catering to wealthy North Americans. But the differences remain, and the two have less to do with each other than the joint name Los Cabos would suggest. San José is still the older sister, more cultured and staid, while Cabo is the wild child, dedicated to sports, beaches, and parties. San José savors organic cuisine and ambles along the colonial streets of its arts district, while Cabo is busy sunbathing on yachts and drinking in nightclubs. San José has the surfing beaches, but Cabo has the port. San José is upscale Mexican; Cabo is gringo all the way.

The good news is, you don't have to choose. However different they may be, the two Cabos are only a half-hour drive apart on a zippy four-lane highway. It's common to make your base in one and make day trips to the other, or split the difference and bed down in one of the super-luxurious beachfront resorts along the so-called Corridor between them. The string of beaches fringing the coast here doesn't discriminate—each town has its own, but, as in many things, the best lie somewhere in between.

SAN JOSÉ DEL CABO ★★★

180km (112 miles) SE of La Paz; 33km (20 miles) NE of Cabo San Lucas; 1,760km (1,091 miles) SE of Tijuana

No matter how sprawling its big-box outskirts, San José remains, at its heart, an old-fashioned colonial town. Low-slung, heavy stone colonial houses painted tropical fruit colors and fixed with wrought-iron balconies open on to courtyards humble and grand; in the town's small *centro histórico*, little has changed since 1730, when Jesuit missionaries founded the town. Today it's a redoubt of Mexican artisans and artists and North American and European expatriates, pursuing late-life ambitions in the arts, food, and hospitality in the sun, and remaking San José in their own upscale boho image.

The latest manifestation of San José's destiny is the Art District (p. 51), an officially designated and funded section of the *centro* of galleries, shops, and restaurants in historic buildings; the Thursday Art Walk (p. 51) is the district's weekly social event, with food and drink specials and gallery open houses.

Essentials

GETTING THERE & DEPARTING

BY PLANE   San José's main airport, and that of Southern Baja, is the **Los Cabos International Airport** (© 624/146-5097; www.sjdloscabosairport.com); the airport code is SJD. **Aeroméxico** (© 800/237-6639 in the U.S., 01-800/021-4000 in Mexico, or 624/146-5098 or 146-5097; www.aeromexico.com) flies nonstop from Mexico City, and has connecting flights and codeshares from other cities; **American Airlines** (© 800/223-5436 in the U.S., or 624/146-5300 or 146-5309; www.aa.com) flies from Dallas/Ft. Worth, Los Angeles, and Chicago; **US Airways** (© 800/235-9292 in the U.S., or 624/146-5380; www.usairways.com) operates nonstop flights from Phoenix; **Alaska Airlines** (© 800/252-7522 in the U.S., or 624/146-5100 or 146-5101; www.alaskaair.com) flies from Los Angeles, San Diego, Seattle, and San Francisco; **Continental** (© 800/537-9222 in the U.S., or 624/146-5040 or 146-5080; www.continental.com) flies nonstop from Houston and Newark; **Delta** (© 800/241-4141 in the U.S., or 624/146-5003; www.delta.com) has flights from Atlanta and Los Angeles; **Frontier** (© 800/432-1359 in the U.S., or 624/146-5421; www.frontierairlines.com) has nonstop service from Denver; **United Airlines** (© 800/538-2929 in the U.S., or 624/146-5433; www.united.com) flies nonstop from Los Angeles and San Francisco; **Volaris** (© 866/988-3527 in the U.S. or 800/122-8000; www.volaris.com) flies nonstop from Mexico City and Tijuana; **WestJet** (© 888/937-8538 in the U.S. and Canada or 800/514-7288; www.westjet.com) flies nonstop from Vancouver.

BY CAR   From San Diego, drive south on Hwy. 1 all the way to the tip of Baja California—the drive takes about 2½ days, as we don't recommend night driving. From La Paz, take Hwy. 1 south; the drive takes 3 to 4 hours. Or take Hwy. 1 south just past the village of San Pedro, and then take Hwy. 19 south (a less winding road) through Todos Santos to Cabo San Lucas, where you pick up Hwy. 1 east to San José del Cabo. From Cabo San Lucas, it's a half-hour drive to San José; the total time is about 3 hours.

BY BUS   The **Terminal de Autobuses (bus station),** on Valerio González, a block east of Hwy. 1 (© 624/142-1100), is open daily from 5:30am to 10pm. Buses between Cabo San Lucas and La Paz run almost hourly during the day. For points farther north, you'll usually change buses in La Paz. The trip to Cabo San Lucas takes 40 minutes, to La Paz, 3 hours. Buses also go to Todos Santos; the trip takes around 3 hours.

ORIENTATION

ARRIVING   Los Cabos International Airport (© 624/146-5111; www.sjd loscabosairport.com; airport code SJD) serves both Cabos and the Corridor in between. San José is 13km (8 miles) from the airport and Cabo San Lucas is a 48km drive (30 miles). Upon arriving in Los Cabos, pass Customs and baggage claim, and turn right once you exit the sliding doors. Be prepared for a gauntlet of shouting timeshare pitchmen, who will say anything to get you to go on a tour with them. Ignore them, and march straight through to the **Josefinos** (© 624/146-5354) shuttle desk for your ticket, inside the terminal on your left as you exit Customs. At about $15 per person, depending on the location of your hotel, shuttles are the

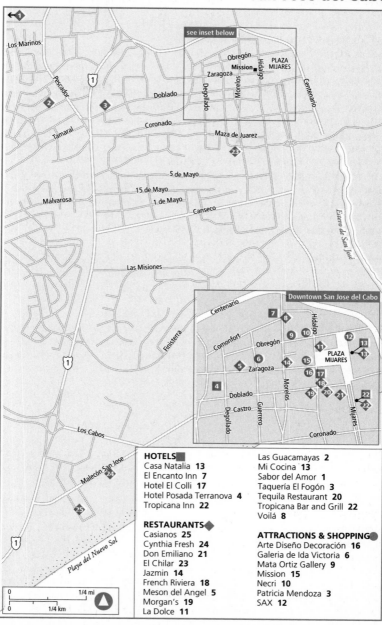

4

HOTELS
Casa Natalia **13**
El Encanto Inn **7**
Hotel El Colli **17**
Hotel Posada Terranova **4**
Tropicana Inn **22**

RESTAURANTS
Casianos **25**
Cynthia Fresh **24**
Don Emiliano **21**
El Chilar **23**
Jazmin **14**
French Riviera **18**
Meson del Angel **5**
Morgan's **19**
La Dolce **11**

Las Guacamayas **2**
Mi Cocina **13**
Sabor del Amor **1**
Taquería El Fogón **3**
Tequila Restaurant **20**
Tropicana Bar and Grill **22**
Voilá **8**

ATTRACTIONS & SHOPPING
Arte Diseño Decoración **16**
Galeria de Ida Victoria **6**
Mata Ortiz Gallery **9**
Mission **15**
Necri **10**
Patricia Mendoza **3**
SAX **12**

cheapest way to get to your hotel from the airport. (A private van for up to five passengers is $85 and is faster than a regular shuttle). Taxis charge about $35 to San José and upwards of $60 to San Lucas.

If you're planning on exploring at all, it's very helpful to have a car in Los Cabos, and a rental is not terribly expensive when booked in advance (see "Getting Around: By Car," p. 182). The major car-rental agencies all have counters at the airport, open during flight arrivals: **Alamo** (© 624/146-1900); **Avis** (© 624/146-1066; avissjd@avis.com.mx); **Dollar** (© 624/146-5060; aeropuerto@dollarloscabos.com); **Fox** (© 624/146-5333); **Hertz** (© 624/146-1803); **National** (© 624/146-5021); **Thrifty** (© 624/146-5030); and **U-Save** (© 624/146-5083). They're all open roughly the same hours, about 8am to 6 or 7pm, and advance reservations are not always necessary, although your spontaneity may cost you.

If you arrive at the **bus station,** it's too far from the hotels to walk with luggage. A taxi from the bus station to downtown or the hotel waterfront costs $5 to $10.

VISITOR INFORMATION San José's city **tourist information office** (©/fax 624/142-3310 or 146-9628) is in Plaza San José on Bulevar Mauricio Castro. It offers maps, free local publications, and other basic information about the area. It's open Monday through Friday from 8:30am to 3pm. Prior to arrival, contact the **Los Cabos Tourism Board** (© 866/567-2226 in the U.S., or 624/143-4777; www.visitloscabos.org).

CITY LAYOUT San José technically spreads from the airport halfway to San Lucas, but for our purposes, it's limited to *el centro,* or downtown, with restaurants, the Art District, historic inns and budget hotels, and the **hotel waterfront** (*zona hotelera*), lined with all-inclusive resorts.

From the highway, **Zaragoza** is the main street leading into town, all the way to the central **Plaza Mijares,** surrounded on two sides by most of the *centro's* attractions. **Paseo San José,** the principal avenue of the *zona hotelera,* runs parallel to Zaragoza and the beach a mile to the south. **Bulevar Mijares,** peppered with restaurants and shops, connects the two areas north to south.

GETTING AROUND

Driving is the most convenient way to get beyond San José's *centro,* but it's not necessarily the easiest. Arm yourself with a good map from the tourist office or your hotel; tiny, white-on-white street signs are made for pedestrians, not drivers. Luckily, the town is a grid, so if you miss your street, you can take the next one in your direction. At night, watch out for speed bumps and *vados,* their treacherous opposites. No local bus service connects the *centro* and the beach, but it's about a 30-minute walk from the downtown to the sand, and **taxis** (© 624/142-0580) connect the two for about $7 each way. For day trips to **Cabo San Lucas,** ask your concierge if your hotel has a daily shuttle, or just catch a **bus** (see "Getting There & Departing," above) or a cab.

Addresses without Numbers

In Mexico, addresses often do not have street numbers. Instead, you'll see the designation "s/n," meaning *"sin número,"* or "without a number." For example, Calle Morelos s/n means that the address is located on Calle Morelos, but it doesn't have a specific street number. When possible, we give the cross street of an address to help you locate the property.

[Fast FACTS] SAN JOSÉ DEL CABO

Area Code The local telephone area code is **624**.

Banks Banks exchange currency during business hours, which are generally Monday through Friday from 8:30am to 6pm, and Saturday from 10am to 2pm. Several major banks with ATMs are on Zaragoza between Morelos and Degollado and in the downtown. A plaza with a bank, ATM, American Express office, and currency exchange is at the south end of Bulevar Mijares.

Emergencies Dial ✆ **066,** or the local police number at City Hall (✆ **624/142-0361**).

Hospital Hospital General is at Retorno Atunero s/n, Col. Chamizal (✆ **624/142-0013**).

Internet Access Most hotels provide some sort of Wi-Fi and/or provide a computer for guest use. Many cafes and restaurants offer Wi-Fi, too.

Pharmacy **Farmacia ISSSTE,** Carretera Transpeninsular Km 34,

Plaza California Local 7 (✆ **624/142-2645**), is open daily from 8am to 8pm.

Post Office The *correo,* Bl. Mijares 1924, at Valerio González (✆ **624/142-0911**), is open Monday through Friday from 8am to 4:30pm, Saturday from 9am to 1pm. For more substantial mailings, **Mail Boxes Etc.,** Plaza Las Palmas Km 31 (✆ **624/142-4355**), is open Monday through Friday from 8:30am to 5:30pm and Saturday from 9am to noon.

Attractions

San José's *centro* doesn't have much of a draw, per se. The sprawling, oddly quiet Plaza Mijares spreads over three blocks, and although lined with shops and restaurants, it feels empty all year except for the Feria de San José, when it fills with music stages, food stalls, and revelers. The most pleasant end for a stroll or a sit is on the western side, where the city's refurbished 1730 **mission** stands. The ceramic tile painting above the entrance graphically memorializes the 1734 revolt over polygamy that lead to the local padre's martyrdom; it looks like he didn't stand much of a chance.

The lovely narrow streets extending westward from Plaza Mijares make up San José's **Art District** ★, a tiny neighborhood of colonial houses made into galleries, studios, shops, and restaurants. Whether or not you're an art aficionado, it's a pleasant place to spend an afternoon, strolling the candy-colored blocks and enjoying a coffee or leisurely lunch. The street view, while lovely, isn't the whole story. Some courtyards here host shops and galleries stuffed with art and handicrafts, while others have hidden restaurants where you can eat in secluded, quiet style. From the square, walk west on Obregón and wander. Highlights include the **Galería de Ida Victoria** (Guerrero 1128 at Obregón; ✆ 624/142-5772; www.idavictoriaarts.com; Nov–Aug Mon–Sat 10am–7pm), the **Mata Ortiz Gallery** (Obregón 10 btw. Morelos and Hidalgo; ✆ 624/142-4969; www.mataortiz.com; Mon–Sat 10am–8pm), and **Patricia Mendoza** (Obregón at Hidalgo; ✆ 624/105-2270; www.patriciamendoza-gallery.com; daily winter 10am–2pm and 5–8:30pm, summer 11am–2pm and 6:30–9pm); pick up a map of the whole district at the tourist office on the square or one of the many restaurants throughout.

On Thursday nights between November and June, the whole town turns out for the district's **Art Walk,** a strolling open house of galleries, studios, restaurants, and bars. Check the Art District website (www.artcabo.com) for information on smaller events as well.

Beaches & Outdoor Activities

Los Cabos is a hotspot for active adventures, and through competitive and professional local tour operators and outfitters, it's easy to arrange hiking, Hummer off-roading, visits to hatching sea turtles (in summer), ATV and dune buggy excursions, surfing excursions with or without rentals and lessons, parasailing, stand-up paddle boarding, kayaking, snorkeling, scuba diving, sailing, WaveRunners, and anything else you can think of. These companies are based in Cabo, but all will arrange hotel pickup in San José. Our picks for Los Cabos are **Baja Outback** (© 624/142-9215; www.bajaoutback.com), **Baja Wild** (© 624/172-6300; www.bajawild.com), **Cabo San Lucas Tours** (© 800/822-4577; www.cabosanlucastours.net), and **Tío Sports** (see "Cabo San Lucas," later in this chapter); check their websites and the sections below for specific offerings and prices.

BEACHES

The best beaches in the area that are safe for swimming aren't in San José; they're in the beautiful coves along the Corridor, the 35km (22-mile) coast between the two Cabos (p. 60). Beach aficionados should consider renting a car for a day or so (from $50 per day; p. 183). Frequent bus service between San José and Cabo San Lucas also makes it possible to visit Playa Médano or Playa del Amor in Cabo (see "Getting There & Departing," above).

Estero San José, a natural freshwater estuary on which the ancient Pericúe Indians built their civilization centuries ago, hosts at least 270 species of birds. The estuary is a protected ecological reserve, and merits a sunset beach walk from the Hotel Presidente InterContinental to the river mouth where the spring-fed estuary meets the Sea of Cortez. Natural beaches along the edge of the estuary are usually safe for swimming. A local environmental group, Angels of the Estuary, is active in keeping the estuary clean and protecting it from industrial pollution and invasive species; find out about upcoming activities on their website, www.delestero.org (in Spanish).

Just to the east of the estuary, across the mouth of the marina harbor, **La Playita** is San José's only true swimming beach. Located about 3km (2 miles) southeast of the *centro* in the community of Puerto Los Cabos, it's a safe and well-kept stretch of sand with a designated swimming area, as well as a natural beach for surfing or fishing.

Playa Costa Azul, just south of town on Highway 1, is Los Cabos's best surfing beach (see "Surfing," below), but you don't have to be a surfer to enjoy the scene. Stretch out on the sand and watch the show, or settle in with a beer at **Zipper's** ★

 Swimming Safety

One of the great ironies of Los Cabos is that many of its endless and spectacular beaches are unsafe for swimming. Strong currents, frequent riptides, and the absence of lifeguards mean that much of that delectable coast is "look, don't touch." Check conditions before entering the surf, and stick to the beaches we list here: La Playita outside of San José, Palmilla ★★★, Chileno ★★, Santa Maria ★, and Barco Varado in the Corridor (p. 61), and Médano ★★ and Playa del Amor ★★★ in Cabo San Lucas (p. 71).

festivals & special events
IN LOS CABOS

San José del Cabo celebrates the feast of its patron saint on March 19. The patron saint of San Bartolo, a village 100km (62 miles) north is feted June 19, and the patron of Santiago, 55km (34 miles) north, July 25. They're all occasions for a rip-roaring Mexican country good time, with music, dancing, horse races, rodeos, rides, religious processions, and lots and lots of sweets for sale from streetside booths. San José's fiesta, in particular, is a reason in itself to make the trip, together with thousands of others from all over southern Baja who come to town for a whole week of partying.

(Km 28.5 on Transpeninsular Hwy.; © **624/172-6162;** daily 11am–10pm), a classic beachside burger joint.

For a list of other nearby beaches worth exploring if you have a rental car, see "Beaches & Outdoor Activities" under "Cabo San Lucas," later in this chapter.

LAND SPORTS

ADVENTURE TOURS   **Baja Wild** offers daylong tours by Jeep or Hummer into the desert and to beaches accessible only by 4x4, as well as desert hikes to a waterfall. **Baja Outback** is more nature-oriented, with offerings including visits to mountain villages and sea turtle releases, all accompanied by local naturalists. **Cabo San Lucas Tours** will take you ATV riding or bungee jumping, as well as on a variety of dune buggy tours.

GOLF   Los Cabos has become Latin America's leading golf destination, with a collection of top signature courses and others under construction. The lowest greens fees in the area are at the 9-hole **Mayan Palace Golf Los Cabos,** in San José at Paseo Finisterra 1 (© **624/142-0900** or 142-0901), which is the first right turn east of the yellow Fonatur statue in the highway roundabout. The 7th hole offers a wonderful view of the ocean on your left and mountains facing you as you approach the green. The 9th is a good finishing hole, with a wide, sloping fairway with sand traps to the top, right, and bottom of the green. Fees are 787 pesos for 9 or 18 holes in low season, 1,225 pesos for 18 in high season, not including equipment; your cart is free after 1pm. For more information about playing golf in Los Cabos, see "The Lowdown on Golf in Cabo" on p. 64.

HORSEBACK RIDING ☺   Hire horses near the Presidente InterContinental, Fiesta Inn, and in the Costa Azul canyon for $15 to $20 per hour. Most people choose to ride on the beach, but a trip up the arroyo is less of a cliché and offers spreading desert views. For a more organized riding experience—English or Western—there's **Cuadra San Francisco Equestrian Center,** Km 19.5 along the Corridor, in front of the Cabo Real resort development (© **624/144-0160;** www.loscaboshorses. com). Master horseman Francisco Barrena has more than 35 years of experience in training horses and operating equestrian schools, and will assist riders of any level in selecting and fitting a horse to their skill level. A 2-hour canyon ride in and around Arroyo San Carlos or Venado Blanco costs $100; a 1-hour ride to the beach or desert is $60. Private tours go for $60 per hour, and equestrian aficionados may schedule a dressage class for $75.

WATERSPORTS

For **sea kayaking, snorkeling, scuba diving,** and **whale-watching,** see "Cabo San Lucas," later in this chapter.

FISHING   The least expensive way to enjoy deep-sea fishing is to pair up with another angler and charter a *panga*, a 7m (23-ft.) skiff used by local fishermen, from Pueblo la Playa, the beach near the new Puerto Los Cabos Marina. Several *panga* fleets offer 6-hour sportfishing trips, usually from 6am to noon, for $200 to $500. Two or three people can split the cost. For information, visit the fishermen's cooperative in Pueblo la Playa (no phone) or contact **Gordo Banks Pangas** (© **800/408-1199** from the U.S., or 624/142-1147; www.gordobanks.com). For larger charter boats, you'll depart from the marina in Cabo San Lucas (later in this chapter).

SURFING   Though surfers have been flocking to Baja for at least 25 years, nowadays it seems there are more and more of them as surfing becomes one of Los Cabos's main attractions. In spring and summer, the breaks are to the east, from San José up the East Cape, and in fall and winter on the Pacific side, up the West Cape. As every break has its secret—from rocks covered in sea urchins to territorial locals—your best bet is to hook up with a reputable surf shop or guide to take you to the break that's right for you. **Baja Outback** and **Baja Wild** organize full-day trips out to the Capes, and half-day excursions to Costa Azul (Mar–Nov), including board rentals and lessons, for kids as well.

While famous breaks on the East and West Cape are just an hour's drive away, **Playa Costa Azul,** at Km 29 on Hwy. 1 just south of San José, is the most popular surf beach in Baja Sur. The **Costa Azul Surf Shop,** Km 28, Playa Costa Azul (© **624/142-2771;** www.costa-azul.com.mx), offers surfing lessons, surfboard and snorkeling equipment rentals, and specialized surf excursions to any of the 15 local breaks. Excursions include transportation and a DVD video of the day, and all rental boards are handcrafted in the owner's San José workshop. Just $20 per day will get you a board, leash, shade umbrella, beach chair, and rack for your rental car. One-hour lessons are $55, and other special packages are available. **Cabo Surf Hotel** (© **624/172-6188;** www.cabosurfhotel.com), on **Playa Acapulquito** next to Costa Azul, also offers custom board orders, surf lessons, and daily board rentals for $35 (and overnight accommodations, p. 176) from its **Cabo Surf Shop** (© **624/172-6188;** www.cabosurfshop.com).

Shopping

San José's *centro histórico* is the best place in Los Cabos to shop for high-quality crafts, art, jewelry, and souvenirs. (Cabo is the best place to shop for the tacky stuff.) The jewelry shops lining Plaza Mijares are a good place to start, as are the streets fanning out west and south, and of course the galleries in the Art District are only too happy to have you stop by. You'll find crafts and some ceramics on Zaragoza along with some kitsch, and refined galleries on Obregón; while there's nothing really cutting-edge here, thanks to Mexico's strong and vivid arts tradition the art here is better and more original than the usual resort-town junk seascapes. The following businesses accept credit cards (American Express, MasterCard, and Visa).

Arte Diseño Decoración   This interior design shop stocks everything from locally made soaps and Damiana tea to embroidered linens and hand-painted talavera ceramics. Although it's not from Baja, you are forgiven for coveting the fine Oaxacan embroidery, appropriated by the area's top resorts for tablecloths and throw pillows.

Open Monday through Saturday from 9am to 10pm and Sunday until 9pm. Zaragoza, at the corner of Hidalgo across from the cathedral. ℭ **624/142-3090.**

Necri ★ The new location of this San José institution specializes in ceramics and pewter, crowded into the front room and courtyard of a lovely old colonial house. Shipping is available. Open Monday through Saturday from 9am to 9pm. Obregón 17. ℭ **624/130-7500.**

SAX For original and well-priced jewelry, visit this small shop where two local sisters create one-of-a-kind pieces using silver and semiprecious stones. They'll even create a special-request design for you and have it ready in 24 hours. Open Monday through Saturday from 10am to 9pm, closed Sundays. On Mijares next to Casa Natalia. ℭ **624/142-6053.** www.saxstyle.com.

Where to Stay

Of the two distinct destinations of Los Cabos, San José is best for accommodations in renovated historic buildings with colonial atmosphere. Though plenty of luxury resorts are along the hotel waterfront, if a resort is what you want, you're better off in the Corridor or Cabo San Lucas. Prices are high in San José, as throughout Los Cabos, but most hotels include breakfast. High season generally denotes December through April, and low season is May through November. Rates listed below do not include tax, which is 13%.

EXPENSIVE

Casa Natalia ★ After the L.A. chic of the high-walled courtyard, shot through with palms and a long pool, you might be a tiny bit disappointed by the rooms here. If the courtyard is the "after" in a design magazine, the rooms are stuck at "before," with stucco walls, dull stone bathrooms, and incongruous royal-blue sofas. But they're spacious and clean, with spotless king-size beds, and each includes a private terrace overlooking the pool. With breakfast (included in most rates) delivered to you in the morning, you could certainly do worse. Surrounded by teak decks, the pool is the most stylish in San José, and the acclaimed Mi Cocina restaurant (p. 58), also in the courtyard, will lull you with excellent margaritas served under the stars. Casa Natalia is part of an informal network of expat women hotel owners, and the staff can help you arrange stays at the other four hotels in the group (p. 57).

Plaza Mijares 4, 23400 San José del Cabo, B.C.S. www.casanatalia.com. ℭ **888/277-3814** in the U.S., 866/826-1170 in Canada, or 624/142-5100. Fax 624/142-5110. 16 units. High season $150–$285 double, $395 spa suite; low season $135–$195 double, $285 spa suite; prices do not include mandatory $15/daily service charge. AE, MC, V. Children 12 and under not accepted. Free parking. **Amenities:** Gourmet restaurant (see Mi Cocina in "Where to Eat," on p. 56); bar; concierge; heated outdoor pool w/waterfall and swim-up bar; access and transportation to private beach club; room service. *In room:* A/C, fan, TV/DVD, movie library, CD player, Internet, hair dryer, bathrobes, spa services, no phone.

MODERATE

El Encanto Inn ★ 🐾 Somewhere between Santa Barbara and the set of a John Wayne movie lies the universe of this historic inn, made up of two sections on opposite sides of a quiet street in the Art District. The Garden building, with the least expensive standard rooms and garden-view suites, is perfectly respectable, but our pick is the motel-style Poolside building, which surrounds a grassy courtyard with a small pool and a fountain, opening up on to a small private plaza with a mission-style stone chapel complete with an old wooden wagon in front. It's a unique space, a country hotel within this historic city center. Rooms are decorated with rustic wood and contemporary iron furniture, with colorful tile accents in the spacious bathrooms; those in the Garden area have two double beds, while suites in both areas have king-size beds and a sitting room. The owners, Cliff and Blanca (a lifelong resident of San José), can help arrange fishing packages and golf and diving outings. Rates include a full breakfast.

Morelos 133 (btw. Obregón and Comonfort), 23400 San José del Cabo, B.C.S. www.elencantoinn.com. ℂ **624/142-0388.** 26 units. $86 double; $105–$240 suite. MC, V. Limited street parking available. **Amenities:** Restaurant; *palapa* bar; small outdoor pool; spa. *In room:* A/C, fan, Direct TV.

Tropicana Inn ★★ This hacienda-style hotel on Bulevar Mijares fronts a spacious walled courtyard whose centerpiece is a large, inviting pool and shady *palapa;* guest rooms open, motel-style, onto the courtyard via an arcade on its side. Each smallish terracotta-tiled room has two double beds, fresh in white linens accented with hot-pink serapes, a window looking out on the courtyard, and a rustic-tiled bathroom with shower. For a romantic treat, splash out on the duplex Troje suite, an incongruous century-old wooden *palapa* cottage from Michoacán with a king-size bed and views of the garden and pool. In the morning, freshly brewed coffee, sweet rolls, and fresh fruit are set out for hotel guests. Room service from the adjacent Tropicana Bar and Grill is available till 11pm.

Bl. Mijares 30 (1 block south of the town square), 23400 San José del Cabo, B.C.S. www.tropicanainn. com.mx. ℂ **624/142-0907** or 142-1580. Fax 624/142-1590. 40 units. High season $132 double, $200 Troje suite; low season $119 double, $180 Troje suite. Rates include continental breakfast. AE, MC, V. Free parking. **Amenities:** Restaurant; bar; outdoor pool; room service; spa room; Wi-Fi. *In room:* A/C, TV, hair dryer, minibar.

INEXPENSIVE

Hotel El Colli Cheap and cheerful, this no-frills pension in a renovated historic building at Hidalgo and Doblado has possibly the best location in San José, and hands-down the best prices. Simple rooms with queen-size or single beds are spread over three floors; some have small balconies. Those streetside can be very noisy on weekends or during the March Fiesta de San José, so ask for a back room when you book. New bathrooms feature open tiled showers and stone counters; this is not a place for designer soaps but complimentary bottled water will do in a pinch. A few croissants for breakfast next door at the French Riviera pastry shop, and you could be backpacking in Europe.

Hidalgo s/n at Doblado, 23400 San José del Cabo, B.C.S. www.hotelcolli.com. ℂ/fax **624/142-0725.** 32 units. 600–800 pesos double. MC, V. *In room:* A/C, TV, Wi-Fi.

Hotel Posada Terranova This small, family-owned hotel is so famous for its traditional Mexican breakfasts and charming outdoor dining terrace that locals often forget it's even a hotel. However, while local Mexicans and expats love it for weekend brunch, the budget traveler will appreciate its newly-renovated rooms, featuring two double beds with high-style chocolate-toned headboards, white-tiled bathrooms with glass showers, its convenient location at the edge of the Art District, and, yes, its *huevos rancheros* and fresh-squeezed OJ in the morning.

Degollado btw. Doblado and Zaragoza, 23400 San José del Cabo, B.C.S. www.hterranova.com.mx. ℂ **624/142-6714.** Fax 624/130-7232. 21 units. 800 pesos double. Rates include continental breakfast. MC, V. Free parking. **Amenities:** Restaurant; bar; room service. *In room:* A/C, fan, satellite TV and DVD player.

When Esther, Nathalie, Sandra, Jenny, and Lisa get together, things happen. The high-powered women owners of El Ángel Azul (La Paz, p. 100), Casa Natalia (San José del Cabo, p. 55), Los Milagros (Cabo San Lucas, p. 78), the Hotelito (Todos Santos; www.the hotelito.com; ☎ 612/145-0099), and Rancho Pescadero (Pescadero, p. 111) have joined forces to offer guests integrated services and each other a network of support in Baja's male-dominated tourism industry. They can book you at each other's hotels, help arrange transportation, and probably tell you a few stories, too.

Where to Eat

What San José lacks in party-hearty nightlife, it easily makes up in culinary sophistication. It's hard to get a bad meal here, and easy to get a great one. This book simply doesn't have enough room to go into detail about every restaurant that's worth your attention, such as **Morgan's** (☎ 624/142-3825) Tuscan-inspired steakhouse; the Art District Mexican **Jazmin** (☎ 624/142-1760); the oh-la-la pastry bar **French Riviera** (☎ 624/104-3125); the dirt-cheap and delicious **Taquería El Fogón** (☎ 624/168-8982); the romantic colonial **Meson del Angel** (☎ 624/142-2828); the all-organic **Sabor de Amor** (☎ 624/142-3794); the old-school Italian favorite, **La Dolce** (☎ 624/142-6621); and the patio-style Euromexican flavors of **Voilá** (☎ 624/130-7569). Below is a cross section of what's available. *¡Buen provecho!*

EXPENSIVE

Casianos ★★ CONTEMPORARY MEXICAN   Lots of restaurants think of food as an art form, but at Casianos it's more like improv theater. There's no menu, and all the choosing you'll have to do is how many courses of the eponymous chef's "spontaneous cuisine" you'd like to try. The conceit is that everything is made up on the spot, allowing the kitchen to express the full flower of its creativity and you to express your personal preferences; in reality, it's more like a traditional daily market menu with an element of surprise. While last night's shrimp roll with epazote (a traditional Mexican herb) and foie gras with sweet potato blintzes will officially never be seen again, expect local fish and vegetables prepared in creative riffs on traditional Mexican cuisine, unusual wine pairings, and the unexpected.

In the back of the strip mall at Bahía de Palmas, on San José's Malecón btw. Las Mañanitas and Desire hotels. ☎ **624/142-5928.** www.casianos.com. Reservations recommended. Tasting menus $72–$92. AE, MC, V. Mon–Sat 6–10pm.

Don Emiliano MEXICAN   For nearly a decade, celebrity chef Margarita Carrillo traveled the world with the Mexican government, supervising meals for heads of state—rest assured, she knows Mexican cuisine inside and out. Now she and her family run this famed temple to traditional foods. Sparkling seasonal menus rooted in such Mexican traditions as Day of the Dead and Independence Day bring rare mole sauces and stuffed chiles drenched in walnut-cream sauce and pomegranate seeds (*chile en nogada*), while traditional staples such as flavored tamales and grilled farm cheese atop roasted tomatillo salsa grace the menu on a regular basis. Service can be hit-or-miss, but the food shouldn't disappoint.

Bl. Mijares 27 in downtown San José. ☎ **624/142-0266.** www.donemiliano.mx. Main courses 218–312 pesos; 5-course tasting menus 592 pesos without wine pairing, 998 pesos with. AE, MC, V. Daily 6–10pm.

4

LOS CABOS | San José del Cabo

El Chilar ★★ CONTEMPORARY MEXICAN   A Mexico City–trained chef has brought some city slick to San José's dining scene. One of the very best in Los Cabos, this off-the-beaten path jewel features a new menu every month, studded with innovative pairings and constructions like a napoleon of octopus and *nopal* cactus, dressed with a smoky chile oil, and snapper served with a roast-pineapple chutney, in a new spin on Mexican street food's classic *pastor*. It's all served up in a cozy little dining room of a reincarnated private home, a low-key setting for high-style food. For what's really a tiny little place, the wine list is impressive, as is the tequila offering: 70 labels and counting.

Benito Juárez 1497, at Morelos, south of the center near the Telmex tower. ⓒ **624/142-2544** or 146-9798. www.elchilar.net. Main courses 175–200 pesos. DC, MC, V. Mon–Sat 3–10pm.

Mi Cocina ★★ ⊡ CONTEMPORARY MEXICAN/INTERNATIONAL   Bathed in moonlight under a row of swaying palms, the restaurant of Casa Natalia hotel may have the most romantic setting in San José. Despite some signs it may be resting on its laurels (a chilling of service, in particular), it's still one of San José's top tables. Recent hits from a rotating menu include the sophisticated roasted chicken with chocolate, a European play on traditional Mexican mole that separates the flavors of the original for maximum punch. Save room for dessert; choices include rum pineapple or a chocolate fondant with homemade ice creams in shades of basil, coconut, and guava. The full-service *palapa* bar offers an excellent selection of wines, premium tequilas, and single-malt Scotches. A special martini—like the Flor de México, an adaptation of the cosmo, using *jamaica* (hibiscus-flower infusion) rather than cranberry juice—caps a special night.

In Casa Natalia (p. 55), Plaza Mijares 4. ⓒ **624/142-5100.** www.casanatalia.com/dining.htm. Main courses 175–260 pesos. AE, MC, V. Daily 6:30–10pm.

Tequila Restaurant ★★★ MEDITERRANEAN   Contemporary Mexican-influenced Mediterranean cuisine is the star attraction here, although the spacious garden setting is a close second, with comfortable tables shaded by palms and mango trees, lit at night by colored lanterns strung among them. A signature dish of fat and fragrant local shrimp in a sauce of (what else?) tequila is a must; fresh fish gets a light touch, while tender octopus stew is a balancing act of flavors from sweet to savory. Homegrown organic greens, harvested from owner Enrique Silva's ranch, garnish most entrees. The accompanying whole-grain bread arrives fresh and hot with a pesto-infused olive oil, and attentive service complements the fine meal. After dinner, Cuban cigars and an unsurprisingly vast selection of tequilas are available, as is an extensive wine list emphasizing California vintages.

Manuel Doblado s/n, near Hidalgo. ⓒ **624/142-1155** or 142-3753. www.tequilarestaurant.com. Reservations recommended. Main courses 180–320 pesos. MC, V. Daily 6–10:30pm.

MODERATE

Flora's Field Kitchen ★★★ 📗 NEW AMERICAN   What's in a name? Flora's Field Kitchen is a restaurant kitchen—a good one—set amid the fields and flora of Gloria Greene's organic farm, ten minutes to the north of San José. From the simple concept of farm to table comes one of Los Cabos's most exciting dining experiences, a daily menu of simple American country favorites rendered thrilling in a beautiful location with a unique concept. From farm-raised pork chops and applesauce to weekly fried local organic free-range chicken, everything is fresh and genuine. Lunch is a la carte; dinner is a fixed menu, available in advance on their Web page. A perfect

GOING green IN LOS CABOS

The last years have brought a tinge of green to these desert shores, and now it's relatively easy to find locally-grown organic vegetables, from nearby Miraflores and the West Cape's Pescadero, and vegetarian menus in Los Cabos (although organic meat is still something of a specialty item).

FARMERS' MARKETS

San José: November to May, Saturdays 9am–3pm; a 10-minute walk from Plaza Mijares. Follow Morales N. to the large Avenida Centenario, take the dirt road to the right and follow it alongside Centenario until it turns left, and follow it to the market. www.sanjomo.com.

The Corridor: November to May, Fridays 9am–1pm, in the parking lot of Las Tiendas de Palmilla shopping center, inland from Hwy. 1 at the Palmilla exit (follow signs to Farmers' Market).

Cabo San Lucas: November to May, Wednesdays and Saturdays 9am–noon, outside the Pedregal resort.

ORGANIC AND/OR VEGETARIAN RESTAURANTS

San José: Cynthia Fresh (on Hwy. 1 south of the *centro,* just below Mega Supermarket; ✆ **624/155-5874**), Flora's Field Kitchen (see directions p. 58; ✆ **624/355-4564**), Sabor de Amor (Julia Navarrete, enter from Av. Pescador; ✆ **624/142-3794**).

Cabo San Lucas: El Ameyal (in El Ameyal resort and spa, Hwy. 1 Km 3.5; ✆ **624/144-4727**).

GROCERIES

Cabo San Lucas: Tutto Bene (Marina Blvd. at Camino de Cerro; ✆ **624/144-3300**; www.tuttobene.com.mx) sells organic dry products like cereal and crackers, as well as additive-free juices.

night begins with a farm-arita or a farm julep, listening to live jazz as the sun goes down, and ends, of course, with chocolate cake.

10 min. driving from San José: Take the Puerto Los Cabos Bridge toward Puerto Los Cabos, turn left at the 1st roundabout, go straight through the 2nd roundabout, and start following arrow signs for Flora farm. At the 3rd roundabout go straight, at the 4th roundabout left. 500m (550 yd.) ahead, you will see a dirt road to your left and a sign that says FLORA FARM. ✆ **624/355-4564.** www.flora-farm.com. Lunch $10–$12; dinner $25. MC, V. Tues–Sun noon–10pm.

Tropicana Bar and Grill MEXICAN/TEX-MEX   If it's a Mexican "fiesta" night on the town you're looking for, the Tropicana delivers. Dated but still Mexi-fabulous, its old-fashioned over-the top hacienda grandeur—Spanish colonial wrought iron, serape tablecloths, and de rigeur mariachis in a high-ceilinged baronial hall, or at streetside tables—makes it a fun night out no matter what you eat. But the food's not bad either. Traditional standbys like chiles en nogada and fajitas are served up in generous portions; the *molcajete,* a mixed grill of chorizo, beef and pork slathered in a spicy tomatillo sauce and served in a mortar (or *molcajete*), is a crowd-pleaser.

Bl. Mijares 30, 1 block south of the Plaza Mijares. ✆ **624/142-1580** or 142-0907. Breakfast 50–80 pesos; main courses 150–250 pesos. AE, MC, V. Daily 8am–midnight.

INEXPENSIVE

Las Guacamayas ★★ 📷 TACOS   This off-the-beaten-path dive is home to the most delectable tacos in all of Los Cabos. If you can get over the plastic chairs, occasional wandering roosters, and low-hanging fruit trees in this packed-nightly courtyard, you'll be mesmerized by this meticulously operated gringo and Mexican hot spot. Traditionalists wisely go for the *tacos al pastor*—shaved pork tacos with onion, cilantro, and pineapple in a corn or flour tortilla, but the *quesadillas chilangas*—crispy fried tortillas stuffed with an assortment of fillings—are a blissful indulgence. Pace yourself. The addicting flavors and rock-bottom prices may inspire you to stay all night.

Driving east (toward Aeropuerto) on Hwy. 1, turn left at the PESCADOR street sign. The street winds into the Chamizal neighborhood. Take your 2nd left and look for the neon sign. Guacamayas is on the right side. No phone. Tacos, stuffed potatoes, and more 15–70 pesos. No credit cards. Mon and Wed–Thurs 6pm–midnight; Fri–Sat 6pm–4am.

San José After Dark

The nightlife in San José may seem a bit more understated than its wild-nights counterpart in Cabo. However, a new crop of swanky clubs, wine bars, and neighborhood hangouts, all pumped with music till 2 or 3am on the weekends, does offer a nighttime release for the local hospitality industry jet set and visitors alike. Those intent on American music and bump-and-grind dance clubs will have better luck in Cabo.

Baja Brewing Company   A new addition to the arts district, this hangout is run by a trio of buddies from Colorado who recognized a need for artisan brews in Baja. In addition to the beers—which run the gamut from the light-bodied Cabotella, a German-style lager, to the Escorpion Negro, a dark beer with a light toasty flavor—the pub-style pizzas also make a great late-night snack. Live rock and jazz musicians often perform on the weekends. Sit inside by the brewing tanks, or on a pleasant patio set back from the street. Open daily noon to 2am. Morelos btw. Comonfort and Obregón. *©* **624/146-9995.** www.bajabrewingcompany.com.

Tropicana   This bar, featuring American sports events and live mariachi music nightly from 6 to 9pm and live Mexican and Cuban dance music from 9:30pm until about 1am on weekends, stays open Tuesday through Sunday from 7am to 2am. Bl. Mijares. *©* **624/142-1580.**

THE CORRIDOR: BETWEEN THE TWO CABOS ★★

The 35km (18-mile) Corridor between the towns of San José del Cabo and Cabo San Lucas contains some of Mexico's most lavish resorts. Most growth at the tip of the peninsula is occurring along the Corridor, which already has become center stage for championship golf. The five major resort areas are **Palmilla, Querencia, Cabo Real, Cabo del Sol,** and **Punta Ballena,** and each is an enclosed master-planned community sprinkled with multimillion-dollar homes (or the promise of them). All but Punta Ballena have championship golf, and all but Querencia, which is a private residential community, have ultra-luxury resorts within their gates. If you plan to explore the region while staying at a Corridor hotel, you'll need a rental car (available at the hotels) for at least 1 or 2 days. Even if you're not staying here, the beaches are a must; plan at least one day trip to Palmilla or Chileno.

Beaches & Outdoor Activities

All 35km (22 miles) of the Corridor are fringed by beautiful public beaches. But strong currents and wandering riptides mean only four of them are consistently safe for swimming. Of these, the loveliest by half is **Playa Palmilla ★★★**, which fronts the glitzy One&Only Palmilla resort 8km (5 miles) west of San José. To reach Palmilla Beach, enter the lush Palmilla community at Km 27.5 on the highway, take the road toward the beach, then take the fork to the left (without entering the hotel grounds), and park in the lot. Moving westward along the coast, **Playa Chileno ★★** is a long golden cove bordered by rocky promontories that frame clear water and gentle, rolling waves. There's snorkeling by the rocks, and rare bathrooms and showers in the cement building on your left. To get there, follow signs at Km 15; you'll make a series of strange 180-degree curves, and reach the parking lot soon after. Snorkeling is terrific at **Playa Santa Maria ★**, in a small rocky cove that gets crowded on weekends. Coming from Cabo (because there are no signs coming from San José), watch for two small signs after the bridge; there will be a bus stop on the right and a dirt road immediately after. Follow the dirt road to the parking lot. **Playa Barco Varado** is the closest of the Corridor beaches to Cabo; it's known for tidepools along the shoreline. At Km 10, follow signs for the Sheraton Hacienda del Mar, but don't turn in to the resort; take the first left after it and follow the road to the parking lot. None of the above have shade; bring an umbrella or slather on the sunscreen.

Although a few travel agencies run snorkeling tours to some of these beaches, there's no public transportation. Your options for beach exploring are to rent a car or have a cab drop you off at the beach of your choice.

GOLF

Los Cabos has become the golf capital of Mexico. The master plan for Los Cabos golf calls for a future total of 207 holes. Fees listed below are for 18 holes, including golf cart, water, club service, and tax. Summer rates are about 25% lower, and many hotels offer golf packages. (For specifics on the various courses, see "The Lowdown on Golf in Cabo," below.)

The 27-hole course at the **Palmilla Golf Club** (© 624/144-5250; www.palmillagc.com; daily 7am–7pm) was the first Jack Nicklaus Signature layout in Mexico, on 360 hectares (900 acres) of dramatic oceanfront desert. The course offers your choice of two back-9 options, with high-season greens fees of $220 (lower after 1pm), and low-season greens fees running between $130 and $180. Guests at some hotels pay discounted rates.

Just a few kilometers away is another Jack Nicklaus Signature course, the 18-hole Ocean Course at **Cabo del Sol,** the posh resort development in the Corridor (© 866/231-4677 in the U.S., or 624/145-8200; www.cabodelsol.com). *Golf Magazine* has ranked this course among the world's best. The 7,100-yard Ocean Course is known for its challenging 3 finishing holes; greens fees start at $205 afternoons and range to $355 in the morning. Tom Weiskopf designed the new 18-hole Desert Course, for which greens fees are $99 in the afternoon, $225 in the morning.

The 18-hole, 6,945-yard course at **Cabo Real,** by the Meliá Cabo Real Hotel in the Corridor (© 877/795-8727 in the U.S., or 624/173-9400; www.caboreal.com; daily 6:30am–6pm), was designed by Robert Trent Jones, Jr., and features holes that sit high on mesas overlooking the Sea of Cortez. Fees run $280 for 18 holes high season, $180 in low season. After 3pm, rates drop to $140 in the low season and $180 in the high season. Kids 16 and under play for $92 year-round.

The consensus among avid golfers is that two of the area's best courses are the Fazio-designed Querencia and the recently reopened El Dorado, a Jack Nicklaus design. However, both courses are private and open only to Querencia and El Dorado members and homeowners. As Los Cabos becomes increasingly exclusive, and as

The Two Cabos & the Corridor

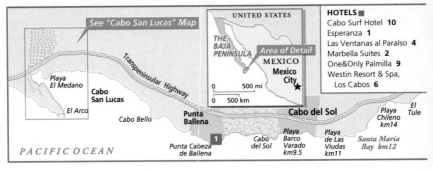

more luxury travelers look to own a piece of it, expect to see more private members-only golf clubs within opulent master-planned residential communities. In fact, the trend already is well underway within the new communities of Chileno Bay, Puerto Los Cabos, Cabo Pacífica, and El Dorado.

Shopping

Las Tiendas de Palmilla   Top brands, tropical style, art galleries, and fine dining are all on offer in San José's upscale shopping mall. Among other shops, Casa Vieja sells fine linen dresses and Pineda Covalín silk scarves, Tiki Lounge is the local Tommy Bahama outpost, Q Boutique houses Diamonds International's connoisseur collection, and the Guadalajara-headquartered Antigua de México sells furniture from the state of Jalisco. On weekends, a farmers' market in the parking lot also has handicrafts and homemade snacks among the organic chard and carrots. Store hours vary. ✆ **624/144-6999.** www.lastiendasdepalmilla.com.

Where to Stay

In addition to the properties listed here, the Corridor has a number of all-inclusive resorts, which, while all very expensive, may be a better deal for people who plan to eat in. Try the **Zoetry Casa del Mar** (www.zoetryresorts.com; ✆ **888/227-9621** in the U.S.), next door to Ventanas del Paraíso at Km 19.5, Cabo Real. Most resorts offer golf and fishing packages, as well as free parking. All properties in this section offer free Wi-Fi. Rates listed below do not include tax, and most hotels will add on a 15% service charge to your bill.

VERY EXPENSIVE

Esperanza ★   If you're expecting the royal treatment, you're in the wrong place. But lamenting the lack of glitz is missing the point—Esperanza aims for the anti-luxe crowd, offering the lowest-key (and most expensive) relaxation without any of the glam. Standard "casita" rooms are long on comfort, with Frette linens, dual shower heads, and large terraces outfitted with whirlpools, but the most splash you'll get here are in the dramatic views of the Punta Ballena cliffs and the sea beyond. Grounds are similarly understated, with landscaping more reminiscent of a college campus than a luxury resort, and serve to highlight the spectacular rocky shore. Two beaches and five pools offer ample entertainment, and the fantastic spa, with steam cave and sunken

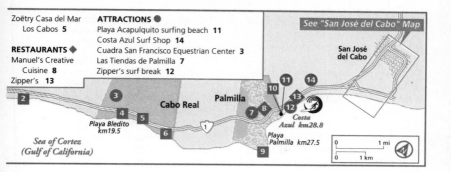

See "San José del Cabo" Map

Zoëtry Casa del Mar
Los Cabos **5**

RESTAURANTS ◆
Manuel's Creative
   Cuisine **8**
Zipper's **13**

ATTRACTIONS ●
Playa Acapulquito surfing beach **11**
Costa Azul Surf Shop **14**
Cuadra San Francisco Equestrian Center **3**
Las Tiendas de Palmilla **7**
Zipper's surf break **12**

San José
del Cabo

Cabo Real   Palmilla

Playa Bledito
km19.5

Sea of Cortez
(Gulf of California)

Costa
Azul km28.8

Playa
Palmilla km27.5

0   1 mi
0   1 km

---

outdoor soaking tubs, is not to be missed. The Mediterranean-influenced restaurant, very practically dubbed El Restaurante, combines good food with good value, a rarity in these rarefied parts.

Carretera Transpeninsular Km 7 on Hwy. 1, at Punta Ballena, Cabo San Lucas, B.C.S. www.esperanza resort.com. ℂ **866/311-2226** in the U.S., or 624/145-6400. Fax 624/145-6499. 57 units. High season $1,200 double; low season $800 double; suites and villas vary. AE, MC, V. Children in rental villas only, and excluded from hotel pool. **Amenities:** Oceanfront restaurant; sushi and ceviche bar; art gallery; private beach w/club; concierge; fitness center; golf privileges; market; outdoor pool; room service; full-service European luxury spa; yoga studio w/complimentary daily classes. *In room:* A/C; TV w/DVD; movie library, MP3 docking station; minibar; hair dryer; in-suite bar; Wi-Fi.

Las Ventanas al Paraíso ★   This celebrated resort is renowned for its architectural design, and it is striking. Adobe structures and rough-hewn wood accents are just right for the xeriscaped desert grounds; cactus gardens feature playful faux-cactus sculptures out of reclaimed metal; pebble mosaics flow from paths to guest rooms like flotsam on the tide. Richly furnished white-on-white "suites" (some of which are actually just very large rooms) are tricked out with everything and more: telescopes for whale-watching, a flight of complimentary tequilas; botanical guides; and hand-painted ceramic sinks. Larger suites offer extras such as rooftop terraces, sunken whirlpools on a private patio, or a personal pool; this is especially a plus here as resort pools are smallish and the beach, like many in Los Cabos, is unsafe for swimming. Las Ventanas has been protecting sea turtle nests on its property since 1997, and in summer, lucky guests can help release hatchlings into the sea.

Hwy. 1 Km 19.5, 23410 San José del Cabo, B.C.S. www.lasventanas.com. ℂ **888/767-3966** in the U.S., or 624/144-2800. Fax 624/144-2801. 71 suites. High season $855 gardenview double, $1,210 oceanview double, $1,625 split-level oceanfront suite with rooftop terrace, $3,585–$6,835 luxury suites (1–3 bedrooms); low season $655 gardenview double, $825 oceanview double, $1,210 split-level oceanfront suite with rooftop terrace, $2,535–$5,185 luxury suites. Spa and golf packages and inclusive meal plans available. AE, DC, MC, V. Free valet parking. **Amenities:** Oceanfront restaurant; terrace bar w/live music; seaside grill; fresh-juice bar; CD library; access to adjoining championship Cabo Real golf course; movie library; pet packages w/treats and massages; 7 outdoor pools; room service; shuttle services; deluxe European spa w/complete treatment and exercise facilities; watersports; sportfishing; luxury yachts. *In room:* A/C, TV/DVD, hair dryer, minibar, MP3 player, Wi-Fi.

One&Only Palmilla ★★★   Exclusive, exquisite, expensive. But you get what you pay for at this super-luxe resort on Punta Palmilla. Lush palm-filled grounds are spread over a steep hillside; hotel buildings line the cliff edge with a 270-degree view

THE LOWDOWN ON golf IN CABO

Los Cabos, one of the world's finest golf destinations, offers an ample and intriguing variety of courses to challenge golfers of all levels.

The reason so many choose to play here is not just the selection, quality, and beauty of the courses, but the reliable weather. The courses highlighted below compare to the great ones in Palm Springs and Scottsdale, with the added beauty of ocean views and a wider variety of desert cacti and flowering plants.

Course fees are high in Cabo—generally more than $200 per round. But these world-class courses are worth the world-class price. Courses generally offer 20% to 30% off rates if you play after 2 or 2:30pm. This can be a great time because play is generally faster.

The golf offerings in Los Cabos have continued to expand; an untold number of courses are in various phases of construction. At **Puerto Los Cabos,** a relatively new mega-development northeast of San José del Cabo, two 18-hole courses have recently opened: the public course designed by Jack Nicklaus and a private course by Greg Norman. **Club Campestre,** in the heart of San José, will have an 18-hole Jack Nicklaus course. The **Chileno Bay Project,** in the center of the Corridor, has set aside 4km (2½ miles) of coastline for luxury-home sites and two championship courses by Tom Fazio. At the other end of the peninsula, near Cabo San Lucas on the Pacific side, the **Quivira Los Cabos** development will soon be launching two more championship courses designed by Jack Nicklaus.

The area's premier courses open to the public are listed below in order of location, from north to south.

Palmilla Golf Club   The original Cabo course is now a 27-hole layout. The original 18 holes are known as the Arroyo; the newest holes are the Ocean 9. It's a bit of a misnomer—although the newer holes lie closer to the water, only one has a true ocean view, with spectacular play directly down to the beach. You must play the Arroyo for your first 9 holes and then choose between Mountain and Ocean for your back 9. If you play this course only once, choose the Mountain, which offers better ocean views. The signature hole is the Mountain 5; you hit over a canyon, and

of the Sea of Cortez. Princely rooms have inlaid stone floors and carved wooden furnishings, and open onto spectacular sea views from a daybed-furnished terrace; suites include a private pool. By day, watch whales spouting from your perch in the cliff-top Jacuzzi; by night, enjoy the resort's magical, luminary landscape transformed by lanterns and candles. Standard rooms are most convenient to the larger pool and gorgeous Palmilla swimming beach; from suites expect a ten-minute walk. Agua Restaurant is enchantingly beautiful but very expensive and with only so-so food; you're better off splurging at Jean-Georges Vongerichten's Market, which while lacking the tropical breezes of its neighbor, surpasses it in cuisine.

Carretera Transpeninsular Km 7.5, 23400 San José del Cabo, B.C.S. www.oneandonlypalmilla.com. ✆ **866/829-2977** in the U.S., or 624/146-7000. Fax 624/146-7001. 173 units. High season $1,195–$1,470 double, $1,695–$3,895 suite; low season $575–$725 double, $875–$3,250 suite. AE, DC, MC, V. **Amenities:** 2 restaurants; 2 bars; pool bar; bicycles; CD library; children's center; championship Palmilla golf course; 2 outdoor infinity pools; room service; deluxe spa w/treatment and exercise facilities; sportfishing; 6 tennis courts; watersports; yoga garden. *In room:* A/C, TV/DVD, CD player, hair dryer, minibar.

then down to the green below over a forced carry. The 14th hole here is considered one of the world's most beautiful golf holes, a forced carry from the hillside tee boxes to an island. From there, players line up on a green set on the side of a steep arroyo. The hole opens up to spectacular vistas and seems a lot longer than it plays. This is target golf, on a Jack Nicklaus course that was constructed with strategy in mind. A mountaintop clubhouse provides spectacular views. Although it is currently a semiprivate club, most Corridor hotels have membership benefits.

Cabo del Sol   The Ocean Course at Cabo del Sol was the second Jack Nicklaus course constructed in Los Cabos. It is much more difficult than the Palmilla course, with less room for error.

Don't be fooled by the wide, welcoming 1st hole. This is challenging target golf, with numerous forced carries—even from the red tees. Seven holes are along the water. At the par-3 signature 17th hole, the golfer is faced with a 178-yard shot over sandy beach and rocky outcroppings to a tiny green framed by bunkers on one side and a drop to the

ocean on the other. The finishing hole, guarded by desert and cactus on the right and rock cliffs leading to the sea on the left, is modeled after the 18th at Pebble Beach.

Cabo del Sol offers another option, the Desert Course, which is Tom Weiskopf's first course design in Mexico. It is spread out over 56 hectares (140 acres) of gently rolling desert terrain and provides sweeping ocean views.

Cabo Real   This Robert Trent Jones, Jr., design is known for its holes along the Sea of Cortez; exceptional among these is the frequently photographed 12th hole, which sits high on a mesa facing the sea. Jones designed the course to test low handicappers, but multiple tees make it enjoyable for average players as well. While the first 6 holes are in mountainous terrain, others skirt the shore. Rolling greens and strategically placed bunkers on narrow terrain work their way up to the 6th tee, 138m (460 ft.) above sea level. The most celebrated holes, the 15th and 16th, sit right on the beach between the Meliá Cabo Real Golf & Beach Resort and Las Ventanas al Paraíso.

EXPENSIVE

Marbella Suites ★ 🍴   Offering the million-dollar views of its ritzy neighbors for a fraction of the price, the Marbella is a rare find on the Corridor's Gold Coast. This rambling cliff-side hotel was renovated in 2010, and now its tidy suites are clean and bright looking, with terra-cotta tiles and handy kitchenettes with tables that enable you to do your own thing at mealtimes. Or try the moderately priced restaurant with sunset views. The Marbella's private beach is not safe for swimming, but you can walk along the sand to one that is, or take advantage of the large pool with swim-up bar. The up-and-down orientation here means lots of stairs, so it's not a good choice for people with mobility problems.

Hwy. 1 Km 17, in Cabo Real, San José del Cabo, B.C.S. www.marbellasuites.com. © **866/654-6160** in the U.S., or 624/144-1059. Fax 624/144-1060. 41 units. $172–$257 double. AE, DC, MC, V. Free parking. **Amenities:** Restaurant; bar; 2 Jacuzzis; 2 outdoor pools; spa room. *In-room:* A/C, fridge, hair dryer, kitchenette.

your home AWAY FROM HOME?

If you spend any time eavesdropping at local coffee shops and gringo bars, you'll find the Baja peninsula is full of Americans, Canadians, and Europeans who came for a visit and never left. Owning property in Mexico is no longer as simple as plunking an RV on the beach, a la 30 years ago, but if you fall in love with Los Cabos—or Baja in general—you never have to leave either.

Mexico has made it easy for foreigners to own their dream home on its shores. Through a *fideicomiso,* which is essentially a renewable trust, your home, condo, fractional ownership, or land by the sea is within reach. If you want to learn more about what's available in Los Cabos, check out the **Baja Real Estate**

Guide (www.bajarealestateguide.com), a Los Cabos listings magazine that's not sponsored by any one particular real estate company and therefore showcases an unbiased range of options. Second, choose a reputable real-estate brokerage, such as **Snell Real Estate** (© **866/650-5845** in the U.S., or 624/105-8100; www.snellrealestate.com). A good agent will walk you through the process and help you find the ownership option that's right for you.

Another great resource for investors thinking about buying in Mexico is Mitch Creekmore and Tom Kelly's book, *Cashing in on a Second Home in Mexico: How to Buy, Rent, and Profit from Real Estate South of the Border.*

Westin Resort & Spa, Los Cabos ★★ ☺ The architecturally dramatic Westin sits at the end of a long, paved road atop a seaside cliff. Vivid terra-cotta, yellow, and pink walls rise against a landscape of sandstone, cacti, and palms, with fountains and gardens lining the long pathways from the lobby to the rooms. Guest rooms all have an ocean view and are sleek and spacious, with fluffy Heavenly Beds and walk-in showers separate from the bathtubs. The seaside 18-hole putting green, first-rate fitness facility, and freshly renovated La Cascada restaurant set this property apart from other Corridor resorts. Plus, it's one of the best among our selections for families vacationing along the Corridor; it offers a wealth of activities for children—not to mention Heavenly Dog Beds for beloveds of the canine species.

Hwy. 1 Km 22.5, San José del Cabo, B.C.S. www.westin.com/loscabos. © **800/228-3000** in the U.S., or 624/142-9000. Fax 624/142-9010. 243 units. High season $199 partial oceanview double, $349 oceanview double, $729 suite; low season 25% discount. AE, DC, MC, V. **Amenities:** 6 restaurants; 2 bars; children's activities; concierge; nearby Palmilla and Cabo Real golf courses; 18-hole putting course; 3 outdoor pools; room service; full fitness center and spa; 2 tennis courts; Xplora Adventours services. *In room:* A/C, TV, hair dryer, Internet ($15/day), minibar.

Where to Eat

Manuel's Creative Cuisine ★★★ NEW AMERICAN   This is the area's hottest new restaurant, specializing in borderline sculptural presentations of luxurious foods. Manuel personally shops for the organic vegetables served here and brings in his own fish when he can, but that's about the end of the simple life, and the beginning of the "creative" in the restaurant's name. The kitchen is a hotbed of poaching, reducing, encrusting, slow-braising, and teasing new meanings out of familiar foods; for example, a "mushroom cappuccino" features garlic foam and porcini powder. But even the classics are special here, like a juicy rack of lamb served with cous cous and pomegranate sauce, or oxtail ravioli that strike the right balance of savory, herbed flavor and texture. Order a margarita just for the garnish: a frozen lime splayed to look like a sunflower.

Tiendas de Palmilla, Hwy. 1 Km 27.5. ℂ **624/144-6171.** www.manuelsrestaurant.com.mx. Reservations recommended. Main courses 140–290 pesos. MC, V. Mon–Sat 6–10pm.

CABO SAN LUCAS ★★

176km (109 miles) S of La Paz; 35km (22 miles) W of San José del Cabo; 1,803km (1,118 miles) SE of Tijuana

Cabo's been a hot spot for 70 years, from its start as a golden-age sportfishing mecca in the 1950s through the 1980s party era of a million spring breakers. Since then it has transformed into one of Mexico's most exclusive destinations, and today's Cabo is a golden peninsula of expensive resorts, American-style restaurants, and all the diversions under the sun. But it's as appealing today as way back when, with beautiful beaches, singular sunsets, and the magic that happens where the Pacific meets the Sea of Cortez.

BEACHES Slip on your shades and start posing at **Playa El Médano,** Cabo's sexiest strip of sand. Whatever your pleasure—swimming, snorkeling, or sipping tropical drinks at a beachside bar—it's here. Across the bay, the surreal cliffs of **Playa del Amor** (Lovers' Beach) make a stunning set for your day in the sun, and kayakers paddle through the giant rock arch of El Arco. Rainbow-colored coral and frilly fish brighten the ocean floor at **Playa Chileno, Playa Santa Maria,** and **Pelican Rock,** where you can snorkel right from shore.

THINGS TO DO The waterbound fun starts in **Cabo's port,** where boats dock for fishing, snorkeling, diving, and kayaking adventures, as well as pirate-themed cruises aboard a historic tall ship. Inland adventurers can hike Baja's **desert canyons** and **waterfalls,** or blow through them in a Humvee. Get your history fix at the stone-walled **Iglesia de San Lucas,** founded by Spanish missionaries in 1730.

EATING & DRINKING Cabo's coastal cuisine is all about **seafood,** and the very best in town is served up Japanese-style at the refined **Nick-San,** where the elite meet over local sashimi of moon scallops and wahoo or a refined sea bass *misoyaki.* Put on your drinking shoes for a visit to **Maro's Shrimp House,** for a stab at a succulent pile of crustaceans and the house cocktail, the Bulldog—down 19 and they'll paint your name on the wall. Mexican foodies can't miss **La Fonda,** a temple of Aztec delicacies like ant eggs and modern-day mole sauces that draw a loyal local crowd.

NIGHTLIFE & ENTERTAINMENT The Southern sun bakes Cabo during the day, but after hours, it's the nightlife that sizzles. Start the evening at **Land's End** with cocktails as the sun sets crimson over the Pacific. A jazz set and a margarita at **Two for the Road** get the night started, and **Marina Boulevard's** tequila-fueled dance parties keep it moving into the wee hours.

Essentials

GETTING THERE & DEPARTING

BY PLANE See "Getting There & Departing," earlier, under "San José del Cabo."

BY CAR From La Paz, the best route is Hwy. 1 south past the village of San Pedro, and then Hwy. 19 south through Todos Santos to Cabo San Lucas, a 2-hour total drive.

BY BUS The bus terminal (ℂ **624/143-5020**) is on Héroes at Morelos; it is open daily from 7am to 10pm. Buses go to La Paz every 2 hours starting at 7:15am, with the last departure at 8:15pm. To and from San José, the more convenient and economical **Suburcabos** public bus service runs every 15 minutes and costs 23 pesos.

ORIENTATION

ARRIVING   At the Los Cabos International airport, either buy a ticket for a *colectivo* (shuttle) from **Josefinos** (✆ 624/146-5354), the authorized transportation booth inside the building ($15 per person, $85 for a private van of up to five passengers), or arrange for a rental car, the most economical way to explore the area. Up to four people can share a private taxi, which costs about $60.

Cabo San Lucas also has its own general aviation **airport** (✆ 624/124-5500; CSL), about 5km (3 miles) out of town. To get there, take Hwy 1 toward the Wal-Mart shopping center, and turn left at the traffic light, onto Constituyentes (marked for La Paz as well). Turn right at the first light, following signs for AEROPUERTO. Drive straight about 3km (2 miles) through an unpromising village of rough-looking shacks, and it's at the end of the road. It's served by **Aereo Calafia** and **Aeroservicios Guerrero,** with flights up the peninsula and to the mainland Pacific coast. Be aware that these flights rarely take off as scheduled, so be patient and just plan to arrive in your final destination at least 30 to 45 minutes later than expected.

The walk from the **bus station** to most of the budget hotels is manageable with light luggage or backpacks, and taxis are readily available.

VISITOR INFORMATION   The many "visitor information" booths along the street in Cabo are actually timeshare sales booths, and their staffs will pitch a visit to their resort in exchange for discounted tours, rental cars, and other giveaways. Don't sign up unless you feel like sitting through a daylong sales pitch. The actual **Los Cabos Tourism Office** (✆ 624/146-9628) is 35km (22 miles) away in San José, in the Plaza San José, and is open daily from 8am to 3pm. The good news is, who needs it? The English-language *Los Cabos Guide, Los Cabos News, Destino Los Cabos,* and the irreverent and entertaining *Gringo Gazette* ★ have up-to-date information on new restaurants and clubs, and are distributed free all over town.

CITY LAYOUT   Cabo spreads out north and west of the harbor, edged by foothills and desert mountains to the west and south. The main street leading into town from the airport and San José is Lázaro Cárdenas. As it nears the harbor, Marina Boulevard branches off from it and curves south around the waterfront, becoming the main tourist artery, lined with shopping centers and touts pushing gold jewelry, timeshares, and Viagra. It's obnoxious, but not sleazy, and is a pleasant place for a walk on Sundays, when it's pedestrian-only. To its north is Plaza Amelia Wilkes, better known simply as "the plaza," bordered east-west by Hidalgo and Cabo San Lucas and north-south by 5 de Mayo and Madero; this is the less flashy center of town, a good place to start a stroll through shops, restaurants, and cafes.

 Festivals & Events in Cabo San Lucas

October 18 is the feast of the patron saint of Cabo San Lucas, celebrated with a fair, feasting, music, dancing, and other special events. However, the biggest event of the year for more than 25 years, also in late October, is **Bisbee's Black & Blue,** which draws thousands of party-ready anglers in the quest for the $100,000 purse that comes with catching the biggest marlin.

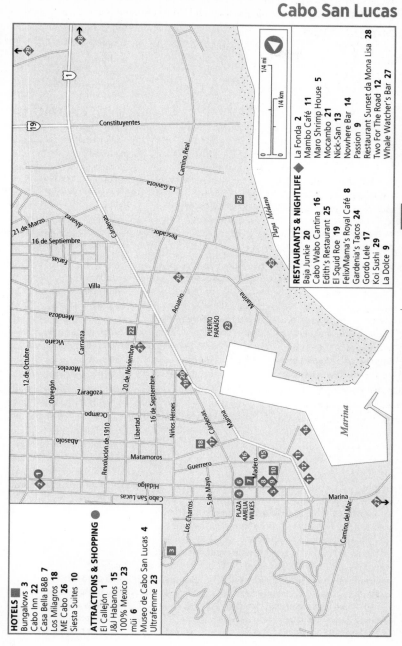

RESTAURANTS & NIGHTLIFE ◆
Baja Junkie **20**
Cabo Wabo Cantina **16**
Edith's Restaurant **25**
El Squid Roe **19**
Felix/Mama's Royal Café **8**
Gardenia's Tacos **24**
Gordo Lele **17**
Koi Sushi **29**
La Dolce **9**
La Fonda **2**
Mambo Café **11**
Maro Shrimp House **5**
Mocambo **21**
Nick-San **13**
Nowhere Bar **14**
Passion **9**
Restaurant Sunset da Mona Lisa **28**
Two For The Road **12**
Whale Watcher's Bar **27**

HOTELS ■
Bungalows **3**
Cabo Inn **22**
Casa Bella B&B **7**
Los Milagros **18**
ME Cabo **26**
Siesta Suites **10**

ATTRACTIONS & SHOPPING ●
El Callejón **1**
J&J Habanos **15**
100% Mexico **23**
müi **6**
Museo de Cabo San Lucas **4**
Ultrafemme **23**

GETTING AROUND

While downtown Cabo is walkable, having a car will enable you to get more easily off the beaten path. Taxis are easy to find but are expensive within Cabo, in keeping with the high cost of everything else. Expect to pay about $15 to $25 for a taxi between Cabo and the Corridor hotels.

For day trips to San José del Cabo, catch a bus (see "Getting There & Departing" under "San José del Cabo," earlier) or a cab. You'll see car-rental specials advertised in town, but before signing on, be sure you understand the total price, including insurance and taxes. Rates can run between $50 and $75 per day, with insurance an extra $10 per day.

[FastFACTS] CABO SAN LUCAS

Area Code The telephone area code is **624.**

Beach Safety Before swimming in the open water, check if conditions are safe. Riptides and large waves are common. **Médano Beach,** close to the marina and town, is the principal beach that's safe for swimming. The ME Cabo resort on Médano Beach has a roped-off swimming area to protect swimmers from personal watercraft and boats. **Playa del Amor** is also usually safe, but use your best judgment. Colored flags to signal swimming safety aren't generally found in Cabo, and neither are lifeguards, so be aware.

Currency Exchange Banks exchange currency during normal business hours, generally Monday through Friday from 9am to 6pm and Saturday from 9am to 2pm. Currency-exchange booths, found throughout Cabo's main tourist areas, aren't as competitive but are more convenient. ATMs are widely available and even more convenient, dispensing pesos—and in some cases dollars—at bank exchange rates.

Emergencies & Hospital In Cabo, **Amerimed** (*©* **624/143-9671**) is a 24-hour, American-standards clinic with bilingual physicians and emergency air-evacuation services, and

it accepts major credit cards. Most of the larger hotels have a doctor on call.

Pharmacy A drugstore with a wide selection of toiletries as well as medicine is **Farmacia Aramburo,** in Plaza Aramburo, on Lázaro Cárdenas at Zaragoza (*©* **624/143-1489**). It's open daily from 8am to 10pm and accepts MasterCard and Visa.

Post Office The *correo* (*©* **624/143-0048**) is at Lázaro Cárdenas and Francisco Villa, on the highway to San José del Cabo, east of the bar El Squid Roe. It's open Monday through Friday from 8am to 4:30pm, and Saturday from 9am to 1pm.

Beaches & Outdoor Activities

Although superb sportfishing is still a draw, there is more to do in Cabo than drop your line and wait for the Big One. World-class scuba diving, kayaking, and surfing are minutes away from Cabo harbor. Glass-bottom, daytime, and sunset cruises for all budgets let you enjoy the water without getting your feet wet. And a wealth of beaches are nearby. On land, take a walk—or ride—on the wild side, exploring Baja's southern deserts and oases on foot, ATV, Hummer, or horseback. Tamer but no less challenging are Los Cabos's top-ranked golf courses, with great sea views up and down the Corridor. And January through March, drop whatever else you had planned and motor out to Baja's migrating gray whales, for one of the most spectacular nature encounters anywhere.

Cabo is a port town, and no trip here is truly complete without getting out on the water at least once. If your boat is carrying fish, you can expect a visit from Pancho, too, an enormous male sea lion who keeps fit leaping onto the backs of fishing boats for treats! For most fishing cruises and excursions, try to make reservations at least a day in advance; keep in mind that some trips require a minimum number of people. Most sports and outings can be arranged through your hotel concierge; fishing also can be arranged directly at one of the fishing-fleet offices at the marina, which is on the south side of the harbor, while scuba and snorkeling go through the three dive outfitters in a building between the marina and Marina Boulevard.

Most businesses in this section are open from 10am to 2pm and 4 to 7pm.

ATV TRIPS Expeditions on ATVs to visit La Candelaria, an isolated Indian village in the mountains 40km (25 miles) north of Cabo, are available through concierge and travel agencies. Lush with palms, mango trees, and bamboo, the settlement gets its water from an underground river that emerges at the pueblo. A 200-kilogram (440-lb.) weight limit per two-person vehicle applies. **Cabo Sports** (✆ 624/143-3399; www.cabosports.com) offers day trips to La Candelaria. Departing at 9am, the 5-hour La Candelaria tour costs around $90 per person or $110 for two on the same ATV.

DRIVING TOURS **Baja Outback** (✆ 624/142-9215; fax 624/142-3166; www.bajaoutback.com) offers a variety of vehicular adventures, including popular H2 Hummer tours in which you drive off-road to cruise desert and beachfront terrain in style. Communication devices link up to 10 vehicles in the caravan, allowing you to listen to the narrations of the guide as you drive. The choice of four routes includes treks to Todos Santos, the East Cape, Santiago and Cañón de la Zorra, and Rancho la Verdad. Tours depart at 9am and return at 3pm, with prices ranging from $95 to $245, depending upon the route, and include lunch. Inquire about multiday tours that focus on the Jesuit missions, migrating whales, and Baja cuisine. Visa, Master-Card, and American Express are accepted, and you must have your valid driver's license. Special group rates are also available.

If speed limits aren't your thing, **Wide Open Baja Racing Experience** (✆ 888/788-2252 or 949/340-1155 in the U.S., or 624/143-4170; office in Plaza Náutica; www.wideopencabo.com) gives you the chance to drive actual Chenowth Magnum race cars at their 600-hectare (1,500-acre) racing ranch on the Pacific coast. There's a varied terrain to drive, with twists, turns, sand washes, and plenty of bumps for thrill-seekers. The $250 price includes shuttle transportation from downtown Cabo to the ranch, driver orientation, and safety equipment.

BEACHES

All along the curving sweep of sand known as **Playa El Médano (Dune Beach)** ★★, on the northeast side of the bay, you can rent snorkeling gear, boats, WaveRunners ($70–$90 per hour), kayaks, pedal boats, and windsurf boards. (You can also take windsurfing lessons.) This is the town's main beach; it's a great place for safe swimming, happy-hour imbibing, and people-watching from one of the many outdoor restaurants, such as the **Office** (✆ 624/143-3464; www.theofficeonthebeach.com) or **Baja Cantina** (✆ 624/143-1591), the less-expensive option, which is just as good and has a better atmosphere for all-day lounging along its shore. Médano has great views of Land's End, the rocky promontory that extends out from the harbor into the Pacific, and the lovely beaches that line it. Land's End's beaches are accessible from town by low tide—just walk along the bottom of the cliffs from the east end of the harbor—but involve a little scrambling over rocks. It's easier to hire a water taxi ($10-$14) to bring you out to **Pelican Rock** ★★, with great snorkeling just twenty yards from shore, or **Playa del Amor (Lovers' Beach)** ★★★, with rolling waves that are usually safe to swim in. From there, it's a surreally picturesque stroll to Divorce Beach, across the sandy break in the cliffs to the Pacific side—but recent drownings here are a reminder that Divorce Beach is under no circumstances safe for swimming. For more area beaches, see "Beaches & Outdoor Activities" under "San José & the Corridor," earlier in this chapter.

CRUISES

Glass-bottom boats leave from the town marina daily every 45 minutes between 9am and 4pm. They cost $14 per person for a 1-hour tour, which passes sea lions and pelicans on its way to the famous **El Arco (Rock Arch)** at Land's End, where the Pacific and the Sea of Cortez meet. Boats can drop you off at Playa del Amor (Lovers' Beach) if you wish to snorkel or sun; make sure you understand which boat will pick you up—it's usually a smaller one run by the same company that ferries people back at regular intervals. Check the timing to make sure you have the correct boat, or expect an additional $10 charge for boarding a competitor's boat.

A number of **daylong** and **sunset cruises** come in a variety of flavors. They cost $30 to $50 per person, depending on the boat, duration of cruise, and amenities; most include at least snacks and many serve meals and have an open bar. A sunset cruise on the 13m (43-ft.) catamaran *Pez Gato* (© 624/143-3797; www.pezgato cabo.com) departs from the Tesoro Resort dock (Dock no. 4, 50m/164 ft. from the main dock) between 5 and 6pm, depending on the season. A 2-hour cruise costs $30, open bar included. Their January to March whale-watching tours ($30, including drinks, children 5 to 11 half-price) leave at 10am and 2pm and return two hours later. The swanker *Tropicat* (owned by the same company) hosts jazz and wine cruises for $50. And *Ecocat* (© 624/157-4685; http://caboecotours.com) claims to be the largest catamaran in Mexico, offering a selection of cruises from $30 to $50. **Pirate cruises ★** ($30–$78 adults, kids 4–12 half-price) are designed with kids in mind, offering the same sunset, whale-watching, and daytime excursions as the cats, but under sail on tall ships, with costumed crew and a pirate show. Choose from the 19th-century *Sunderland* (© 624/105-0955; www.thecabopirateship.com) and the *Buccaneer Queen* (© 800/745-2226 in the U.S., or through Cabo San Lucas Tours, © 800/822-4577; www.cabotallships.com).

LAND SPORTS

Aside from the obvious—golf and horseback riding—Cabo is hot on mountain biking, rock climbing, and hiking as well.

GOLF   Most of Los Cabos's world-famous golf is in the Corridor, driving east toward San José (see "The Lowdown on Golf in Cabo" earlier in this chapter). But an 18-hole course designed by Roy Dye is at the **Cabo San Lucas Country Club,** formerly the Raven Club (© 888/328-8501 in the U.S., or 624/143-4653; fax 624/143-5809; www.golfincabo.com). The entire course overlooks the juncture of the Pacific Ocean and Sea of Cortez, including the famous rocks of Land's End. It includes a 607-yard, par-5 7th hole. High season greens fees are $150 for 18 holes, $120 for the noon rate, and $79 after 2pm. In summer, greens fees drop significantly.

The lowest greens fees in the area are at the public 9-hole **Mayan Palace Golf Los Cabos** (© 624/142-0900 or 142-0901) in San José del Cabo (p. 53). Greens fees are just 1,225 pesos for 18 holes with equipment; rates drop to 787 pesos for 18 holes in summer. All greens fees include the use of a cart.

HIKING   An increasing array of adventure tours and extreme sports are available in the Los Cabos area. **Baja Outback** (© 624/142-9200; www.bajaoutback.com)

leads daylong tours into the foothills of the Sierra de la Laguna, 2 hours north of Los Cabos, focusing on waterfalls or canyons and stopping in traditional mountain villages, for $115 including lunch; private two-person tours are also available. **Baja Wild** (✆ **624/142-5300;** www.bajawild.com) offers canyons and waterfalls in one tour ($110), skipping the cultural visits. The range runs north to south in the Baja peninsula and reaches elevations of more than 2,100m (7,000 ft.), accommodating a unique biosphere where oak and pine trees flourish. Although you sense you are in Baja's desert landscape, you'll be awed by the amount of wildlife you'll see: frogs, doves, Monarch butterflies, deer, giant golden eagles, lizards, and much more. There are also cool, spring-fed mountain pools to soothe your muscles after the 8km (5-mile) round-trip hike. Group sizes are limited to about eight, and transportation to the hiking area is by air-conditioned minivan.

HORSEBACK RIDING For horseback riding, **Cuadra San Francisco Equestrian Center** (p. 53) comes highly recommended. You can also rent **horses** through **Rancho Colín** (✆ **624/143-3652**) for $25 per hour. Tours for sunset riding on Sea of Cortez beaches cost $35 per hour, the 2-hour desert and beach trail ride is $60, and the 3½-hour tour through the mountains is $80. The ranch is open daily from 8am to noon and 2 to 5pm, and is across from the Hotel Club Las Cascadas.

YOGA Many hotels offer yoga, but if yours doesn't, the **San Lucas Yoga Shala** (Matamoros btw. Obregón and Carranza; ✆ **624/144-7419**) offers kundalini, hatha, and vinyasa classes.

WATERSPORTS

Tío Sports (✆ **624/143-3399;** www.tiosports.com) on Playa Médano arranges a variety of land- and water-based adventure and nature tours; stand-up paddleboarding; parasailing; and kayak, catamaran, snorkeling, and diving trips. The website gives current prices.

SEA KAYAKING Cabo's bays and cliffs are a marvelous backdrop for a kayak trip. The most popular excursion is a half-day, out from the marina to the sea lion colony at El Arco, stopping for snorkeling at Pelican Rock, for $70 to $85 (experienced kayakers can go without a guide, renting kayaks for $15/hour). If you've got a full day to invest, you can visit Twin Dolphin, Chileno, and Santa Maria bays for snorkeling and lunch, or go out to the coral reef at Cabo Pulmo marine park. Tours run $140 to $185 per person and include transportation, lunch, and gear. **Tío Sports** can set you up on Médano Beach; for out-of-the-bay tours, contact **Baja Wild** (✆ **624/142-5300;** www.bajawild.com) or **Baja Outback** (✆ **624/142-9200;** www.bajaoutback.com).

SNORKELING/DIVING The meeting of the Pacific and the Sea of Cortez makes for amazing sea life here, from the teeming coral reef of Cabo Pulmo on the East Cape to the mantas and sharks of the Pacific. You can dive with sea lions right in Cabo's bay, float across a 180m (600-ft.) sand waterfall, and swim through a school of thousands of grouper forming a wall in the water—all in a 10-minute boat ride from the marina. Nearby, snorkeling at Pelican Rock, right offshore near Playa del Amor, is easy and full of colorful parrotfish, angelfish, and anemones. There's also good snorkeling at Santa Maria and Chileno bays. Two-tank local dives go for $75 to $90 plus $25 to $50 equipment rental, while snorkel trips cost $25 to $45, including all equipment and a naturalist guide. With kids, consider one of the cheesy but fun pirate-themed snorkel tours of the *Buccaneer Queen* (✆ **800/745-2226** in the U.S., or through Cabo San Lucas Tours, ✆ **800/822-4577;** www.cabotallships. com).

TAKING THE plunge

The proximity of dive sites to the marina, the high local standard of dive companies, and the incredible marine diversity here make Cabo a great place to try scuba diving. All of Cabo's principal dive outfitters offer PADI diver training courses in English. For beginners, a one-day Introduction to Scuba Diving Course (half-day, $100–$115) is a first taste of the underwater world; if you've got the time, Scuba Diver (3 days, $300 plus materials) or Open Water Diver (4 days, $425–$450 plus materials) certifications will qualify you to dive for the rest of your days. The first day of each course is spent learning how to use the regulator and vest to breathe underwater and control buoyancy, and going over safety questions. Then it's out on the water, where you'll dive one-on-one with instructors, practicing skills while you watch eels and mantas cruising by. You can watch study DVDs in your hotel room at night, so when it's time for your test, you'll pass with flying colors. Your certification allows you to dive anywhere in the world—but you may be happiest with Cabo.

Farther afield, the area's best dive sites are at **Gordo Banks, Los Frailes,** and **Cabo Pulmo.** Gordo Banks is an advanced dive site where you can see whale sharks and hammerhead sharks. It's a deep dive—27 to 30m (90–98 ft.)—with limited visibility (9–12m/30–40 ft.). Most dives are drift dives, and wet suits are highly recommended. Los Frailes is often home to schooling white-tip sharks. And Cabo Pulmo, a protected marine park 72km (45 miles) northeast of San José, has seven sites for divers of all experience levels, the northernmost living coral reef in the Americas, and some of the most beautiful stretches of Baja beach; with tropical reef fish, rays, corals, eels, and sea turtles, it's a paradise for divers and snorkelers alike. Three-tank Cabo Pulmo and Frailes dives cost $175 to $235, Gordo Banks, a two-tank site, $175. Cabo's dive companies are all located in the Gali Plaza building on Marina Boulevard, right behind the marina. **Manta Scuba** (© 624/144-3871; www.caboscuba.com) has full-size two-engine dive boats, and factory-trained technicians maintaining their gear. **Amigos del Mar** (© 624/143-0505; www.amigosdelmar.com) has dive boats with toilets and a full-service dive shop. Manta offers hotel/dive packages with **Bungalows** hotel (p. 78), two dives, accommodations, and breakfast for $100 per person. They're also the only company that goes to Cabo Pulmo by boat (2 hr.); the others travel by car and use local boats there. For more on Cabo Pulmo, see chapter 5.

SPORTFISHING ★★★   Fishing is Cabo's original claim to fame, and it still lives up to its reputation: Bringing in a 45-kilogram (100-lb.) marlin is routine. Angling is good all year, though the catch varies with the season. Sailfish and wahoo are best from June through November; yellowfin tuna, May through December; yellowtail, January through April; and black and blue marlin, July through December. Striped marlin, dorado, and mahimahi are prevalent year-round. Decades of overfishing in the Sea of Cortez continue to put pressure on populations; you can be part of the solution by practicing catch-and-release with big fish (p. 95).

You can call on a concierge or a travel agent, but it's more fun to make your own arrangements for a fishing trip. Just go to the marina on the south side of the harbor, where you'll find several fleet operators with offices near the docks. The *panga* fleets east of San José in La Playita offer the best deals; 5 hours of fishing for two or three people costs $210 to $450, plus a 20% tip (see **Gordo Banks Pangas;** © **624/142-1147;** www.gordobanks.com; Visa and MasterCard accepted). In Cabo, try **Pisces Fleet,** located in the Cabo Maritime Center, behind Tesoro Resort and next to Captain Tony's on the marina (© **624/143-1288;** www.piscessportfishing.com; daily 10am–4pm; Visa and MasterCard accepted), or **Minerva's Baja Tackle** (on the corner of Marina Blvd. and Madero; © **624/143-1282;** www.minervas.com; daily 6am–8pm; American Express, MasterCard, and Visa accepted). A day on a fully equipped cruiser with captain and guide starts at around $985 for up to six people. For deluxe trips with everything included aboard a 12m (40-ft.) boat, you'll have to budget around $1,500 and up. If you're traveling in your own vessel, you'll need a fishing permit, which you can get at Minerva's. Depending on the size of the boat, it will cost $37 to $109 per month. Daily permits (136 pesos) and annual permits are also available.

SURFING Stellar surfing can be found from November through April all along the Pacific beaches north and west of town, and the East Cape is the ultimate North American surfing destination from May through October. (Also see "Surfing" in "San José del Cabo," p. 54, for details on Costa Azul breaks.)

The areas to the east and west of Los Cabos, known as the East Cape and the Pacific side, respectively, have yet to face the onslaught of development that's so rapidly changed the tip. An hour-long drive up the western coast to the little towns of Pescadero and Todos Santos is a great surf journey, as well as a summer trek up the Sea of Cortez coastline toward Cabo Pulmo. See chapter 5 for more on Pescadero, Todos Santos, and Cabo Pulmo, and visit **www.costa-azul.com.mx/areas_maps.htm** for a detailed look at the different breaks, excursions, rental equipment, and lessons available for the time of year you're planning to visit.

WHALE-WATCHING ★ ☺ From January through March, migrating gray and humpback whales visit Baja to breed and bear their calves, in one of the world's great wildlife spectacles. Practically every local tour company advertises whale-watching tours that range from an hour to an overnight. The difference is location: While you can see whales and their calves right off of Los Cabos and the Corridor, you won't get very close to them and they're likely to be on the move. The best whale-watching action is up the Pacific coast in the bays of Mid-Baja, where whale families come right up to your *panga* to "play."

If time is limited, whale-watching in the waters off Cabo is fun and educational. Options include Zodiac-style rafts, sportfishing boats, glass-bottom boats, and cruise catamarans, all of which depart from the Cabo San Lucas Marina and cost $35 to $70, depending on the type of boat and whether the price includes snacks and beverages. **Baja Wild** does a half-day trip for $70, $50 for children; **Cabo San Lucas**

Letting One Get Away

As fish stocks in the Sea of Cortez decline, sportfishermen and women are doing their part and letting go. "Catch and release" fishing allows you to reel in as many of the big guys as you can, provided you use equipment and practices that allow them to be released in good condition back into the sea. (You'll get a certificate to take home.) Green-thinking businesses are encouraging sustainable sportfishing by supporting captains who participate—you can be a part of the solution, too.

surf & SLEEP

If you can't get enough of the surf, stay where the breaks are.

The **Cabo Surf Hotel & Spa** (*©* **858/964-5117** in the U.S., or 624/142-2666; www.cabosurfhotel.com) has 16 beachfront rooms in a secluded, gated boutique resort. It's 13km (8 miles) west of San José del Cabo, across from the Querencia golf course, on Playa Aca-pulquito, the most popular surfing beach in Los Cabos. Along with a choice of rooms and suites, it's equipped with an oceanfront terrace restaurant, surf shop, and the Mike Doyle Surf School, which offers day lessons and more intensive

instruction. Rates range from $265 to $375 for a double and $290 to $625 for suites and villas. Promotional rates are available during summer months, which is optimum for surfers who seek the Sea of Cortez's summertime swells.

Of course, if you're coming to Baja strictly for the surf, you may join the other hard-core wave-riders and camp along the sugary beaches of the East Cape in the summer and the Pacific in the winter. Most beaches—especially the ones fronting secluded surf breaks—are safe and accommodating for overnight stays.

Tours offers all kinds of watercraft on half-day tours between $33 and $63 for adults, half-price for children. Cabo San Lucas Tours also offers a 14-hour day trip to Magdalena Bay twice a week in season, that includes van transfers, lunch, and two hours on a boat for $200. If money is no object, for $440 you can take Baja-based airline **Aereo Calafia**'s (*©* **624/143-4302**; www.tourballenas.com) tour, in which you fly 75 minutes from San Lucas to Magdalena, board a *panga*, and spend 3 hours watching gray whales and humpbacks loll around the coastal lagoons before returning the same day. You also can spot whales from the shore in Los Cabos; good spots include the beach by the Westin Resort & Spa, at Esperanza Resort in the Punta Ballena community, and along the beaches and cliffs of the Corridor. For more information, see "Whale-Watching in Baja: A Primer," in chapter 6.

Exploring Cabo San Lucas

HISTORIC CABO SAN LUCAS

Plaza Amelia Wilkes is the town's main square, and it's a funny hodgepodge, containing a gazebo, some giant chicken topiary, and a whale skeleton. Buildings on the streets facing the plaza are gradually being renovated to house restaurants and shops, and the picturesque neighborhood is miles more colorful than the touristy strip to the south. The **Museo de Cabo San Lucas** (*©* **624/105-0661**; Mon 10am–noon, Tues–Fri 10am–7pm, Sat 10am–2pm and 4–8pm, Sun 4–8pm) is at the north side of the square at Lázaro Cárdenas 10; it's got exhibits on local natural history and archaeology and the remains of a prehistoric zebra. The Spanish missionary Nicolás Tamaral established the stone **Iglesia de San Lucas (Church of San Lucas)** on Calle Cabo San Lucas near Plaza Wilkes in 1730; a large bell in a stone archway commemorates the completion of the church in 1746. (If you visited the mission church in San José, you may remember Father Tamaral met his fate at the hands of Pericué people in a dispute over the church's ban on polygamy.)

DAY TRIPS

Most local hotels and travel agencies can book day trips to the city of La Paz for around $60, including beverages and a tour of the countryside along the way. Usually there's a stop at the weaving shop of Fortunato Silva, who spins his own cotton and weaves it into wonderfully textured rugs and textiles. Day trips are also available to Todos Santos ($60), with a guided walking tour of the Cathedral Mission, museum, Hotel California, and various artists' homes. For more information, see chapter 5.

Shopping

If you're after a beer-themed T-shirt, Cabo San Lucas can't be beat. But it's not a complete retail desert. In addition to top-end international shopping malls like **Plaza Paraíso** (on Lázaro Cárdenas, fronting the marina; (C) **624/144-3000;** www.puerto paraiso.com), where you can replace your missing Burberry bikini or buy a diamond ring, try these shops for unique, high-quality products.

El Callejón Cabo's best selection of fine Mexican furniture and decor items, plus gifts, accessories, tableware, fabrics, and lamps. Open Monday through Friday 10am to 7pm and 10am to 5pm on Saturdays. Hidalgo 2518 near 12 de Octubre in front of La Fonda Restaurant. (C) **624/143-3188.**

J & J Habanos This is Cabo's go-to cigar shop, selling premium Cuban and fine Mexican cigars; it even has a walk-in humidor. Open Monday through Saturday 9am to 10pm, Sunday 9am to 9pm. Madero btw. Marina Blvd. and Guerrero. (C) **624/143-6160** or 143-3839. www.jnjhabanos.com.

Müi Mexican-made women's fashion, with city-slick leather bags and shoes in earth and jewel tones just right for Cabo, as well as traditional straw bags and crazy bead jewelry. Open Monday to Saturday 10am to 7pm. Lázaro Cárdenas at Hidalgo. No phone.

100% Mexico All of the items in the store—including Oaxacan weavings, Pueblan talavera, and lacquered boxes from Guerrero—are certified by *Fondo Nacional Para El Fomento de las Artesans* (FONART), Mexico's national artisan foundation. Open daily from 9am to 9pm. Near the main entrance of Plaza Paraíso. (C) **624/105-0443.** www.100mexico.com.

Ultrafemme Mexico's largest duty-free shop has an excellent selection of fine jewelry and watches, including Rolex, Cartier, Omega, TAG Heuer, Tiffany, and Tissot; perfumes, including Lancôme, Chanel, Armani, Carolina Herrera; and other gift items, all at duty-free prices. Open daily 10am to 9:30pm. On the 1st floor of the Luxury Avenue section of Puerto Paraíso. (C) **624/145-6090.** www.ultrafemme.com.mx.

Where to Stay

Cabo hotels have three price "seasons": extra-high, at Christmas, New Years, and usually a week in March; high, from December to April; and surprisingly low, from May to November. Several full-service beachfront resorts lining Playa Médano, in the spirit of the very expensive Corridor hotels but closer to town, offer good package deals through online travel search engines. The 14% tax is not included in the rates listed below.

VERY EXPENSIVE

ME Cabo ★★ If you've come to Cabo to party, this is your place. Upgraded rooms, an adult-focused floor called "the Level," and the presence of the swank Nikki Beach stake a glam claim on this beachfront property. Its location on Médano Beach is central to any other action you may want to seek, but with Nikki Beach and Passion (see "Cabo San Lucas After Dark," below), you'll find plenty right here. Rooms are awash in fiery red and white, with sleek, contemporary decor. All suites have ocean views, and private terraces look across to the famed El Arco. Master suites have separate living-room areas. Guests gather by the beachfront pool where oversize daybeds perfectly accommodate this lounge atmosphere. There are also VIP tepees, and the live DJ music keeps the party here going day and night.

Playa El Médano s/n; 23410 Cabo San Lucas, B.C.S. www.me-cabo.com. ⓒ **624/145-7800.** Fax 624/143-0420. 151 units. High season $469–$679 double, $1,129 chic suite, $1,629 loft suite; low season $349–$559 double, $1,009 chic suite, $1,509 loft suite. AE, MC, V. Free parking. **Amenities:** Nikki Beach Restaurant & Beach Club; Passion bar/dance club; concierge; Jacuzzi in some rooms; 2 outdoor pools; room service. *In room:* A/C, TV, hair dryer, minibar, Nintendo Wii in some rooms, Wi-Fi.

EXPENSIVE

Casa Bella B&B ★ 🛏 This hacienda-style boutique hotel is right on the main plaza in Cabo San Lucas, yet its walled grounds keep it private and tranquil. Built in the 1960s as a family home, it was converted to a hotel in 2003; rooms are attractively furnished with antiques but are otherwise quite ordinary, with double or king-size beds and pretty, but windowless, tiled bathrooms. Quite extraordinary, on the other hand, is the central courtyard and pool, with landscaped tropical gardens and a wealth of nooks and patios to retreat with a book. The common living area has the only TV on the property, and a small, lovely terraced dining area serves the complimentary continental breakfast as well as other meals.

Hidalgo 10, Col. Centro, 23410 Cabo San Lucas, B.C.S. www.casabellahotel.com. ⓒ **626/209-0215** in the U.S., or 624/143-6400. Fax 624/143-6401. 12 units. High season $160–$250; low-season specials available upon request. Rates include continental breakfast. AE, MC, V. Street parking available. Closed Aug–Sept. **Amenities:** Restaurant; concierge; outdoor pool; room service. *In room:* A/C, no phone; Wi-Fi.

MODERATE

Bungalows ★★ 🛏 This is Cabo's most spacious, comfortable, full-service inn, one of the most special places to stay in all of Los Cabos. In a quiet residential neighborhood uphill from town, each "bungalow"—actually small apartments in a gated compound—is a charming retreat decorated with terra-cotta tiles, hand-painted sinks, wooden chests, blown glass, and other creative touches; balconies catch a refreshing breeze off of the bay. Rooms surround a lovely heated pool with cushioned lounges and tropical gardens, and each one has a kitchenette, purified water, and DVD. A hearty breakfast of French toast or eggs with fresh-ground coffee and fresh juices is served on the brick-paved patio. Wi-Fi is strongest in rooms near the main house.

Miguel A. Herrera s/n, btw. Constitución and Libertad, three blocks uphill from Plaza Amelia Wilkes, Cabo San Lucas, B.C.S. www.cabobungalows.com. ⓒ/fax **624/143-5035** or 143-0585. 16 units. High season $135–$175 suite; low season $95–$150 suite. Extra person $20. Rates include full breakfast. MC, V. Street parking available. **Amenities:** Breakfast room; concierge; outdoor pool; Wi-Fi. *In room:* A/C, TV/DVD, hair dryer, kitchenette, movie library.

Los Milagros The stylishly whitewashed, two-level buildings housing the 12 suites and rooms of Los Milagros (the Miracles) border a grassy garden area or the small pool. Spiffy terra-cotta tiled rooms are fresh with contemporary iron queen or full-size beds; they're small, but you can hang out on the rooftop terrace too. Some units have kitchenettes, the master suite has a sunken tub, and there's coffee service in the mornings on the patio. Evenings are romantic: Candles light the garden, and classical music plays. Request a room in one of the back buildings, where pomegranate trees buffer others' conversations. It's just 1½ blocks from Cabo Wabo Cantina (p. 83). Los Milagros is part of an informal network of expat women hotel owners, and the staff can help you arrange stays at the other four hotels in the group (p. 57).

Matamoros 116, 23410 Cabo San Lucas, B.C.S. www.losmilagros.com.mx. ℂ/fax **718/928-6647** in the U.S., or 624/143-4566. 12 units. $85 double; $100 kitchenette suite; $125 master suite. Ask about summer discounts, group rates, and long-term discounts. No credit cards, but payable through PayPal. Free secure parking. **Amenities:** Small outdoor pool; rooftop terrace. *In room:* A/C, TV, Wi-Fi.

INEXPENSIVE

Cabo Inn ★ 🏠 This three-story hotel on a quiet street offers a rare combination of low rates, friendly management, and a modicum of style. Rooms are basic and very small, with either two twin beds or one queen-size; although this was a bordello in a prior incarnation, everything is kept new and updated, from the mattresses to the minifridges. Wall murals and painted window borders add a spark of personality. The rooms surround a courtyard where you can enjoy satellite TV, a barbecue grill, and free coffee. The third floor has a rooftop terrace with *palapa* and a small swimming pool; also on this floor is a colorful, *palapa*-topped, open-air room with hanging *tapetes* (woven palm mats) for additional privacy, equipped with a king-size bed and Jacuzzi. A large fish freezer is available, and most rooms have kitchenettes. The hotel is just 2 blocks from downtown and the marina. A lively restaurant next door will even deliver pitchers of margaritas and dinner to your room.

20 de Noviembre and Leona Vicario 20, 23410 Cabo San Lucas, B.C.S. www.caboinnhotel.com. ℂ/fax **619/819-2727** in the U.S., or 624/143-0819. 23 units. Year-round $40–$48 single; $55–$90 double; $120 up to 6 people; $120 suite with Jacuzzi. No credit cards. Street parking. **Amenities:** Barbecue; small rooftop pool and sunning area; communal TV. *In room:* A/C, fridge.

Siesta Suites 🗝 Long on amenities, short on chic, the Siesta Suites is a great perch for fishermen, spring breakers, and anyone else who's not overly concerned with the style of their accommodations. The very clean rooms at this motel-style lodge are colorful and functional, with funky painted wood furniture, tile floors, foam mattresses, and tacky polyester bedspreads; they're "suites" because most include a kitchenette and a small eating area (some rooms substitute an additional bed for the kitchen facilities). Additionally, a huge gas grill is available for guests on one of the many terraces and barbecues are encouraged. At the adjacent Salvatore's, a popular Italian-American restaurant, is a tiny plunge pool for guests to cool off in.

Calle Emiliano Zapata btw. Guerrero and Hidalgo, 23410 Cabo San Lucas, B.C.S. www.cabosiestasuites. com. ℂ **866/271-0952** in the U.S., or 624/143-2773. 20 suites. $69–$80 double; $440–$535 weekly rates. DC, MC, V; AE for prepay only. **Amenities:** Barbecue pit; restaurant; outdoor pool; Wi-Fi and computer in lobby. *In room:* A/C, fan, TV, kitchenette (in some), fridge.

Where to Eat

Cabo has a lot of bad, overpriced food and a lot of good food that's good value. It can be hard to know what's what from the outside, so make sure you get a recommendation before just walking in—locals know the difference, so ask around before you end up in a tourist trap. We've listed a selection of local favorites here, and some insider tips on Cabo's best restaurants at all price levels. For cheap eats, the absolute local favorite is **Gardenia's Tacos,** a bare-bones eatery on Paseo Pescadores (same street as McDonald's) that serves Cabo's best tacos; other cheap (tacos and quesadillas from 15 pesos) and safe snacks are served up out of the **white trucks** in front of the Marina Mercado down Marina Boulevard, open roughly 5am to 2pm. Note that three of our picks are on the same block, Hidalgo just south of Plaza Amelia Wilkes, so if you can't get into one, you can try the others easily. Other streets to explore for other good restaurants include Hidalgo and Lázaro Cárdenas, plus the marina at the Plaza Bonita. Many restaurants automatically add a 15% tip to the bill.

VERY EXPENSIVE

Edith's Restaurant ★★ SEAFOOD/STEAKS/MEXICAN Lanterns light the open-air way for highly trained waiters, and bouquets of fresh lilies perfume the entrance and washrooms. No detail is overlooked and everyone in the house is in full celebration mode. You will be, too, after a celestial pitcher of margaritas or a bottle from Edith's carefully stocked cellar. The menu gives a nod to classic top-end American steakhouses, accompanying local specialties like lobster with mashed potatoes and stir-fried vegetables; portions are similarly north of the border. And if Mexican food is what you crave, both the Tampiqueña and the Pancho Villa offer a generous sampling of some of Mexico's most prized traditional dishes, which are abundant enough for two, especially when kicked off with the squash-blossom quesadillas or a Caesar salad.

Camino a Playa Médano. ✆ **624/143-0801**. www.edithscabo.com. Reservations strongly recommended. Main courses $20–$84. MC, V. Daily 5–11pm.

Nick-San ★★★ JAPANESE/SUSHI Cabo's celebrated sushi temple has the very freshest and most delicate fish, straight out of the Pacific to your plate. While much of the menu is well-presented sushi and sashimi, including Cabo catches like wahoo, red snapper, and moon scallops, the rest is creatively cooked presentations, like an inspired *chasoba*, green tea pasta with a green curry and sautéed shrimp, or the spare sea bass *misoyaki*, with a miso and white mushroom sauce. While during the day the restaurant doesn't show to its best advantage—low ceilings and spare decor are reminiscent of an employee cafeteria—at night, lit low, this is one of the most elegant rooms in Cabo, and it's a see-and-be-seen scene par excellence.

Marina Blvd., Plaza de la Danza, Local 2. ✆ **624/143-2491**. www.nicksan.com. Reservations recommended. Sashimi, rolls, and main courses 265–500 pesos. MC, V. Tues–Sun 11:30am–10:30pm.

EXPENSIVE

La Fonda ★★ MEXICAN Chef Christophe Chong didn't learn how to make his Prehistoric Appetizers during his studies at the California Culinary Institute—the maguey worms and ant eggs are 100% Mexican. The goes for the non-creepy-crawly part of the menu too: delectable Oaxacan moles with chocolate and sesame seeds, *pipian* moles made of pumpkin seeds, chiles rellenos, and a poblano soup right out of his Mexican grandmother's recipe book. In its soul, this is a neighborhood place, but it's become a favorite of locals from all over Los Cabos, a hot spot for an authentic Mexican night on the town, complete with strolling musicians. Reservations are highly recommended; bear in mind this is about a 20-minute walk up from the main plaza, so you may want to take a taxi or drive.

Hidalgo btw. Obregón and 12 de Octubre, about 6 blocks uphill from Plaza Amelia Wilkes. ✆ **624/143-6926**. Reservations recommended. Main courses 175–275 pesos. AE, MC, V. Mon–Fri 3–10:30pm; Sat–Sun 2–10:30pm.

Maro Shrimp House SEAFOOD A raucous gringo crowd wolfs down the grilled shrimp and lobster here like they're going out of style, but they're not. This place is the reincarnation of a local favorite that closed a few years ago, brought back to life by Maro, one of its former employees. He's sticking to a formula that works: no-nonsense seafood sold by weight and washed down with cold beer and the house specialty cocktail, a Bulldog. It's tequila, beer, and fizzy lemonade, sort of a tequila shandy, served over purified ice in a huge goblet; beat the current record of 18 (in a row!) and get your name painted on the wall. It's a loud and casual joint, decked with folding chairs and strung with Christmas lights; non-seafood eaters can try tacos or a steak.

Hidalgo just south of Madero and Plaza Amelia Wilkes. (✆) **624/143-4966.** Main courses 182–260 pesos. MC, V. Daily noon–10pm.

MODERATE

Felix/Mama's Royale Café ★★ BREAKFAST/MEXICAN What is Mama's in the mornings becomes Felix at night: It's one space, two restaurants, and three tasty meals a day. This is a family place, but the family is two generations of rebel cooks from the California Bay Area, and the counterculture element shows, in kooky menu art and sideways offerings like a Tropical Guess What cocktail: "tequila, orange juice, orange liqueur and something else." Despite this, the food is surprisingly traditional and solidly prepared: American brunches of French toast stuffed with cream cheese and topped with pecans, strawberries, and orange liqueur; several variations of eggs Benedict; home fries and fruit crepes during Mama's hours, and seafood cocktails, guacamole, homemade salsas, and 13 varieties of shrimp during Felix time. The shady patio decked with cloth-covered tables, and the bright, inviting dining room are both comfortable places to settle in, all day long.

Hidalgo at Zapata s/n. (✆) **624/143-4290.** www.mamascabosanlucas.com. Reservations not accepted. Breakfast 100–180 pesos; lunch and dinner main courses 150–250 pesos. MC, V. Daily 7:30am–1pm.

Koi Sushi 🍴 SUSHI Champagne tastes on a beer budget? If you're jonesing for sushi, Koi has got you covered. A former chef from Nick-San has gone way off the beaten path—to the food court of the Wal-Mart shopping center heading out of town—to open up this well-regarded new sushi joint. Tucked in next to a burger stand, and with just a few tables next to its open kitchen, it's a real insider tip. Choose from a standard but delicately prepared and imaginatively presented selection of nigiri (45 pesos for 2 pieces), hand rolls (45–70 pesos), and sashimi, fresh off the boat, or do as the locals do and go off-menu, and ask for the chef's special rolls, different every day.

Plaza San Lucas food court, Hwy. 1 Km 2. (✆) **624/144-7377.** Sashimi and main courses 75–150 pesos. No credit cards. Daily noon–9:30pm.

La Dolce ★★ ITALIAN The very definition of a crowd-pleaser, La Dolce is Cabo's favorite Italian restaurant and one of its top tables in any category. With a traditional pan-Italian menu and a pizza oven besides, it's not trying to win any prizes for gastronomic innovation—and that's just the way regulars like it. Homemade pastas take advantage of the abundance of fresh seafood, in preparations like *spaghetti al cartoccio* (baked with shellfish in a tinfoil envelope) and *linguine ai calamari* (with sautéed cuttlefish), but there's plenty of turf amid the surf, with lasagna, pesto, and a beef filet *al gorgonzola* that draws rave reviews. As befits such a popular place, you are advised to reserve for dinner or risk being shut out.

Hidalgo btw. Madero and Zapata. (✆) **624/143-4122.** Reservations essential. Pasta 128–196 pesos; meat and seafood 180–280 pesos; pizza 118–160 pesos. MC, V. Daily 5pm–midnight.

INEXPENSIVE

Gordo Lele ★ ◙ TACOS   Lele likes the Beatles. Actually, Lele loves the Beatles. His little storefront *taquería* is a shrine to all things John, Paul, George, and Ringo, with the soundtrack to match, and if you're lucky, Lele will sing along. The tacos are pretty good, too, served up hot and juicy and in unusually generous portions—Lele-size, to wit—garnished with avocado and corn, on plastic plates covered handily with plastic liners. *Tortas* (sandwiches) are enough for a full meal, and you can get them to go as well. This is a Cabo institution, and there are always a few locals hanging around, trading jokes and snacking—ask them to explain the Elvis tablecloths, a riddle in an enigma in a mystery.

Matamoros just north of Cárdenas. No phone. Tacos 15–25 pesos; *tortas* 30–50 pesos. No credit cards. Mon-Sat noon-7pm.

Mocambo ★ SEAFOOD   The location of this long-standing Cabo favorite is not inspiring—it's basically a large cement building—but the food obviously is. The place is always packed, generally with locals tired of high prices and small portions. Ocean-fresh seafood is the order of the day, and the specialty platter can easily serve four people. The restaurant is 1½ blocks inland from Lázaro Cárdenas.

Av. Leona Vicario and 20 de Noviembre. ℂ **624/143-6070.** Reservations not accepted. Main courses $5–$30. MC, V. Daily noon-10pm.

Cabo San Lucas After Dark

Cabo San Lucas is the nightlife capital of Baja. After-dark fun starts with the casual bars and restaurants on Marina Boulevard or facing the marina, and transforms into a tequila-fueled dance-club scene after midnight. You can easily find a happy hour with live music and a place to dance, or a fiesta with mariachis.

MEXICAN FIESTAS & THEME NIGHTS   Some larger hotels have weekly fiesta nights and other buffet-plus-entertainment theme nights that can be fun as well as a good buy. Check travel agencies and the **Solmar** (ℂ **624/143-3535**) and **Finisterra** (ℂ **624/143-3333**) hotels. Prices range from $25 (not including drinks, tax, and tips) to $50 (which covers everything, including an open bar with domestic drinks).

SUNSET WATCHING   At the end of the day, the place to be is Land's End, where the two seas meet and the sun goes down. **Restaurant Sunset Da Mona Lisa** (ℂ **624/145-8160**), located on the eastern side of Cabo San Lucas Bay, is Los Cabos's premier place for sunset watching. Spectacular Arch views, dramatic terraces, and a decent Italian and seafood menu make this the ultimate place for watching the sun dive past the horizon. It's open from 8am to 11pm daily. Another option is the **Whale Watcher's Bar,** in the Hotel Finisterra (ℂ **624/143-3333**). Its location at

---

Hey, that Guy's Doing the Cabo Wobble!

Before the **Cabo Wabo Cantina** became a legend, its founder (and former Van Halen singer), Sammy Hagar, had to come up with a name. The story goes that as Hagar was driving into town he noticed a local "staggering" and "bashing about." He exclaimed, "That guy's doing the Cabo Wobble!" and the term Cabo Wabo was born. Visitors can still witness the famous "Cabo Wobble," or try it themselves.

Land's End offers a world-class view of the sun sinking into the Pacific. Mariachis play on Friday from 6:30 to 9pm. The bar is open daily from 10am to 11pm. "Whale margaritas" cost $4, beer $3. Happy hour from 4 to 6pm has two-for-one drinks.

HAPPY HOURS & HANGOUTS

If you shop around, you can usually find an *hora feliz* (happy hour) somewhere in town between 10am and 7pm. The most popular places for tourists to drink and carouse until all hours are still long-standing favorites like El Squid Roe and the Cabo Wabo Cantina, but insiders flock to newer joints like **Nowhere Bar** (Plaza Marina, on Marina Blvd.; ✆ **624/143-4493;** www.nowherebar.com) and **Baja Junkie** (on Lázaro Cárdenas where it splits off to Marina Blvd.; ✆ **624/143/4740;** www.baja junkie.com).

Cabo Wabo Cantina ★   Owned by Sammy Hagar (formerly of Van Halen) and his Mexican and American partners, this "cantina" packs them in, especially when rumors (frequent, and frequently false, just to draw a crowd) fly that a surprise appearance by a vacationing musician is imminent. One of Cabo's few air-conditioned dance venues, it's especially popular in the summer months. There's live music daily, and Sammy himself performs every year on his birthday, October 13. Beer goes for $4, margaritas for $6. For snacks, the Taco Wabo, just outside the club's entrance, stays up late, too. The cantina is open daily from 9am to 2am. Vicente Guerrero at Lázaro Cárdenas. ✆ **624/143-1188.** www.cabowabo.com.

El Squid Roe   This is the kind of faux-shack nightclub with old license plates on the walls and a sign out front proclaiming: "beer makes people see double and feel single." You have been warned. Skin-to-win is the theme as the dancing on tables moves into high gear around 9pm. The scene is mostly tourists jerking to American hip-hop from early evening to around midnight, and at 1am, the local Mexican crowd—just getting their night started—flow in and the hips don't stop shaking until first light. This is a spring break must—and a non-spring break mustn't. Open daily from noon to 4am; there's a kitchen, too. Marina Blvd., opposite Plaza Bonita. ✆ **624/143-0655.** www.elsquidroe.com.

Two for the Road ★ 🍸   In a forest of rock and dance clubs, this little jazz spot is a welcome break. Marty and Kathy hold court over an older crowd, performing jazz standards while the audience sips martinis; when visiting musicians join the show, it's a jam session. Hotel Tesoro Local A-15, on Marina Blvd.. ✆ **624/143-7759.**

DANCING

Mambo Café ★★ 📷   Ready, set, rumba! Make no mistake: You go to Mambo Café to dance, to salsa, cumbia, reggaeton, and whatever else the high-energy bands are playing tonight. Tiered levels of seating lead to the expansive dance floor, where the dancers are as much of a show as the live music. It's open Wednesday through Sunday from 9pm. Thursday is ladies' night, which means women drink free from 9 to 11pm. Marina Blvd. Local 9–10, next to the Tesoro Resort. ✆ **624/143-1484.** www.mambocafe.com.mx. Cover varies by night.

Passion ★★   Passion is the hunting grounds of Cabo's young and sexy, the most consistently cool of Los Cabos's nightclub scenes. Champagne cocktails, the house music of resident and guest DJs, and a low-lit atmosphere prime Los Cabos's jet set for dancing and partying all the way through. Open Sunday to Wednesday, 10am to 2am, and Thursday to Saturday, 10am to 4am. In the ME Cabo resort, on Médano Beach. ✆ **624/145-7800.**

4

THE SOUTHERN LOOP: TO LA PAZ & TODOS SANTOS

Barely outside the city limits of Los Cabos, the urban sprawl gives way to desert, shopping malls to cactus, and the domesticated coastline of WaveRunners and sunset bars is once again wild. Here you'll find the peninsula's best surfing and snorkeling, some of its best diving and hiking, and a wealth of genuine cultural attractions in Southern Baja's expat arts center, Todos Santos, and bayside state capital, La Paz. And it's nearly all accessible via a well-maintained highway loop that makes the region an easy series of day trips from Los Cabos or a destination of its own using either Los Cabos International airport or La Paz.

Just north of San José and south of La Paz along the Sea of Cortez, the **East Cape** is a string of spectacularly wild, empty beaches, cut through the rocks where the mountainous desert meets the sea. Its geography is dramatic, and challenging. Where Hwy. 1 cuts inland south of La Paz, at La Ribera, the only access to the East Cape's coast is a dirt road; it takes about 4 hours to cover the 100km (62 miles) between Buenavista and San José—the remote location for some of Baja's most beautiful coastline, including Cabo Pulmo, the site of a national marine park and the peninsula's best snorkeling.

La Paz, the state capital, spreads across the hills leading down to its spectacular natural Sea of Cortez port. The city is big enough that it has nothing to prove, but still small enough to allow for easy exploration and a friendly, neighborhood feel. Its city charms are legion—it's the day-trip destination of choice for all those expats in Todos Santos—and it's the only place in southern Baja where you can go diving and to the ballet in the same day. Offshore islands rich in wildlife above and below the waterline, pristine beaches, and crystalline water are all within easy reach of downtown, and it's easy to spend the day here roughing it on the waves, and the evening at a sophisticated restaurant, listening to jazz.

All that changes when you get to **Todos Santos,** on the Pacific side. This palm grove and mission town set uphill from the beaches is an oasis both for its underground aquifers and its aboveground civilization. Founded in 1723 by missionaries, it was a buggy outpost for centuries until it was re-colonized by surfers in the 1980s, and more recently by ever-increasing waves of U.S. and Canadian expatriates who continue to expand the town's cultural offerings with a conquistador's zeal. Just about every month sees the opening of a restaurant, cafe, or bar; the town of about 4,000 now has at least 20 art galleries, nine hotels, and a film festival, and tourism is a major earner. Todos Santos was named one of 30 *"Pueblos Magicos"* ("Magical Towns") by the Mexican government in 2006, a designation that confers official bragging rights to one of Mexico's most picturesque towns, as well as one that imposes restrictions on development.

North of Cabo San Lucas, the **Pacific coast** is one long, foamy stretch of sand and waves, dotted with surfers and sea lions and golden as the sun goes down. The so-called "Pacific Side" is Southern Baja's original surf destination, a string of winter-time breaks whose names are traded by word of mouth; there have been fishing boats and surf camps here for generations, but little else. While real-estate fever hit here as much as anywhere—you'll see FOR SALE signs all the way from Cabo to Todos Santos—this area has remained virtually undeveloped, and the few outposts of tourism, in Cerritos and Pescadero, are still extremely low-key. This is the place for walking the beach, catching a few waves, and sipping a beer as the sun goes down—and not much else.

EAST CAPE: OFF THE GRID ★

Long a favored destination of wave-hungry surfers, die-hard anglers, and motivated escape artists, the East Cape is not for couch potatoes. Most settlements here have no electricity or paved roads, which has kept development to a minimum; to get here, residents either challenge the dusty dirt roads by car, cruise by in sailboats or yachts, or fly their private planes to airstrips at out-of-the-way lodges. The reward for your effort, though, is some of the peninsula's most dramatic landscapes—and chances are, you'll have it all to yourself: secret surf spots, desolate beaches, a coral-reef marine park, road runners, majestic cliffs, empty coves, lone burros, cactus forests, palm groves, craggy mountains, and more.

Essentials
GETTING THERE
The paved and well-maintained Hwy. 1 travels up the coast from San José to La Paz, hitting the coast at Los Barriles after an hour and a half (La Paz is another 1½ hr. up the road). A few paved roads cut through to the coast, between Las Cuevas and La Ribera, for example, or part of the way from San José Viejo to La Fortuna. But for most of the East Cape's off-the-beaten-path beaches and communities, you'll have to take the unpaved coast road. From La Ribera to Cabo Pulmo it's graded gravel, and in pretty good shape; southward, it's slow going, but you should manage it in an ordinary car as long as there haven't been any rainstorms. Plan an hour and a half from Los Barriles to Cabo Pulmo, and 2½ hours from Cabo Pulmo to San José.

VISITOR INFORMATION
The East Cape doesn't have its own tourism bureau, but the **Visit Los Cabos** office in San José (© 866/567-2226 in the U.S., or 624/143-4777; www.visitloscabos.org) has some useful information. Locally, **Wolf Property Management** (© 624/188-3029) in Los Barriles and the dive shop at the **Cabo Pulmo Beach Resort** (© 562/366-0398 in the U.S.) are good, if informal, sources.

GETTING AROUND

You'll need a car to explore this region; there's no public transportation at all. The good news is, automotive mobility enables you to stop at any of the wild and deserted beaches that strikes your fancy as you're rolling down the road.

What to Do in the East Cape

BEACHES & RESORT TOWNS

Beaches are the East Cape's raison d'être, and it's got enough of them to fill their own guidebook. Starting from San José and traveling east up the coast road, you'll encounter the following:

Laguna Hills is an area once loved for its empty beaches and pristine beachfront wilderness. Today, solar-powered homes and El Encanto de La Laguna, a timeshare development, speckle the landscape beneath three mountain peaks. However, Laguna Hills still retains its out-of-the-way charm, and it's a great jumping-off point for summer surf seekers. Slightly northeast, the stretch of **Zacatitos beach** is heaven. Although only surfers and a community of homes are there now, locals believe it's being scoped out as a potential development site. The beautiful bay of **Los Frailes** is just outside of the Cabo Pulmo National Marine Park, and it's an angler's dream come true.

Cabo Pulmo ★★★ is a tiny beach town 72km (45 miles) northeast of San José, and here the Sea of Cortez breaks on a coral reef, allowing only the finest bits of sand and smooth pebbles to pad the spectacular coastline. The coral itself is a sight to behold, but the real attraction is the flourishing fish life in this protected marine park. More than seven dive sites, desert hiking trails, secret coves, and some of the most beautiful stretches of beach in Baja make this a superb place to get away from it all.

There's not much in the way of resorts in **La Ribera,** but this slow-paced fishing village is tops for relaxing by the sea. It's also home to the **Buena Fortuna Botanical Garden** (No phone; siempresemillas@yahoo.com), which is open to visitors every day but Saturday.

Down the hill from the highway, **Buena Vista** is an unremarkable fishing town with one great reason to visit: the **hot springs** in the sea water along the shore, which feed the treatments at the **Buena Vista Spa Hotel** (Hwy. 1 Km 105; ✆ **800/752-3555** in the U.S., or 624/141-0033; www.hotelbuenavista.com) but are available for free along the beach—just feel for the jets of warm water with your feet. The hills give way to sandy flats as you roll into **Los Barriles ★** off Hwy. 1. The exquisite beaches, gentle breezes, excellent fishing, and subdued vibe draw expats in droves; winter winds make this a top kite-and windsurfing spot. Los Barriles has the East Cape's most developed infrastructure, with supermarkets, restaurants, and ATMs. Nearby in Santiago, the **Cañon de la Zorra** is an easy hike to a spectacular desert waterfall.

The remote coastal retreat of **Punta Pescadero ★★** is simple in its finery, located on a point named for the top-notch fishing offshore, about 14km (8¾ miles) from Los Barriles.

WATERSPORTS

SNORKELING & SCUBA DIVING ★★★   **Cabo Pulmo National Marine Park** is Baja's most vibrant marine sanctuary, and the northernmost living coral reef in the Americas. All the dive companies in Los Cabos make dive trips here, but why not save yourself the drive and stay? You'll find all manner of reef fish, sharks, sea

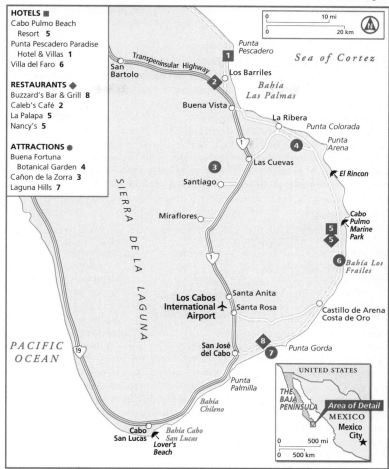

HOTELS ■
Cabo Pulmo Beach
  Resort **5**
Punta Pescadero Paradise
  Hotel & Villas **1**
Villa del Faro **6**

RESTAURANTS ◆
Buzzard's Bar & Grill **8**
Caleb's Café **2**
La Palapa **5**
Nancy's **5**

ATTRACTIONS ●
Buena Fortuna
  Botanical Garden **4**
Cañon de la Zorra **3**
Laguna Hills **7**

turtles, and mantas, as well as a sea lion colony and the wreck of *El Vencedor*. Arrange two-tank dive trips ($149) with **Cabo Pulmo Dive Center** (✆ **624/141-0726;** www.cabopulmo.com). There's great snorkeling offshore from the beach, all the way south from the dive center to where the coast curves into a protected bay, or go on a snorkel tour for $79.

SURFING ★   The summer surf breaks all the way from San José to Punta Frailes. Shipwrecks (15km/9miles up the gravel road) and Nine Palms (near the grove of palms at Santa Elena) beaches are the most consistent; for directions and tips, check www.costa-azul.com.mx/areas_maps.

WINDSURFING & KITEBOARDING ★★ The straight, stiff winds blow coastward across the sandy bay of Los Barriles from November through March, making this one of Baja's kiteboarding and windsurfing hot spots. Rent gear and take lessons from **Exotikite** (© **624/165-2612;** www.exotikite.com) or stop by the stands on the beach.

Shopping

You can forget about souvenirs here, unless you catch a giant marlin and take a picture. There's not much to buy, but stock up on essentials at **Chapito's Supermarket** in Los Barriles (Calle Los Barriles, on the way into town from the highway; © **624/141-0202**).

Where to Stay

While the East Cape has few hotels, many, many area vacation homes are for rent at every price range and often with beach access or a swimming pool. Contact **Wolf Property Management** in Los Barriles to start (© **624/188-3029;** www.wolf-pm-rentals.com).

EXPENSIVE

Punta Pescadero Paradise Hotel & Villas ★ Well-appointed rooms and bathrooms, a full restaurant serving three meals, and you could be at any plush resort. Step outside, however, and you're in a wild, deserted beachside paradise, with sweeping sea views and not another development in sight. You're just 15km (9 miles) from Los Barriles and Hwy. 1, a stone's throw by East Cape standards, but if you'd rather fly than drive there's a 1,050m (3,500-ft.) landing strip on the property.

East Cape. www.puntapescaderoparadise.com.© **800/332-4442** in the U.S., or 624/141-0101. 24 units. High season $174 double; low season $150 double; Christmas holidays $299 double. MC, V. **Amenities:** Outdoor pool; beach. *In room:* TV, fridge.

Villa del Faro ★★ 👔 This solar-powered family compound proves that being off the grid doesn't mean roughing it. There's no phone and the water is trucked in, but this magical desert oasis is all about comfort, with a private swimming beach, a pool, and a gourmet restaurant. Five guest casitas are spread about the property, guaranteeing maximum privacy and minimum environmental impact. Villa del Faro is a member of Responsible Hotels of the World.

East Cape. www.villadelfaro.net; reservations through rental@villadelfaro.net. No phone. 5 units. Casitas $140-$425. Rates include a full breakfast. MC, V. 1 hr. from SJD airport; at Punto Fraile; directions on website. **Amenities:** Restaurant; private beach; outdoor pool. *In room:* TV (in some), fireplace (in some), kitchenette (in some), library (in some).

MODERATE

Cabo Pulmo Beach Resort 🌿 Simple casitas are arranged along neat sand paths along the beachfront; the effect is that of an upscale campground, where the only sounds are singing birds and the sea. The concrete bungalows, all with full kitchen, have tiled floors and screened eating areas, and some have outdoor showers, hammocks, and patios. This is a great choice for divers and snorkelers, with easy access to gear and excursions through the resort's dive center (see "Watersports," on p. 86). Cabo Pulmo is solar-powered, with generator backup.

Cabo Pulmo. www.cabopulmo.com. © **562/366-0722** in the U.S., or 624/141-0726. Bungalows $89-$229. MC, V. **Amenities:** Restaurant; beach; dive center. *In room:* A/C (upon request), kitchen or kitchenette.

Where to Eat

Dining up the East Cape is in keeping with the bare-bones free spirit of the place. This isn't a place for fussy preparations or fine wine. Expect laid-back locales, limited menus, and the very freshest fish.

MODERATE

Buzzard's Bar & Grill ☺ AMERICAN   The only restaurant in Laguna Hills is this solar-powered beach bar, serving up a fun menu of gringo brunch specialties like blueberry pancakes, as well as burgers, and coconut shrimp.

Laguna Hills. ✆ **624/113-6383.** www.buzzardsbar.com. Mon–Sat 8am–8:30pm, Sun 9am–2pm. Main courses 90–115 pesos. No credit cards. From San José, drive east about 15 min., past La Playita, and follow signs at next turnoff.

Nancy's ★★ CONTEMPORARY MEXICAN   American-run Nancy's is the classiest place in Cabo Pulmo, with a daily menu of stepped-up local seafood and vegetables served on a pleasant *palapa*-shaded terrace with terra-cotta tiles and a fireplace.

Cabo Pulmo. ✆ **624/141-0001.** Main courses 150–220 pesos. No credit cards. Thurs–Tues 9am–9pm.

INEXPENSIVE

Caleb's Café BAKERY   Los Barriles's breakfast favorite has fresh baked sweets, sandwiches, and potato salad, free Wi-Fi, and the best Sunday-morning sticky buns of your life.

Los Barriles. ✆ **624/141-0531.** Breakfast 60–90 pesos; lunch 80–100 pesos; sticky buns 36 pesos. MC, V. Tues–Sun 7am–3pm.

La Palapa ★ MEXICAN   Right on the beach at Cabo Pulmo, this simple restaurant is a local favorite for fish tacos, enchiladas, and beer. The food is excellent, if simple, and its location will keep you from having to pack a picnic.

Cabo Pulmo. No phone. Main courses 55–130 pesos. No credit cards. Daily noon–9pm. From main road in Cabo Pulmo, follow signs to Alicia's beach; La Palapa is at the end of the road on the left.

LA PAZ ★★

177km (110 miles) N of Cabo San Lucas; 196km (122 miles) NW of San José del Cabo; 1,578km (978 miles) SE of Tijuana

La Paz has no picturesque colonial downtown, no sunbathing boardwalk, no magical postcard views. And yet *bajacalifornianos* up and down the peninsula claim it as their favorite place. Why? La Paz means "peace," and this breezy provincial city has got it in spades. Although it's the capital of the state of Baja California Sur, and home to nearly 200,000 people, it's slow-paced and relaxed. Beautiful deserted beaches just minutes away complement the lively palm-fringed *malecón* that fronts the town center, and the busy port—Baja's principal shipping center—lends the place a decidedly marine air. But most importantly, this easygoing city maintains an "old Baja" atmosphere, a beloved bastion of a tourist-less past.

Despite its name, La Paz has historically been a place of conflict between explorers and indigenous populations. Beginning in 1535, Spanish conquistadors and Jesuit missionaries arrived and exerted their influence on the town's architecture and traditions. Mass pearl harvesting lasted from the time conquistadors saw local Indians wearing pearl ornaments through the late 1930s. All the pearls eventually were wiped out. John Steinbeck immortalized a local legend in his novella *The Pearl*.

February features the biggest and best *Carnaval,* or Mardi Gras, in Baja, as well as a month-long **Festival of the Gray Whale** (starting in Feb or Mar). On May 3, **La Fiesta de La Paz** celebrates the city's founding by Cortez in 1535 and features *artesanía* exhibitions from throughout Southern Baja. The annual **marlin-fishing tournament** is in August, with other fishing tournaments in September and November. And on November 1 and 2, the **Days of the Dead,** altars are on display at the Anthropology Museum.

The slow-paced charms of this city are matched by vast opportunities for outdoor adventure close by. Adventurous travelers enjoy hiking, rock climbing, Baja's best scuba diving, "big one" sportfishing, and sea kayaking excursions from several hours to several weeks. The uninhabited island of Espíritu Santo and Los Islotes islets, just offshore, were once hiding places for looting pirates but now draw kayakers, snorkelers, and beachcombers. You can swim with sea lions during the day, then camp overnight, posh safari-style, at **Baja Camp** (www.bajacamp.com).

The University of Southern Baja California adds a unique cultural presence that includes museums and a theater and arts center; there are also galleries and a natural foods street market downtown twice a week. Recent years have seen a flowering of restaurant culture, too, and the new generation of interesting eats is another great reason to make this a base. From accommodations to taxis, La Paz is also one of Mexico's most outstanding beach vacation values and a great place for family travelers.

Essentials

GETTING THERE & DEPARTING

BY PLANE   La Paz's General Manuel Márquez De León International Airport (LAP; ☏ **612/164-6307**) is 18km (11 miles) northwest of town along the highway to Ciudad Constitución and Tijuana. Both **Alaska Airlines** (☏ **800/252-7522** in the U.S.; www.alaskaair.com) and **Delta** (☏ **800/241-4141** in the U.S.; www.delta.com) have nonstop flights from Los Angeles. **Aeroméxico** (☏ **800/237-6639** in the U.S., or 612/122-0091; www.aeromexico.com) connects through Tucson and Los Angeles in the United States, and flies from Mexico City and other points within Mexico.

Airport *colectivos* (175 pesos per person) run only from the airport to town, not vice versa. **Taxi** service (300 pesos, 600 pesos for a van) is available as well. If you fly to Los Cabos International airport in San José, there's a convenient **shuttle** (3 hr.; ☏ **888/829-9925** in the U.S., 01-800/026-8331 in Mexico; www.shuttletolapaz.com) to La Paz bus station on the *malecón* for 325 pesos one-way.

Most major rental-car agencies have booths inside the airport. **Budget**'s airport number is ☏ **612/124-6433** or 122-3107 in town; you can contact **Avis** at ☏ **612/124-6312,** or 122-2651 in town, or **Hertz** at ☏ **612/124-6330** at the airport, or 128-4865 in town.

BY CAR   From San José del Cabo, Hwy. 1 north through the East Cape is the more scenic route, passing through **San Bartolo ★★**, a mountain town where heavenly homemade macaroons made of thick, fresh-cut coconut, and pralines made from *cajeta* (goat's-milk caramel) will for some be worth the longer drive, about 3½ hours.

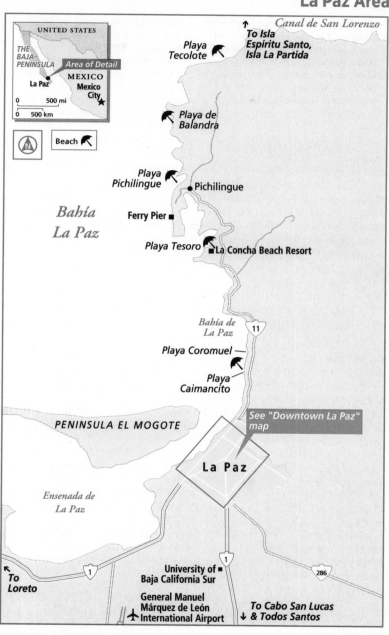

TAKING YOUR CAR TO THE mainland

Those planning to take their U.S. or Canadian cars on the ferry to the Mexican mainland must obtain a temporary import permit, as explained in "Getting There: By Car," in chapter 8. Additionally, every traveler going to the mainland needs a Mexican Tourist Permit (FMM), available upon your entry into Mexico.

Reserve your space on the ferry as early as possible and confirm your reservation 24 hours before departure; you can pick up tickets at the port terminal ticket office as late as the morning of the day you are leaving. The dock is at Pichilingue, 18km (11 miles) north of La Paz.

Buses to Pichilingue depart from the beach bus terminal of **Transportes Aguila** (✆ 612/122-7898) on the *malecón* at Independencia on the hour, from 7am to 8pm, and cost $2 each way.

A faster route from the south heads north from Cabo San Lucas on Hwy. 19 through Todos Santos to San Pedro, where Hwy. 19 rejoins Hwy. 1 and runs north into La Paz, about 2½ hours. From Northern Baja, Hwy. 1 south is the only choice; the trip from Loreto takes 4 to 5 hours.

BY BUS   The bus station is on the *malecón* at Álvaro Obregón and Cinco de Mayo (✆ 612/122-7898). The station is open daily from 6am to 10pm, and taxis line up in front. Buses to the beach at Pichilingue depart seven times a day from 8am to 5pm and cost 22 pesos one-way; buses to San José del Cabo leave from 6am to 9pm, and to Cabo San Lucas (236 pesos one-way) from 5:45am to 6pm. For schedule information all the way from Tijuana down the peninsula, check at the station or with **Transportes Aguila** (✆ 800/824-8452; www.autotransportesaguila.net).

BY FERRY   **Baja Ferries** serves La Paz from the mainland Pacific ports of Topolobampo (6 hr., daily at 3pm from La Paz, at 11pm from Topolobampo) and Mazatlán (15 hr., Sun–Fri, alternating days from La Paz at 5 or 7:30pm and Mazatlán at 4pm). Tickets are available at the Baja Ferries office in La Paz, on the corner of Allende and Marcelo Rubio (✆ 800/337-7427; www.bajaferries.com) or by phone through their call center. The local office is open daily 8am to 6pm. They do not accept foreign credit cards for payment, so if you don't have a credit card backed by a Mexican bank, to buy a ticket, you'll have to make a deposit into the Baja Ferries bank account. This is easier than it sounds; go to the office, pick up a deposit slip, go to the bank and have it validated, and bring it back in exchange for your tickets.

Passengers pay one fee for themselves (Topolobampo 790 pesos, Mazatlán 890 pesos for a seat, half price for children ages 3–11, and an additional 770 pesos for a cabin with four beds and one bathroom) and another for their vehicles (1,050 pesos to Topolobampo, 2,462 pesos to Mazatlán). The 1,000-passenger ferries, which are accessible to people with disabilities, offer restaurant and bar service, as well as a coffee shop and live music, and a hot meal is included in the cost of the ticket. Cabins and bathrooms are very clean with good showers.

Buses line up in front of the ferry dock at Pichilingue to meet every arriving ferry. They stop at the beach bus station on the *malecón* at Independencia; it's within walking distance of many downtown hotels if you're not encumbered with heavy luggage. Taxis also meet each ferry and cost about $10 to downtown La Paz.

ORIENTATION

CITY LAYOUT Although La Paz sprawls well inland from the *malecón* (the seaside boulevard, Álvaro Obregón), you'll probably spend most of your time in the older, more congenial downtown section within a few blocks of the waterfront. The main plaza, Plaza Pública (or Jardín Velasco), is bounded by Madero, Independencia, Revolución, and Cinco de Mayo. The plaza centers on an iron bandstand where public concerts frequently take place in the evening, and the *malecón* is dotted with the bronze sculptures of Guadalajara artist Alejandro Colunga. A 24-hour **taxi stand** is on the *malecón* at 16 de Septiembre, or call one at ✆ **612/122-0308.**

VISITOR INFORMATION The visitor information center of the Hoteliers' Association (✆ **612/125-6844;** www.vivalapaz.org or www.visitlapaz.net) is in the 1910 former city hall at Dominguez and 16 de Septiembre, two blocks up from the *malecón.* They have very helpful English-speaking staff on duty from 9am to 5pm. You can also find the excellent and detailed **gotbaja La Paz map** (www.gotbajamaps. com) and the English-language **Baja Citizen** community newspaper (www.baja citizen.com) in hotels and restaurants.

GETTING AROUND

Because most of what you'll need and want in town is on the *malecón,* or a few blocks inland, it's easy to get around La Paz on foot. Public buses go to some of the beaches north of town (see "Beaches & Outdoor Activities," below), but to explore the many beaches within 81km (50 miles) of La Paz, your best bet is to rent a car or hire a taxi. Several car-rental agencies have offices on the *malecón.*

[FastFACTS] LA PAZ

Area Code The telephone area code is **612.**

Banks Banks generally exchange currency during normal business hours: Monday through Friday from 9am to 6pm and Saturday from 10am to 2pm. ATMs are readily available and offer bank exchange rates on withdrawals.

Emergencies Dial ✆ **066** for general emergency assistance, or ✆ **060** for police. Both calls are free.

Hospitals The two hospitals in the area are **Hospital Especialidades Médicas,** at Km 4.5 on the highway toward the airport (✆ **612/124-0400**), and **Hospital Juan María de Salvatierra** (✆ **612/122-1497**), Nicolás Bravo 1010, Col. Centro. Both are open 24 hours, and the former offers access to emergency air evacuation.

Marinas La Paz has a growing number of marinas: **Marina de La Paz,** at the west end of the *malecón* at Legaspi (✆ **612/125-2112;** marina lapaz@prodigy.net.mx); **Marina Palmira,** south of town at Carretera a Pichilingue Km 2.5, Edificio la Plaza (✆ **877/217-1513** in the U.S., or 612/121-7000; eloisa@marinapalmira. com); and **Marina Costa Baja,** Carretera a Pichilingue Km 7.5 (✆ **866/899-7567** in the U.S.; www. costabajaresort.com). The large ships arrive at the commercial port of **Pichilingue,** Carretera a Pichilingue Km 2.5, Puerto Pichilingue (✆ **612/122-7010**), 17km (11 miles) from La Paz.

Municipal Market The public market is 3 blocks inland, at Degollado and Revolución. It mainly sells produce, meats, and utilitarian wares. Hours are Monday through Saturday 6am to 6pm and Sunday 6am to 1pm.

Parking In high season, street parking may be hard to find in the downtown area, but there are several guarded lots, which cost from $2 to $5, and side streets are less crowded. Most hotels and resorts have parking.

Pharmacy   As a city, La Paz has plenty of pharmacies, including a 24-hour one across from the Salvatierra Hospital. Downtown, try the **Farmacia America,** at Revolución and Delgollado (② **612/122-3343**).

Post Office   The *correo* is 3 blocks inland, at Constitución and Revolución (② **612/122-0388**); it's open Monday through Friday 8am to 5pm, Saturday 8am to 1pm.

Tourism Office
Located at 16 de Septiembre at Dominguez in the old city hall (② **612/125-6844**), it's open daily from 9am to 5pm.

Beaches & Outdoor Activities

La Paz combines the unselfconscious bustle of a small capital port city with beautiful, isolated beaches not far from town. Well on its way to becoming the adventure-tourism capital of Baja, it's the starting point for whale-watching, diving, freediving, sea kayaking, climbing, and hiking tours throughout the peninsula. Arrange any of those activities, plus beach tours, sunset cruises, and visits to the sea lion colony, through recommended tour operators **Baja Expeditions** (② **800/843-6967** in the U.S., or 612/125-3828; www.bajaex.com); **Baja Diving,** Obregón 1665-2 (② **612/122-1826**; fax 612/122-8644; www.clubcantamar.com); **DeSea Baja Adventures,** Marina Palmira L3, Carretera a Pichilingue Km 2.5 (② **310/691-8040** in the U.S., or 612/121-5100; www.deseabaja.com); **Fun Baja,** Reforma 395, on the corner of Guillermo Prieto (② **612/121-5884** or 125-2366; www.funbaja. com); or in travel agencies along the *malecón*. You can also arrange activities through agencies in the United States that specialize in Baja's natural history. (See "Special-Interest Tours," in chapter 2.)

BEACHES

La Paz is not itself a beach city, but within a 10- to 45-minute drive from the center you'll find some of the loveliest beaches in Baja, reminiscent of the Caribbean with clear, calm turquoise waters.

The white-sand beaches that line the *malecón* are the most convenient in town, but locals don't generally swim there—La Paz is a commercial port and the water in the bay is not particularly clean. The best beach nearby is immediately north of town at **La Concha Beach Resort;** nonguests may use the hotel restaurant/bar and rent equipment for snorkeling, diving, skiing, and sailing. It's 10km (6¼ miles) north of town on the Pichilingue Highway, at Km 5.5. The other beaches are farther north of town, but midweek you may have these far-distant beaches to yourself.

At least 10 public buses depart from the *malecón* between 8am and 5:30pm for beaches to the north. From the bus station at the corner of Independencia, buses stop at the small **Caimancito** (5km/3 miles), **Coromuel** (8km/5 miles), **Tesoro** (14km/8¾ miles), and **Pichilingue** (17km/11 miles, just north of the ferry terminal) beaches. Pichilingue, Coromuel, and Tesoro beaches have *palapa*-shaded bars or restaurants, and umbrellas and beach chairs for rent.

But with a little extra effort, you can reach the most beautiful of these outlying beaches, playas **Balandra ★** and **Tecolote ★★★**, approximately 29km (18 miles) from La Paz at the end of a paved road. The water is a heavenly cerulean blue, the beaches look out upon Isla Espíritu Santo, and several local restaurants specialize in lobster. To get there on your own, take a bus to Pichilingue; from there, take a taxi the remaining 13km (8 miles), or rent a car and follow the signs.

THE BAY OF LA PAZ PROJECT: saving THE SEA OF CORTEZ

Although the best whale-watching is in the Pacific, it's the Sea of Cortez that once inspired Jacques Cousteau to call it the "world's aquarium." Apart from gray and humpback whales—plus remarkable pelagic and reef life—divers have spotted blue whales and even orcas in this extraordinary body of water, also known as the Gulf of California. Sadly, marine populations have declined between 70% and 90% since the 1960s, and, until now, nothing has been done to ensure that future generations will have fish in the sea.

SeaWatch, a La Paz–based organization dedicated to exposing and stopping destructive fishing practices in the Sea of Cortez for the past 15 years, has launched a public awareness campaign in Southern Baja to stop commercial fishermen from wiping out reefs and snaring hammerhead schools in nets. The **Bay of La Paz Project,** under the auspices of SeaWatch and three NGOs (Niparajá, the Billfish Foundation, and Pro-Natura), hopes to limit commercial fishing in various high-pressure areas over time, thereby allowing fish populations the chance to reproduce. If you would like to know more or find out how you can help, visit **www.seawatch. org** or call ✆ **503/616-4421.**

If you want to take a general tour of all the beaches before deciding where to spend your precious vacation days, **Viajes Lybs** (✆ **612/122-4680**) offers a 4-hour beach tour for $25 per person, with stops at Pichilingue, Balandra, and Tecolote.

CRUISES

A popular and very worthwhile cruise is to **Isla Espíritu Santo ★★★** and **Los Islotes ★★.** You visit the largest sea lion colony in Baja, stunning rock formations, and remote beaches, with stops for snorkeling, swimming, and lunch. (See "Snorkeling with Sea Lions," below.) Both boat and bus tours are available to **Puerto Balandra,** where bold rock formations rise up like humpback whales and frame pristine coves of crystal-blue water and ivory sand. Tour operators (see above) can arrange these all-day trips, weather permitting, for about $80 per person, or arrange them yourself at **www.playaeltecolote.com**.

GOLF

La Paz's first golf course, the Arthur Hills–designed par 72 **Paraíso del Mar** (✆ **612/165-1818;** www.paradiseofthesea.com), is on Isla Mogote, a 5-minute water taxi ride across the bay. *Golf Magazine* named its cactus-rich landscape one of the top five new international golf courses for 2010.

WATERSPORTS

SCUBA DIVING ★★★   Scuba diving conditions are best from July through October, when visibility is excellent and the water is warm. (Winter water is cold, sometimes down to 20°C/68°F or colder, and changing temperatures can mean poor visibility in spring.) Certified divers will get the most out of La Paz's amazing dive sites, including the sea lion colony at Los Islotes, distant Cerralvo Island, the sunken ship *Salvatierra,* an 18m (59-ft.) wall dive, and several sea mounts (underwater mountains) and reefs; a little farther afield, you can see hammerhead sharks and manta rays. **Baja Expeditions, Fun Baja,** and **Baja Dive** all offer a variety of dive

LA PAZ'S top dive spots

La Paz is among the world's great dive destinations: More than 25 dive sites surround the islands outside La Paz's bay, such as Espíritu Santo, San José, and Cerralvo. What sets La Paz diving apart is the big stuff: giant mantas, sea lions, and impressive numbers of sharks, including whale sharks and hammerheads. Here are the area's most notable dive sites:

o **El Bajito:** Just next to the Los Islotes sea-lion colony is this beautiful dive site where crevices in the seafloor are covered in soft corals.

o **El Bajo:** Advanced divers revel in the underwater mountain rising to 18m (60 ft.) below the surface, with a relatively flat top. It's especially notable for its schooling hammerhead sharks; groups of several to hundreds travel clockwise around the seamount. You're also likely to see Panamic green morays; over 50 live in a small canyon on the mountain. Additional sea mounts nearby have peaks at between 18 and 45m (60–150 ft.) from the surface; visibility is good year-round.

o **La Reina & La Reinita:** Enjoy a wreck dive and wall diving to 45m (150-ft.) depths at these islets in front of Cerralvo Island, 1½ hours from La Paz. You'll see brain coral, tropical fish, rays, and several types of morays here. During the summer you can see giant sea horses. Whale encounters are common in the channel during the winter calving season.

o **Los Islotes:** Divers here can view the underwater rock caves and frolic with the friendly colony of sea lions. The two large rock islands, one of which is a natural arch whose center you can dive through, are a 1½-hour boat ride from La Paz, north of Espíritu Santo, and offer depths of 4.5 to 30m (15–100 ft.).

o **Salvatierra Wreck:** In 1976, this 75m (250-ft.) ferryboat sank after colliding with a nearby reef. It now lies on a sandbar at a depth of 18m (60 ft.) in the San Lorenzo Channel and the southern end of Espíritu Santo. Filled with sea life, it makes for a fascinating dive and a good site for novice divers.

o **San Francisquito:** Similar to El Bajo, this popular site for advanced divers, with varied depths, has an abundance of sea life.

o **Whale Island:** This small, whale-shaped island has dive-through caves, crevices, rocky reefs, and a coral forest at depths from 6 to 18m (20–60 ft.). Between the caves is a sand shelf containing a large "garden" of conger eels, which extend their bodies vertically from the seafloor and sway in the currents while feeding on passing morsels. This area is tranquil and protected from wind; its mild current makes it a good choice for beginning divers, or for a second dive of the day.

o **Lapas 03 and the Fang Ming:** These two rusting Chinese long liner boats were sunk in 1999 to promote artificial reef development for sport diving. They're at a depth of 21m (70 ft.) and offer full penetration diving over numerous levels.

expeditions, starting at $105 per person for an all-day outing and two-tank dive. Day boat trips run approximately $110 for two-tank dives, $125 to $175 for three-tank dives. **Fun Baja** runs scuba safaris as well, combining diving and camping at the island of Espíritu Santo in a luxury camp with beds and meal service for $440 to $999 with dives, $289 to $599 for non-divers coming along for the ride. **DeSea Baja Adventures** also has private boats with guides for underwater photo or video diving, and private dive masters or instructors for yachts or charters, and **freediving,** including instruction in yoga-based breathing exercises, mental control, and the physiology of breath hold.

Every March, groups of **whale sharks** are spotted in the waters of La Paz's bay. These enormous, plankton-feeding creatures, the world's largest fish, stay close to the surface, so they're easy to spot from light aircraft that make the rounds each morning to find them for snorkel tours. All Cabo and La Paz dive outfitters make the trip; for about $80 per person, you'll spend an hour or so paddling around sharks up to 10m (33 ft.) long.

SEA KAYAKING ★★★ Kayaking in the many bays and coves near La Paz is a paddler's dream, and because some of the area's special sites for swimming and snorkeling are accessible only by kayak, daylong or multiday trips can't be beat. In the waters near La Paz, the water clarity gives the sensation of being suspended in the air. Bring your own equipment, or let the local companies take care of you. Several companies in the United States (see "Special-Interest Tours," in chapter 2) can book trips in advance. Locally, **Baja Quest** and **Sea & Adventures** (© **800/355-7140** in the U.S.; www.kayakbaja.com) arrange extended kayak adventures, from $250 for a 2-day trip to Espíritu Santo to $1,150 for a week paddling between La Paz and Loreto, as well as simple gear rental.

SPORTFISHING La Paz, justly famous for its sportfishing, attracts anglers from all over the world. Its waters are home to more than 850 species of fish. The most economical approach is to rent a *panga* boat with a captain and equipment. It costs $125 for 3 hours, but you don't go very far out. Super *pangas,* which have a shade cover and comfortable seats, start at around $180 for two persons. Larger cruisers with bathrooms start at $240.

You can arrange sportfishing trips locally through hotels and tour agencies. **La Paz Sportfishing's** (© **310/691-8040;** www.lapazsportfishing.com) rates start at $250 per day for two people. English-speaking David Jones of **Fishermen's Fleet** (© **612/122-1313;** fax 612/125-7334; www.fishermensfleet.com) uses the locally popular *panga*-style fishing boat. Average price is $225 for the boat, but double-check what the price includes—you may need to bring your own food and drinks.

WHALE-WATCHING ★★★ ☺ Although it is across the peninsula on the Sea of Cortez, La Paz has the only major international airport in the area and thus has become a center of Baja's winter whale-watching excursions. Most tours originating in La Paz go to Bahía Magdalena, where the whales give birth in calm waters. Twelve-hour tours from La Paz start at around $115 per person, including breakfast, lunch, transportation, and an English-speaking guide. **Baja Expeditions** offers the widest variety of tours, including family-focused overnights at Magdalena ($480 per person for 2 nights), overnights at San Ignacio lagoon ($420 per person for 2 nights), and a charter flight tour from San Diego ($2,395 per person for 4 nights all-inclusive). **Fun Baja** travels to Magdalena, as does **DeSea Adventures.**

SNORKELING WITH sea lions

Prime among the many treasures of Baja are the colonies of sea lions that live in the Sea of Cortez. These playful, curious sea creatures prove a powerful lure for many travelers to this area. One of the largest colonies is found at Los Islotes, a cluster of tiny rock islands north of La Paz, where a colony or "rookery" of some 250 California brown sea lions lives year-round.

Many tour operators in La Paz offer trips to Los Islotes, generally in *pangas*—the trip, by boat, takes about 2½ hours from La Paz. Here, the sea lions lay in the sun along the jagged rock shelves, bark out greetings to visitors, and occasionally belly-flop into the water.

Trip participants don wet suits or skins, life jackets, and snorkels to join the sea lions, which will sometimes instigate play by mimicking your movements in the water.

California sea lions are considered to be the smartest of the pinnipeds, the class of mammals with flippers.

However, they're also kind of like seafaring guard dogs. While they are adorable, don't let their big brown eyes fool you: They are wild animals and should be treated as such. No feeding, no touching, and don't get too close to their rocky home. The chocolate-brown "bulls" can weigh up to 455 kilograms (1,000 lb.) and can occasionally become aggressive, so keeping your distance from the males and the females and pups they're protecting is a good idea. For example, if a sea lion blows bubbles in your face, consider it a warning that you're too close.

Among the operators offering sea lion snorkeling trips is **Cortez Club**, at the La Concha Beach Resort (© **612/121-6120;** www.cortezclub.com). The full-day excursion departs at 8:30am and costs $83 per person, which includes wet suit, snorkel gear, and a box lunch, which you'll eat on the beach at Isla Partida. Dive trips are also available, with depths at Los Islotes averaging 7½ to 15m (25–49 ft.).

You can go whale-watching without joining a tour by taking a bus from La Paz to Puerto López Mateos or Puerto San Carlos at Bahía Magdalena (a 3-hr. ride) and hiring a boat there for about $30. It's a long trip to do in a day, but there are a few modest hotels in San Carlos. Check at the La Paz tourist office for information.

For a more in-depth discussion, see "Whale-Watching in Baja: A Primer," on p. 141.

A Break from the Beaches: Exploring La Paz

Most tour agencies offer city tours of all of La Paz's major sights. Tours last 2 to 3 hours, include time for shopping, and cost around $15 per person.

HISTORIC LA PAZ

When Cortez landed here in 1535, he named it Bahía Santa Cruz. The name didn't stick. In April 1683, Eusebio Kino, a Spanish Jesuit priest, arrived and dubbed the place Nuestra Señora de la Paz (Our Lady of Peace). It wasn't until 1720, however, that Jaime Bravo, another Jesuit priest, set up a permanent mission. The mission church stands on La Paz's main square on Revolución and Independencia.

Museo de Antropología (Anthropology Museum) ★ This museum features large, though faded, color photos of Baja's prehistoric cave paintings. There are also

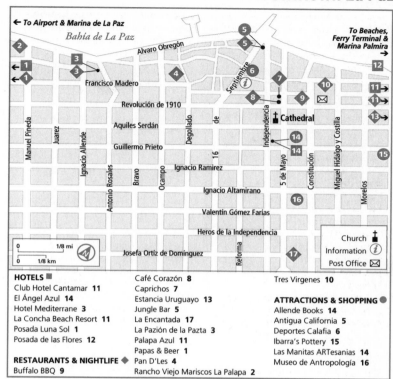

← *To Airport & Marina de La Paz*

Bahía de La Paz

Alvaro Obregón

To Beaches, Ferry Terminal & Marina Palmira →

Francisco Madero

Revolución de 1910

Aquiles Serdán

Guillermo Prieto

Ignacio Ramirez

Ignacio Altamirano

Valentín Gómez Farías

Heros de la Independencia

Josefa Ortíz de Domínguez

✝ Cathedral

Manuel Pineda

Juarez

Ignacio Allende

Antonio Rosales

Bravo

Ocampo

Degollado

16 de Septiembre

Independencia

5 de Mayo

Constitución

Miguel Hidalgo y Costilla

Morelos

Reforma

0   1/8 mi
0   1/8 km

Church ✝
Information ⓘ
Post Office ✉

HOTELS ◼	Café Corazón **8**	Tres Virgenes **10**
Club Hotel Cantamar **11**	Caprichos **7**	
El Ángel Azul **14**	Estancia Uruguayo **13**	**ATTRACTIONS & SHOPPING** ●
Hotel Mediterrane **3**	Jungle Bar **5**	Allende Books **14**
La Concha Beach Resort **11**	La Encantada **17**	Antigua California **5**
Posada Luna Sol **1**	La Pazión de la Pazta **3**	Deportes Calafia **6**
Posada de las Flores **12**	Palapa Azul **11**	Ibarra's Pottery **15**
	Papas & Beer **1**	Las Manitas ARTesanias **14**
RESTAURANTS & NIGHTLIFE ◆	Pan D'Les **4**	Museo de Antropología **16**
Buffalo BBQ **9**	Rancho Viejo Mariscos La Palapa **2**	

exhibits on various topics, including the geological history of the peninsula, fossils, missions, colonial history, and daily life. All information is in Spanish.

Corner of Altamirano and Cinco de Mayo. ⓒ **612/122-0162** or 125-6424. Free admission (donations encouraged). Daily 9am–6pm.

Shopping

La Paz has little in the way of folk art or other treasures from mainland Mexico. But the dense cluster of streets behind the **Hotel Perla,** between 16 de Septiembre and Degollado, abounds with small shops—some tacky, others quite upscale. This area also holds a very small but authentic **Chinatown** dating to the time when Chinese laborers were brought to settle in Baja. Serdán Street, from Degollado south, offers dozens of sellers of dried spices, piñatas, and candy. On Tuesdays, there's a natural products **street market** in front of Buffalo BBQ from 9am to noon; on Saturdays, it decamps to the street in front of Corazón Café.

Allende Books   La Paz's English-language bookstore carries fiction, nonfiction, and Baja-themed books, as well as travel guides. They accept Visa, MasterCard, and

U.S. dollars. Open Monday to Saturday 10am to 6pm. Independencia 518 at Guillermo Prieto, at El Ángel Azul. ℂ **612/125-9114.**

Antigua California   This shop manages to stay in business as others come and go. It carries a good selection of folk art from throughout Mexico. It's open Monday to Saturday from 9:30am to 8:30pm, Sunday from 10:30am to 2:30pm. Paseo Álvaro Obregón 220, at Arreola. ℂ **612/125-5230.**

Deportes Calafia   A sport outfitter with a focus on scuba diving and camping, this is the place to stock up on gear before you hit Espíritu Santo. They accept Visa and MasterCard, and are open Monday to Saturday 9:30am to 8:30pm. 16 Septiembre btw. Obregón and Dominguez. ℂ **612/122-6177.**

Ibarra's Pottery   Here, you not only shop for tableware, hand-painted tiles, and decorative pottery, you can watch it being made. Each piece is individually handpainted or glazed, and then fired. Open Monday to Saturday from 9am to 3pm. Call ahead to schedule a tour. Guillermo Prieto 625, btw. Torre Iglesias and República. ℂ **612/122-0404.**

Las Manitas ARTesanias   Crafts, textiles, ceramics, and hand-embroidered clothes line the walls at this small, American-run folk art shop. Open Monday to Saturday, 10am to 2pm. Independencia 518 at Guillermo Prieto, at El Ángel Azul. ℂ **612/135-5939.**

Where to Stay

For water sports enthusiasts, Baja Diving also has a 40-unit sports lodge and beach resort at Pichilingue, very convenient for boat trips, **Club Hotel Cantamar** (www.clubcantamar.com; ℂ **612/122-7010**). Rates for a double room run about $78. Sea & Adventures runs a hotel geared to kayakers at the **Posada Luna Sol** (www.posadalunasol.com; ℂ **800/355-1740** in the U.S., or 612/122-7039 in La Paz), on the *malecón* at the Marina La Paz, with rooms starting at $65.

EXPENSIVE

Posada de las Flores ★   La Paz's most elegant hotel is a renovated villa overlooking the *malecón* and the bay. Each room is individually decorated with high-quality Mexican furniture and antiques, hand-loomed fabrics, and exquisite artisan details. Bathrooms are especially welcoming, with marble tubs and thick towels. Breakfast is served from 8 to 11am daily. Telephone, fax, and Internet are available through the office.

Av. Álvaro Obregón 440, the northern end of the *malecón*, 23000 La Paz, B.C.S. www.posadadelasflores.com. ℂ **877/245-2860** in the U.S., or 612/125-5871. 8 units. August $180 double, $290 suite; Sept–July $150 double, $250 suite. Rates include full breakfast. MC, V. Street parking. Children 11 and under not accepted. **Amenities:** Teatime; small outdoor pool; Wi-Fi. *In room:* A/C, TV, bathrobes, complimentary wake-up coffee service on request, hair dryer, minibar.

MODERATE

El Ángel Azul   Housed in a restored 19th-century courthouse by the cathedral, this is an old-fashioned bed-and-breakfast with one unbeatable perk: its green and cheerful courtyard, strewn with comfy garden chairs and brimming with cactus, agave, palms, hummingbirds, and tomato plants that supply the organic breakfast. All rooms open on to the courtyard, and as such can be a bit dark; queen-size beds feel a little worn. The best room, the honeymoon suite, is worth the extra money, for its upstairs windows and small private terrace. El Ángel Azul is a member of the UN Foundation for Sustainable Tourism, and is also part of an informal network of expat women hotel owners, and the staff can help you arrange stays at the other four hotels in the group (p. 57).

Independencia 518 at Guillermo Prieto, 23000 La Paz, B.C.S. www.elangelazul.com. © **612/125-5130.** 10 units. High season $100 double; $165 suite; low season $90 double, $165 suite. Rates include full breakfast. MC, V. Street parking. Children 12 and under not accepted. **Amenities:** Bar; courtyard garden; Wi-Fi. *In room:* A/C.

Hotel Mediterrane ★   At the best location in town, right on the *malecón*, this unique inn channels the Mediterranean with white-on-white decor and a European attitude. All white-tiled rooms face an interior courtyard, and have colorful Mexican serapes draped over the king-size beds. The adjacent Pazión de la Pazta restaurant (see "Where to Eat," below) is one of La Paz's best. Rates include the use of kayaks on the bay, a block away, and Wi-Fi. Those not traveling with their laptops can use the computer center, included with the rates. This is a gay-friendly hotel.

Allende 36, btw. the *malecón* and Dominguez, 23000 La Paz, B.C.S. www.hotelmed.com. ©/fax **612/125-1195.** 9 units. High season $85–$95 double; low season $75–$85 double. Weekly discounts available. Street parking. AE, MC, V. **Amenities**: Restaurant; computer center; kayaks; room service; Wi-Fi. *In room:* A/C, TV/DVD, minifridge (in some), MP3 docking station (in some).

La Concha Beach Resort ★★   Ten kilometers (6 miles) north of downtown La Paz, this resort's setting is perfect: on a curved beach ideal for swimming and water-sports. All rooms face the water and have double beds, balconies or patios, and small tables and chairs. Condos with full kitchens and one or three bedrooms are available on a nightly basis in the high-rise complex next door. If available, they're worth the extra price for a perfect family-vacation stay. The hotel offers scuba, fishing, and whale-watching packages. Children 13 and under are not allowed in the condos.

Carretera Pichilingue Km 5, 23000 La Paz, B.C.S. www.laconcha.com. © **800/999-2252** in the U.S., 612/121-6161 in Mexico. 113 units. $98 double; $177 junior suite; $222–$291 condo year-round. AE, DC, MC, V. Free guarded parking. **Amenities:** Restaurant (w/theme nights); 2 bars; babysitting; beach club w/ scuba program; Internet; Jacuzzi; beachside pool; room service; free twice-daily shuttle to town; complete watersports center w/WaveRunners, kayaks, and paddleboats. *In room:* A/C, TV, minibar.

Where to Eat

La Paz has a growing assortment of small, pleasant restaurants that are good and reasonably priced. In addition to what's listed here, try **Caprichos,** Madero at 5 de Mayo (© **612/125-8105**), **Estancia Uruguayo,** Revolución 785 at Salvatierra (© **612/122-5412**), and **Tres Vergines,** Madero 1130 (© **612/123-2226**). Reservations are generally unnecessary.

MODERATE

Buffalo BBQ ★★ ☺ARGENTINE/GRILL   Indoor seating plays second fiddle to the courtyard, which fronts a fiery grill on which prime cuts are turned into delicacies. The hamburgers are big, flavorful, and come in so many delectable styles—from the special-sauced New Mexico burger to the standard cheeseburger—that a carnivore may just call this heaven. Otherwise, Buffalo BBQ's steaks, ribs, and wine list are a worthy tribute to the chef's Argentine roots.

Madero 1240 at Constitución. © **612/128-8755.** www.bbqbuffalogrill.com. Hamburgers and main courses 110–250 pesos. AE, MC, V. Tues–Fri 6–11pm; Sat–Sun 2–11pm.

Café Corazón ★★★ ◙ CONTEMPORARY MEXICAN   This hot new restaurant has everything going for it: a historic 20th-century courtyard, a fun, sunny vibe, and an irreverent menu designed by Armando Montaño, of San José's famed El Chilar. To wit: Enchiladas Corazón play on traditional Oaxacan mole, by substituting duck for chicken and adding fig to the mix; the result is like a Mexican Peking duck, delicious and thoroughly original. The music here is the best in town, and there's an inviting and creative kids' menu too.

Revolución 385, at Constitución. ℭ **612/128-8985.** Main courses 114–155 pesos. AE, MC, V. Mon–Sat 8am–11pm.

La Pazión de la Pazta ★★ THAI/ITALIAN/SWISS   What unites the Swiss Flädlisuppe, Thai Tom Ka Gai, and baked lasagna on the menu here is the cosmopolitan owner-chef's passion for all of them, without regard for traditional rules. At night, this place shines with black-and-white tiles and candlelight. La Pazión's streetside cafe is also appealing for breakfast or you can simply opt for an espresso and croissant. The restaurant is in front of the Hotel Mediterrane.

Allende 36. ℭ **612/125-1195.** www.hotelmed.com. Breakfast $2–$4; main courses $8–$15. AE, MC, V. Restaurant Wed–Sun 4–11pm; cafe daily 7am–3pm.

INEXPENSIVE

Palapa Azul SEAFOOD   Just outside of town where the bus stops on Tecolote beach, the Palapa Azul offers a completely authentic Baja experience. It's packed with hungry crowds on weekends, but if you get there early enough you can get a head start on their fresh, famous oysters.

Km 26 Carretera at Pichilingue. ℭ **612/122-1801.** Main courses $4–$10. No credit cards. Hours vary; call for schedule.

Pan D'Les BAKERY   Bringing a bit of old-world charm to historic La Paz is the new Pan D'Les bakery. Pedestrians on Calle Madero can smell the aroma of baguettes, ciabattas, and bagels baking from blocks away. Owner Les Carmona makes all the bread from scratch with fresh ingredients. In addition to bread, the shop offers decadent sweets like chocolate rum balls, creampuffs, and éclairs.

Madero at Ocampo. ℭ **612/119-8392.** www.eatingthroughlapaz.blogspot.com. Breads and muffins 9–40 pesos. No credit cards. Mon–Sat 8am–1:30pm. Hours may vary, so call ahead to double-check.

Rancho Viejo Mariscos La Palapa 🍴 MEXICAN/DINER   Eggs, with a view. There's more to it than that, of course—La Palapa has a full menu of Mexican standards, and you're welcome to sit inside as well. But the draw here is the top-floor balcony with a close-up view of the marina, a sunny place to start the day. This is also one of the cheapest sit-down places in town.

Pineda at the *malecón.* ℭ **612/126-1885.** Breakfast egg dishes 25–60 pesos; main courses 45–110 pesos. No credit cards. Daily 7am–midnight.

La Paz After Dark

A night in La Paz logically begins in a cafe along the *malecón* as the sun sinks into the sea. Have your camera ready.

A favorite ringside seat at dusk is a table at **La Terraza,** next to the Hotel Perla (ℭ 612/122-0777). La Terraza makes good, schooner-size margaritas. **Papas & Beer** (ℭ 612/128-5145; www.lapaz.papasandbeer.com) is the star attraction for the late night set at the trendy Vista Coral entertainment center, located at the very start of the *malecón* at Marquez de Léon. **Jungle Bar** (ℭ 612/125-7666), on the *malecón* at 16 de Septiembre, has spring-break-style Ladies' Night and shot specials, open until 2am Sunday to Wednesday, and till 4am Thursday to Saturday. For a lower-key night on the town, **La Encantada** gallery and wine bar (ℭ 612/185-3469), on Dominguez between 5 de Mayo and Callejón Constitución, showcases local jazz musicians in the garden until 10:30pm Monday to Saturday.

For dancing, two of the hottest clubs are **Casa de Villa** (© 612/128-5799), where current pop music has young *paceños* (La Paz locals) dancing till late on the second-floor terrace above La Paz–Lapa on the *malecón*, and **Las Varitas,** Independencia and Dominguez (© **612/125-2025;** www.lasvaritas.com), which plays Latin rock, *ranchera,* and salsa. Both are open from 9pm to 3 or 4am Thursday through Saturday (occasionally open earlier in the week as well), with cover charges around $5 (the charge may be waived or increased, depending on the crowd).

TODOS SANTOS: ART OASIS ★★★

68km (42 miles) N of Cabo San Lucas; 74km (46 miles) SW of La Paz; 1,200km (745 miles) SE of Tijuana.

Todos Santos is an oasis in the true sense of the word—in this desert landscape, Todos Santos enjoys an almost continuous water supply from the peaks of the Sierra de la Laguna mountains. It's just over an hour's drive up the Pacific coast from Cabo San Lucas and an hour southwest across the desert from La Paz; you'll know you've arrived when the arid coastal scenery suddenly gives way to verdant groves of palms, mangos, avocados, and papayas. But it's also an oasis of culture in an otherwise barren landscape: With dozens of galleries and restaurants, cultural events, and a growing contingent of wealthy, aging counterculture expats on the voter rolls, it's built its identity and staked its future on being Baja's art town—and it's paying off.

During the Mission Period of Baja, this oasis valley was deemed the only area south and west of La Paz worth settling because it had the only reliable water supply. In 1723, an outpost mission was established, followed by the full-fledged Misión Santa Rosa de Las Palmas in 1733. At the time, the town was known as Santa Rosa de Todos Santos; eventually shortened to its current name, it translates as "All Saints."

Over the next 200 years, the town alternated between prosperity and difficulty. Its most recent boom lasted from the mid–19th century until the 1950s, when the town flourished as a sugar-cane production center and began to develop a strong cultural core. The local history museum, **La Casa de La Cultura** (no phone), on Avenida Juárez, charts much of the history of Todos Santos and exhibits artwork from local artists, past and present. Many of the buildings now being restored and converted into galleries, studios, shops, and restaurants were built during this era. It wasn't until the 1980s that a paved road connected Todos Santos with La Paz, and road-trip tourism began to draw new attention to this tranquil town.

The last ten years have seen winter surfers squeezed out in favor of a better-paying clientele, and although it would be pushing it to say "Todos" has gone chic, it is an undeniable fact that with more than 20 art galleries, at least that many restaurants, a film festival, and a wine bar, the dusty town has put on some polish. While a number of farms are still in the palm oasis and taco stands sit on Hwy. 19 as it continues south of town, Todos Santos has embraced its official designation as a Mexican "Magical Town" and oriented its future surely toward tourism, albeit of an arty, elite sort. Artists, entrepreneurs, and foreign residents have snapped up many of the town's colonial-style buildings for galleries and restaurants; there are several places that serve sushi, and there seems to be an espresso machine on every corner. High-quality art and jewelry on offer, very good hotels, excellent restaurants, and live music and arts events have now made Todos Santos a destination in its own right. Whether that's a good thing, depends on who you ask.

Essentials

GETTING THERE

BY CAR From La Paz, take Hwy. 1 south. Just south of San Pedro, Hwy. 1 splits into two directions. Take Hwy. 19 to Todos Santos and stay on it, heading south until you reach Todos Santos. From Cabo San Lucas, take Hwy. 19 north. Your hour-long journey will take you through a few small towns, but you'll mostly be surrounded by dramatic desert landscape.

BY BUS **Transportes ABC** (*©* **800/025-0222;** www.transportes-abc.com) offers first-class bus service from both **La Paz** and **Cabo San Lucas.** Tickets cost about 70 pesos from either city. Todos Santos's **bus station** is a stick *palapa* on Colegio Militar and Zaragoza; it's an easy if slightly uphill walk to most hotels listed here (the exception is Posada La Poza, which is out of town).

VISITOR INFORMATION

Todos Santos is the only town in Baja to gain the designation of *"Pueblo Magico"* or "Magical Town" from Mexico's tourism secretariat (towns in other states include Tequila, Jalisco, and Taxco, Guerrero), and you'll know why the minute you walk along its tranquil streets. To get acquainted before your trip, visit the town's official website, **www.todossantos.cc**, for weather, maps, and information on restaurants, galleries, and nightlife.

When you get into town, pick up a copy of the free magazine *El Calendario de Todos Santos*, which can be found at coffee shops and hotels or by calling *©* **612/145-0129.** This community publication not only features restaurant and calendar listings, but has info on fun expat activities like book groups, dharma talks, and yoga.

GETTING AROUND

You won't need a car to explore town, but if you want to go to the beach or stay at Posada la Poza, wheels are essential. Taxis in town can take you to one of the local beaches for 60 to 80 pesos. **Fox** car-rental service is at Márquez de León 3 (*©* **612/145-0615**) car-rental service.

[Fast FACTS] TODOS SANTOS

Area Code The telephone area code is **612.**

Banks Banks generally exchange currency during normal business hours: Monday through Friday from 9am to 6pm and Saturday from 10am to 2pm. An ATM is at the Banorte on Márquez de León between Juárez and Colegio Militar.

Emergencies Dial *©* **066** for general emergency assistance, or

© **060** for police. Both calls are free.

Hospitals **St. Luke's Hospital** (*©* **612/145-0600**), at Colegio Militar between Márquez de León and Hidalgo, has a 24-hour emergency room.

Pharmacy **Farmacia Guadalupe** (*©* **612/145-0300**) on Juárez at Delgollado (Hwy. 19) carries standard prescriptions.

Post Office The *correo* is up Hwy. 19

from downtown, on Calle Villarino between Pedrajo and Olachea.

Tourism Office So far, Todos Santos doesn't have an official tourism office, but plenty of information is available at **gotbaja maps,** Calle Juárez, next to Heartease and Tecolote Books (*©* **612/178-0067**) and online at **www.todos santos.cc**.

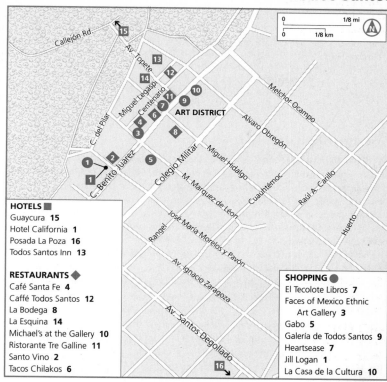

What to Do in Todos Santos

The great pleasure of Todos Santos is strolling its historic streets, browsing in the more than 20 art galleries, and eating and drinking at its many delightful cafes, restaurants, and bars. These are mainly concentrated in the north of town, in the area around Plaza Centenario bordered by Calle Juárez to the south, Calle Obregón to the east, Calle Morelos to the west, and Calle Pilar to the north. Don't miss the noted **Galería de Todos Santos,** corner of Topete and Legaspi (© **612/145-0500**), which features a changing collection of works by regional artists. It's open daily from 11am to 4pm (closed Sun May–Nov) and doesn't accept credit cards. Also of note are the galleries of **Jill Logan ★**, Juárez at Morelos (© **612/145-0151**) and **Gabo ★**, Márquez de León between Colegio Militar and Juárez (© **612/145-0514**), two of the brightest stars in Todos' art firmament. You can also see their work on display at the Hotel California and Tre Galline.

During the **Festival Fundador** (Oct 10–14), which celebrates the founding of the town in 1723, streets around the main plaza fill with food, games, and wandering troubadours. Many of the shops and the Café Santa Fe close from the end of September through the festival. The **Arts Festival** (www.todossantos-baja.com/todos-santos/art/art-festival.htm), held in February, seems to be gaining importance, with film, dance and music performances, and more. And the Todos Santos **Film Festival** ★ (www.todossantoscinefest.com), in the first week of March, has become a bona fide event in Latin American film.

Although most tours of Todos Santos start from outside town, family-run **Todos Santos Eco Adventures** (☎ **619/446-6827** in the U.S., or 612/145-0189; www.tosea.net) will take you bird-watching, hiking, or walking along the cliffs and beaches. **Cabo San Lucas Tours** (☎ **866/348-6286** in the U.S., or 01-800/822-4577; www.cabosanlucastours.net) leads art tours of the town that start in San José, and La Paz-based dive operator **Fun Baja** (☎ **612/106-7148;** www.funbaja.com) offers walking tours of Todos Santos, as well as Pescadero, with offbeat stops like a strawberry farm.

Shopping

El Tecolote Libros ★★★ 🎒 Though tiny, El Tecolote carries an exceptional selection of Latin American literature, poetry, children's books, and reference books centering on Mexico. Both English and Spanish editions, new and used, are in stock, along with maps, magazines, cards, art supplies, and used DVDs and books. A wonderfully eclectic gift shop in the back room focuses on the most authentic Mexican folk art with a supernatural bent. Information on upcoming writing workshops and local reading groups is posted here. Open Monday to Saturday 10am to 4:30pm, Sunday noon to 3pm. Corner of Juárez and Hidalgo. ☎**612/145-0295.**

Faces of Mexico Ethnic Art Gallery Push past the front room, crowded with T-shirts, for a look at an impressive collection of centuries-old *exvotos,* or portraits made to commemorate a saint's miraculous intervention. Owner Kersten Kiehnle is the son of famed explorer Constantine Kiehnle, who amassed the collection in the early 1900s. Many church patrons have purchased them for decorations in their parishes in the U.S. There's also a wall covered in traditional masks from around the country. Hours are Monday to Saturday 10am to 5pm. Márquez de León btw. Juárez and Centenario. ☎**612/145-0717.**

Heartsease This spa boutique sells all-natural soaps and skin-care products created by Canadian expat Gwenn McDonald. Look for items like castor oil conditioner, mini perfumes, and after-sun balm; either McDonald or a helpful employee can explain the healing effects. A masseuse offers services on the premises. Open daily from 10am to 5pm, closed July through September. Juárez btw. Hidalgo and Topete. ☎**612/132-0095.**

Where to Stay

EXPENSIVE

Guaycura ★★ Todos Santos's newest and chicest hotel brings a touch of urban sophistication to these dusty streets. Guaycura is a brand-new renovation of an early 20th-century school building, now cool and classy with terra-cotta floors, a rooftop pool, and large, mod rooms and suites with wrought-iron canopy beds, beamed ceilings, and stylish accents in pink and brown. Terraces furnished with comfy sofas have views over the palm oasis; some of the bright bathrooms boast hand-hammered copper tubs. The courtyard restaurant is for breakfasting in the shade, and a tiny, glamorous rooftop pool is for soaking up the sun.

Legaspi at Topete, 23305 Todos Santos, B.C.S. www.guaycura.com.mx. ☎**877/448-2928** in the U.S., or 612/175-0800. 14 units. $195–$280 double; $370–$450 suite. AE, MC, V. **Amenities:** Restaurant; bar; rooftop pool; spa room; Wi-Fi. *In room:* A/C, TV/DVD, minibar, MP3 docking station.

IS IT OR ISN'T IT? THE real story OF THE HOTEL CALIFORNIA

It's every hotel owner's dream: You can check out any time, but you can never leave. Despite an unequivocal denial by Eagles frontman Don Henley, the legend persists that the 1976 hit song "Hotel California" was inspired by the Todos Santos hotel, and the story has spawned its own tiny Todos cottage industry. A wedding planner calls the hotel "such a lovely place" for your destination wedding, with "plenty of room . . . [for] living it up." Across the street, tourists quaff drinks at Tequila's Sunrise. Henley says the song was inspired by 1970s L.A., and that the hotel in the lyric is a metaphor for the drug culture. Hotel owner Debbie Stewart is coy; she points to Todos Santos's "dark desert highway" and the next-door "mission bell," and suggests one of Henley's co-Eagles may have once stayed here even if Henley didn't. But, she admits, deserved or not, the hotel's fame is only half the rent. "We're really happy it brings people to the door—but those people will take a picture and then go away. We still have to keep them here."

Posada La Poza ★   The Posada la Poza (Inn at the Spring) was designed by its Swiss owners as an oasis within the oasis of Todos Santos, a place of peace in touch with nature. The grounds, about 2km (1½ miles) outside of town, are at the manmade sandy edge of a pond fronting the beach, where 130 species of birds have been sighted, many with the binoculars and bird books provided for hotel guests. A sprawling cactus and palm garden is the setting for eight comfortable rooms, decorated Swiss-style with bright colors and art by owner Libusche; also European-style, toilets are separate from bathrooms in all guest rooms. Enjoy the saltwater swimming pool with a Jacuzzi and small waterfall, and the exercise facility (on a lovely garden patio). Hiking and walking paths surround the hotel, and the pond has a kayak; bring bug repellent for twilight excursions from your room. A full breakfast of Swiss muesli, eggs, pastry, and fruit is included.

Apdo. Postal 10, Col. La Poza, 23305 Todos Santos, B.C.S. Follow blue signs with red arrows from Hwy. 19 southwest of town. www.lapoza.com. © **612/145-0400.** 8 units. Low season $160 double, $340 suite; high season $195 double, $420 suite. Rates include full breakfast. MC, V. Children 11 and under are not permitted. **Amenities:** Restaurant; loaner boats for pond; exercise facility; hiking paths; outdoor Jacuzzi; saltwater pool. *In room:* A/C, CD player, binoculars (for bird-watching), minibar, no phone, Wi-Fi.

MODERATE

Hotel California ☺   In a town of artists, Hotel California is an art hotel and an institution, decked from floor to ceiling with paintings, sculpture, furniture, and design elements that represent a lifetime of collecting. The effect is Philippe Starck in the desert, funky and wild and bejeweled with color and light. Cheaper, wood-floored streetfront rooms have less charm, but shell out a few tens more for a room in back and you'll want to take the place home with you (you can—almost everything here is for sale as well). The hotel has a small, secluded pool, as well as the Coronela Bar and Restaurant, with live music on the weekends, the Emporio Hotel California art and decor shop, and the new bistro **Santo Vino** (see "Where to Eat," on p. 108).

Calle Juárez, corner of Morelos, 23305 Todos Santos, B.C.S. www.hotelcaliforniabaja.com. © **612/145-0525** or 145-0522. 11 units. High season $110–$190 double; low season $100–$180 double. MC, V. **Amenities:** 2 restaurants; bar; tequila bar; boutique; library; outdoor pool; room service. *In room:* A/C, no phone, Wi-Fi.

Todos Santos Inn ★   A historic Spanish colonial house that has served as a general store, cantina, school, and private residence, this still feels like an aristocratic country home. Four rooms and four suites border a lush courtyard and brick terrace, pool, and garden. Rooms are aging well, with luxurious white bed linens, netting draped romantically over the beds, talavera tile bathrooms, antique furniture, and high, wood-beamed ceilings. (The suites are air-conditioned but have neither television nor telephone.) A high point is the Inn's clubby bar, **La Copa,** open to the public Mondays through Saturdays from 3 to 11pm.

Calle Legaspi 33, at Topete, 23305 Todos Santos, B.C.S. www.todossantosinn.com. © **612/145-0040.** Fax 612/145-0040. 8 units. Low season $95–$165 double; shoulder season $125–$225 double; high season $165–$325 double. MC, V. **Amenities:** Restaurant; bar; outdoor pool. *In room:* A/C, fan, hair dryer, MP3 docking station, no phone, Wi-Fi.

Where to Eat

In addition to the full-service restaurants listed here, Todos Santos has some delightful cafes, where you can get a light meal, pastries, and great coffee in a setting that will make you want to stay all day. Try **Caffé Todos Santos** ★ (© 612/145-0300), on Calle Centenario 33, with a terrace and Italian coffee prepared by the owners of Tre Galline (below), or **La Esquina** (© 612/145-0851), a spacious palm garden hangout on the way out of town at Calles Topete and Horizonte, with free Wi-Fi and a long list of smoothies. At cocktail hour, **La Bodega** wine bar (© 612/152-9370; Mon 5–8pm and Tues–Sat 11am–7pm) is a fine place for an aperitif, with live music and Baja wine tastings Mondays 5 to 8pm. For a unique dining experience, make sure to reserve at **Michael's at the Gallery** (© 612/145-0500) on Juárez between Hidalgo and Obregón, where artist and chef Michael Cope prepares Asian fusion cuisine amid his artwork on Friday and Saturday nights.

EXPENSIVE

Café Santa Fe ★★ ITALIAN   Much of the attention the town has received in recent years can be directly attributed to this outstanding cafe, and it continues to live up to its lofty reputation. Owners Ezio and Paula Colombo refurbished a large stucco house on the plaza, creating an exhibition kitchen, several dining rooms, and a lovely courtyard adjacent to a garden of hibiscus, bougainvillea, papaya trees, and herbs. The excellent northern Italian cuisine emphasizes local produce and seafood; try ravioli stuffed with spinach and ricotta in a Gorgonzola sauce, or ravioli with lobster and shrimp accompanied by an organic salad. In high season, expect a wait for a table.

Calle Centenario 4. © **612/145-0340.** Reservations recommended. Main courses 230–510 pesos. MC, V. Wed–Mon noon–9pm. Closed Sept–Oct.

Ristorante Tre Galline ★★ 🍴ITALIAN   When an earthquake destroyed Magda Valpiani's family restaurant in northern Italy, she and her husband took it as a sign to set out on a new adventure. They packed a shipping container to the brim with their personal treasures—including table settings and a pasta machine—headed to Mexico, and signed the papers for their new restaurant within hours of stepping into the former art gallery. The result couldn't be more authentically Italian, with home-made pastas, home-cured bresaola, and cheeses imported from the old country. Dishes like polenta with Gorgonzola and *caponi di bietola,* beet greens stuffed with a savory grain-and-cheese mixture, are Northern Italian home cooking at its best, while *tortelli di camote,* a sweet potato play on classic pumpkin tortellini, and mango-lime-orange-basil gelato show they're picking up some new tricks in their new home. The owners were active in Slow Food in Italy, and they bring the philosophy to Todos Santos.

Calle Juárez and Calle Topete. © **612/145-0274.** Main courses 180–300 pesos. MC, V. Mon–Sat 2–10pm.

MODERATE

Santo Vino CONTEMPORARY MEXICAN   This little place at the corner of the Hotel California is making a splash with strange and creative flavor pairings and an intimate bistro feel. The menu, designed by Hotel California chef Dany Lamote, is full of unexpected plays on Mexican classics, sexing up ceviche with tequila, sweet potato with chile, and enchiladas with lamb. Skip the uninspired hotel-food starches and concentrate on what's really exciting here: meats, fish, and the original and delicious starters, like shrimp croquettes with orange-chipotle cream and a chilled avocado soup with chile oil that goes down like butter. Bread is fresh made and different every day.

Calle Juárez btw. Márquez de León and Morelos, at the east end of the Hotel California building. © **612/145-0792.** Main courses 150–160 pesos. MC, V. Mon–Sat 4–10pm.

INEXPENSIVE

Tacos Chilakos TACOS   This authentic taco stand is the best cheapie in Todos Santos, hands down. Look for a streetside *palapa* roof with a set of plastic tables on the sidewalk, sit right down and order some tasty *arrachera* beef tacos or burritos *d'machaca,* with dried and shredded beef mixed with jalapeños and onions. Don't fear the hot sauce—it's not that hot. If you only have one opportunity to try street food during your trip to Baja, this is the spot.

Juárez at Topete. No phone. Tacos and tortas 14–35 pesos. No credit cards. Mon–Sat 9am–9pm.

THE PACIFIC SIDE: ENDLESS SUMMER ★★★

If it's ever occurred to you that it might be a good idea to chuck it all in and spend the rest of your days bumming around the beach, it turns out, you're not alone. That's what the Pacific beaches north of Cabo San Lucas were made for, and they're getting good use. The Pacific side, a rough designation for the stretch of coast from Cabo up to Todos Santos, sometimes feels like one long surf break, with an occasional taco stand thrown in for laughs. But look closer, and you'll find some variety: inland desert expanses you can explore by dune buggy, an art gallery-cum-seafood bar in the road-side sand, an oasis given over to organic vegetable farms that supply many of the local tables, an all-green yoga retreat. Cerritos Beach is the center of gravity here, such as it is: a loose grouping of homes and surf camps, a beachside bar and restaurant, and waves people will drive the whole peninsula for (and a swimming beach, too). While it's close enough to Cabo or to Todos Santos to make either your base, if you stay at the beach, you can lose yourself completely in the sound of the surf.

The Pacific Side offers a great deal of tranquillity and plenty of opportunities for Zen-like moments. You can get your "om" on at a retreat like **Prana del Mar ★★★** (*©* 415/310-2909 in the U.S.; www.pranadelmar.com) at Km 105 on Hwy. 19 in Migriños. For about $2,000 you can spend 7 days enjoying twice-daily yoga classes, organic meals, and ocean-side meditation; Prana del Mar is totally off-the-grid and one of the most sustainable hotels in Baja. Or, if you're interested in turning your downward dog into a new career, you can attend a 16-day yoga teacher training at the **Yandara Yoga Institute** (*©* 877/490-9883; www.yandara.com) in Todos Santos. The $2,330 tuition includes certification, tuition, meals, and accommodations.

Essentials

GETTING THERE

It's a piece of cake to get to the Pacific Side from Cabo San Lucas or Todos Santos: There's just one road, Hwy. 19. Be aware that a long and drawn-out road upgrade from two to four lanes means that parts of this highway are often closed, and lane changes to the wrong side of the road are poorly marked. The road is still agreeably flat and straight, but know that when you give in to the urge to let the throttle out, the next construction site is just around the bend. Be especially cautious at night.

GETTING AROUND

You'll do well to have a car here, but it's not absolutely necessary. If you stay in Todos Santos, you can make day trips to Cerritos and Pescadero by taxi; see "Todos Santos," earlier in this chapter.

What to Do on the Pacific Side

BEACHES

The Pacific Side is one long beach, extending from west of Cabo San Lucas all the way up to Todos Santos. Due to riptides, big surf, and the occasional rogue wave, most of the Pacific coast is unsafe for swimming, and all of it is wild. **Cerritos Beach ★★★** (Hwy. 19 Km 66) is a notable exception: It's a favorite of surfers and swimmers alike, and has the endless summer vibe that's made the Pacific Side a favorite of beach bums for decades now. To get there, turn in on the dirt road just after Km 66, and drive toward the magnificently overblown orange cliff-top mansion (see "Where to Stay," below) with the bell tower. As you get closer, you'll see a few orange *palapa*-roofed buildings on the beach, which house the **Costa Azul** surf shop (*©* 866/546-2102; www.costa-azul.com.mx) and the **Cerritos Beach Club** (*©* 624/143-4851; www.cerritosbcs.com), a central-casting surfer bar and grill with tables in the sand from which you can watch the show.

OFF-ROAD DRIVING

Get the adrenaline pumping without getting wet on a dune buggy tour: Drive automatic-transmission open-frame buggies through desert canyons and along the wind-swept Pacific shore with **Baja Buggys** (*©* 888/497-4283 in the U.S., or 624/105-9318; www.bajabuggys.com), located at Puente Migriño, Hwy. 19 Km 100. Two-hour outings leave Monday to Saturday at noon and 3pm, and cost $140 single, $180 double.

SURFING

Cerritos is the Pacific Side's most famous, and crowded, surfing beach, great for beginners and beloved of experts too. But winter breaks are all up and down the coast, including **Migriño** (Km 100), **Gaspareño** (Km 73), **San Pedrito** (Km 59), and **Punta Lobos** (Km 54). Most beach access roads are unpaved and unmarked but easy to find, as there aren't that many of them; beaches are generally 2 to 3km (1–2 miles) from the highway. See www.costa-azul.com.mx/areas_maps for details. You can rent boards and take lessons at the **Costa Azul** surf shop (see above) or through **Rancho Pescadero** (see "Where to Stay," below). At the former, be aware of hefty replacement fees should you ding a board; examine your gear well.

Where to Stay

EXPENSIVE

Hacienda Cerritos ★ 👔 Live like a billionaire for under $300 a night at this private megamansion-turned-guesthouse on the cliffs overlooking Cerritos beach. The magnificent Spanish colonial knockoff is owned by American real estate mogul Roger Pollock, who is renting over-the-top suites with carved wooden beds, fireplaces, and hand-tiled bathtubs to the public, along with the run of the private beach, two outdoor Jacuzzis, and pool with 270-degree views of the Pacific. There's no restaurant, but you're welcome to use the gigantic chef's kitchen, or just order in for pizza.

Atop the cliff at Playa Cerritos, Km 66 Hwy. 19. www.haciendacerritos.com. ⓒ**612/107-9935.** 12 units. $289 suites. MC, V. **Amenities**: Bar; private beach; helicopter pad; 2 Jacuzzis; communal kitchen; outdoor pool. *In room:* Fireplace, kitchenette (in some), Wi-Fi.

Rancho Pescadero ★★★ A hipsterrific hideout without pretensions, this beachside retreat is an oasis of cool. Airy beach-view rooms sport stylish polished-concrete floors and canopy beds, while more traditional garden rooms showcase high-quality local art. The poolside scene, with low Middle Eastern–style cushion seating and a low-key bar, is convivial and fun. Imaginative touches include loaner beach bags, straw hats, fishing poles, and even dogs for beach walks, and game sets (Jenga!) in rooms. Rates include a light breakfast, delivered in a wicker basket to your door. Rancho Pescadero offsets 20% of its electricity use with solar power, and grows produce for its restaurant in the on-site organic farm; it's part of a loose network of women hotel owners, and the staff can help you book at the other four hotels in the group (p. 57).

Pescadero, Km 62 Hwy. 19; turn in at the Pemex station and follow signs. www.ranchopescadero.com. ⓒ **910/300-8891** in the U.S., or 612/135-5849. 28 units. Low season $185–$275 double, $295–$385 suite; high season $250–$325 double, $345–$465 suite. DC, MC, V. **Amenities:** Restaurant; bar; Jacuzzi; 2 outdoor pools; spa; surfing lessons (for a fee); watersports equipment rentals; free daily yoga class. *In room:* A/C, fans, hair dryer, MP3 docking station, no phone, limited Wi-Fi.

INEXPENSIVE

Pescadero Surf Camp 🏄 This surf camp is a comfortable step up from the beach camping that's a way of life for most surf mongers. And, in the winter, when the waves—and sometimes winds—are at their strongest, it's nice to have a roof overhead. The property's pool has a BYOB swim-up bar that's ideal for cooling off between surf excursions, and a large outdoor kitchen provides a space to prepare your own meals. Owner Jaime Dobies also offers 1½-hour lessons for $50, board rental for $20 a day, boogie and skim board rental for $10 a day, and daylong guided surf safaris starting at $100 per person. He also repairs boards, should your baby get dinged in action.

Pescadero, Km 64 Hwy. 19; turn in at the Pemex station and follow signs. www.pescaderosurf.com. © **612/134-0480.** 9 units. $30–$85 double; $10 campsite. DC, MC, V. **Amenities:** Outdoor pool. *In room:* Minifridge.

Where to Eat

Most of the culinary action is up the road in Todos Santos, but a handful of places to eat are between Cabo San Lucas and Todos Santos. It's worth noting that Pescadero is a major center for organic vegetable farming, so this is a great area to refuel on your leafy greens.

Art & Beer 📷 SEAFOOD   It's an art gallery, it's a biker stop, it's a restaurant, it's an institution. Art & Beer may be Baja's weirdest night out, but it's a must on your trip up the Pacific Side for artisan cocktails, decent eats, and a taste of Baja's off-road hippie days, by now long gone. Try juicy marinated *chocolata* clams and a classic Mexican *michelada,* beer over ice with lime juice and salt, or the daily vegetarian special. You can also buy the outsider art and sculpture on display here; take it with you with a beer "to go." There's a 40-peso minimum consumption charge, per person, to enter.

Hwy. 19 Km 69. No phone. Main courses 175–225 pesos. No credit cards. Daily 1–10pm.

Napoli Pizzeria ★★ 🎁 PIZZA   This half-open *palapa* hut looks like every other roadside taco stand in Baja, but there's not a taco in sight. Instead, its wood oven is firing out the best pizzas in Baja: super-authentic extra-thin crispy-crust pies that are a hit with everyone from surfers to local gastronomes. The Roman-style potato pizza, with rosemary, is a particular treat; wash it down with a cold beer. Killer hot sauce packs a very Mexican kick.

Hwy. 19 south of Pescadero, on inland side of road next to Mini-Super Cristal. No phone. Pizzas 50–150 pesos. No credit cards. Daily 1–10pm.

MID-BAJA: LORETO, MULEGÉ & SANTA ROSALÍA

Baja's midsection is something of a test, a destination that separates the tourists from the travelers. Halfway between the busy border at Tijuana and the glitz and glamour of Los Cabos, however you got here, it's been a long trip. The vast majority of Baja visitors don't make it this far, and many who do just keep on driving through. They're missing out.

That's because this remotest of Baja regions is also its least developed, the closest to a state of nature you'll find in 1,120km (758 miles) of road. Jagged, lonely mountain ranges meet the Sea of Cortez at deserted beaches and impassable cliffs. Hours of wild desert suddenly erupt into bloom at a rare oasis. Birds on land and whales in the water make this special place their migratory home. If you're looking for peace, quiet, and a deep connection to the natural world, your journey ends here.

While the region's greatest charms are exactly where there's been no development, there are a few population centers that make a good base for exploration. Overlooked by many travelers (except avid sportfishermen and the off-road racers who pass through several times a year), the historic mission town of **Loreto,** the original capital of the Californias, is a head-quarters for fishing, diving, and kayaking in the Loreto Bay National Marine Park, and its offshore islands Coronado and Carmen, as well as for multiday hiking trips into the Sierra Giganta. **Mulegé** is, literally, an oasis in the Baja desert. The only freshwater river (Río Mulegé) in the peninsula flows through town, creating a wildlife-filled estuary. It's a start-ing point for the beaches, diving, and windsurfing of Bahía Concepción, as well as for hiking excursions to the ancient cave paintings of the Sierra de Guadalupe. And the port town of **Santa Rosalía,** while a century or so past its prime, makes a worthy detour, with its pastel clapboard houses and unusual steel-and-stained-glass church, designed by Gustave Eiffel (of Eiffel Tower fame).

The region's best-known attraction, and unquestionably its most thrill-ing, is the annual wintertime breeding and calving migration of gray whales to mid-Baja's bays and lagoons. From San Ignacio, Guerrero Negro, and Bahía Magdalena, you can commune with these giant creatures in their natural environment. If you're lucky, they'll come right up to the boat and look you in the eye: man and nature, face to face. See "Whale-Watching in Baja: A Primer," on p. 141.

LORETO & THE OFFSHORE ISLANDS ★★

389km (241 miles) NW of La Paz; 533km (330 miles) N of Cabo San Lucas; 1,125km (698 miles) SE of Tijuana

Little Loreto sits so unassumingly on the edges of its bay that it's easy to forget its historical importance. Loreto was the center of the Spanish mission effort during colonial times, the first capital of the Californias, and the first European settlement in the peninsula. Founded on October 25, 1697, it was Father Juan María Salvatierra's choice as the site of the first mission in the Californias. (California, at the time, extended from Cabo San Lucas to the Oregon border.) He held Mass beneath a figure of the Virgin of Loreto, brought from a town in Italy bearing the same name. For 132 years, Loreto served as the state capital, until an 1829 hurricane destroyed most of the town. The state capital moved to La Paz (chapter 5) the following year.

During the late 1970s and early 1980s, the Mexican government saw in Loreto the possibility for another mega-development along the lines of Cancún, Ixtapa, or Los Cabos. It invested in a golf course and championship tennis facility, modernized the town's infrastructure, and built an international airport and full marina facilities at Nopoló, 26km (16 miles) south of town. The economics, however, didn't make sense at the time, and few hotel investors and even fewer tourists came. A new timeshare development out of town seems far from the shot in the arm that Loreto's tourism anticipated; so far, the only discernable effect on the town is the timeshare salesmen annoying locals and visitors. And so Loreto, rather than becoming the next "new" destination, remains as it has been—at its heart, a pretty simple fishing town with a historic center and a very beautiful bay.

But its simplicity is its appeal. There's no high culture here, and no mainstream tourism, and it's easy to find a place to be by yourself on the sand or the waves. Recently, Loreto has received international accolades as a top new destination—and

> ### ⚠ Loreto's Timeshare Troubles
>
> With the opening of Loreto's first time-share development an hour south of town in 2011, the town has been invaded by out-of-town sales representatives willing to say just about anything to get you to visit the development. Firsthand reports tell of pitchmen representing themselves as tour guides, taxi drivers, even representatives of the marine park; they offer free whale-watching trips, boat tours, and overnights at the hotel. Don't be fooled: The tour takes at least 6 hours, and you'll be subject to a hard sell. You can tell the sales reps by the "Villa del Palmar" logos on their shirts, and by the fact that when you brush them off, they tend to get snotty—Loreto locals never do. At time of research, the Hotel Association was working on guidelines to keep the salesmen from harassing tourists; with any luck, by the time you read this, they'll be under control.

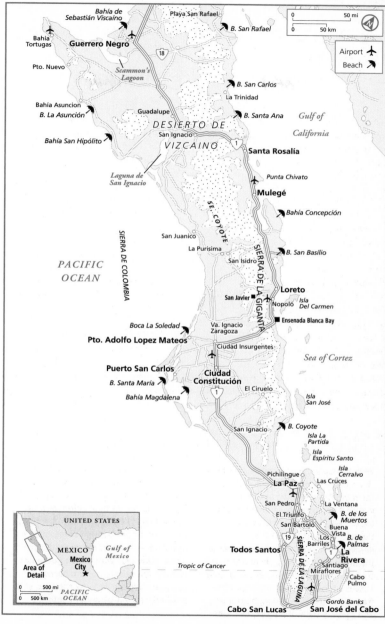

Bahía de
Sebastián Vizcaíno

Playa San Rafael

B. San Rafael

Bahía
Tortugas

Guerrero Negro

Pto. Nuevo

*Scammon's
Lagoon*

B. San Carlos

La Trinidad

Bahía Asuncion
B. La Asunción

Guadalupe

B. Santa Ana

*Gulf of
California*

DESIERTO DE

Bahía San Hipólito

San Ignacio

VIZCAINO

Santa Rosalía

*Laguna de
San Ignacio*

Punta Chivato

Mulegé

Bahía Concepción

SIERRA DE COLOMBIA

San Juanico

La Purisima

San Isidro

B. San Basílio

*PACIFIC
OCEAN*

San Javier

Loreto

*Isla
Del Carmen*

Nopoló

■ **Ensenada Blanca Bay**

Boca La Soledad

Va. Ignacio
Zaragoza

Pto. Adolfo Lopez Mateos

Ciudad Insurgentes

Puerto San Carlos

**Ciudad
Constitución**

Sea of Cortez

B. Santa María

El Ciruelo

Bahía Magdalena

*Isla
San José*

San Ignacio

B. Coyote

*Isla La
Partida*

*Isla
Espíritu Santo*

Pichilingue

*Isla
Cerralvo*

La Paz

Las Crúces

San Pedro

La Ventana

El Triunfo

*B. de los
Muertos*

San Bartolo

Buena
Vista

Los
Barriles

*B. de
Palmas*

Todos Santos

**La
Rivera**

Santiago

Miraflores

Tropic of Cancer

Cabo
Pulmo

Gordo Banks

Cabo San Lucas

San José del Cabo

0   50 mi
0   50 km

Airport ✈
Beach ↗

UNITED STATES

MEXICO

*Gulf of
Mexico*

**Mexico
City** ★

**Area of
Detail**

0   500 mi
0   500 km

*PACIFIC
OCEAN*

it's easy to see why. The Sea of Cortez and its offshore islands are teeming with wild-life—whales, dolphins, giant grouper, sea turtles—and the deserted crescents of turquoise in every cove are some of Baja's most secluded beaches. The natural port of Puerto Escondido shelters a growing yachting community; and the area is so lovely that most of the sailboats stay put year-round. Fishermen pull in big-game catches all year, kayakers launch here for trips to Isla del Carmen and Isla Danzante, or down the remote mountain coast to La Paz, and history buffs, birders, and desert campers head for the mountains to visit some of the oldest Jesuit missions and the ranch communities that still inhabit them. It's no wonder the American and Canadian expats who settled in here decades ago want to keep the place a secret—it's still one of Baja's best.

Essentials

GETTING THERE & DEPARTING

BY PLANE   The **Loreto International Airport** (airport code: LTO; ✆ 613/135-0499 or 135-0498) is 6km (3¾ miles) southwest of Loreto. For such a new and beautiful building, it doesn't have many flights: **Alaska Airlines** (✆ 800/252-7522 in the U.S.; www.alaskaair.com) flies nonstop four times weekly from Los Angeles, and **Aereo Calafia** (✆ 613/135-2503; www.aereocalafia.com) flies from Cabo San Lucas and Ciudad Obregón. When you exit immigration, be prepared for a gauntlet of timeshare sales representatives, who will try to get your attention with calls of "taxi?" or "tours?" Ignore them and walk outside to the real taxis waiting at the curb.

BY CAR   From La Paz (a 4½–5 hr. drive), take Carretera Transpeninsular (Hwy. 1) northwest to Ciudad Constitución; from there, continue northeast on Carretera Transpeninsular to Loreto. This route takes you twice over the mountain range that stretches down the Baja peninsula, through mountain and desert landscapes, and into the heart of the old mission country. From Tijuana, travel south on Carretera Transpeninsular. The drive takes 17 to 20 hours straight into Loreto, and driving after dark is strongly discouraged.

BY BUS   The bus station, or Terminal de Autobuses (✆ 613/135-0767), is on Salvatierra and Paseo Tamaral, a 10-minute walk from downtown. It's open 24 hours. Buses stop in Loreto en route to Santa Rosalía, Tijuana, Mexicali, Guerrero Negro, and La Paz. The trip to Cabo San Lucas on **Autotransportes Baja California** (✆ 800/025-0222; www.abc.com.mx) takes about 8 hours and costs 586 pesos. You can usually get a ticket for any bus, except during Easter, summer, and Christmas holidays, when buses tend to be more crowded. The bus terminal is a simple building and the staff there is very friendly and helpful.

ORIENTATION

ARRIVING   At the airport, taxis (✆ 613/135-1255) line up on the street to receive incoming passengers. They charge an astonishing 260 pesos to Loreto (300 pesos returning from Loreto to the airport), a 10-minute ride. (You'll save money with a *colectivo,* or group taxi, at 80 pesos per person, but you'll have to wait until the driver has four passengers to go to town.) The expensive taxi price is not an anomaly; the taxi union has set shockingly high rates in Loreto, so if you're planning to do much automotive exploring, your best bet is to rent a car.

If you do, it's best to book it in advance because the airport is so small that car-rental desks aren't always staffed on your arrival. **Budget Baja** has a counter at the airport (✆ 613/135-0937) and a branch office in town, on Hidalgo between Pípila

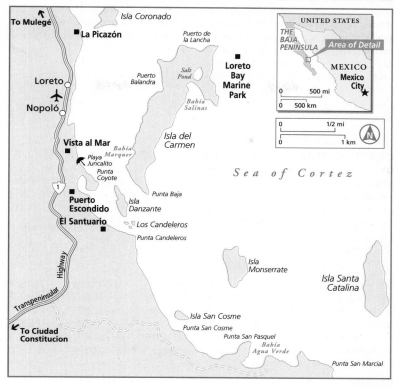

and López Mateos (𝄢 613/135-1149; daily 8am–8pm). Advance reservations are not always necessary, but will save you time.

If you arrive at the **bus station,** it's about a 10-minute walk to the downtown area and a little farther to the hotels by the water. A taxi from the bus station to the hotels costs 50 to 100 pesos.

VISITOR INFORMATION   The city **tourist information office** (𝄢 613/135-0036 or 135-0411) is in the southeast corner of the Palacio de Gobierno building, across from the town square. It offers maps, local free publications, and other basic information about the area. It's open Monday through Friday from 8am to 3pm. Information, which may be outdated, is also available at **www.gotoloreto.com** and **www.loreto.com**. The Loreto Adventure Network is an association of green-minded hotels, restaurants, and tour operators. Their website, **www.loretoadventure network.com** is a trove of helpful information.

CITY LAYOUT   Loreto is laid out between the entrance to Hwy. 1 and Bulevar López Mateos (the *malecón,* or beachside promenade), a distance of about 12 blocks. Salvatierra is the main street that connects them, running through the main square and up under a block-long arbor to a cobbled section of colonial road through Loreto's tiny historic district, with mahogany and teak homes dating from the 1800s, and the central plaza, with restaurants, an elegant hotel, a town hall straight out of a Western movie, and the old mission. Where Salvatierra is pedestrian-only, it's paralleled by Hidalgo, another main drag. The town's social life revolves around the central plaza, the old mission, and the *malecón*, where you'll find many hotels, seafood restaurants, fishing charters, bars, and the marina.

GETTING AROUND

Although street numbers are being assigned, many addresses in Loreto still use cross-streets for reference instead. There is no local bus service around town. Taxis or walking are your only options, and, luckily, the town is quite small and manageable for walking. The main taxi stand is on Salvatierra, in front of the El Pescador supermarket.

[Fast FACTS] LORETO

Area Code The telephone area code is **613.**

Banks Loreto has only one bank. Come here to exchange currency. **BBVA Bancomer** (☎ **613/135-0315** or 135-0014) is on Francisco I. Madero, across the street from the Palacio Municipal (City Hall). Bank hours are Monday through Friday from 8:30am to 4pm. This is also the only ATM in town. A *casa de cambio* (money-exchange house) is on Salvatierra, near the main square.

Beach Safety The beaches are generally safe for swimming, with the main beach along the *malecón* (seafront promenade).

Emergencies Dial ☎ **060** or ☎ **613/135-0035** for emergency assistance. In addition, 613/135-1566 will put you in touch with paramedics and the fire department.

General Store **Super El Pescador,** on Salvatierra and Independencia (☎ **613/135-0060**), is the best place to get toiletries, film, bottled water, and

other basic staples as well as newspapers and telephone calling cards.

Internet Access Practically every restaurant, hotel, and RV park in Loreto offers free Wi-Fi to patrons. One of the more popular places to hook up is **Augie's Bar and Bait Shop** (☎ **613/135-1224**) on the *malecón.*

Marinas Loreto's marina for *pangas* (small fishing boats) is along the *malecón.* Cruise ships and other large boats anchor at Puerto Loreto, also known as Puerto Escondido, 26km (16 miles) south of Loreto. For details about the marina and docking fees, contact the Capitanía de Puerto in Loreto (☎ **613/133-0992** or 135-0465).

Medical Care Medical services are offered at the **Centro de Salud** hospital (☎ **613/135-2035**), on Hwy. 1 between Loreto and the airport. The center is open 24 hours for emergencies (a standard visit costs $10), and from 8 to 10am and 3 to 5pm for general consultations, which cost $5. Two

English-speaking doctors in town are Dr. Collins (cell-phone ☎ **613/104-3600**) and Dr. Fernando (cell-phone ☎ **613/109-0165**).

Parking Street parking is generally easy to find in the downtown area.

Pharmacy The **Farmacia del Rosario** (☎ **613/135-0670**) is at Independencia and Zapata; **Farmacia de los Americas** (☎ **613/135-0670**) is on the west corner of Independencia and Juárez. Both are open daily 8am to 10pm.

Post Office The *correo* (☎ **613/135-0647**) is at Deportiva between Salvatierra and Benito Juárez, and is open Monday through Friday from 8am to 4:30pm and Saturday from 9am to 1pm.

Taxis Taxis can generally be found parked on the north side of Loreto's main street, just east of the El Pescador market, and near large hotels. The two taxi companies in Loreto are **Sitio Loreto** (☎ **613/135-0424**) and **Sitio Juárez** (☎ **613/135-0915**).

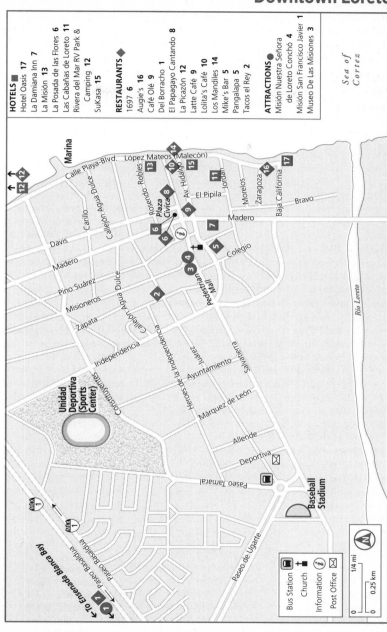

HOTELS ■
Hotel Oasis **17**
La Damiana Inn **7**
La Misión **13**
La Posada de las Flores **6**
Las Cabañas de Loreto **11**
Rivera del Mar RV Park & Camping **12**
Sukasa **15**

RESTAURANTS ◆
1697 **6**
Augie's **16**
Café Olé **9**
Del Borracho **1**
El Papagayo Cantando **8**
La Picazón **12**
Latte Café **9**
Lolita's Café **10**
Los Mandiles **14**
Mike's Bar **5**
Pangalapa **5**
Tacos el Rey **2**

ATTRACTIONS ●
Misión Nuestra Señora de Loreto Conchó **4**
Misión San Francisco Javier **1**
Museo De Las Misiones **3**

Marina

Sea of Cortez

Calle Playa-Blvd.
López Mateos (Malecón)
Rosendo Robles
Av. Hidalgo
El Pipila
Calle Agua Dulce
Callejón Agua Dulce
Carillo
Davis
Madero
Pino Suárez
Misioneros
Zapata
Independencia
Plaza Cívica
Colegio
Madero
Jordan
Morelos
Zaragoza
Baja California
Bravo
Pedestrian Mall
Heroes de la Independencia
Juárez
Ayuntamiento
Salvatierra
Márquez de León
Allende
Deportiva
Paseo Tamaral
Constituyentes
Paseo de Ugarte

Rio Loreto

Unidad Deportiva (Sports Center)

Baseball Stadium

To Ensenada Blanca Bay
paseo Basdiua
paseo Basdiua

Bus Station
Church
Information
Post Office

1/4 mi
0
0.25 km
0

119

If you're driving between Loreto and points south, schedule in a lunch stop at **Vista al Mar ★**, known by local gringos as the **Clam Shack**. In front, it's a low concrete building with a Pacifico beer sign hanging out front; in back, it's an expat's favorite barefoot beachside restaurant. Specialties are the marinated *chocolata* clams, and for those who prefer their shellfish cooked, a highly rated clam soup. Vista al Mar is on the coast side of Hwy. 1, midway between Nopoló and Puerto Escondido, about 15 minutes south of Loreto.

What to Do in Loreto

There's a different outdoor activity for every day of Loreto's year: whale-watching from January to April, kayaking May to June and October to December, dorado and billfish fishing in summer, scuba diving and snorkeling in May and July to August, mule expeditions into the mountains November to June, and sportfishing and excursions to San Javier mission, cave paintings, and Loreto's offshore islands year-round. For a small town, Loreto has a lot of very good tour operators. Some of our favorites are **Baja Big Fish** (seasonal summer office in Mediterraneo restaurant on the *malecón;* ✆ 613/135-1603; www.bajabigfish.com), a sportfishing company with a strong commitment to sustainability; **Dolphin Dive Center** (on Juárez just off the *malecón;* ✆ 613/135-1914; www.dolphindivebaja.com), Loreto's most established dive operator; **Land & Sea Eco Adventures** (next door to the Damiana Inn on Madero at Hidalgo; ✆ 613/135-0680; www.loretoecotours.wordpress.com), with gifted naturalist guides; and **Tour Baja** (✆ 800/398-6200; www.tourbaja.com), offering sailing, kayaking, pack trips, and some of the entire peninsula's most exciting active adventures since 1983.

Bear in mind that if you'll be on the water or the offshore islands, you'll need a Loreto Bay National **Marine Park bracelet** as proof you've paid your daily entry fee (23 pesos). Tour operators will take care of it for you, but if you're on your own, stop into the park office at the marina to pay.

Beaches & Cruises

BEACHES The main beaches at either end of the *malecón* are popular places for Loretanos, especially on Sundays; they're safe for swimming. But the region's most beautiful, pristine beaches, glittering with white sand, turquoise water, and spectacular marine life, are on **Isla Coronado ★★★**, a half-hour boat ride away, and **Isla del Carmen ★★**—if you're here for more than 1 day, you won't want to miss out, especially on Coronado, which is an easy trip. The best anchorage is on the western shores of both islands. To get there, see "Boat Trips," below.

BOAT TRIPS Loreto offers island exploration tours that take in one, or a combination, of the five islands located just offshore. They usually offer the opportunity to visit sea lion colonies and do some snorkeling and beachcombing for around $60 for three people. Arrange cruises through your hotel—every hotel has a deal with a local fisherman—or through one of the operators listed above. **Land & Sea Eco Adventures** will take you to Coronado's beaches for $65, including snorkeling, a desert nature walk, and lunch (add $20 for an excellent barbecue and beer); they also run boat and hiking tours to Isla del Carmen. Ask about visits to the farther-flung islands—each one is unique and offers a spectrum of activities such as sea kayaking, snorkeling, diving, hiking, or simply exploring the local desert flora and fauna (see "A Visit to Isla del Carmen," below).

Land Sports

BIRD-WATCHING The **estuary ★** just out of town south of the Hotel Oasis is an Eden of wildlife in the early mornings. Hire a *panga* at the marina or through your hotel for sunrise bird- and dolphin-watching, or just stroll down along the shore. Don't forget your camera! Farther afield, **Land & Sea Eco Adventures** offers seasonal bird-watching at Misión San Javier, and **Baja By Kayak** (© **613/135-1887;** www.bajabykayak.com) arranges birding overnights to Laguna San Ignacio.

GOLF The 18-hole **Campo de Golf Loreto,** Bulevar Misión San Ignacio, Fraccionamiento Nopoló (© **613/133-0554**), is 18 holes of natural landscaping, incorporating desert, mangroves, and artificial lakes that attract migrating birds. The front 9 holes are a links-style course with gently sloping fairways, and the back 9 incorporate the mangroves and water features.

HIKING & MOUNTAIN BIKING As hiking goes, the Sierra de la Giganta has virtually no formal trails, so a local's perspective is invaluable and will land you in many magical spots in these towering mountains. **Tour Baja** offers a range of adventure tours, including hiking, mountain biking, kayaking, sailing, and horseback riding, and they were adventurers in this rugged territory long before they decided to become guides. Their **Pedaling South ★** tour offers vehicle-supported guided mountainbike treks for all skill levels. Choose from tours into the mountains, along the coast, and to the San Javier Mission, and combine your favorite with snorkeling or kayaking. Call Tour Baja for information on mule packing and day-hike trips into the mountains. A 3-day guided mountain-bike trip costs $95 per hiker per day, and a mountainbiking excursion costs $125 per day or $95 if you bring your own bike (with a minimum of three people). **Land & Sea Eco Adventures** will organize custom hiking tours with a strong emphasis on understanding the natural environment of the desert, including desert survival tips, for $50 per day.

HORSEBACK RIDING Tour Baja's **Saddling South** offers pack trips on horse- and muleback into the Sierra de La Giganta range and through historic ranches along the way. If you're looking to experience life on the California frontier, this is for you. One to 6-day **mule treks ★★** to the cave paintings of San Ignacio are highly recommended. The cost is $125 per day for a minimum 3-day and maximum 8-day tour.

 Festivals in Loreto

The feast of the patron saint of Loreto is celebrated September 5 to September 8, with a fair, music, dancing, and other cultural events, closing with the procession of the miraculous figure of the Virgin of Loreto. During the month of October, Loreto celebrates the anniversary of its founding with a series of cultural events that include music and dance. There is also a reenactment of the landing of the Spanish missionaries that is part of a popular festival held from October 19 to October 25.

TENNIS   You can play tennis at the Nopoló Sports Center's **Loreto Bay Tennis Center** (© 877/522-9466), which was dedicated by John McEnroe. There are eight courts, a pool, a sun deck, a stadium that holds 250 people, a racquetball court, and a pro shop. Check in before your visit to find up-to-date prices. The center is open daily from 7am to 8pm.

Watersports & Activities ★★★

The Sea of Cortez is the star in Loreto, and the five islands just offshore make for some of the best kayaking, sailing, diving, and fishing in North America. Paddling alongside jagged mountains and crystal bays, diving with mantas and giant squid, and pulling in mega marlin are all in a day's fun. Freediving, or breath-hold diving as opposed to diving with tanks, is becoming more popular as well. Loreto is the nearest major airport and city to Bahía de Magdalena (Magdalena Bay), the southernmost of the major gray whale calving lagoons on the Pacific coast of Baja, and Loreto was their stage in winter 2007 during the filming of a documentary called *Whales.*

SEA KAYAKING   Kayaking season is October through December and May through June, and although Loreto attracts mostly expert kayakers, options are available for novice recreational paddlers as well. **Tour Baja** offers Paddling South multi-tiday trips ($1,045–$1,195) in one- or two-person fiberglass sea kayaks. Puerto Escondido is also an ideal starting point for experienced kayakers who want to reach Isla Montserrat; call Tour Baja for details. **Land & Sea Eco Adventures** offers kayaking day trips to Coronado ($90) and Danzantes ($115). **Sea Trek Kayak** (© 415/332-8494 in the U.S.; www.seatrekkayak.com), out of Sausalito, California, has been running weeklong island-hopping kayak camping trips here for 25 years; $995 per person includes all food, lodging, guides, fees, and gear.

SNORKELING & DIVING   Several companies offer snorkeling; most island exploration trips include snorkeling, and trips to Isla del Carmen, Isla Coronado, Isla Monserrate, and Isla Catalina all include snorkeling opportunities. The going rate is $65 including gear, snacks, and tips. Some fishing trips carry snorkeling gear on board to give anglers a chance to check out the underwater world.

For scuba diving, contact **Dolphin Dive Center.** It offers several diving sites where you can admire the underwater bounty of the Sea of Cortez. The two-tank trips cost $99 to $120 per diver, and a PADI dive master guides all tours. Snacks, Loreto Bay Marine Park fees, weights, two tanks, and a boat are included, but any equipment needed comes at an extra charge (air costs $5/tank, wet suit $10, BC [buoyancy compensator] $10, regulator with dive computer $12, mask/fins/snorkel $10). If you're new to scuba and would like to get certified, or if you want an advanced certi-fication, Dolphin Dive Center also offers several PADI resort courses, which range from $150 for a daylong resort course to $650 for dive-master certification.

For something more unusual and boldly adventurous, take advantage of the run of giant Humboldt **squid** that pass inshore to spawn between Isla del Carmen and Isla Danzante from May through October. Dolphin arranges nighttime encounters with these ink-squirting apex predators, which can grow up to 90 kilograms (200 lb.) and travel in packs called shoals, with divers protected in shark-proof cages, for $200, with a minimum of three divers.

SEA TURTLE MONITORING   The Sea of Cortez is an important habitat for endangered sea turtles, but scientists still don't know how far they travel from these shores. **Tour Baja** and **Baja By Kayak** (© 613/135-1887; www.bajabykayak.com)

A VISIT TO isla del carmen ★★

Isla del Carmen rises like a rust-colored slice of Dakota badlands out of the slate-blue sea. It's the largest of Loreto's offshore islands, and it's privately owned, so you'll have to go through one of a number of tour companies in Loreto to go ashore. Choose your company based on your preferred activity and mode of exploration (usually kayaking or snorkeling, sometimes hiking).

The island was once the site of an impressive salt-mining operation, but increased competition—not to mention the opportunity to earn a dollar from granting landing permissions to tourism purveyors—encouraged the company to shut down and refocus its economic endeavors. You can see the ghost of the salt-mining town, completely abandoned in 1983, at the northeastern tip of the island.

Volcanic in origin, Isla del Carmen also has deposits of *coquina,* a limestone-like rock of cemented shell material that was quarried by the Jesuit missionaries for use in constructing the church and other buildings in Loreto.

One favorite cove on Isla del Carmen is Puerto Balandra, where bold rock formations rising up like humpback whales frame crystal-blue water and ivory sand.

The craggy desert terrain offers a cornucopia of plant life, including elephant trees, desert asparagus (pickleweed), mesquite trees, jojoba, agave, cardón cacti, and passionflower vines. Be careful of the cholla cacti, whose spines enter your skin in a crisscross pattern. To remove them, cut the spines from the plant and then pull them out one at a time.

The topography on the island alternates between salt-crusted ground, spongy surfaces—a sure sign that snakes, iguanas, and burrowing animals are nearby—and the rocky remains of former riverbeds. The large variety of fauna includes a population of mountain goats that were introduced to the island to provide a meat supply for its inhabitants, and now are game for paying hunters. You'll spot feral cats, blacktailed hares, and birds ranging from osprey to gila woodpeckers, among other wildlife.

are contributing to sea turtle research by capturing, measuring, and tagging sea turtles near Danzante and Coronado islands, and for $125, you can help. The classic trip is a camping overnight, and you can expect a short night, as nets are checked every hour, and when turtles arrive, the action begins. Tour Baja also offers daytime turtle trips.

SPORTFISHING The fishing near Loreto is exceptional, with a different game fish for every season. Winter and spring months are great for yellowtail, sea bass, roosterfish, and grouper; and summer is the time for big marlin, sailfish, tuna, and dorado. This is a protected marine park, and the catch is limited to fin fish, not more than 10 per day and five per species; marlin, shark, swordfish, and sailfish count as five, with only one allowed, and dorado, roosterfish, shad, and tarpon count as five, with only two allowed. Catch-and-release fishing is unlimited, and strongly encouraged. **Baja Big Fish** is the go-to operator for sustainable fishing practices; they offer fly-fishing as well.

The least expensive way to enjoy deep-sea fishing is to pair up with another angler and charter a *panga* from the **Loreto Sportfishing Cooperative** at the main pier in Loreto. Prices range from $150 to $180 per boat, depending on the size and availability of shade. You can also arrange your trip in advance through most resorts and tour operators or contact the fleets directly. People with their own boats can launch at the ramp just north of the *malecón* in town or at Puerto Loreto, 26km (16 miles) south of town; you'll need a fishing license from the marine park office at the marina, 136 pesos daily and 258 pesos a week. If you plan on running out to Isla del Carmen, it's better to launch from Puerto Loreto, which cuts 10km (6 miles) off the crossing. For tackle, head to Deportes Blazer (✆ **613/135-0911**) on Hidalgo, the catchall sporting-goods store in town.

WHALE-WATCHING ★★★ ☺ Loreto is the nearest major airport and town to Bahía Magdalena (Magdalena Bay), the southernmost of the major gray whale calving lagoons on the Pacific coast. For more information on popular whale-watching spots and tour operators elsewhere than Loreto, see the "Whale-Watching in Baja: A Primer" section later in this chapter. All hotels and tour operators can arrange (long) day trips to Magdalena Bay, for between $70 and $150, depending on whether lunch and an English-speaking guide are included. It's a 2-hour car or van ride each way, with about 2 hours on the water and lunch in between. To visit the whales at San Ignacio Lagoon, plan an overnight. **Baja By Kayak** has 2-night trips from Loreto for $995 to $1,150.

While the gray whales are Baja's number one attraction between January and March, they're not the only giant marine mammals in town. Right in Loreto Bay are large populations of migrating blue whales—the largest animal in the world—humpback, pilot, and sperm whales, local finback whales, orcas, and dolphins. They won't come up and commune with boat passengers the way the gray whales do, but it's still an awe-inspiring nature experience, without the commute. **Land & Sea Eco Adventures** runs daylong excursions into the bay for $130, while **Dolphin Dive Center** charges $150, including a naturalist guide and lunch on an island beach.

Historic Loreto & Other Interesting Sites

For cultural day trips in the area other than those listed below, contact **C&C Tours** (✆ **613/133-0151;** www.loretovacations.com). Among the guided excursions they offer are the Historic Loreto City Tour (220 pesos, morning and evening options available), a long day hiking in Tabor Canyon ($18), a beach tour of Mulegé with a restaurant lunch (220 pesos, see "Mulegé" later in this chapter), whale-watching tours, and folkloric dance classes.

MISIÓN NUESTRA SEÑORA DE LORETO CONCHÓ The first mission in the Californias was started here in 1697. The catechization of California by Jesuit missionaries was based from this mission and lasted through the 18th century. The inscription above the entrance reads "Cabeza y Madre de las Misiones de Baja y Alta California" (Head and Mother of the Missions of Lower and Upper California). The current church, a simple building in the shape of a Greek cross, was finished in 1752 and restored in 1976. The original Virgen de Loreto, brought to shore by Padre Kino in 1667, is on display in the little chapel behind the courtyard on the right as you enter—this is the icon that Steinbeck describes in the *Log from the Sea of Cortez.* The mission is on Salvatierra, across from the central square.

MISIÓN SAN FRANCISCO JAVIER ★★★ About 2 hours of dirt-road driving from Loreto and in a section of the old Camino Real used by Spanish missionaries and explorers, this is the best-preserved, most spectacularly set mission in Baja—high in a mountain valley oasis, beneath volcanic walls. Founded in 1699 by the Jesuit priest Francisco María Píccolo, it was completed in 1758 and was the second mission established in California. The church was built with blocks of volcanic stone from the Sierra de la Giganta Mountains. It is very well preserved, with its original walls, floors, gilded altar, and religious artifacts, and the surrounding ranches—filled with onion fields and olive-tree orchards—make for a pastoral setting and a nice stroll. At research time, a marketplace for local products was also in the works.

Day tours from Loreto, organized by several local tour operators, visit the mission, with stops along the way to view aboriginal cave paintings and an oasis settlement with a small chapel. The trips can be arranged through most hotels and tour operators, including **C&C Tours,** for 500 pesos, **Dolphin Dive Center,** for $60, and **Sea and Land Eco Tours,** which includes visits to organic ranches and/or bird-watching on request, for $85. All tours include lunch and an English-speaking guide. If you are driving a high-clearance four-wheel-drive vehicle and are an experienced off-road driver, you can get there yourself by traveling south on the Carretera Transpeninsular and taking the detour marked SAN JAVIER on Km 118, 3.2km (2 miles) south of Loreto. The 40km (25-mile) drive takes about 2 hours, the first half on pavement and the second on washboard road. If you fall in love with San Javier, you won't be the first. Stay a little longer, at simple ecotourism cabanas in the fresh mountain air. Contact **Hotel Oasis** (p. 127) or **Raíces Vives** (© 505/280-4761 in the U.S., or 613/109-8583; www.livingrootsbaja.org) for reservations.

MUSEO DE LAS MISIONES ★ This museum explains the Misión Nuestra Señora de Loreto church (see above). It has a small but complete collection of historical and anthropological exhibits, set around a charming colonial courtyard. You'll learn about the indigenous Guaycura, Pericúe, and Cochimí populations, along with the accomplishments of the Jesuit missionaries—including their zoological studies, scientific writings, architectural sketches, and details of the role they played in the demise of indigenous cultures. Also on display are several religious paintings, original wooden beams and tools, and sculptures dating to the 18th century. The museum, located at Salvatierra 16 (© **613/135-0441**), has a small shop where the INAH (Instituto Nacional de Antropología e Historia) sells books about the history of Mexico and Baja California. It's open Tuesday through Sunday from 9am to 6pm, closing for 45 minutes for lunch at 1pm. Admission is 37 pesos.

Shopping

Quite frankly, you won't be coming to Loreto to shop, and if you do, you're going to be disappointed. Loreto has little in the way of shopping, either for basics or for folk art and other collectibles from mainland Mexico. A handful of the requisite shops selling souvenirs and some *artesanía* are all within a block of the mission. More known for its atmosphere than its material holdings is the Sunday **farmers' market/flea market** (6am–noon). It's Loreto's weekly community get-together, held in the arroyo just south of town. Follow the crowds.

Caballo Blanco There's beach fiction up front, Baja guides in the back, and an old-fashioned small-town vibe throughout Loreto's English-language bookstore. It's open daily 8am to 9pm, although it may open later on Sundays when the owners go to brunch at Lolita's. Hidalgo 85 at Madero. © **613/116-5374.**

El Alacrán This shop has a quality selection of arts and crafts, as well as interesting books about Baja, fine silver jewelry, and handmade and cotton clothing. Open Monday through Saturday from 9:30am to 1pm and 3 to 7pm. The gallery next door showcases fine art by Carlos Díaz Uroz in acrylics on handmade paper and canvas. Salvatierra and Misioneros. © **613/135-0029.**

La Casa de la Abuela "Grandma's House" is Loreto's oldest, originally built in 1744 and rebuilt after the 1877 earthquake. Its old-fashioned wood-floored rooms are stuffed with saddlery, clothes, and folk art from throughout Mexico. It's open Wednesday through Monday from 9am to 10pm. No credit cards. Salvatierra and Misioneros, across from the Mission. No phone.

Silver Desert Exquisite—and original—silver jewelry is the order of the day here. Open daily from 9am to 2pm and 3 to 9pm. Salvatierra 36, next to the bank, and on the main plaza across from Posada de las Flores. ✆ **613/135-0684**.

Where to Stay

In general, accommodations in Loreto are the kind travelers to Mexico used to find all over: inexpensive and unique, with genuine and friendly owner-operators. And, as Mid-Baja is a mecca of sorts for RV explorers, **Rivera del Mar RV Park & Camping** (www.riveradelmar.com; ✆ 613/135-0718) has deluxe hookups just 2 blocks from the beach. Also of note, as people fall in love with Loreto and build their dream homes there, vacation-rental properties are on the rise, and Kathy and Hector at **Rentals Loreto** (✆ **613/135-2505;** www.rentalsloreto.com) have the best selection in town. Beachfront homes that sleep up to eight can go for about $170 a night and most also rent by the week.

EXPENSIVE

La Misión Loreto's newest hotel is also its most luxurious, a palatial monolith that presides over the *malecón* like a queen over her subjects. The rooms are deluxe, with bayview balconies, carved-wood and wrought-iron furnishings, and crisp white sheets dressed up with lots of pillows, but the location, despite its proximity, feels a bit disconnected from the rest of town—great if you want a resort vacation, but if you want to get into the local color, you may be better off elsewhere. The restaurant, despite its excellent location and high style, is overpriced, but the belly-up bar is elegant and lively and the rooftop spa, with Thai, hot stone, and aromatherapy massages, is a treat.

On the *malecón* btw. Robles and Juárez, Loreto, B.C.S. www.lamisionloreto.com. ✆ **877/535-2646** in the U.S., or 613/134-0350. 68 units. $115–134 double; $156–425 suite. Meal plans available. AE, MC, V. **Amenities:** Restaurant; bar; concierge; fitness center; Jacuzzi; outdoor pool; room service; deluxe spa. *In room:* A/C, fan, TV, hair dryer, minibar, Wi-Fi.

La Posada de las Flores ★★ The most luxurious place to stay in Loreto conveniently sits on the main plaza, in the heart of historic Loreto. When you're in the lobby, look up—the rooftop pool has a glass bottom. That's the only offbeat touch here; the rest is strictly classic Mexican colonial, with fine arts and crafts, heavy wood doors, talavera pottery, painted tiles, candles, and scenic paintings. Large bathrooms have thick white towels and bamboo doors, with Frette bathrobes hanging in the closet. Every detail has been carefully selected, including the down comforters and numerous antiques tucked into corners. The **spa ★★** is locally celebrated, and open to the public. Only children 13 and over are welcome.

Salvatierra and Francisco I. Madero, Centro, 23880 Loreto, B.C.S. www.posadadelasflores.com. ✆ **619/378-0103** in the U.S., or 613/135-1162. Fax 613/135-1099. 15 units. August $180 double, $290 suite; Sept–July $150 double, $250 suite. Rates include continental breakfast. MC, V. Street parking. No children 12 and under permitted. **Amenities:** Breakfast restaurant; rooftop glass-bottom pool. *In room:* A/C, TV, minibar, Wi-Fi.

MODERATE

Hotel Oasis The fisherman's old-style favorite, this beachfront hotel caters to their needs with specialized services, excursions, and its own fleet of boats and equipment. In operation since 1962, Hotel Oasis has a friendly and knowledgeable staff. The simple but spacious rooms have two double beds and a private balcony or terrace, with either pool or ocean views. Summer rates with mandatory meal service are more expensive. It's on the beach at the south end of the *malecón*, close to restaurants, shops, and the historic downtown. Their restaurant gets high marks from guests, and it even serves a 5am fisherman's breakfast. The hotel can also book a stay for you at Casa de Ana, a simple guesthouse in the mountains at San Javier.

On the south end of the *malecón* at Baja California, 23880 Loreto, B.C.S. www.hoteloasis.com. ℂ **800/482-0247** in the U.S., or 613/135-0211. Fax 613/135-0795. 39 units. $120–$150 double; $164 suite. Bed-and-breakfast, as well as full meal plans available. MC, V. Private parking. **Amenities:** Restaurant; bar; fishing services including boat and gear rentals; heated outdoor pool. *In room:* A/C, TVs and phones on request.

Las Cabañas de Loreto ★★ 📷 There's no better place in Loreto to put your feet up and stay a while. This family-run beachside compound extends a real Baja welcome to its guests, from stocking refrigerators with breakfast and beer to hosting impromptu birthday parties in its outdoor dining area and singalongs at the fire pit. Four simple guest rooms are clustered around the courtyard; they all have kitchenettes where you can make your own breakfast. The two generations of owners have their own specialties, so you'll get expert advice on sportfishing, watersports, and wildlife viewing, the last from photographer Rick Jackson, whose photographs decorate the rooms and many restaurants in town. Book early, especially in billfishing season. No kids 11 and under.

Morelos at the *malecón*, Loreto, B.C.S. www.lascabanasdeloreto.com. ℂ **613/135-1105.** 4 units. $95 double. MC, V. **Amenities:** Jacuzzi; book and movie library; loaner bicycles, snorkel gear, wetsuits, beach chairs and umbrellas; outdoor pool, fire pit, and communal kitchen. *In room:* A/C, fans; TV/DVD; kitchenette; safe; Wi-Fi.

INEXPENSIVE

La Damiana Inn ★ 🖋 The location of the La Damiana Inn—in the heart of town on Calle Madero—is reason enough to book a reservation, but its warmth and style make it one of the best accommodations values in Loreto. This former family home was built in 1917. Today, its six bedrooms are outfitted with air-conditioning and ceiling fans and twin, queen- or king-size beds (make sure to be specific about what you want when you book). The pretty garden out back can be used for communal or group dinners, cooked up in the guest kitchen or catered upon request. Wi-Fi throughout the hotel, laundry facilities (for a fee), a shared living room, a bookshelf full of beach reading, and free cuddles from the friendly house dog are the extras that make La Damiana Inn seem like a gracious friend's home.

Madero 8 Sur, btw. Hidalgo and Jordan, Centro, 23880 Loreto, B.C.S. www.ladamianainn.com. ℂ**613/135-0356.** 6 units. $62 double; $70 suite. MC, V. Pets accepted upon prior approval. **Amenities:** Bicycles; library; phone for local calls; TV in common area; Wi-Fi. *In room:* A/C, fan, no phone.

SuKasa ★★ 🛍 This is the place for travelers who want to have their own homey space right on the *malecón*. The name doesn't mislead—SuKasa feels like *su casa* and comes with friendly owners, swaying hammocks, and well-appointed Mexican decor. Two fully furnished bungalows, with kitchens, master bedrooms, and charming living areas; one pristine casita with full kitchen; a sprawling two-story main house that's available for rent by the week; and one modern and spacious yurt make for a charming resort retreat. The property is shrouded in towering palms and desert blooms, right across the street from the water. SuKasa arranges fishing packages with Baja Big Fish. Smoking is prohibited on the property.

Malecón. 23880 Loreto, B.C.S. www.loreto.com/sukasa.© **613/135-0490.** 5 units. $75 bungalow; $85 casita; $55 yurt. MC, V. **Amenities:** Bicycles; barbecue grill; kayaks; Wi-Fi. *In room:* A/C, ceiling fan, TV/ VCR, kitchen, no phone.

Where to Eat

Big flavors come in humble packages in Loreto, but for the lack of polish there's a lot of variety. In addition to the below hubs, the fried shrimp tacos at **Tacos el Rey** on Benito Juárez are legendary, but get there early—when they're out, the place closes. **Pangalapa** on Hidalgo is a favorite among Mexican locals, for authentic food and low prices under a streetside *palapa* hut, and everyone agrees that Loreto's best Mexican breakfast is at **Los Mandiles** on the *malecón.* For coffee lovers, the town now has two espresso machines, at **Lolita's Café,** Salvatierra, just off the *malecón* (daily 7am–3pm), and **Latte Café,** on Madero between Hidalgo and Salvatierra, next door to Café Olé. For more tips and updated details check the website of the **Loreto Restaurant Association** (www.loretorestaurants.com).

EXPENSIVE

La Picazón ★★★ 📷 SEAFOOD   At the end of a long graded desert road, behind a stand of cacti and steps from the water's edge, this is Loreto's favorite place to watch the sun go down over a plate of just-caught fish. Come by car (about a half-hour) or by boat from Coronado Island, order by 6pm and linger as long as you want over scallops, shrimp, snapper in garlic sauce or encrusted in fresh coconut, the popular mixed seafood wrap, or just a pair of frosty king-size margaritas—it's all good. (Taxis charge about 400 pesos for the round-trip from town, including time waiting while you eat.) The secluded beach is the spot for an after-lunch constitutional. At dinner, arrive early to stake your claim to a waterside table.

Calle Davis norte 27, Camino al Bajo Km 7.© **613/109-5078.** Main courses 100–225 pesos. No credit cards. Mon–Sat noon–6pm (last order at 6pm, though the restaurant stays open till the last guest leaves).

MODERATE

1697 ★ ITALIAN/MEXICAN   An Irish chef and his Mexican wife have put together a very good menu of Mexican and Italian specialties at reasonable prices, presented in a pleasant low colonial building at a corner of the main plaza. The good news: Excellent crispy pizza, fresh and generous salads, and Loreto's only microbrew, straight from San José's Baja Brewing Company, will end up on your table at this convivial, candlelit garden eatery. The bad news is that the service is painfully slow and sometimes sloppy. Decide for yourself if the food and ambience, some of Loreto's best, are worth the wait.

Calle Davis 18 norte.© **613/135-2538.** Pizzas 105–145 pesos; main courses 135–210 pesos. MC, V. Tues–Sun 6–10pm.

Del Borracho ★ 😊 BURGERS/SANDWICHES   If you're a *Three Amigos* fan from way back, this obscure tribute to the bar in the classic comedy is a must. The movie sometimes plays on loop in the background of this Old West–style wooden saloon outside of town while chili dogs, milkshakes, sandwiches, and burgers make the rounds among a happy-bellied gringo crowd chugging draft beer. Del Borracho's non-cinematic claim to fame is the $3.50 bowl of blow-your-mind clam chowder that comes with a side of homemade bread every Friday. Ask about the smoked fish for sale from the Loreto Smokehouse and Fish Factory; and, of note for sports fans, Del Borracho has the NFL Sunday Ticket.

.5km (⅓ mile) down the road to San Javier, Ladrillera Rancho Viejo, 3km (2 miles) south of Loreto. ℰ **613/137-0112.** Main courses $3–$5. No credit cards. Daily sunrise–sunset. Closed mid-May to Oct.

El Papagayo Cantando ★ SEAFOOD   In a vast gated garden tucked just off the main plaza, "The Singing Parrot" is a green and lovely spot for a special occasion. The unusually vast and kitschy-looking menu covers everything from jalapeño poppers to Italian *panini* to roast chicken, but the raves here are about the seafood, as fresh as any in Loreto and prepared in a dizzying variety of ways. Choose from the catch of the day rubbed in *achiote* and served with risotto, lobster grilled over mesquite coals, coconut shrimp, shrimp bisque, or a humble shrimp tostada, laid out with tomato and avocado on a crispy tortilla. Reservations advised at night and on weekends.

Salvatierra and Davis, 1 block east of the Plaza. ℰ **613/135-2216.** Main courses 130–495 pesos. No credit cards. Fri–Wed 3–10pm.

INEXPENSIVE

Café Olé LIGHT FARE   This *palapa*-topped cheapie is a good option for gringo or Mexican breakfasts, served all day long. Try eggs with *nopal* cactus, pancakes, or a not-so-light lunch of a burger and fries. Tacos and some Mexican standards are also on the menu, as are fresh fruit smoothies, or *licuados*. There's no sign, but it's next door to Latte Cafe, with which it shares outdoor tables.

Madero 14. ℰ **613/135-0496.** Breakfast 25–55 pesos; lunch 32–78 pesos. No credit cards. Mon–Sat 7am–10pm; Sun 7am–1pm.

Loreto After Dark

Although selection is limited, Loreto after dark seems to offer a place for almost every nightlife preference. Happy hour starts in the late afternoon and ends shortly after sundown at gringo bars like **Augie's** (on the *malecón* btw. Jordan and Hidalgo), **Del Borracho** (5km/3 miles out of town on the San Javier road), and **Mike's Bar** (Hidalgo btw. Pipila and Madero). Of these, Mike's is the only one open past sunset. In addition, as is the tradition throughout Mexico, Loreto's central plaza offers a **free concert** in the bandstand most Sundays. However, Loretanos and their families are so hospitable that the best party may be the one to which you're unexpectedly invited.

MULEGÉ: OASIS IN THE DESERT ★

998km (619 miles) SE of Tijuana; 137km (85 miles) N of Loreto; 496km (308 miles) NW of La Paz; 710km (440 miles) NW of Cabo San Lucas

Verdant Mulegé offers shady cool in an otherwise scorching part of the world. Founded in 1705, it is home to one of the most well-preserved and beautifully situated Jesuit missions in Baja. Mulegé lies between two hills, in a valley where a river runs down to the ocean. The landscape here consists of immense palms, orchards, and tangles of bougainvillea. Several well-preserved Indian caves with stunning paintings can be reached by guided hikes into the mountains. Unfortunately, much of the area is littered with trash, a sign that the beauty of this land is taken for granted by some.

Besides the respite inherent in the views, Mulegé (pronounced moo-leh-*hay*), at the mouth of beautiful Bahía Concepción, has great diving, kayaking, and fishing—and the RV following to prove it. After an '80s heyday as the next Baja new place, Mulegé has settled into a dotage of U.S. and Canadian retirees. Accommodations are limited and basic, and trailer parks are nearby. Good beach camping is also available just south of town along the Bahía Concepción, as is a landing strip for small planes.

Essentials

GETTING THERE & DEPARTING

BY PLANE   The closest international airport is in Loreto (p. 116), 137km (85 miles) south. From Loreto, you'll need to rent a car or hire a taxi for the 1½-hour trip; taxis average 800 pesos each way.

Small regional or private charter planes can get you all the way to town: **El Gallito,** a well-maintained, graded, 1,200m (4,000-ft.) airstrip, adjoins the Hotel Serenidad, Carretera Transpeninsular Km 30 (www.hotelserenidad.com/airstrip.htm, or use radio frequency UNICOM 122.8). For additional information, contact the Comandancia del Aeropuerto in Loreto (✆ **613/135-0565**), from 7am to 7pm daily.

BY CAR   From Tijuana, take Carretera Transpeninsular (Hwy. 1) direct to the Mulegé turnoff, 998km (619 miles) south (approx. 16 hr.). From La Paz, take Carretera Transpeninsular north, a scenic route that winds through foothills and then skirts the eastern coastline. The trip takes about 6 hours; it's roughly 496km (308 miles).

BY BUS   Mulegé's new **bus station** (✆ **615/135-2552**), on the highway north of the entrance to town by La Noria restaurant, can accommodate travelers in standard and luxury buses up and down the peninsula. A ticket to or from Loreto ranges from 120 to 200 pesos, and a ride to Santa Rosalía ranges from 60 to 100 pesos, depending on whether you select the standard or luxury option. Schedules are highly variable, but buses stay for about 20 minutes while dropping off and picking up passengers. Tickets to Tijuana average 300 pesos; the one-way fare to La Paz is about 200 pesos.

ORIENTATION

ARRIVING   If you arrive by bus, you will be dropped off at the entrance to town. From there, you can walk the few blocks downhill and east into town, or take a taxi. Taxis also line up around the plaza and usually charge around $2.50 to $6 for a trip anywhere in town.

VISITOR INFORMATION   There is no official office, but tourist information is available at the office of the centrally located **Hotel Las Casitas,** Calle Francisco Madero 50 (✆ **615/153-0019**). Several maps that list key attractions, as well as a local biweekly English-language newspaper, the *Mulegé Post,* are available throughout town. Also of interest to serious travelers to Mulegé is Kerry Otterstrom's self-published book *Mulegé: The Complete Tourism, Souvenir, and Historical Guide,* available at shops and hotels in town.

The State Tourism Office of Baja California Sur can be reached by calling ✆ **612/124-0199.**

CITY LAYOUT   Mulegé has an essentially east-west orientation, running from the Carretera Transpeninsular in the west to the Sea of Cortez. The Mulegé River (also

known as Río Santa Rosalía) borders the town to the south, with a few hotels and RV parks along its southern shore. It's easy to find the principal sights downtown, where two main streets will take you either east or west; both border the central plaza. The main church is several blocks east of the plaza, breaking with the traditional layout of most Mexican towns. The Bahía Concepción is 11km (6¾ miles) south.

GETTING AROUND   There is no local bus service in town or to the beach, but you can easily walk or take a taxi. Taxis line up around the central plaza, or you can call the taxi dispatch at ✆ **615/153-0420.**

Bicycles are available for rent from **Cortez Explorers,** Moctezuma 75-A (✆ **615/153-0500;** www.cortez-explorers.com). Prices start at $20 for the first day, then drop to $15 per day for the first week, and are less per day after that. It also has full dive- and snorkel-equipment rentals. It's open Monday through Saturday from 10am to 1pm and 4 to 7pm.

Mulegé is so small that it's easy to find anything you're looking for, even though most buildings don't have numbered addresses.

Area Code The telephone area code is **615.**

Banks This little town nearly made it a decade into the 21st century without having its own bank. Luckily, cash-strapped visitors can now visit the **Bancomer** on Zaragoza between Martínez and Madero.

Beach Safety Beaches in the area are generally tranquil and safe for swimming. The more protected waters of Bahía Concepción are especially calm. Avoid swimming at the mouth of the Mulegé River, which is said to be polluted.

Internet Access Most of the hotels in town offer Internet access and Wi-Fi for hotel guests and visitors.

Medical Care Emergency medical services are offered by the **Mexican Red Cross** (© **615/153-0110**) and the **Health Center ISSSTE** (© **615/153-0298**).

Parking Street parking is generally easy to find in the downtown area. Note, however, that Mulegé's streets are very narrow and difficult for RVs and other large vehicles to navigate. Also, many streets are one-way.

Pharmacy Farmacia Ruben, Calle Francisco Madero s/n, at the northwest corner of the central plaza (no phone), is a small drugstore with a sampling of basic necessities and medicines. The owner speaks some English. Across the plaza, **Supermercado Alba** (no phone) has a somewhat wider selection of other goods and toiletries. Both are open Monday through Saturday from 9am to 7pm.

Post Office The *correo* is at the intersection of calles Francisco Madero and General Martínez, on the north side of the street, opposite the downtown Pemex station (© **615/153-0205**). It is open Monday through Friday from 8am to 3pm, and Saturday from 8 to 11am.

Beaches & Outdoor Activities

Mulegé has long been a favorite destination for adventurous travelers looking for a place to relax and enjoy the diversity of nature. Divers, sportfishermen, kayakers, history buffs, and admirers of beautiful beaches all find reasons to stay in this oasis just a little longer.

BEACHES To the north and east of Mulegé lies the Sea of Cortez, known for its abundance and variety of species of fish, marine birds, and sea mammals. To the north are the mostly secluded beaches of **Bahía Santa Inez** and **Punta Chivato,** both known for their beauty and tranquillity. Santa Inez is reachable by way of a long dirt road that turns off from Carretera Transpeninsular at Km 151. Twenty-five kilometers (16 miles) south is the majestic **Bahía Concepción ★★**, a 48km-long (30-mile) body of water protected on three sides by more than 80km (50 miles) of beaches, and dotted with islands. The mountainous peninsula borders its crystal-clear turquoise waters to the east. Along with fantastic landscapes, the bay has numerous soft, white-sand beaches such as **Santispác, Concepción, Los Cocos, El Burro, El Coyote, Buenaventura, El Requesón,** and **Armenta.** Swimming, diving, windsurfing, kayaking, and other watersports are easily enjoyed, with equipment rentals locally available. Here's a rundown on some of the area beaches with restaurant service:

o **Punta Arena** is accessible off Carretera Transpeninsular, at Km 119. A very good *palapa* restaurant is there, along with camping facilities and primitive beach *palapas.*

HOTELS ■
Casa Granada **6**
Clementine's **6**
Hotel Hacienda Mulegé **4**
Hotel Las Casitas **5**
Hotel Serenidad **6**

RESTAURANTS ◆
El Candil **3**
Hotel Serenidad **6**
Las Casitas **5**
Los Equipales **2**
Taquería Doney **1**

To La Paz

Transpeninsular Highway

La Playa

La Río

Río Mulegé

Panteon

Police ■

Museo Regional de Historía ■

Cananea

Moctezuma

General Martínez

Madero

Romero Rubio

Zaragosa

Mission Rd.

Bus 🚌
Church ✝
Post Office ✉

Ice House Rd.

UNITED STATES
Area of Detail
Mulegé
BAJA CALIFORNIA SUR
MEXICO
Mexico City ★
0   500 mi
0   500 km

Misión Santa Rosalía de Mulegé ✝

Baseball Field ■

To Santa Rosalía

0   200 yds
0   200 m

133

o **Playa Santispác,** at Km 114, has a nice beachfront, lots of RVs in the winter, and two good restaurants (Ana's is the more popular).

o **Playa El Coyote** is the most popular and crowded of the Bahía Concepción beaches. The restaurant El Coyote is on the west side of Carretera Transpeninsular at the entrance to this beach, .8km (½ mile) from the water; Restaurant Bertha's serves simple meals on the beachfront.

o **Playa Buenaventura,** at Km 94, is the most developed of the beaches, with a large RV park, motel, convenience store, boat ramp, and public restrooms, along with George's Olé restaurant and bar.

FISHING All of the hotels in town can arrange guided fishing trips to Punta Chivato, Isla San Marcos, or Punta de Concepción, the outermost tip of Bahía Concepción.

The best fishing in the area is for yellowtail, which run in the winter, and summer catches of dorado, tuna, and billfish like marlin and sailfish. Prices run $120 per day for up to three people in a *panga,* $180 for four in a small cruiser, or $200 and up for larger boats.

HIKING & PAINTED CAVE EXPLORATIONS ★★★ The cave paintings in the Sierra de Guadalupe are one of this region's main attractions. UNESCO declared the huge, complex murals a World Heritage Site, and the locals take great pride in protecting them. You are allowed to visit the caves only with a licensed guide.

The most popular series of caves near Mulegé is in **La Trinidad ★★★**, a remote rancho 29km (18 miles) west of town. Among the representations of the cave murals are large deer silhouettes and a human figure called the "cardón man" because of his resemblance to a cardoon cactus. After your guide drives you there, the hiking begins (count on trekking about 6km/3¾ miles and getting wet). To reach the caves, several river crossings are necessary in spots deep enough to swim. Indeed, at one point, rock walls fringe a tight canyon, and there is no way through except by swimming. This river in Cañón La Trinidad allegedly is the source of the river that flows through Mulegé, although it disappears underground for many miles in between.

Another favorite cave-art site is **San Borjitas ★**. To get there, you travel down a four-wheel-drive road to Rancho Las Tinajas, where your guide will take you on foot or by mule to the caves.

For 400 pesos per person (6 hr., minimum five people, lunch included), you can arrange for a guide in Mulegé to take you to La Trinidad; San Borjitas will cost around $50 per person (7 hr., two meals included). Check at Hotel Las Casitas for guide recommendations. One recommended guide is **Salvador Castro (𝒞 615/153-0232)** and his Mulegé tours, and Hotel Las Casitas owner **Javier Aguiar Zuniga** also guides tours locally (𝒞 **615/152-3023**).

The full-immersion cave painting tour is a customizable 1-to-6-day **mule trek ★★★** into the Sierra de San Francisco, offered by **Tour Baja's Saddling South. Mulegé Tours ★★** (𝒞 **615/153-0232**; at the Las Casitas Hotel in downtown Mulegé; www. mulegetours.com) guides tours (400 pesos) to the La Trinidad cave paintings. The tour lasts approximately 12 hours and takes you to the foothills of the Sierra Guadalupe, between Loreto and Bahía de los Angeles, where you hike through the desert canyons before you reach the site. There is also an INAH museum in the area, which has displays and additional information about the cave paintings and the research that has been done on them. Near Loreto are a few minor cave painting sites, which you can access in a fun day tour from **Sea & Land Eco Adventures** for $95.

BAJA'S cave paintings: A WINDOW IN TIME

The mountains that run through the Baja peninsula are dotted with ancient rock painting sites, at least 1,500 years old and some perhaps as old as 7,500, tucked into caves and under rock overhangs in steep, inaccessible canyons. A visit to them is a trip back into an unknown past, and a connection with the universe of Baja's earliest inhabitants. The spectacular murals, with representations of larger-than-life humanlike and animal forms, are the only paintings of this kind in North America, and one site, a grouping of over 300 paintings known as the Great Mural Region, is the largest concentration of ancient rock art in the world.

The entire region where these paintings are located covers almost 19,000 sq. km (7,500 sq. miles) in the central part of the Baja peninsula, concentrated in the San Francisco de la Sierra and Santa Martha mountain ranges. It is believed that thousands of years ago, the shallow pools and oases that existed in this region allowed groups of people to survive here. The paintings were "discovered" in the modern era by Jesuit missionary Francisco Javier Clavijero in 1789. Since then, scholars around the world have attempted to date and interpret the images. The paintings, in ocher, red, white, yellow, and black, show scenes that could be ritual ceremonies, pilgrimages, hunting, or battle. Faceless humanlike figures painted in red and black stand with their arms extended and are often depicted with unusual headpieces above their heads; other figures appear to be jaguars, reptiles, deer-headed snakes, and human hands. Often the figures appear overlaid on one another, meaning they were likely painted by various artists at different periods of time.

The Great Mural Region has been designated by UNESCO as a world cultural heritage site. Mexico's National Institute of Anthropology (INAH) oversees the sites now and opens only selected sites for public viewing; entry to most is allowed only with authorized guides.

In mid-Baja, you can visit sites near Mulegé, Loreto, and San Ignacio. San Ignacio's sites, in the Sierra de San Francisco, are the most spectacular, but they require camping overnight, and as such are less accessible than the Sierra de Guadalupe paintings near Mulegé, which can be seen on a challenging day hike. Due to the summer rains and heat, it is recommended that you visit between October and May.

If you're driving through San Ignacio, you can find guides to take you to La Cueva del Ratón, **La Cueva de las Flechas** ★, and **La Cueva Pintada** ★★★; it's a long and difficult trek. Near Mulegé, drive and hike to **La Trinidad** ★★★, Piedras Pintas, or **San Borjita** ★

SCUBA DIVING & SNORKELING   Although diving in the area is very popular, be aware that visibility right in Mulegé is marred by the fresh and not-so-fresh water that seems to flow into the sea from the numerous septic tanks in this area (do not swim or snorkel close to town). But as you head south into Bahía Concepción, excellent snorkeling can be had at the numerous shallow coves and tiny offshore islands. Explore the middle of the sandy coves for oysters and scallops. For bigger fish and colorful sea life, you'll have to swim out to deeper waters along the edges of each cove.

Boat diving around Mulegé is concentrated around Punta de Concepción or north of town at Punta Chivato and the small offshore islands of Santa Inez and San Marcos.

Numerous sites are good for both snorkeling and scuba diving. The marine life here is colorful—you're likely to see green moray eels, angelfish, parrotfish, and a variety of lobster, as well as dolphins and other sea mammals. The best diving is between August and November, when the visibility averages 30m (98 ft.) and water temperatures are warmer (high 20s Celsius/mid-80s Fahrenheit).

Cortez Explorers, Moctezuma 75-A (©/fax **615/153-0500;** www.cortez-explorers.com), maintains its reputation as one of the best-run dive operations in the state, with excellent prices, exceptional service, and a commitment to sustainability. Cortez Explorers runs trips from a large, custom dive boat and uses only well-maintained, current equipment.

Two-tank dive trips generally involve a 45-minute boat ride offshore and cost $90 to $135 per person, depending on the equipment needed. Snorkeling trips go for $45 to $95 (based on the need to rent equipment and how far you're going). Wet suits and jackets are available, and you'll need them in winter.

SEA KAYAKING   Kayaks are the most popular and practical way to explore the pristine coves that dot this shoreline, and Bahía Concepción is a kayaker's dream—clear, calm water and lots of tempting coves to pull into, with white, sandy beaches. Rent a kayak at El Candil restaurant for $29 per day and explore on your own.

WINDSURFING   Bahía Concepción, south of Mulegé, gets quite windy in the afternoon and has numerous coves for beginners to practice in. It has yet to pull the hard-core kite-boarding crowd that such places as Los Barriles and La Ventana have, but it's a worthy place to stop and rig up nevertheless.

Exploring Mulegé

MISIÓN SANTA ROSALÍA DE MULEGÉ   Founded in 1706 by Father Juan de Ugarte and Juan María Basaldúa, the original mission building was completed in 1766 to serve a local Indian population of about 2,000. In 1770, a flood destroyed nearly all the common buildings, and the mission was rebuilt on the site it occupies today, on a bluff overlooking the river. Built of stone, it is notable for its "L" formation. Its tower is several meters behind the main building. Although not the most architecturally interesting of Baja's missions, it remains in excellent condition and still functions as a Catholic church, although mission operations halted in 1828. Inside is a perfectly preserved statue of Santa Rosalía and a bell, both from the 18th century.

The mission is also a popular tour site. A lookout point 30m (98 ft.) behind the mission provides a spectacular vantage point for taking in the view of a date palm oasis backed by the Sea of Cortez.

MUSEO REGIONAL DE HISTORÍA (REGIONAL MUSEUM OF HISTORY)
In 1907, a state penitentiary was built on a hill overlooking the town of Mulegé. It was known as a "prison without doors" because it operated on an honor system—inmates were allowed to leave every morning to work in town, on the condition that they return when the afternoon horn sounded. Apparently, the honor system worked—few escaped, and when they did, the other prisoners joined the chase to keep from losing their own privileges. It functioned that way until the mid-1970s. About 20 years ago, a local historian and citizen's group established this small museum inside.

The museum (no phone) details the prison's operations and houses an eclectic collection of local historical artifacts. Admission is by donation, and hours are supposed to be Monday through Friday from 9am to 1pm, but have been known to vary. The museum is at the end of Calle Cananea.

Where to Stay

Accommodations in Mulegé are basic but generally clean and comfortable. If you need more pampering, check in at the deluxe **Posada de las Flores ★★** (www.posadadelasflores.com; **☎ 615/155-5600**), 42km (26 miles) north of Mulegé at Punta Chivato.

INEXPENSIVE

Casa Granada ★★ ✦ The rambling gated stone house on Mulegé's estuary feels very much like a private home, with a pretty landscaped garden, upstairs terraces, and a friendly house dog. Guest rooms in the house are simple but very light and bright, with terra-cotta tiles and big windows, and bathrooms dressed up with talavera tiles. But for just $10 more, it's worth the money to spring for a ground-floor casita with its own spacious walled courtyard, decked with flowing ivy and outfitted with a barbecue and outdoor kitchen. There are views in all directions, from the desert hills across the estuary to the Sea of Cortez. Coffee is free; breakfast is extra.

No. 1 Estero de Mulegé, CP 23900 Mulegé, B.C.S. www.casagranada.net. ☎ 615/153-0688. 6 units. $55 double; $65 casita; extra person $10. No credit cards. Free parking; private airstrip nearby. **Amenities:** Free coffee; bicycles; kayaks. *In room:* A/C, fans, kitchen and barbecue (in casitas), Wi-Fi.

Clementine's ★ Although it bills itself as a traditional bed-and-breakfast, the main attraction here are the seven concrete-and-stone casitas spread around the sprawling property, all equipped with full kitchens and many with pleasant outdoor patios or gardens. They're a terrific choice for families: You can cook your own meals, and most of the one-bedroom houses have a futon or sleeping loft for kids. Rooms in the main house are a little dark, and the "breakfast" is very light indeed. All beds here are queen-size, except in Casa Chuparosas, which has a queen, a full, and a twin.

Mulegé, B.C.S. www.clementinesbaja.com or Clifftaylor1942@hotmail.com. ☎ 615/153-0319. 11 units. $50–$65 double; $90–160 casita. Rates include a light breakfast. No credit cards, pay cash on-site or PayPal in advance. 2-day minimum, reservations essential. Free parking. Airstrip nearby. **Amenities:** Gas grill; communal kitchen; kayaks and rowboats. *In room:* A/C, kitchenette (in some), Wi-Fi.

Hotel Hacienda Mulegé A former 18th-century hacienda with double courtyards and a small, shaded swimming pool makes for a comfortable and value-priced place to stay. You couldn't be more centrally located in Mulegé, and the Hacienda is known for its popular bar, which also has satellite TV featuring sporting events. (The bar closes for the night between 10 and 11pm, so it shouldn't keep you awake.) The cozy restaurant with stone walls and a fireplace also has a pleasant patio. Rooms surround the courtyard and have beds with foam mattresses and brightly colored Mexican accents. Bathrooms are simple but large, with showers.

Calle Francisco Madero 3, Mulegé, B.C.S., a half-block east of the central plaza. ☎ 800/346-3942 in the U.S., or 615/153-0021. Fax 615/153-0046. 22 units. $45 double. No credit cards. Free parking. **Amenities:** Bar; Internet cafe; small outdoor pool; room service. *In room:* A/C, TV.

Hotel Las Casitas This long-standing favorite welcomes many repeat visitors, along with the local literati—it is the birthplace of Mexican poet Alan Gorosave. Rooms are in a courtyard just behind (and adjacent to) the Las Casitas restaurant, one of Mulegé's most popular. The very basic accommodations have high ceilings, tile bathrooms, and rustic decor. Plants and birds fill a small central patio for guests' use, but the more socially inclined gravitate to the restaurant and bar, which is open daily from 7am to 10pm. The place is especially lively on weekends—on Friday evenings there's a Mexican fiesta. The inn and restaurant are on the main east-west street in Mulegé, 1 block from the central plaza.

Calle Francisco Madero 50, Col. Centro, 23900 Mulegé, B.C.S. www.baja-web.com/mulege/casitas. © **800/346-3942** in the U.S., or 615/152-3023. Fax 615/153-0190. 8 units. $30 double; $35 triple. MC, V. **Amenities:** Restaurant; bar. *In room:* A/C, TV, Wi-Fi.

Where to Eat

The must-have meal in Mulegé is the traditional pig roast. It's an event, with the pig roasted Polynesian-style in a palm-lined open pit for hours, generally while guests down a few beers and the mariachis wail. The classic roast at the **Hotel Serenidad** (© **615/153-0530**) is still number-one: Every Saturday at 7:30, it's all you can eat including a small margarita and dessert for 206 pesos. The pig crackles as well at **Las Casitas** restaurant (see below).

Mulegé's best tacos are reportedly found at the stand adjoining Las Casitas or at the popular **Taqueria Doney,** at Madero and Romero Rubio, just as you enter town, past the *depósito* (warehouse) on the right.

MODERATE

Las Casitas ★ SEAFOOD/MEXICAN   At Las Casitas, a popular mainstay with both locals and visitors, nearly every night of the week has a special. Tuesdays it's $12 lobster; Fridays there's a Mexican buffet and fiesta, complete with mariachis. And of course Saturdays are the date for Mulegé's famous pig roast party. Dine either in the interior stone-walled dining area or on its adjoining, plant-filled patio. The bar has a steady clientele day and night and often features special sporting events on satellite TV. Menu offerings are standard fare with an emphasis on fresh seafood, but the quality is good and you can see the extra-clean exhibition kitchen as you enter.

Calle Francisco Madero 50. © **615/152-3023.** Breakfast $2–$4.50; main courses $3.50–$11. MC, V. Daily 7am–10pm.

INEXPENSIVE

El Candil MEXICAN   Filling platters of traditional Mexican fare at reasonable prices are the specialty of this casual restaurant, which has been run by the same family for more than 3 decades. Tacos are always popular, but the best of the house is the heaping Mexican combination plate.

Zaragoza 8, near the central plaza. © **615/153-0185.** Main courses $2–$8. No credit cards. Mon–Sat 11am–11pm; Sun 1–8pm.

Los Equipales ★★ MEXICAN/SEAFOOD   This is one of Mulegé's ever-popular hangouts, with home-style cooking matched by family-friendly service. Its second-story location offers diners the only lofty view in town, and this is also the only place in Mulegé that serves complimentary chips and salsa with the meal. The specialties are traditional Mexican fare and Sonoran beef, especially barbecued ribs, but shellfish lovers should head straight for the generously sized shrimp dinner. Tropical drinks, such as mango margaritas, are also popular.

Calle Moctezuma, 2nd floor. © **615/153-0330.** Main courses $3–$10. MC, V. Daily 8am–10pm.

Mulegé After Dark

Mulegé's nightlife, if you can call it that, centers on the bars of the **Hacienda Hotel** and **Las Casitas,** in town. Also of note is the gringo-heavy bar at the **Hotel Serenidad.**

SANTA ROSALÍA

61km (38 miles) N of Mulegé

Located in an arroyo (dry riverbed) north of Mulegé, Santa Rosalía looks more like an old Colorado ghost town than a Mexican port city. In fact, this was a mining town, built way back in 1855. Founded by the French, Santa Rosalía has a decidedly European architectural bent, although culturally, it's Mexican through and through. Beat-up pastel clapboard houses surrounded by picket fences line the streets, giving the town its nickname, *ciudad de madera* (city of wood)—for Mexicans, the wood structures are rather exotic and much remarked-upon, although for North American visitors they're likely to look like home. Santa Rosalía's large harbor and the rusted relic of its copper-smelting facility dominate the central part of town bordering the waterfront, and the highlight of downtown Santa Rosalía is, without a doubt, the old **El Boleo bakery** (see below).

The town served as the center for copper mining in Mexico for years; a French company, Compañía de Boleo (part of the Rothschild family holdings), obtained a 99-year lease in the 1800s. Mexican President Porfirio Díaz originally granted the lease to the German shipping company Casa Moeller, which sold the mining operation rights to the Rothschild family but retained exclusive rights to transport ore from the mine. The agreement was that in exchange for access to the rich deposits of copper the company would build a town, the harbor, and public buildings, and establish a maritime route between Santa Rosalía and Guaymas, creating employment for Mexican workers. Operations began in 1885 and continued until 1954, when the Mexicans regained the use of the land through legislation. The French operation built more than 644km (399 miles) of tunnels in the surrounding hills, primarily by Indian and Chinese laborers. Following the reversion of the mining operations to the Mexican government, the facility was plagued with problems, including the alleged leakage of arsenic into the local water supply, so the plant was permanently closed in 1985.

Today, Santa Rosalía, with a population of 14,000, is notable for its man-made harbor—the recently constructed Marina Santa Rosalía, complete with concrete piers, floating docks, and full docking accommodations for a dozen ocean cruisers. Santa Rosalía is the main seaport of Northern Baja, directly across from Guaymas on the mainland. A ferry link established during the mining days still operates between the two ports. Because this is the prime entry point of manufactured goods into Baja, the town abounds with auto-parts and electronic appliance stores, along with shops selling Nikes and sunglasses.

The town has no real beach to speak of, and fewer recreational attractions. The rusted, dilapidated smelting foundry, railroad, and pier all border the docks and give the waterfront an abandoned, neglected atmosphere.

Exploring Santa Rosalía

Here, in this bustling ghost town, wooden saloons, wraparound verandas, and mountainous terrain make for a paradoxical contrast to the Mexicans milling in the streets. The most attractive of the clapboard houses, painted in a rainbow of colors—mango, lemon, blueberry, and cherry, are in the streets bordering the museum. The wood used to construct these houses was the return cargo on ships that transported copper to refineries in Oregon and British Columbia during the 1800s.

The principal attraction in Santa Rosalía is the **Iglesia de Santa Barbara ★**, a Gothic-inspired structure of galvanized steel designed by Gustave Eiffel (of Eiffel Tower fame) in 1884. It was originally created for the 1889 Paris World Expo, where it was displayed as a prototype for what Eiffel envisioned as a sort of prefab mission. The concept never took off, and the structure was left in a warehouse in Brussels, where it was later discovered and sent to Baja by officials of the mining company. Section by section, the church was transported then reassembled in Santa Rosalía in 1897. Step inside for the full effect of intricate stained-glass windows under a post-industrial arched roof.

Along with the church, the other site to see is the **ex-Fundación del Pacífico** (former Foundry of the Pacific), or **Museo Histórico Minero de Santa Rosalía** (✆ **615/153-0471**). In a landmark wooden building overlooking the sea, it houses a permanent display of artifacts from the days of Santa Rosalía's mining operations. Inside the museum building are miniature models of the town, old accounting ledgers and office equipment, and samples of the minerals extracted from local mines. It's open Monday through Saturday from 8:30am to 2pm and 5 to 7pm. Admission is free.

Other sites of note are the **Plaza Benito Juárez,** or central *zócalo* (square) that fronts the **Palacio Municipal,** or City Hall, an intriguing structure of French colonial design. The streets of Constitución, Carranza, Plaza, and Altamirano border the square.

Where to Stay & Eat

Dining is limited here, but lunch at **El Muelle** restaurant, on Obregón (no phone), right across from the central plaza, leaves no complaints. The tacos; enchiladas in spicy, fresh tomato sauce; and breaded fish bathed in peppers and cheese are all good reasons to visit, but the main draw is the creamy, chipotle smoked tuna dip that comes with chips before the meal. Follow it up with dessert bread from El Boleo, below.

El Boleo ★★★ BAKERY   This may well be the best bakery in Baja; it's certainly the most famous. Everything is prepared in the wooden oven, dating from 1901, according to techniques brought over by the town's French fathers. They're celebrated here for their baguettes, but you can get baguettes at home—instead, try a Mexican *concha*, a *budin*, or a *pitahaya*, a dense sweetbread stuffed with almond paste. El Boleo is 3 blocks west of the church.

Avenida Obregón at Calle 4. ✆ **615/152-0310.** Bread and pastries 10–25 pesos. No credit cards. Mon-Sat 9:30am–7:30pm.

Hotel Francés   Founded in 1886, the Hotel Francés once set the standard of hospitality in Baja Sur, welcoming European dignitaries and hosting the French administrators and businessmen of the mining operations. Today it has a worn air, but still has the most welcoming accommodations in Santa Rosalía. Rooms are in the back, with wooden porches and balconies overlooking a small courtyard pool. Each room has individually controlled air-conditioning, plus windows that open for ventilation. Floors are wood-planked, and the small bathrooms are beautifully tiled. You have a choice of two double beds or one king-size. Telephone service is available in the lobby. The popular restaurant serves breakfast until noon.

15 Calle Jean Michel Cousteau s/n, 23920 Santa Rosalía B.C.S. ✆/fax **615/152-2052.** 17 units. 650 pesos double. MC, V. Free parking. **Amenities:** Restaurant (7am–noon); small courtyard pool. *In room:* A/C, TV, Wi-Fi, no phone.

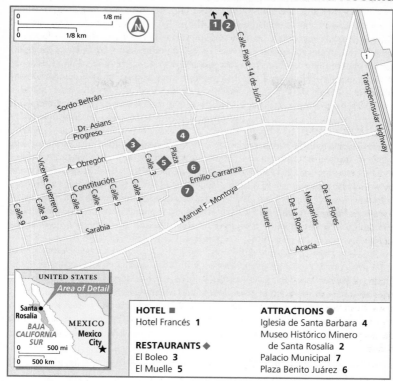

HOTEL ■	**ATTRACTIONS** ●
Hotel Francés **1**	Iglesia de Santa Barbara **4**
	Museo Histórico Minero
RESTAURANTS ◆	de Santa Rosalía **2**
El Boleo **3**	Palacio Municipal **7**
El Muelle **5**	Plaza Benito Juárez **6**

WHALE-WATCHING IN BAJA: A PRIMER ★★★

Between January and March, and sometimes as early as December, thousands of gray whales migrate from the Bering Strait to the lagoons and bays of Baja's Pacific coast to give birth and start their calves in life. For reasons that remain completely mysterious, the calving whales and their newborn babies, rather than being shy of humans, appear to seek out contact with visitors, and the result is one of the most awe-inspiring wildlife encounters anywhere. You can experience it in a day trip or a longer overnight in the **El Vizcaíno Biosphere Reserve,** at **Bahía Magdalena** on the Pacific (about a 2-hr. drive from Loreto), **Laguna San Ignacio** (on the Pacific, near San Ignacio, a 4- to 5-hr. drive from Loreto or 2 hr. from Santa Rosalía), and **Laguna Ojo de Liebre** (near Guerrero Negro, 6 hr. from Loreto or 4 from Santa Rosalía).

What You'll See

Gray whales are the favorite species for whale-watchers because they tend to swim and feed mostly in coastal shallows, occasionally resting with their abdomens on the bottom, while their close relatives prefer to frequent the deeper realms of the ocean.

Whale-watching in one of Baja's lagoons is truly exciting—at times, gray whales appear to be on all sides. In the lagoons and bays, gray whales are often so "friendly" and curious that they come up to the whale-watching boats and stay close by, sometimes allowing people to pet them.

You'll certainly experience the full scale of normal whale behavior at its most awesome. Watchers might be showered with a cloud of water from a whale spouting (clearing its blowhole) or might witness an enormous male spyhopping—lifting its head vertically out of the water, just above eye level, to pivot around before slipping back into the water. Perhaps the most breathtaking spectacle of all is a breach, when a whale propels itself out of the water and arches through the air to land on its back with a splash.

Which Town? Which Tour?

Bahía Magdalena ★ is the most easily accessible for a day tour from mid-Baja, but it's not as intense an experience as the other two lagoons—it's much bigger, so whales are less concentrated, and they're less likely to come up to you. Still, it's one of Baja's classic whale sites, and you won't leave disappointed. It's easy to get here from Loreto, but three nearby towns, two on the bay's shore, also offer whale-watching tours. **Puerto López Mateos,** on the northern shore, is the closest town to the whales' calving areas. Accommodations and dining are limited to a few modest options, but several boat operators offer tours. **Puerto San Carlos** offers a more developed tourism infrastructure, with well-appointed hotels and restaurants, trailer parks, travel agencies, a bus station, and other services. **Ciudad Constitución,** the largest of the three towns, is 61km (38 miles) inland. It has a well-developed tourism infrastructure, with tour organizers that offer daily whale-watching tours during the season.

Laguna San Ignacio ★★★ is accessed via **San Ignacio ★**, 74km (46 miles) to the northeast, a small town built by the Spaniards in the middle of a palm oasis, rich in Jesuit history. This lagoon is an excellent spot for whale-watching; in San Ignacio, the whales have a reputation for being especially "friendly"—they'll seek you out more than the whales in Magdalena, occasionally allowing you to touch them. It's also a base for expeditions to some of the world's most amazing cave paintings (see "Baja's Cave Paintings: A Window in Time," p. 135), and a great spot for bird-watching, in whale season and outside. **Baja by Kayak** does combination whale-watching and bird-watching tours, 3 nights all inclusive for $995, out of Loreto. **Ecoturismo Kuyima ★** (© 615/154-0070; www.kuyima.com), on the shores of the lagoon, will put you up in comfortable, clean tents or cabanas, and feed you at its restaurant. Camping is $40 for a double tent, or sign up for an all-inclusive 4-day whale extravaganza that includes cabana accommodations, meals, three whale excursions, and tours of the lagoon for $495 per person.

Laguna Ojo de Liebre is accessible via **Guerrero Negro,** which sits on the dividing line between Southern and Northern Baja. It has a modest but well-developed tourism infrastructure in an otherwise industrial town (it's the site of the world's largest evaporative saltworks). The lagoon where gray whales calve and spend the winter has remained pristine, and has witnessed a remarkable comeback of this almost-extinct species. This lagoon is the farthest north and thus the most accessible for a whale-watching road trip from the U.S.; it's known for "friendlies" and high concentrations of whales. But Guerrero Negro is the most touristy-feeling of the lagoon towns—upwards of 4,500 tourists a year come here in the 3-month season—and there's not much there other than whale-watching. The most established tour company running boats on the lagoon is **Mario's Tours** (© 615/157-1940; www.mariostours.com); they charge $49 adults, $39 kids for 3 hours including a visit to a shore bird colony. Book tours

Should I Take a Tour or Hire a Boat?

You may get a better deal if you drive to the lagoon and head down to the local pier to hire a local *panga* operator. Expect to pay anywhere from $45 to $60 per person for a day trip with a local guide (plus a tip for good service). An organized tour can run almost double that price, but the services and respect for the whales that come at a higher price tag are worth it in most cases. It's always a good idea to check for licensed, experienced operators (they must have photo-ID credentials showing they are official tour guides) who know how to approach the whales with calm, caution, and respect for the environment. The most important thing about whale-watching is to enjoy it while practicing guidelines that ensure both your safety and the safety of the whales. (We've recommended several tour operators and organizations above.)

through the **Ejido Benito Juárez** (www.elejidobenitojuarez.com), the community association that oversees the lagoon, $40 for adults, $30 for kids, or **Malarrimo Eco-tours** (© 615/157-0100; www.malarrimo.com), 4 hours for $49 adults, $39 kids. Both can book you into very simple motel-like accommodations as well.

If whale-watching is a centerpiece of your Baja vacation, you'll want to plan at least one overnight at **Guerrero Negro** or **San Ignacio,** either on your own or with a tour. If you're going to Bahía Magdalena, **Loreto** may actually be the wisest base to choose, with its well-developed tourist infrastructure and good hotels and restaurants. From there, it's just a 2-hour drive to the bay, and en route you get a chance to view the spectacular desert landscape. All hotels and tour operators in Loreto offer day trips, for between $70 and $140, including transportation both ways, 2 hours on the water, and lunch; a taxi from Loreto to López Mateos costs 800 pesos. And you can even visit Magdalena in a day from Cabo San Lucas—flying tours on Baja-based airline **Aereo Calafia** (© 624/143-4302; www.aereocalafia.com) fly 75-minutes to the bay, where you board a *panga* and spend 3 hours watching gray whales and humpbacks before returning the same day. This tour is $440, including air transportation, the tour, and lunch. (For whale-watching tours that depart from La Paz, see chapter 5; for Los Cabos, see chapter 4.)

GETTING THERE

BAHÍA MAGDALENA To get to Puerto López Mateos, take the only road going west from Loreto for about 121km (75 miles). When you arrive in the town of Insurgentes, turn right and continue 2.4km (1½ miles) to the Puerto López Mateos exit. Turn left and continue 34km (21 miles) to Puerto López Mateos. To get to Puerto San Carlos, take the same road west to Insurgentes, and then drive south about 24km (15 miles) until you reach Ciudad Constitución. From Ciudad Constitución, take the exit marked PUERTO SAN CARLOS, and continue the remaining 63km (39 miles) to town. Both routes are well paved and maintained.

LAGUNA SAN IGNACIO Right on Highway 1, the town of San Ignacio is 796km (494 miles) south of Ensenada and 271km (168 miles) northwest of Loreto. North-south buses stop at the gas station.

LAGUNA OJO DE LIEBRE Right on Highway 1, Guerrero Negro is 651km (404 miles) south of Ensenada and 416km (258 miles) northwest of Loreto. You can also fly there from Santa Rosalía on Aereo Calafia, or take an ABC or Transportes Aguila bus from all points north and south.

NORTHERN BAJA: THE BORDER, THE BEACH & THE BARREL

The birthplace of the margarita, the front line in the drug war. An alt-culture heaven of galleries, restaurants, and offbeat bohemian cool, a cruise ship hell of tourist traps and junky souvenirs. Wine-country idyll, urban sprawl. So which is it? The bad-news border region's reputation precedes it—it was previously Mexico's most-visited destination—and everyone's got an opinion. But Baja's most populated and dynamic area is changing faster than anyone can get a handle on it, and the truths of yesterday are now, often as not, tired clichés. All that's true about Northern Baja is that it's all true, and to figure it out, you've got to see for yourself.

First stop, **Tijuana.** Mexico's fifth-largest city is unique in all the world, an amazingly vivid and diverse twin to its sister city north of the border, San Diego. At least a hundred thousand people cross the border every day—it's the world's busiest international crossing—mixing the cultures and concerns of north and south. It's not an easy place. Human trafficking and the miseries of the frontier are ever-present in the city's shadows, and drug-war violence, although absent from anywhere you're likely to visit and decreasing overall, casts a pall. But life on the edge fertilizes immense creativity, which flowers in the city's culture of visual art, music, lively hipster nightlife, and food. Much of its inspiration comes from Tijuana's uneasy position as the gateway between north and south, and a warts-and-all nostalgia for its bad old days.

Rosarito is Tijuana's beach resort, an urban retreat formerly known as a Prohibition-era getaway for gin-swilling Hollywood stars, and most recently as the location for much of the filming of *Titanic.* Its glory is fading, but it's a place for a tranquil beach weekend away from the city lights. Continuing south past surf breaks, golf courses, and fish-taco stands is this region's main seaside attraction, **Ensenada,** a favored port of call that's slowly moving from its gringo-weekend roots toward a more sophisticated foodie future. It's home to some of Mexico's most exciting restaurants,

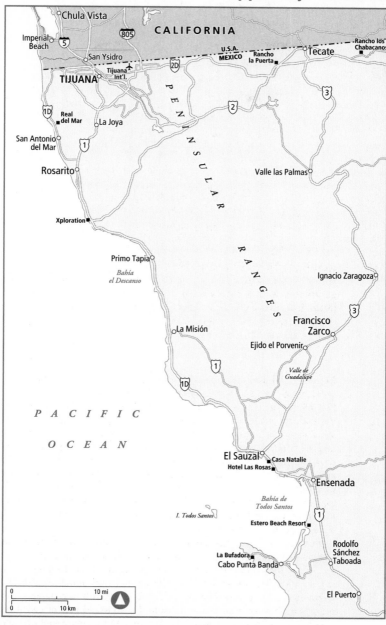

many linked spiritually to Baja's up-and-coming wine country, the **Valle de Guadalupe.** Rolling hills, organic farms, and top-flight wineries have led critics to predict its future as "the next Provence," but for now it's a place for an idyllic country getaway that feeds equally the spirit and the taste buds.

North of the Valle de Guadalupe, **Tecate** is Northern Baja's other border town, Tijuana's opposite in so many ways. It's quiet, it's peaceful, there's not much to do—and that's just what's so appealing about it. And should you need even more relaxation, nothing beats the flat-lining pulse of **San Felipe**'s beaches. While munching a shrimp taco and sipping a cool Tecate beer, perhaps you'll agree that Northern Baja isn't so bad after all.

Exploring Northern Baja

If you have a car, it's easy to venture into Baja Norte from Southern California for a few days' getaway. Whether you drive your own car or a rented one, you'll need Mexican auto insurance in addition to your own; it's available at the border in San Ysidro or through the car-rental companies (see "Getting Around," in chapter 8).

It takes relatively little time to cross the international border in Tijuana, but be prepared for a delay of an hour or more on your return to the United States through San Diego—with increased security measures for entering the U.S., this is an especially diligent point of entry. Even the crossing at less popular Tecate can take an hour or more, and evenings and weekends make for a longer wait anywhere you cross. If you take local buses down the Baja coast (which is possible), the delays come en route rather than at the border.

TIJUANA: TWO WORLDS COLLIDE ★★

26km (16 miles) S of San Diego

Tijuana is dead. Long live Tijuana! Despite drug-war violence, flatlined tourism, and a reputation that's gone from shady to disastrous, Tijuana is actually alive and well, possibly better than ever. Crime is down 40% in the last 2 years, and a new police chief has defied narco-cartels to bring the city's police force back in line. The creative, middle, and upper classes are out again in the city's busy social life. While drug-war killings are still a dark presence (Tijuana's per-capita murder rate is approximately equivalent to Detroit's, but lower than that of New Orleans), they're confined to parts of town tourists will never see. But that good news hasn't made it across the border, and ticky-tacky U.S. tourism, once the city's mainstay, has evaporated. In its place has come a flowering of genuine local culture, based in Tijuana's urbanity and cross-border way of life, that's making this city of nearly two million one of the most important cultural hubs in Mexico.

Tijuana is a city that has seen its share of booms and busts. Its reputation for hustling and decadence stems from its early notoriety as a playground of illicit pleasures during the U.S. Prohibition, when scores of visitors flocked here to the site of the world's largest saloon bar, the Whale, and Caesar's, birthplace of the Caesar salad (see "Where to Eat," later in this chapter). Not long after, the $10-million Hotel Casino de Agua Caliente—the first "megaresort" in Mexico—attracted Hollywood stars and other celebrities with its casino, greyhound racing, and hot-springs spa.

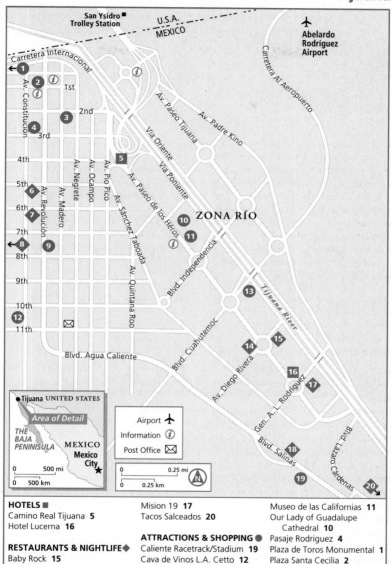

HOTELS ■
Camino Real Tijuana **5**
Hotel Lucerna **16**

RESTAURANTS & NIGHTLIFE ◆
Baby Rock **15**
Caesar's **6**
Calle 6 **7**
El Lugar del Nopal **8**
La Cantina de los Remedios **14**
La Querencia **18**

Mision 19 **17**
Tacos Salceados **20**

ATTRACTIONS & SHOPPING ●
Caliente Racetrack/Stadium **19**
Cava de Vinos L.A. Cetto **12**
Centro Cultural Tijuana
   (CECUT) **11**
Cerveza Tijuana Brewery **13**
HSBC Bank Building **3**
Jai Alai Frontón Palacio **9**

Museo de las Californias **11**
Our Lady of Guadalupe
   Cathedral **10**
Pasaje Rodriguez **4**
Plaza de Toros Monumental **1**
Plaza Santa Cecilia **2**

⚠ bad REPUTATION

The U.S. Department of State issued a Travel Advisory for Mexico on April 22, 2011. The section on Tijuana reads: "Targeted [transnational criminal organization] assassinations continue to take place in Northern Baja California, including the city of Tijuana. You should exercise caution in this area, particularly at night. In late 2010, turf battles between criminal groups proliferated and resulted in numerous assassinations in areas of Tijuana frequented by U.S. citizens. Shooting incidents, in which innocent bystanders have been injured, have occurred during daylight hours throughout the city. In one such incident, an American citizen was shot and seriously wounded." It's important to note here that "U.S. citizens" are not the same thing as tourists; there are citizens of both nationalities living in mixed communities on both sides of the border. To go back to the Travel Advisory, "there is no evidence that U.S. tourists have been targeted by criminal elements due to their citizenship." It's extremely unlikely that your visit to Tijuana's restaurants, galleries, and shopping will end in drug-war bloodshed.

Still, Tijuana has a street crime problem equivalent to that of many U.S. cities, and you should exercise the same caution here that you would there. Stay away from deserted streets, especially at night. Don't walk around visibly intoxicated or showing lots of cash or jewelry. Park in well-lit, guarded parking lots. Avoid driving at night, and when driving between Tijuana and Ensenada, stick to the toll road, and obey instructions at any checkpoints you may encounter. And if you should be the victim of a robbery or carjacking, don't resist. The Ministry of Tourism has set up toll-free numbers to call from the U.S. and Canada (☎ **866/201-5060**) and Mexico (☎ **078**) staffed 24 hours daily with English-speaking operators who can coordinate help from the police.

A final word from the State Department: "Millions of U.S. citizens safely visit Mexico each year, including more than 150,000 who cross the border every day for study, tourism or business and at least one million U.S. citizens who live in Mexico."

From the 1970s through the 1990s, TJ (as it's nicknamed by many American visitors) became known as a party mecca for vacationing college students and a must-see curiosity for international travelers. But a rash of brutal murders and kidnappings related to Mexico's narco-wars starting in 2006, some involving American citizens, has decimated the city's reputation as a south-of-the-border playground. While tourists have never been involved in the drug violence, bad press and the extreme savageness of some of the killings have scared the vast majority of them away.

Today, tourism in Tijuana is concentrated on a few select groups: medical tourists from the U.S. taking advantage of low Mexican prices (averaging one-fifth of U.S. costs) for medical and dental treatment and prescription drugs; executives of the more than 500 international factories in the border area on business-and-pleasure trips; and adventurous Southern Californians who are close enough to the local scene to get some perspective on the headlines. What they find is a new Tijuana, that's leaving its bad old days behind for a more complex, sophisticated, and ultimately exciting future.

Getting There & Departing

Gone are the days when U.S. citizens could merely flash a smile and a driver's license to drive across the border. As of 2009, all travelers attempting to enter the United States, including U.S. and Canadian citizens, by land or sea must have a valid passport or other WHTI-compliant document (such as the new Passport Card and SENTRI, NEXUS, FAST, and the U.S. Coast Guard Mariner Document; see chapter 8 for more information).

Mexican immigration requires that visitors have passports that are valid for at least 6 months. American and Canadian tourists do not require a visa or a tourist card for stays of 72 hours or less within the border zone (20–30km/12–19 miles from the U.S. border). For travel to Mexico beyond the border zone, Americans must be in possession of a tourist card, also called a Tourist Migration Form (FMM). This document is provided by immigration authorities at the country's points of entry. If you enter Mexico by land, and will be going beyond the border zone or staying there more than 72 hours, it is your responsibility to stop at the immigration module located at the border. For more information on tourist visas, see p. 197 in chapter 8.

BY PLANE The **Tijuana Airport** (*C* 664/607-8201) is about 8km (5 miles) east of the city. All Mexican airlines (**Aeroméxico, Volaris, Interjet,** and **VivaAerobus.com**) fly to Tijuana from points within Mexico. To fly from other countries, you'll fly to **San Diego's Lindbergh Field** in California (*C* 619/400-2404 in the U.S.; www.san.org), about an hour from Tijuana, which has nonstop and connecting flights from all over the United States.

Official taxis from Tijuana's airport cost 200 to 250 pesos to *centro* or Zona Río; buy tickets from the booth near the exit. From San Diego's airport, take the 992 bus ($2.25) or a cab (about $10) the 5 minutes to Santa Fe train station and take the Trolley (see below) to the border to walk across.

BY CAR To drive to Tijuana from the U.S., take highways I-5 or 805 S. to the Mexican border at San Ysidro. The drive from downtown San Diego takes about 30 minutes, or you can leave your car in a San Ysidro parking lot and walk the 20 minutes to Avenida Revolución.

If you choose to leave your car behind, which may be a wise decision since traffic is challenging, you can take the San Diego Trolley (see below) to the San Ysidro border. From there you can follow the signs to walk across the border, or hop one of the **buses** (*C* 664/685-1470), which are located next to the trolley station. Once you're in Tijuana, it's easy to get around by taxis, which are still relatively safe compared to those in other large cities like Mexico City. Cab fares from the border to downtown average 50 pesos. You can also hire a taxi to Rosarito for about 200 pesos one-way.

BY BUS **Greyhound Bus Lines** (*C* 800/231-2222 in the U.S.; www.greyhound.com) offers service nearly 24 hours daily for $13 one-way between San Diego and Tijuana via the San Ysidro border crossing, stopping at Tijuana's Rodriguez airport (TIJ) and ending up at Tijuana's Central de Autobuses, where you can connect to Mexican bus lines for destinations farther down Baja (see "Getting Around: By Bus," p. 185). **Mexicoach** (*C* 619/428-9517 in the U.S., or 664/685-1470 in Mexico) runs a similar service (hourly, 5am–10pm) between San Ysidro and Tijuana for $4 one-way/$6 round-trip. For $13 one-way/$20 round-trip, it will take you as far as Rosarito. Mexican discount airliner **Volaris** also runs a shuttle between San Diego's Santa Fe train station and Tijuana airport for passengers; cost is $15.

BY TROLLEY   From downtown San Diego, you have the option of taking the bright-red **Tijuana Trolley** (🕐 **619/595-4949;** www.sdmts.com) headed for San Ysidro and getting off at the last, or San Ysidro, stop. It's simple, quick (about 1 hr. from Old Town San Diego to San Ysidro), and inexpensive; the one-way fare is $2.50. The last trolley leaving for San Ysidro departs downtown San Diego around midnight; the last returning trolley from San Ysidro is at 1am. On Saturday, the trolley runs 24 hours. From the trolley station, just walk over the border.

Visitor Information

Prior to your visit, you can write for information, brochures, and maps from the **Tijuana Convention & Visitors Bureau,** PO Box 434523, San Diego, CA 92143-4523. You can also get a preview of events, restaurants, and more online at **www. seetijuana.com**. Once in Tijuana, pick up visitor information at the **Tijuana Tourism Board,** Paseo de los Héroes 9365, Zona Río (🕐 **888/775-2417** in the U.S., or 664/687-9600; www.seetijuana.com). You can also try the **National Chamber of Commerce** (🕐 **664/685-8472;** Mon–Fri 9am–2pm and 4–7pm). Its offices are at the corner of Avenida Revolución and Calle 1, and its staff is extremely helpful with maps and orientation, local events of interest, and accommodations; in addition, the Tijuana Tourism Board provides legal assistance for visitors who encounter problems while in Tijuana. For additional information online, visit **www.tijuanaonline.org**. And for Tijuana's offbeat side, the blogs **Tijuego** (www.tijuego.com) and **I♥TJ** (www. tijuanita.com; Spanish only) keep abreast of arts, culture, and nightlife.

Tijuana has a special **tourist assist number** (🕐 **078;** this is a free call) to help visitors with special needs, as well as provide assistance in the event of crime. And in a pinch, don't hesitate to stop one of Tijuana's grey-and-black-uniformed **tourist police;** they're all over Avenida Revolución.

[Fast FACTS] TIJUANA

Area Code   The local telephone area code is **664.**

Banks   Banks exchange currency during business hours, generally Monday through Friday from 8:30am to 6pm and Saturday from 9am to 2pm. Major banks with ATMs and *casas de cambio* (money-exchange houses) are easy to find in all the heavily trafficked areas discussed in this chapter. Although dollars are widely accepted, you're advised to use pesos for a better deal.

Climate & Weather
Tijuana's climate is similar to Southern California's: Don't expect sweltering

heat just because you're south of the border, and remember that the Pacific waters won't be much warmer than off San Diego. The first beaches you'll find are about 24km (15 miles) south of Tijuana.

Embassies & Consulates   The following countries have consulate offices in Tijuana: the **United States** (🕐 **664/ 622-7400**), **Canada** (🕐 **664/684-0461**), and the **United Kingdom** (🕐 **664/686-5320**).

Emergencies   Dial 🕐 **078** to reach **Tourist Assist;** 🕐 **066** to reach the **Police** or **Red Cross.** Both

are free calls. To reach the **Green Angels** (a government service that travels the roadways of Mexico looking for cars with problems, equipped to make minor repairs, and only charging for parts used or gas consumed), servicing the Tijuana area, call 🕐 **078** or 664/624-3479.

Internet   Changes come fast in Tijuana, so the Internet cafe that was there the last time you visited is probably not there anymore. Most hotels offer free Wi-Fi or, if you're just passing through and need to get connected, scan the streets for the occasional

INTERNET or CAFE INTERNET sign. You won't have to go far to get online.

Pharmacy Sanborn's is a 24-hour department store with a 24-hour pharmacy. It has two locations in Tijuana: one downtown at the corner of Avenida Revolución and Calle 8 (© 664/688-1462) and another in the Zona Río (© 664/684-8999) at Paseo de los Heroes and Cuauhtémoc. Numerous discount pharmacies are also found along avenidas Constitución and Revolución.

Taxes & Tipping A value-added tax of 10%, called **IVA** (Impuesto al Valor Agregado), is added to most bills, including those in restaurants. This does not represent the tip; you should add about 15% if the service warrants.

Taxis Call **Yellow Cabs (Taxis Amarillos)** at © 664/682-9892.

Exploring Tijuana

AVENIDA REVOLUCIÓN & DOWNTOWN

The Avenida Revolución of cheap drinks, discount pharmaceuticals, and a rootin'-tootin' gringo good time is as bygone as the days when tourists flooded its streets. Many of its loud and tacky storefronts are now boarded up (nearly half of its retail shops are now vacant), and with a few exceptions, you're not missing anything if you skip it. But the death of Avenida Revolución's tourist traps has given way to a rebirth of sorts of some of the downtown streets that cross it. **Calle 6 ★** (Sixth Street, known as la Sexta) is a hopping string of Tijuana's coolest bars, clubs, and cantinas. **Pasaje Rodriguez ★** (pasajerodriguez.blogspot.com), a narrow street between Revolución and Constitución at Calle 3, has been transformed from a gauntlet of souvenir shops into a new and vibrant arts district, with 24 storefronts made over into galleries, studios, cafes, and bookstores.

A few worthwhile old-school sites are still alive and kicking on "La Revo," however. Starting at the entry to the area from the San Ysidro border crossing and walking south, you'll arrive at **Plaza Santa Cecilia,** also known as Arguello Square, Tijuana's oldest plaza; it's at Calle 1 and Avenida Revolución, near the Tourist Assistance kiosk. Today it's home to some very touristy restaurants and bars, and a clutch of hard-luck mariachis eager to sell you a song (if you can't think of one, ask for "Cielito Lindo"). At the center of the plaza is a monument to Santa Cecilia, the patron saint of musicians.

On Avenida Revolución (at Calle 2) is the **HSBC Bank Building.** One of Tijuana's oldest private buildings, the structure was built in 1929 to resemble the French Nouveau style popular in the early 1900s. A few deserted, depressing blocks south is the original **Caesar's ★,** Av. Revolución 1059, at Calle 5 (© 664/685-1927), the birthplace of the Caesar salad, tossed into the limelight by Caesar Cardini in 1924. The restaurant has been recently revived by the city's top restaurateur family, and it's a Tijuana hot spot once more. See "Where to Eat," later in this chapter.

Although the lightning-paced indoor ballgame jai alai (pronounced "*high* ah-*lye*") is no longer played here, the **Jai Alai Frontón Palacio,** Avenida Revolución at Calle 8 (© 664/685-3687, 688-0125, or 619/231-1910 in San Diego) is still worth a visit for its exquisite neoclassical architecture. Built in 1925, the building, for years, was the site of jai alai matches, an ancient Basque tradition incorporating elements of tennis, hockey, and basketball. Now the arena is used just for cultural events or occasional boxing matches.

ZONA RÍO

Most of the local action, however, isn't downtown at all, but in the **Zona Río,** Tijuana's upscale business district. This is where you'll find most of the city's best restaurants, hotels, and shopping, as well as its more mainstream cultural life. The main drag here is the wide, European-style Paseo de los Héroes, with gigantic *glorietas* (traffic circles), at the center of which stand monuments to leaders ranging from Aztec Emperor Cuauhtémoc to Abraham Lincoln. Admire them on your way to the **Centro Cultural Tijuana** (**CECUT** or **Tijuana Cultural Center**), Paseo de los Héroes at Mina (© **664/687-9600;** www.cecut.gob.mx), the linchpin of Tijuana's burgeoning arts scene and the storehouse of the area's cultural history. You can easily spot the ultramodern complex, designed by Pedro Ramírez Vásquez, by its centerpiece gigantic sand-colored dome housing an OMNIMAX theater, which screens various 45-minute films (subjects range from science to space travel). The center also holds the **Museo de las Californias (Museum of the Californias),** with exhibits that trace the history of the Californias, dating back to prehistoric times. The center is open daily from 10am to 7pm. Admission is 25 pesos adults, 15 pesos children. Also check out the **Baja California Cultural Institute,** which has exhibits showcasing the culture of the region. It's at Av. Centenario 10151.

The oldest church in Tijuana is the **Catedral de Nuestra Señora de Guadalupe (Our Lady of Guadalupe Cathedral),** in front of City Hall, at Paseo Centenario 10150 and Josefa Ortiz de Domínguez, in Zona Río (© **664/607-3775**). First inaugurated in 1902 as a parish church, it was appointed cathedral status in 1964. Expansion work began in 2001 and is still underway. (You can watch the progress at **www.nuevacatedraldetijuana.org.**) When finished, the renovated cathedral will seat 3,000, with standing room for 14,000. Its hallmark will be a brilliant white obelisk bell tower 25 stories high in front of a large statue of the Virgin of Guadalupe, Mexico's patron saint. Mass is celebrated Monday through Friday at 8am and 7pm, Saturdays at 7pm, and Sundays at 9am, noon, and 6pm.

The fertile valleys of Northern Baja produce most of Mexico's wines; many high-quality vintages are exported to Europe but, despite NAFTA, most are not available in the U.S. For an in-town introduction to Baja's wines, stop into **Cava de Vinos L.A. Cetto (L.A. Cetto Winery),** Av. Cañón Johnson 2108, at Avenida Constitución Sur (© **664/685-3031** or 685-1644; www.cettowines.com) or make an appointment for a tasting. Shaped like a wine barrel, this building's striking facade was fashioned from old oak aging barrels in an inspired bit of recycling. The entrance has a couple of wine presses (ca. 1928) that Don Angel Cetto used back in the early days of production. Bottles of Petite Sirah, Nebbiolo, chardonnay, and cabernet sauvignon cost about $8; the special reserves are a little more than $15. The family-owned company also produces tequila and olive oil, for sale here. Wine tastings cost $2 for standard wines, $5 for reserves, for those 18 and older only; those under 18 are admitted free with an adult but cannot taste the wines. L.A. Cetto is open Monday through Saturday 10am to 5pm. Tours and tastings run Monday through Friday 10am to noon and 2 to 5pm.

If you're more of a beer person, don't despair—you're in Tijuana, remember? The **Cerveza Tijuana brewery,** Fundadores 2951, Colonia Juárez about a mile south of CECUT (© **664/638-8662;** www.tjbeer.com), offers guided tours (by prior appointment) that demonstrate the beer-making process the family of brewers learned in the Czech Republic. The lager, dark, and light beers are all available to sample in the adjoining European-style pub, which features karaoke on Thursday, Friday, and Saturday nights. It's open Monday to Wednesday 1pm to midnight, Thursday to Saturday until 2am.

Spectator Sports

BASKETBALL Tijuana basketball has been foundering as much as the city's tourism industry, but a new team hopes to win back fans with a fun attitude and a mascot beloved of old Tijuana. The **Zonkeys**—named for the zebra-painted donkeys you'll still see on Revolución—are the new sports ticket for hip Tijuanans; catch a game at the Municipal Auditorium (© **664/250-9015**), about 3km (2 miles) west of the center at Bl. Díaz Ortaz 12421. Schedules and tickets are online at www.tijuana zonkeys.com.

BULLFIGHTING Whatever your opinion of it, bullfighting has a prominent place in Mexican heritage and is even considered an essential element of the culture in Tijuana. The skill and bravery of matadors is closely linked with cultural ideals regarding machismo, and some of the world's best perform at Tijuana's historic stadium. While the last few years' schedules have been unpredictable, reforms and a new manager announced in the spring of 2011 are hoped to bring a more reliable performance schedule in the future. For up-to-date ticket and season information, contact San Diego's **Five Star Tours** (© **619/232-5049** in the U.S., or 664/622-2203). **Plaza de Toros Monumental,** or Bullring-by-the-Sea (© **664/680-1808;** www. plazamonumental.com), is 10km (6 miles) west of downtown on Hwy. 1-D (before the first toll station), at the edge of both the ocean and the California border. You can also negotiate a fare to Bullring-by-the-Sea, which will range anywhere from $12 to $25, depending on the bargaining mood of the taxi driver.

DOG RACING There's satellite wagering on U.S. horse races at the majestic **Caliente Racetrack,** Bl. Agua Caliente 12027, 4.8km (3 miles) east of downtown, but these days only greyhounds actually kick up dust at the track. Races are held daily at 7:45pm and at 1pm on Sunday. General admission is free. For more information, call © **664/682-3110** or 619/231-1910 in San Diego.

SOCCER Soccer is far and away Mexico's favorite sport, and the largest sporting crowds in Tijuana are to be found cheering on the Xoloitzcuintles (their mascot is the famed Mexican hairless fighting dog), or Xolos, at **Caliente** stadium (Agua Caliente 12027, Colonia Hipódromo). U.S.-side fans organize trips across the border with buses, U.S. parking, and tickets to games; contact Xolos US at © **619/600-5233** in the U.S., or go to www.xolos.us.

Shopping

Tijuana's number-one attraction is shopping, with reasonable to rock-bottom prices on all kinds of merchandise: terra-cotta and colorfully glazed pottery, woven blankets and serapes, embroidered dresses and sequined sombreros, onyx chess sets, Viagra, beaded necklaces and bracelets, silver jewelry, leather bags and huarache sandals, hammered-tin picture frames, thick drinking glasses, novelty swizzle sticks, Cuban cigars, and Mexican liquors such as Kahlúa and tequila. You're permitted to bring $800 worth of purchases back across the U.S. border (sorry, no Cuban cigars allowed), including 1 liter of alcohol or three bottles of wine per person. At **El Campanario,** Av. Revolución 952 (no phone), and **El Girasol,** Av. Revolución 964 (© **664/685-8561**), you'll find a broad selection of quality wares including talavera ceramics from Puebla, Oaxacan black-clay pottery, Huichol bead art, hand-blown glassware from Tonalá, Day of the Dead curios, *alebrijes* (fantasy animal figurines), and works of art made from *milagros,* small silver religious offerings.

Although many of the city's former tourist-oriented shops on Revolución are now closed, there are plenty of alternatives, starting with **Sanborn's,** a branch of the Mexico City department store long favored by American travelers (see "Fast Facts," above). It sells an array of regional folk art and souvenirs, books about Mexico in both Spanish and English, and candies and fresh sweet treats from the bakery—and you can have breakfast in the sunny cafe. It's open daily from 7:30am to 1am.

For a taste of everyday Mexico, visit **Mercado Hidalgo,** in the Zona Río 1 block west of Plaza del Zapato at avenidas Sánchez Taboada and Independencia, a busy indoor-outdoor marketplace where vendors display fresh flowers and produce, sacks of dried beans and chiles by the kilo, and a few souvenir crafts (including some excellent piñatas). Morning is the best time to visit the market, and you'll be more comfortable paying with pesos, since most sellers are accustomed to a local crowd.

Shopping malls are as common in Tijuana as in any big American city; you shouldn't expect to find typical souvenirs there, but shopping alongside residents and other intrepid visitors is often more fun than feeling like a sitting-duck tourist. One of the biggest, and most convenient, is **Plaza Río Tijuana,** Paseo de los Héroes 96 at Avenida Independencia, Zona Río (✆ **664/684-0402**), an outdoor plaza anchored by several department stores and featuring dozens of specialty shops and casual restaurants. **Plaza Agua Caliente,** Bl. Agua Caliente 4558, Colonia Aviación (✆ **664/681-7777**), is a more upscale shopping center, and in addition to fine shops and restaurants, it is known for its emphasis on health and beauty, with day spas, gyms, and doctors' offices in abundance here. Other shopping malls are listed on www.tijuanaonline.org.

Where to Stay

When calculating room rates, always remember that hotel rates in Tijuana are subject to a 12% tax.

EXPENSIVE

Camino Real Tijuana ★★ The Camino Real is a favorite among locals, with the hallmark architectural style and use of bold colors that define this luxury Mexican hotel chain. It's popular especially with business travelers, and its location in the Zona Río makes it ideal for shopping or cultural excursions to the city. It's also close to the most sophisticated dining and nightlife in Tijuana. Rooms are both elegant and spacious. The contemporary lobby showcases renowned Mexican artists, and four restaurants offer both casual and upscale dining options. A variety of packages are available, including weekend escape, seasonal bullfight, and honeymoon packages. Rooms, restaurants, the lobby, and the gym have been renovated.

Paseo de los Heroes 10305, Zona Río, 22320 Tijuana, B.C. www.caminoreal.com/tijuana. ✆ **664/633-4000**. Fax 664/633-4001. 263 units. 1,020–1,350 pesos deluxe double; 1,364–1,819 pesos suite Camino Real club room. AE, MC, V. Valet parking. **Amenities:** 4 restaurants; lobby bar; babysitting; concierge; fitness center; meeting facilities; room service; sauna. *In room:* A/C, TV, hair dryer, minibar, Wi-Fi.

MODERATE

Hotel Lucerna ★ Once the most chic hotel in Tijuana, Lucerna now feels slightly worn, but the place still has personality. The flavor here is Mexican colonial— wrought-iron railings and chandeliers, rough-hewn, heavy wood furniture, brocade wallpaper, and traditional tiles. The hotel is in the Zona Río, away from the noise and congestion of downtown, so a quiet night's sleep is easily attainable, and it's just 2 blocks from the Plaza Río Tijuana shopping center (see above). All the rooms in this five-story hotel have balconies or patios but are otherwise unremarkable. Sunday brunch is served outdoors by the swimming pool. The staff is friendly and attentive.

Av. Paseo de los Héroes 10902, Zona Río, Tijuana, B.C. www.hoteleslucerna.com/tijuana. **664/633-3900.** 168 units. $89 double; $125 suite. AE, MC, V. Meal plans available. Free parking. **Amenities:** Restaurant, coffee shop; gym; outdoor pool; room service. *In room:* A/C, satellite TV, hair dryer, Wi-Fi.

Real del Mar ★★ If being in the center of downtown is a bit too much Tijuana for you, this hotel offers a location that is near enough to the city's action while also being in its own tranquil setting, complete with golf course. Real del Mar is a resort and residential development about 16km (10 miles) south of Tijuana, across the highway from the ocean on the way to Rosarito. In addition to golf, it has an equestrian center, spa, and shopping. You have your choice of two room categories, studios or suites; all suites offer ocean views, fireplaces, living rooms, and small but complete kitchens—ideal for families or extended stays in the area and worth the extra $20. Two restaurants are available for dining: El Patio Brasserie overlooks the golf course and is open for breakfast and lunch, while Rincón de San Roman, under the direction of a Paris-educated chef, serves Continental cuisine for lunch and dinner.

Carretera Escénica Tijuana-Ensenada Km 19.5, 22605 Tijuana, B.C. www.realdelmar.com.mx. **800/803-6038** in the U.S., or 664/631-3670. Fax 664/631-3677. 76 units. $89–$119 studio; $119–139 suite. Rates include wine and beer in the evening and breakfast in the morning. Golf and spa packages available. AE, MC, V. Complimentary on-site parking. Pets are welcome for a $75 one-time sanitation fee. **Amenities:** 2 restaurants; bar; babysitting; equestrian center; exercise room; grocery shopping service; outdoor pool; room service; spa; tennis court. *In room:* A/C, TV, hair dryer, Internet, kitchen.

Where to Eat

The changes in Tijuana apply to its food scene, too; a new generation of restaurateurs is now preparing some of the most exciting food in all of Mexico. The scene is in constant evolution—some might say revolution—but one very good and frequently updated source is the food blog www.streetgourmetla.com. Check in for foodie news before you cross the border.

VERY EXPENSIVE

La Querencia ★★ CONTEMPORARY MEXICAN/MEDITERRANEAN The birthplace of the Baja Med movement, which brings together a Mediterranean focus on high-quality local ingredients with Baja's traditional Mexican flavors, La Querencia is something of an institution in Tijuana. American celebrity chef Rick Bayless filmed a TV episode here, spit-roasting local lamb with Chef Miguel Angel Guerrero. The menu is a salute to Baja's bounty: scallops, octopus, and tacos of manta and giant squid. The dining room is post-industrially spare, with the exception of a collection of taxidermied ducks flying about the airspace, a testament to the chef's love of hunting (you'll often find venison on the menu).

Calle Escuadron 201, btw. Sanchez Taboada and Salinas, Zona Río. **664/972-9935.** www.laquerenciatj.com. Main courses 125–290 pesos. AE, MC, V. Mon–Sat 1pm–midnight.

Mision 19 ★★★ 📷 CALIFORNIAN/CONTEMPORARY MEXICAN Hailed by critics as one of the most important and influential restaurants in Mexico—and indeed, in the Californias—this is the number-one must for visiting foodies. On the second floor of Baja's first LEED Gold-certified green office building, Tijuana native Javier Plascencia presides over a locavore kitchen that's turning out consistently spectacular food, skillfully designed and dramatically presented. Particular raves go to the signature dish, slow-cooked short ribs in a fig leaf with black mole and Mission figs, but there's a wealth of delights to savor: Sonoma *foie gras* with chipotle syrup; licorice-skewered duck with guava dust; milk-fed baby chicken with truffle and thyme. A tip of the hat also to the exceptionally fine cocktails, sophisticated plays on traditional Mexican drinks like *horchata* and *tamarindo*.

Misión de San Javier 10643, Zona Río. ✆ **664/634-2493.** http://mision19.com. Main courses 400–500 pesos; tasting menus 100 pesos per course, from 4 to 8 courses. AE, MC, V. Mon–Sat 1pm–midnight.

MODERATE

Caesar's ★ BISTRO   A Tijuana institution since before the Caesar salad was invented here in 1924, Caesar's went through a desolate period before being bought and completely revived by the Plascencia family restaurant group (see "Mision 19," above). Now it's a grand and lively exception to its abandoned neighbors on Avenida Revolución, a window into the past of Tijuana's elegant, high-living good old days. A long, sconce-lit dining room speaks easy with checker-tiled floors, linen tablecloths, and dark wood banquettes; formally-dressed waiters serve with élan. The signature salad, a perfect specimen, is still elaborately prepared tableside (and despite gringo concerns about the water used to wash lettuce in Mexico, the management guarantees their salads are safe to eat).

Av. Revolución 1059, at Calle 5. ✆ **664/685-1927.** Caesar salad 72 pesos; main courses 120–200 pesos. MC, V. Sun–Thurs noon–10pm; Fri–Sat noon–midnight.

INEXPENSIVE

Tacos Salceados ★★ MEXICAN   Tacos are Tijuana's favorite round-the-clock meal, and Tacos Salceados is Tijuana's hottest place to get them. The lowly taco has been raised to a chef-worthy art form here, with complex sauces and painterly presentations. Don't come expecting any classic meat-in-a-tortilla snacks though; this place is all about breaking the rules. Traditional corn or flour tortillas go wild with marlin, trout, pineapple, or beef tongue fillings. "Quesatacos" switch out the corn tortilla for a crispy cheese shell. Dessert tacos add sweet sauces to salty meat, slicing through beef, for example, with mango. Bring an empty stomach, and cash—the place doesn't take credit cards.

Ermita 807, btw. Díaz Ortaz and Benito Juárez, La Mesa. No phone. Tacos 12–35 pesos. No credit cards. Mon–Sat 6pm–midnight.

Tijuana After Dark

After decades of bar-dancing and tequila shooters, Avenida Revolución is officially dead. In its ashes has risen a new hipster nightlife scene along **Calle 6** ("La Sexta"), populated by Tijuana's young creatives and a host of new cool-kid bars and restaurants. For the several blocks on either side of Revolución, it's a late-night gauntlet of bar after dance club after ironic retrospot. Standing favorites on La Sexta include the venerable and newly cool cantina **Dandy del Sur,** Mexi-kitsch dance club **La Mezcalera,** the five-bars-in-one variety pack **Callejon de la Sexta,** and retro **Pop Diner** (in the Metropoli store), which amid all the irony, is actually a diner too.

The after-dark action in the Zona Río and Plaza Fiesta are more geared toward late-night dining and dance-clubbing than tequila swilling and barhopping. Although the nightlife scene changes regularly, perhaps the most popular dance club is **Baby Rock,** 1482 Diego Rivera (✆ **664/634-2404**), near the Guadalajara Grill restaurant, a cousin to Acapulco's lively Baby O, which features everything from Latin rock to rap. It's open from 9pm to 3am, with a cover charge of $12 on Saturdays. One of the most fun bars in Zona Río is **La Cantina de los Remedios,** 2479 Diego Rivera

Bohemian Tijuana

The flip side of Tijuana's rough and tumble exterior is an almost impossibly active arts scene. It's home to an internationally-renowned graffiti arts community as well as a thriving theater scene, a wildly popular orchestra, as well as countless painters, sculptors, photographers, and musicians. The arts community gathers annually in October at the **entijuanarte** (© 664/621-1493; www.entijuanarte.com) exposition on the grounds of the Centro Cultural Tijuana; it's a place for new music, exciting collaborations, and a showcase for Tijuana's cutting edge. If you miss entijuanarte, you can *bohemear* (literally, to act like a bohemian) any time of the year at **El Lugar del Nopal,** 1328 Priv. 5 de Mayo between calles 6 and 7, 5 blocks from Revolución, Zona Centro (© 664/685-1264; www.lugardelnopal. com), a cafe, gallery, and performance arts space. In addition to hosting live music acts that play everything from Brazilian bossa nova to blues, El Nopal (as it's referred to by locals) offers painting, guitar, and Tango workshops. To get started, the offbeat lifestyle tour group **Turista Libre** (http://turistalibre. com) makes visits to Tijuana galleries, graffiti sites, and hipster events that will give you a taste of *la vida bohemia.*

(© 664/634-3065; www.losremedios.com.mx; Mon–Thurs 1pm–1am, Fri–Sat 1pm–2am, and Sun 1–10pm). Although los Remedios may be best known as a restaurant, nightfall is when the real fun starts; the tequila options here are plentiful—there's a reason it's called "the remedies."

ROSARITO BEACH & BEYOND: BAJA'S FIRST BEACH RESORTS

55km (34 miles) S of San Diego; 29km (18 miles) S of Tijuana

Just a 20-minute drive south of Tijuana and a complete departure in ambience, Rosarito Beach is a tranquil, friendly beach town. It also gained early renown during the U.S. Prohibition, when the elegant Rosarito Beach Hotel catered to Hollywood stars. This classic structure still welcomes numerous guests, despite the fact that its opulence has lost some luster. Hollywood has likewise played a major part in Rosarito's recent renaissance—it was the location for the soundstage and filming of the Academy Award–winning *Titanic.* The Titanic Expo museum—now called **Xploration**—here continues to draw fans of the film. At time of research, a film shoot had closed the studio to the public. Get current ticket and schedule info at © 661/614-0110.

Two roads run between Tijuana and Ensenada (the largest and third-largest cities in Baja)—the scenic, coast-hugging toll road (marked cuota, or 1-D) and the free but slower-going public road (marked libre, or 1). For safety reasons, we recommend you use the toll road—Rosarito is close enough to Tijuana that some of the city's street crime has made it here, and the public road has been the site of some carjackings in recent years. If you're not driving, you can take a shuttle from the last trolley stop in San Ysidro. **Mexicoach** (© 619/428-9517 in the U.S., or 664/685-1470 locally; www.mexicoach.com) offers shuttle rides for about $10.

Visitor Information

Try **Baja California Tourism Information** (© 800/522-1516 in California, Arizona, and Nevada or 800/225-2786 in the rest of the U.S. and Canada, or 619/298-4105 in San Diego; www.discoverbajacalifornia.com). This office provides advice and makes hotel reservations throughout Baja California. You can also contact the local **Secretaria de Turísmo,** Carretera Libre Tijuana-Ensenada Km 28 (© 800/962-2252 in the U.S., 01-800/025-6288 in Mexico; www.rosarito.org). The office is open Monday through Friday from 8am to 8pm, and Saturday and Sunday from 9am to 1pm. Special **tourist aid** service is available by calling © 078 from any phone. And as in Tijuana, you can ask for help from the 18 members of the **tourist police,** identifiable by their gray-and-black uniforms with "Policia Turistica" on the shirt.

FAST FACTS The local state **tourism office** (© 661/612-5222) can be found at Km 28 local 13-b Carretera Tijuana-Ensenada. As in most Mexican cities, the **Cruz Roja** (© 661/612-0414) serves as a triage for larger hospitals and clinics. The main branch in Rosarito is located at Calle del Olivo 100. Smaller clinics include **Ciudad Misericordia,** Carretera Tijuana Ensenada 61 (© 661/614-1726), and the private clinic **Baja Medix,** Mar del Norte 484 (© 661/613-0383), whose staff will contact your U.S. physician and arrange for an ambulance to meet you at the border if necessary. The **post office** (© 661/612-1355) is on Bulevar Juárez near Acacias. Most hotels provide Internet access, but also check out the aptly named **Internet Café** (© 661/612-1008) at Bl. Benito Juárez 23.

Shopping

The dozen or so blocks north of the Rosarito Beach Hotel abound with the stores typical of Mexican border towns: curio shops, cigar and *licores* (liquor) stores, and *farmacias* (where drugs like Viagra, Retin-A, Prozac, and many more are available at low cost and without a prescription). More interesting is Rosarito's traditional **carved wooden furniture**—plentiful downtown along Bulevar Benito Juárez—and **pottery,** best purchased at stands along the old highway, south of town. A reliable but more expensive furniture shop is **Casa Neri** (formerly Casa La Carreta), Km 29.5, on the old road south of Rosarito (© 619/308-7991 in the U.S., or 661/612-0502; www.casaneri.com), where you can see plentiful examples of the best workmanship—chests, tables, chairs, headboards, cabinets, and cradles—and nearly 40 years of family-run custom furniture.

Where to Stay

In the event you go to Rosarito Beach to drink and dance by night and to drink and sunbathe by day, plan to stay at the **Hotel Festival Plaza Resort** (© 800/411-2987 in the U.S.; www.festivalplazahotel.com). If a lobby that appears as though it could be hosed down gives any indication of party-ready quotient, Festival Plaza is off the charts. For something more subdued, see the following recommendations.

Hotel Brisas del Mar ★ 🍴 This clean, friendly hotel is close to everything in Rosarito and just a 3-minute walk to the beach. It's also a good value. The rooms are basic, but highlights of the hotel are its semi-chic lounge-style bar and the friendly, attentive staff. If you don't have to be on the beach, this is the best bet in town.

Bl. Benito Juárez 22, 22710 Playas de Rosarito, B.C. © **800/697-5223** in the U.S., or 661/612-2546. 71 units. High season $60–$80 double; low season $45–$50 double. MC, V. Free secured parking. **Amenities:** Restaurant; bar; heated Jacuzzi; heated outdoor pool and kids' pool. *In room:* A/C, TV.

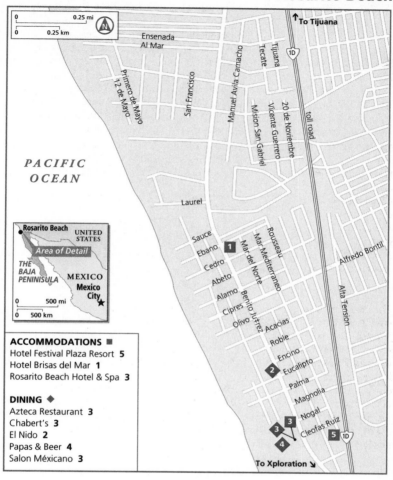

ACCOMMODATIONS ■
Hotel Festival Plaza Resort **5**
Hotel Brisas del Mar **1**
Rosarito Beach Hotel & Spa **3**

DINING ◆
Azteca Restaurant **3**
Chabert's **3**
El Nido **2**
Papas & Beer **4**
Salon Méxicano **3**

Rosarito Beach Hotel & Spa ★★ ◆ The historic Rosarito Beach Hotel recently completed major renovations and the construction of a new condo/hotel, the Pacifico Tower, which brings a needed update to this landmark hotel. The rooms in the original buildings are worn and old but maintain a certain classic charm, but the new rooms have a more modern aesthetic, featuring family-style condo suites with floor-to-ceiling ocean views, kitchens or kitchenettes, modern artwork and furniture over 17 floors. Unique features of artistic construction and lavish decoration remain, setting it apart from the rest along a wide stretch of a family-friendly beach.

Bl. Benito Juárez 31, Zona Centro, 22710 Rosarito, B.C. www.rosaritobeachhotel.com. ✆**800/343-8582** in the U.S., or 661/612-0144. Fax 661/612-1125. 500 units. $109 Playas double; $149–$169 Pacifico double; $289–$319 suites. 2 children 11 or younger stay free in parent's room. Packages available. MC, V. Free

surfing, NORTHERN BAJA STYLE

Surfers flock to the Northern Baja coast for perpetual right-breaking waves, cheap digs and eats, and *Endless Summer*-type camaraderie.

Undoubtedly, the most famous surf spot in all of Mexico is **Killers,** at Todos Santos Island. This was the location of the winning wave in the 1997–98 K2 Challenge (a worldwide contest to ride the largest wave each winter—and be photographed doing it). Killers is a very makeable wave for confident, competent surfers. To get there you need a boat. You can get a lift from the local *panga* (skiff) fleet, for about $100 for the day. That's pretty much the going rate, and the tightly knit Ensenada *pangueros* aren't eager to undercut each other. It's about 15km (10 miles) out to the island; there you'll anchor and paddle into the lineup. You must bring everything you'll need—food, drink, sunscreen, and so on.

Other less radical and easier-to-reach spots include the rocky **Popotla** break, south of Rosarito, where you'll walk to the beach through the Popotla trailer park. **Calafia,** just a few kilometers south of Rosarito, has a reeling right point that can get very heavy. **San Miguel** is the point break just south of the final tollbooth on the highway into Ensenada. It's an excellent wave but generally crowded.

If you're a surfer looking to get your bearings or a beginner wanting to get your feet wet, stop by **Inner Reef** (📞 **661/613-2065;** Km 34.5 on the free road, 9.7km/6 miles south of Rosarito). This tiny shack, painted green with blue flames, sells all the essentials: wax, leashes, patch kits, custom surfboards, rentals, and ding repairs. Owner Mitch Benson is there daily, 9am to 5pm in winter, and 8am to 6pm in summer. He also has a shop in front of Rosarito Beach Hotel.

parking. **Amenities:** 2 restaurants; bar; playground; 2 outdoor pools; wading pool; racquetball court; room service; spa; Wi-Fi in some areas of hotel. *In room:* A/C (in some), fan (in some), TV.

Where to Eat

While in Rosarito, you may want to try **Chabert's** (Continental) or the more casual **Azteca Restaurant** (Mexican), both in the Rosarito Beach Hotel. Early risers out for a stroll can enjoy fresh, steaming-hot tamales (with a variety of stuffings), a traditional Mexican breakfast treat sold from sidewalk carts for around 50¢ each.

El Nido ★★ MEXICAN/STEAKS One of the first eateries in Rosarito, El Nido remains popular with visitors unimpressed by the flashier, neon-lit joints that pop up to please the college-age set. The setting here is Western frontier, complete with rustic candles and rusting wagon wheels; sit outside in the enclosed patio or opt for the dark, cozy interior warmed by a large fireplace and open grill. The mesquite fire is constantly stoked to prepare the grilled steaks and seafood that are El Nido's specialty; the menu also includes free-range quail and venison from the owner's ranch in the nearby wine country. Meals are reasonably priced and generous, including hearty bean soup, American-style green salad, baked potatoes, and all the fresh tortillas and zesty salsa you can eat.

Bl. Benito Juárez 67. 📞 **661/612-1430.** www.elnidorosarito.net. Main courses 115–250 pesos. No credit cards. Daily 8am–11pm.

Rosarito Beach After Dark

The most popular spot in town is **Papas & Beer** (© 661/612-0444; www.papas andbeer.com) on Rosarito Beach. It's a relaxed, bikini-and-board-shorts type club on the beach with blaring hip-hop music and umbrellas in the sand, just a block north of the Rosarito Beach Hotel. Even for those young in spirit only, it's great fun, with open-air tables and a bar surrounding a sand volleyball court. It's open daily all year long from 11am to 3am. Or choose from several other adjacent clubs, each offering booming music, spirited dancing, and all-night-long energy. Cover charges vary depending on the season, the crowd, and the mood of the staff. The **Salon Méxi-cano** (© 661/612-0144), in the Rosarito Beach Hotel, attracts a slightly more mature crowd, with a Mexican fiesta every Friday and Saturday night and karaoke on the nights you're lucky enough to catch it. The Fiesta Mexicana features folkloric dance performances, mariachis, and a buffet-style Mexican dinner.

ENSENADA: PORT OF CALL ★★

135km (84 miles) S of San Diego; 110km (68 miles) S of Tijuana

After the buzz of Tijuana and the city-beach hustle of Rosarito, Ensenada feels different: more relaxed, more genuine. This classic port town, situated on a rocky bay flanked by sheltering mountains, has an unmistakable sincerity. Despite a bilingual, bicultural population, Ensenada has more Mexican charm than any of its neighbors to the north, evoking the dual culture of a border town without the chaos. About 40 minutes from Rosarito, it's the kind of place that loves a celebration. Almost anytime you choose to visit, the city is festive—be it for a bicycle race or a seafood festival.

One of Mexico's principal ports of call, Ensenada welcomes half a million visitors a year who are attracted to its beaches, excellent sportfishing, nearby wineries, and surrounding natural attractions. And the last few years have brought a new and delicious reason to visit: Ensenada is the standard-bearer for a new generation of Mexican culinary culture, the cradle of the Baja Med movement and home to some of the finest restaurants in the country. With a focus on ingeniously simple preparations of ultra-fresh Baja specialties—*mariscos,* cactus, wine—and organically produced local products, Ensenada's restaurants are making international news, but still charging Mexican prices. Get 'em while they're hot.

GETTING THERE   After passing through the final tollbooth, Hwy. 1-D curves sharply toward downtown Ensenada. Watch out for brutal metal speed bumps slowing traffic into town—they're far less forgiving on your chassis than those in the U.S.

VISITOR INFORMATION   The **Tourist and Convention Bureau booth** (© 800/310-9687 in the U.S., or 646/178-8588 or 178-8578) is at the western entrance to town, where the waterfront-hugging Bulevar Lázaro Cárdenas—also known as Bulevar Costero—curves away to the right. The office is open daily from 9am till dusk and can provide a downtown map, directions to major nearby sites, and information on special events throughout the city. As in most of the commonly visited areas of Baja, one or more employees speak English fluently. (There's another office in the Hotel Santo Tomas at Miramar 609). **Taxis** park along the bustling López Mateos, or Avenida Primera (First Ave.).

FAST FACTS   Two accessible **hospitals** in Ensenada are the **Clinica Hospital ISSSTE,** on the corner of bulevares Sangines and Pedro Loyola (© 646/176-5276), and the **Hospital General de Zona IV No. 8,** on Avenida Reforma and

Fraccionamiento Bahía (© **646/172-4500**). The main **post office** is on Avenida López Mateos at Calle Floresta.

Exploring Ensenada

Ensenada is thought of as a "border town," but part of its appeal is its multilayered vitality, born out of city life that's much more than tourism. The bustling port consumes the entire waterfront—beach access is north or south of town—and the Pacific fishing trade and agriculture in the fertile valleys surrounding the city dominate the economy. Make time for a visit to the indoor-outdoor fish market at the northernmost corner of the harbor where each day, from early morning to midday, merchants and housewives gather to assess the day's catch—tuna, marlin, snapper, plus many other varieties of fish and piles of shrimp from the morning's haul.

Together with Tijuana, Ensenada is the center of a culinary revolution in which this northern corner of Baja is outstripping its rivals in Mexico City. Some of the country's best restaurants are part of the Baja Med movement, which marries Mediterranean cooking precepts with Baja's bounty; many of them are here in Ensenada, along the waterfront and on the streets surrounding Avenida López Mateos. Ensenada is already a destination trip for So Cal foodies, and it's only getting better. While you'll get great fish tacos and plenty of tourist food here, this is the place to pony up for the good restaurants.

Avenida López Mateos, or Avenida Primera, is the hub of tourist activity in the city, with shopping and lots of English-speaking businesses. Touring town, your first stop should be the **Bodegas de Santo Tomás Winery,** Av. Miramar 666 at Calle 7 (© **646/178-3333;** www.santo-tomas.com), open 7 days a week. The tour is free, and if you wish to follow it up with a tasting, available 10am to 4pm, 160 pesos gets you a sampling of six wines (or pay 80 pesos for three whites, 100 for three reds). The little modern machinery installed here freed up a cavernous space now used for monthly jazz concerts. Across the street stands La Esquina de Bodegas (the Corner Wine Cellar), former aging rooms for Santo Tomás: The industrial-style building now functions as a gallery showcasing local art, with a skylit bookstore on the second level and a small cafe (punctuated by giant copper distillation vats) in the rear.

Ensenada's primary cultural center is the **Centro Cívico, Social, y Cultural,** Bulevar Lázaro Cárdenas at Avenida Club Rotario. The impressive Mediterranean building was formerly Riviera del Pacífico, a glamorous 1930s bayfront casino and resort frequented by Hollywood's elite. Tiles in the lobby commemorate "Visitantes Distinguidos 1930–1940," including Marion Davies, William Randolph Hearst, Lana Turner, Myrna Loy, and Jack Dempsey. Elegant hallways and ballrooms evoke bygone elegance, and every wall and alcove glows with original murals depicting Mexico's colorful history. Lush formal gardens span the front of the building, and a small art gallery is on one side.

Drive 45 minutes south along the rural Punta Banda peninsula to one of Ensenada's natural attractions: **La Bufadora ★★**, a sea spout in the rocks. With each incoming wave, water is forced upward through the rock, creating a 21m-high (70-ft.) blowhole whose loud grunt gave the phenomenon its name (*la bufadora* means "buffalo snort"). Local fishermen have a more lyrical explanation. According to legend, a mother gray whale and her calf were just rounding Punta Banda, when the curious baby was trapped in a sea cave. The groan that the blowhole makes is the stranded calf still crying for his mother, and the tremendous spray is his spout.

HOTELS■
Estero Beach Resort **19**
Las Rosas Resort & Spa **8**

ATTRACTIONS ●
Bodegas de Santo Tomás Winery **11**
Colores de Mexico **15**
Centro Civico Social y Cultural **18**
Fausto Polanco **17**
Los Castillo **14**

RESTAURANTS & NIGHTLIFE◆
Barra Azul **12**
Belio **1**
El Charro **4**
El Rey Sol **16**
Hussong's Cantina **2**
La Casa del Arte **5**
La Cocedora de Langosta **10**
La Contra **6**
La Guerrerense **13**
Manzanilla **7**
Muelle Tres **9**
Papas & Beer **2**
Ultramarino **3**

From downtown Ensenada, take Avenida Reforma south (Carretera Transpeninsular) to Hwy. 23 west. It's a long, meandering drive through a semi-swamplike area untouched by development; look for grazing animals, bait shops, and fishermen's shacks along the way. La Bufadora is at the end of the road, behind the souvenir stands and fish taco shacks.

Sports & Outdoor Activities

Ensenada is home to a thriving adventure subculture: Off-road racers, climbers, surfers, kayakers, and more flock to Ensenada in search of their adrenaline fix.

FISHING Ensenada, which bills itself as the yellowtail capital of the world, draws sportfishermen in search of the Pacific's albacore, halibut, marlin, rockfish, and sea bass. A wooden boardwalk parallel to Bulevar Lázaro Cárdenas (Costero) near the northern entrance to town provides access to the sportfishing piers and their charter-boat operators. Open-party boats leave early, often by 7am, and charge around $50 per person, plus an additional fee (around $12) for the mandatory fishing license. Nonfishing passengers must, by law, also be licensed. If you don't want to comparison shop, make advance arrangements with **Sergio's Sportfishing Center** (✆ **619/399-7224** in the U.S., or 646/178-2185; www.sergiosfishing.com). In addition to daily fishing excursions, it offers multiday trips to Colonet, San Martín, San Gerónimo, Sacramento Reef, and San Carlos.

HIKING Ensenada is the gateway city to the **Parque Nacional Constitución de 1857.** On the spine of the Sierra de Juárez, the park was once a heavily used mining area, but most of the mines are now defunct. In contrast to the dry and sometimes desolate surroundings of much of the northern peninsula, the 5,000-hectare (12,350-acre) forest preserve averages about 1,200m (3,936 ft.) in altitude and is covered in places with pine forests. To get to the park, take Hwy. 3 south from Ensenada and exit at the graded dirt access road at Km 55. The park entrance road (35km/22 miles to the park entrance) is gravel and generally well maintained but can be really rough after a rainy year. If the entrance is staffed, you'll be asked for a modest entrance fee. For more information, contact the **Baja National Parks Service** at ✆ **646/176-0190** or visit www.conanp.gob.mx.

The **Parque Nacional Sierra San Pedro Mártir** is to Baja California what Yosemite is to Alta California. Almost 72,000 hectares (177,840 acres) of the highest mountains on the peninsula have been preserved here. The highest, **Picacho del Diablo** (Devil's Peak), rises to 3,095m (10,154 ft.) and draws hikers and backpackers to scale its two-pronged summit about 130km (80 miles) south of Ensenada. Views from the top encompass both oceans and an immense stretch of land. You'll find a high alpine realm of flower-speckled meadows, soaring granite peaks, and year-round creeks. Official trails are few and far between, so wander at your own risk, but anyone who's good with a map and compass can have a great time hiking. Cow trails (yes, cows in a national park) are numerous. Four year-round creeks drain the park and make great destinations. Picacho del Diablo is a difficult but rewarding overnight hike and long scramble. Always remember that you're in one of the most rugged and remote places in all of Baja, and with the lack of marked trails, it's quite likely that if you get lost or hurt, nobody will come looking for you. **California Alpine Guides** (✆ **877/686-2546;** www.californiaalpineguides.com), out of Mammoth Lakes, California, is an adventure-tour operator with guides who know what they're doing in the unmarked Baja desert wilderness.

To get to the park, take the Carretera Transpeninsular south from Ensenada, to Km 140, soon after you pass the little town of Colonet. There's a sign for the park entrance; the sign also says OBSERVATORIO. (Fill up with gas in Colonet—there is no more until you exit this way again—and reset your trip odometer at the turnoff.) It's 76km (47 miles) to the park entrance.

For other adventure tours in the region, contact **Mario's Tours,** Bl. Costero 1094–14, Centro (✆ **646/178-3704;** www.mexonline.com/ecotur.htm), which runs hiking, mountain-bike, ATV, and other adventure tours in the region.

SEA KAYAKING The rocky coastline of Punta Banda is a favorite first trip for beginning ocean kayakers due to its several secluded beaches, sea caves, and terrific scenery. Many kayakers use La Bufadora as a launching point to head out the 11km

DIVING WITH great white sharks IN BAJA

For anyone who still draws a pause when they hear the theme from *Jaws,* read no further: This is no adventure for the faint of heart. Off the coast of Baja, one can go cage diving with great white sharks at Isla Guadalupe. More than an extreme sport, this activity actually supports shark science. **Absolute Adventures–Shark Diver** (© 888/405-3268, 415/404-6144, or 235-9410 in the U.S.; www.sharkdiver.com) is led by Patric Douglas, an adventure guide who has teamed up with scientists in Baja Mexico and Southern California to fuse ecotourism with research. Dives take place at Isla Guadalupe, a 158-sq.-km (109-sq.-mile) island 242km (150 miles) offshore from the Pacific coast of Mexico, roughly south of San Diego and west/northwest of Punta Eugenia on the Baja California peninsula. Surrounded by deep water, as much as 3,600m (11,808 ft.) between the island and the mainland, the island is home to a stunning array of wildlife, including one of the world's most accessible populations of great white sharks.

The great white shark (*Carcharodon carcharias*) occurs naturally in all temperate marine waters and is usually between 3 and 4m (10–13 ft.) long, although it can grow to 6.5m (21 ft.) and weigh over 1,800 kilograms (2 tons).

They are among the most feared predators in the world, known for their fearsome sudden attacks. Great whites typically surprise their prey by rushing from below and grasping the victim with a powerful, large bite. If the bite is not fatal, the prey is usually left to weaken or die through blood loss, at which time the white shark returns and consumes its prey. Shark diving allows shark enthusiasts to observe the world of great whites, as well as the array of other marine life in the area, in their natural environment. Absolute Adventures claims to use the largest shark cages in existence—4.5 to 9.3 sq. m (50–100 sq. ft) in size—which are used to create a discernible barrier that the sharks quickly recognize so divers may safely view and photograph the sharks. The four-man shark cages are constructed using high-grade materials and a state-of-the-art fabrication process. The 5-day live-aboard cage-diving expeditions take place on one of their four full-time shark-diving vessels and cost $3,100 per person (all offer air-conditioned staterooms). The program supports large-scale research programs involving researchers from Mexico (Centro Interdisciplinario de Ciencias del Mar) and University of California–Davis, in Northern California.

(7 miles) to the Todos Santos Islands. **Dale's La Bufadora Dive Shop** (© 619/730-2903 in the U.S., or 646/154-2092; www.labufadoradive.com) has kayak rentals and is open weekends or by prior reservation; they can advise you on how to make the crossing. **Ecotur,** Bl. Costero 1094–14, Centro (© 646/178-3704; www.mexonline.com/ecotur.htm), offers guided kayak trips, including a full kayak expedition through the Bay of Los Angeles.

SCUBA DIVING & SNORKELING La Bufadora is a great dive spot with thick kelp and wonderful sea life. Get underwater and zoom through lovely kelp beds and rugged rock formations covered in strawberry anemones and gypsy shawl nudibranchs. You may also spot spiny lobsters and numerous large fish. It's possible to swim right over to the blowhole (see "La Bufadora," p. 162), but use caution in this area—you don't want to end up like that mythical whale calf. **Dale's La Bufadora Dive Shop** is onshore at the best entry point.

Several Ensenada dive shops will arrange boat dives to the Todos Santos islands, which sit at the outer edge of Todos Santos Bay, and other local sites. The diving here is similar to the diving at Catalina or the other California Channel Islands—lots of fish, big kelp, urchins, and jagged rock formations. It's $120 for a two-tank dive.

SURFING   Only the best and boldest surfers challenge the waves off Islas de Todos Santos, two islands about 19km (12 miles) west of Ensenada, considered to be some of the best surf on the coast. Waves at the famous Killers break can reach 9m (30 ft.) in winter, and surfers must hire a *panga* to take them to the waves. You'll find gentler but still challenging waves at San Miguel and Salsipuedes. For local surf reports and gear rental, visit the **San Miguel Surf Shop,** on Avenida López Mateos between Gastelum and Miramar (✆ **646/178-1007**). Longboards and shortboards rent for $25 a day, and for $5 extra, you get a wet suit.

Shopping

Ensenada's slightly more refined equivalent of Tijuana's Avenida Revolución is the crowded Avenida López Mateos (or Av. Primera), which runs roughly parallel to Bulevar Lázaro Cárdenas (Costero); the highest concentration of shops and restaurants is between avenidas Ruíz and Castillo. Beggars fill this street, and sellers are less likely to bargain here than in Tijuana—much of the merchandise is of much higher quality than in the north, and the shopkeepers of lesser stores are used to gullible cruise-ship buyers in Ensenada. Compared to Tijuana, there is more authentic Mexican art- and craftswork in Ensenada, pieces imported from rural states and villages where different skills are traditionally practiced. Off the highway on the way into Ensenada is the can't-miss **Art & Stuff** in El Sauzal (✆ **949/202-5321** in the U.S., or 646/175-8859; Km 103 Carretera Tijuana-Ensenada). This unpretentious and eclectic gallery has a collection worthy of boastfulness and high prices, but the owner is endearingly humble. Local artist Señora Q is the showstopper here with her whimsical interpretations that hint at magical realism on found objects and canvases, and in sculptures.

For jewelry and fine silver adornments, nothing compares to **Los Castillo,** five specialty stores along Avenida López Mateos (✆ **646/156-5274;** www.loscastillo silver.com). This is the official outlet for the Castillo family's jewelry from the renowned silver city of Taxco. You'll find intricate sterling silver designs upon pristine porcelain that create original works of art on fine china, which also can be found at Neiman Marcus in the U.S., ornate sterling silver serving pieces, and jewelry that can't be found anywhere else. A few doors down from Los Castillo, and at the opposite end of the spectrum, **Colores de Mexico** sells designer look-alike bags made of leather. For handcrafted furnishings, **Fausto Polanco** (✆ **646/174-0336;** www.faustopolanco.com.mx), at López Mateos and Castillo, sells fine hacienda-style furnishings at U.S. prices.

Where to Stay

Casa Natalie ★★★ 👰   When it comes to luxury and service in Ensenada, this outpost of understated opulence is unmatched. A guard-gated entrance to Casa Natalie's modern, adults-only sanctuary in El Sauzal, just north of downtown Ensenada, ensures supreme privacy. Once inside, the resort's intimate setting charms and delights. Undoubtedly Northern Baja's finest boutique hotel, Casa Natalie feels light and airy, with lounge-ready seagrass furniture and wispy white drapes that frame the floor-to-ceiling windows, which form a concave half moon to the outside. The living room, chef's kitchen, and dining area, all of which feel more like your own luxury home than an impersonal hotel, open up on a sleek infinity-edge pool, which pours toward the Pacific and is surrounded by teak sun beds with open-air canopies and white privacy curtains.

Seven master suites, all of which face the pool and ocean, embody the casual sophistication so intrinsic to Baja and are named after the peninsula's indigenous plants. *Note:* Casa Natalie is unrelated to Casa Natalia in San José del Cabo.

Carretera Tijuana-Ensenada Km 103.3, El Sauzal, 22760 Ensenada, B.C. www.hotelcasanatalie.com. ✆ **619/246-9772** or 646/174-7373. 8 units. $250–$450 suite. MC, V. No children permitted. **Amenities:** Restaurant; bar; Jacuzzi; heated outdoor pool; room service; full-service spa. *In room:* A/C, satellite TV, CD/DVD player, Wi-Fi.

Estero Beach Resort ★ ☺ About 10km (6¼ miles) south of downtown Ensenada, this sprawling complex of rooms, cottages, and mobile-home hookups has been popular with families and active vacationers since the 1950s. The bay and protected lagoon at the edge of the lushly planted property are perfect for swimming and launching sailboards; there's also a large swimming pool with a swim-up bar, tennis, horseback riding, volleyball, and Ping-Pong and billiards tables. The guest rooms are a little worn, but no one expects fancy here. The beachfront restaurant serves a casual mix of seasonal cuisine including seafood, sushi, Mexican fare, hamburgers, fried chicken, omelets, and even a special kids' menu. Some suites and 5 of the 15 cottages have kitchenettes, and some can easily accommodate a whole family.

Estero Beach. (Mailing address: Apdo. Postal 86, Ensenada, B.C.) www.hotelesterobeach.com. ✆ **646/176-6225.** 100 units. High season $80–$150 double, $80–$120 cottage, $500 suite; low season $70–$110 double, $50–$100 cottage, $400 suite. Mobile-home hookups range from $35–$45 per night and $360–$750 per month. MC, V. From Ensenada, take Carretera Transpeninsular south; turn right at ESTERO BEACH sign. **Amenities:** Restaurant; 2 bars; beach club; Mexican culture museum and shop; outdoor pool w/2 Jacuzzis; tennis, basketball, and volleyball courts. *In room:* TV, kitchenette (in some).

Las Rosas Hotel & Spa ★★ 🖈 One of the most modern hotels in the area, Hotel Las Rosas still falls short of most definitions of luxurious, yet the pink oceanfront hotel 3.2km (2 miles) north of Ensenada is the favorite of many Baja aficionados. It offers most of the comforts of an upscale American hotel—which doesn't leave room for much Mexican personality. The atrium lobby is awash in pale pink and seafoam green, a color scheme that pervades throughout—including the guest rooms, sparsely furnished with quasi-tropical furniture. Some rooms have fireplaces and/or in-room whirlpools, and all have balconies overlooking the pool and ocean. One of the resort's main photo ops is the infinity swimming pool that overlooks and appears to merge with the Pacific Ocean beyond.

Carretera Transpeninsular, 3.2km (2 miles) north of Ensenada. (Mailing address: Apdo. Postal 316, Ensenada, B.C.) www.lasrosas.com. ✆ **646/174-4595.** 47 units. High season $139–$164 double; low season $111–$130 double. Extra child 11 and under $16; extra adult $22. MC, V. **Amenities:** Restaurant; cocktail lounge; cliff-top hot tub; Internet; massage; outdoor pool; room service; tennis and racquetball courts; basic workout room. *In room:* A/C, TV.

Where to Eat

In the last 5 years or so, Ensenada has become a premier foodie destination not only for Mexicans, but for cross-border travelers. The list of great new eats here includes the upscale, seaside **Belio** (Km 104 Carretera Ensenada-Tijuana; ✆ **646/175-8810;** www.beliorestaurant.com), the gallery and jazz spot **La Casa del Arte** (Moctezuma 479; ✆ **646/116-8338;** www.lacasadelarte.com.mx), the shellfish mecca **La Cocedora de Langosta** (Teniente Azueta 187; ✆ **646/178-3742**), the parkside, wine-loving **La Contra** (Moctezuma 623; © **646/178-8213;** www.lacontravinos. com), and the steel-and-neon seafood nightspot **Ultramarino** (Ruíz just off López Mateos; © **646/178-1195**) as well as the hot spots and old favorites listed here.

EXPENSIVE

El Rey Sol ★ FRENCH/MEXICAN   Opened by French expatriates in 1947, the family-run El Rey Sol has long been considered one of Ensenada's finest eateries, right in the heart of the tourist center of López Mateos. Its somewhat dated cuisine and service style are being overshadowed by Ensenada's newcomers, but it's still the pick for an old-fashioned elegant meal. Wrought-iron chandeliers and heavy oak farm tables create a country-French atmosphere, and the service is excellent. House specialties include seafood puff pastry; baby clams steamed in butter, white wine, and cilantro; chicken in brandy and chipotle-cream sauce; and homemade French desserts. Portions are generous and always feature fresh vegetables from the family farm. Don't miss the almond croissant at breakfast.

Av. López Mateos 1000 (at Blancarte). © **646/178-1733.** www.elreysol.com. Reservations recommended for weekends. Main courses $9–$19. AE, MC, V. Daily 7:30am–10:30pm.

Manzanilla ★★★ CONTEMPORARY MEXICAN   At Ensenada's most celebrated restaurant, the look and the food are all about flouting convention: The elegant wooden salon with antique bar is razzed with pink glass chandeliers, and the menu of gorgeous seafood, Sonoran ranch meats, and organic produce from the Valle del Guadalupe is shot through with offbeat touches like squid dyed fuchsia with beet juice and succulent clams paired with Gorgonzola cheese. A dressed-up clam chowder with saffron, *huitlacoche* risotto, or sliced beef tongue with cactus may not be on offer when you arrive, but never fear, the kitchen will give you one of the best meals in Baja. Critics agree, it never misses the mark—Manzanilla is consistently ranked among the best restaurants in Mexico.

Teniente Azueta 139. © **646/175-7073.** www.rmanzanilla.com. Reservations recommended. Main courses 140–330 pesos. MC, V. Wed–Sat noon–midnight.

Muelle Tres ★★★ CONTEMPORARY MEXICAN   This restaurant and oyster bar is right next to the fish market, and it shows. Small, casual, and with an industrial feel, it's the place for farmed clams, scallops, oysters, and mussels, as well as divine *almohaditas de camaron,* literally "little pillows" of puff pastry filled with shrimp and cheese, and a variety of *tiraditos,* or fish carpaccios. While the deep bowls of steamed mussels served five ways—watch out for the *seis chiles*—are well-nigh irresistible, if you're in it to win it, go directly to the tapitas, the chef's tasting menu, for a guided tour through the catch of the day.

Teniente Azueta 187 on the *malecón.* © **646/174-0318.** wwwmuelletres.com. Oysters 60–80 pesos for an order of 6; main courses 50–100 pesos. MC, V. Wed–Sun noon–7pm.

MODERATE

Barra Azul ★★ 🍴 SEAFOOD   Slightly off the main tourist trail, 11 blocks up from the *malecón,* Barra Azul has become a de rigeur stop on Ensenada's foodie trail, for its impeccably fresh and diverse seafood and moderate prices. Oysters of the tempura and raw persuasions are perennial favorites, as are ceviches, molded and stacked like napoleons, and the lion's mane scallops. Dishes are light, so there's room for dessert: crepe cake or a not-so-simple brownie. Look for the bright blue building.

Calle 11 no. 1090, btw. Espinoza and the bridge. © **646/178-4846.** Main courses 90–130 pesos. MC, V. Sun–Mon and Wed–Thurs 2–10pm; Fri–Sat 2–11:30pm.

El Charro ☺ MEXICAN Dating from before Ensenada's fine dining days, El Charro is a casual spot for a family meal. You'll recognize it by its front windows: Whole chickens rotate slowly on the rotisserie in one while a woman makes tortillas in the other. This little place has been here since 1956 and looks it, with charred walls, a ceiling made of split logs, and giant piñatas hanging overhead. The simple fare includes half a roasted chicken with fries and tortillas, or *carne asada* (grilled marinated beef) with soup, guacamole, and tortillas. Kids are welcome. Wine and beer are served, and beer is cheaper than soda.

Av. López Mateos 475 (btw. Ruíz and Gastelum). ⓒ **646/178-2114.** Menu items $5–$12; lobster $20. No credit cards. Daily 11am–2am.

INEXPENSIVE

La Guerrerense ★ 🍴 SEAFOOD This shellfish stand has been serving it up raw for 40 years; it's an Ensenada tradition. That said, nothing it serves is traditional: Tostadas, normally a staid chop of raw fish, avocado, and onion on a crispy tortilla, are reinvented here with sea urchin, sea snail, and a collection of more than 20 homemade salsas seen nowhere else. Purists will go straight for the raw bar specialties, Pismo clams on the half-shell. If you're going to eat raw shellfish on the street, this is the only place you should be doing it.

Av. López Mateos and Alvarado. ⓒ **646/174-2114.** Tostadas and raw bar 15–30 pesos. No credit cards. Wed–Mon 10am–4pm.

Ensenada After Dark

No discussion of Ensenada would be complete without mentioning **Hussong's Cantina,** Av. Ruíz 113, near Avenida López Mateos (ⓒ **646/178-3210**); just like the line from *Casablanca,* "everyone goes to Rick's," everyone's been going to Hussong's since the bar opened in 1892. Nothing much has changed in the last century plus—the place still sports Wild West–style swinging saloon doors, a long bar to slide beers along, and strolling mariachis bellowing above the din of revelers. There's definitely a minimalist appeal to Hussong's, which looks as if it sprang from a south-of-the-border episode of *Gunsmoke.* Beer and tequilas at astonishingly low prices are the main order of business. Be aware that hygiene and privacy are a low priority in the restrooms.

While the crowd at Hussong's (a pleasant mix of tourists and locals) can really whoop it up, they're amateurs compared to those who frequent **Papas & Beer,** Avenida Ruíz near Avenida López Mateos (ⓒ **646/178-4231**), across the street. A tiny entrance leads to the upstairs bar and dance club, where the music is loud, and the young crowd is definitely here to party. Happy patrons hang out of the second-story windows calling out to their friends and stop occasionally to eat *papas fritas* (french fries) accompanied by local beers. Papas & Beer has quite a reputation with the Southern California college crowd and has a branch in Rosarito (p. 161).

TECATE: A BETTER BORDER ★

Tecate is just 45km (30 miles) east of Tijuana and San Diego, but it's a world away from Tijuana's urban sprawl. This provincial border town is Baja's oldest, and before the Tecate brewery opened the taps in 1943, it was a dusty agricultural supply stop and not much more. Since then, a small city has grown up around the sleepy main square, but the center of town still has an old-fashioned, dusty feel, and the taco stands and occasional mariachi band on Parque Hidalgo are as lively as it gets. That's

A NORTHERN BAJA SPA sanctuary

One of Mexico's best-known spas is in Northern Baja, just 58km (36 miles) south of San Diego. The **Rancho La Puerta ★★**, opened in 1940 as a "health camp," was among the pioneers of the modern spa and fitness movement. The location was chosen for its perfect climate. The rates at the time were $18 a week—but you had to bring your own tent.

Much has changed. Today, the ranch occupies 1,200 hectares (2,964 acres) of lush oasis surrounded by pristine countryside, which includes a 2.5-hectare (6-acre) organic garden and La Cocina Que Canta, a spa-cuisine cooking school. Cottages can accommodate up to 150 guests per week, and the ranch has a staff of almost 400. Each cottage has its own patio garden and is decorated with Mexican folk art. Inside the rooms are spacious living-room-size seating areas, desks, CD players, hair dryers, robes, and safes, and most rooms have fireplaces.

Three swimming pools, 4 tennis courts, 5 hot tubs, saunas, steam rooms, and 11 gyms for aerobic and restorative classes are only a part of the facilities. Separate men's and women's health centers offer the full range of spa services. Hiking trails surround the resort, and there's even a labyrinth that is a full-size replica of the ancient labyrinth found in Chartres Cathedral, for moving meditation.

Lounges and shared spaces include the library, with thousands of books to browse and read, an evening movie lounge, recreation room, and for those who can't conceive of totally disconnecting, the E-center, with 24-hour Internet access.

Weeklong programs—Saturday to Saturday—emphasize a mind/body/spirit philosophy, and certain weeks throughout the year are geared specifically to one topic; Specialty Week themes range from couples to Pilates and dance to meditation. Weekly prices begin at $2,835 for most of the year and $3,115 from February through June. Included in the rates are all classes, meals, evening programs, and use of facilities. Personal spa services cost extra. You may be able to book shorter stays (3 nights or more); and rates may be prorated on a nightly basis.

For reservations or to request a brochure, visit **www.rancholapuerta.com**; call ✆ **800/443-7565** in the U.S., or fax 858/764-5500. American Express, MasterCard, and Visa are accepted.

a large part of its appeal—and local tourism authorities are just starting to capitalize on it, with a small but growing series of food, beer, wine, and music events.

GETTING THERE North of the border, you'll take California Hwy. 94 for 66km (41 miles) to Hwy. 188 south to the crossing; south of the border, Tecate lies right at the intersection of highways 2 and 3. It's a 30- to 45-minute drive from Tijuana, 2 hours from Ensenada. Many visitors from the U.S. side of the border opt to park and walk.

The old Ferrocarril Tijuana-Tecate **train** linking the two border towns has been reincarnated as a tourist attraction, with daylong Saturday outings including a 2-hour train ride each way in double-decker cars and a mariachi performance in Tecate. Tickets and schedules are at the train stations in Tijuana (Av. Ferrocarril 1; ✆ 664/324-0360) and Tecate (Bl. Defensores de Baja California 53 next to the Cervecería Tecate; ✆ 665/521-2903; www.fcbc.com.mx). Previously, another rail option was the antique rail cars that ran from San Diego. However, this route is closed

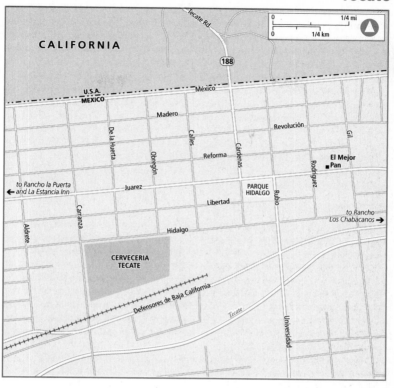

Map labels: California; Tecate Rd.; 188; U.S.A.; MEXICO; México; Madero; Revolución; De la Huerta; Calles; Cárdenas; Obregón; Reforma; Gil; El Mejor Pan; Rodriguez; to Rancho la Puerta and La Estancia Inn ←; Juarez; Libertad; PARQUE HIDALGO; Rubio; to Rancho Los Chabacanos →; Carranza; Aldrete; Hidalgo; CERVECERIA TECATE; Defensores de Baja California; Tecate; Universidad; 0 1/4 mi; 0 1/4 km

indefinitely due to damage from a tunnel fire. Check **sdrm.org** to see if it's been repaired.

VISITOR INFORMATION Tecate's **tourism office** is across from the park on Callejon Libertad (© 665/654-5892). The center of town life is at Parque Hidalgo, five blocks south of the border on Cárdenas; it's a pleasant square lined with restaurants and taco stands, which double as Tecate's only nightlife. South of the square, Benito Juárez is the town's main drag, leading east and west to highways 2 and 3. Up-to-date information on bars, restaurants, and activities (in Spanish) is at **www.entecate.com**.

FAST FACTS A **pharmacy** and **hospital** (© 665/654-5803) are at Juárez and Gil, south of downtown. The **Bancomer** bank on Parque Hidalgo has an **ATM**.

Exploring Tecate

This untouristy town's number-one attraction is the **Cervecería Tecate** ★★ (© 665/654-9478; www.cuamoc.com), brewers of the beer that's made the town famous throughout Mexico and California. Founded in 1943, it makes for an interesting tour for beer nuts and their friends; afterwards, enjoy a free beer in the beer garden. It's at Hidgalo and Obregón, the biggest building in town. Tours run Monday to Friday 9am to noon and 3 to 5pm and Saturday 10am to noon; call a day in advance to make sure there's someone to show you around, and leave jewelry and sandals at home.

For further attractions, you'll have to head out of town, to the 500-year-old **cave paintings** at El Vallecito (© **686/552-8279**), near la Rumorosa 10km (6 miles) out of town along the highway to Mexcali. Although the paintings aren't as old or as vast as those in the Sierra de San Francisco or Guadalupe, they provide one clue that demonstrates a sophisticated understanding of timekeeping: A painting known as El Diablito is positioned so that every year on December 21, the winter solstice, it's illuminated by a ray of sunlight. To get to El Vallecito, take Hwy. 2 to the Vallecitos exit. Entrance is 35 pesos; there are guides and maps for a mile-long self-guided tour.

In August, the Cocinarte **food festival** (© **665/654-1381**; http://cocinarte. canacotecate.org) brings a gastronomic focus to town; in September, it's beer time, with the **Festival de la Cerveza** (© **665/108-9257**; http://tktbeerfest.com). The first weekend of October is Tecate's all-in-one patronage **festival,** a beer-drinking mariachi-playing birthday party for the town.

Where to Stay & Eat

The swankiest digs in town are unquestionably at **Rancho la Puerta ★**, a five-star spa retreat 5km (3 miles) out of town (see "A Northern Baja Spa Sanctuary," below). The beautiful stone chalet at **Rancho Los Chabacanos** (© **665/655-1624**; www. rancholoschabacanos.com), 15 minutes to the east, isn't half bad either, with an organic apricot orchard and ecotouristy pursuits like kayaking and bird-watching, for $80 to $160 a night, and $285 for a two-bedroom villa. If your pockets aren't that deep, **La Estancia Inn** (© **665/521-3066**; www.laestanciainn.com.mx; 3km/2 miles west of town at Benito Juárez 1450) is an upscale motel with guarded parking, a swimming pool, and 89 well-kept rooms for 706 to 807 pesos a night in low season, 848 to 951 pesos in high season.

This is not a foodie town, and most of the culinary action is at the **taco stands** that line the central Plaza Hidalgo. Tecate is known locally for excellent **bakeries,** however, including **El Mejor Pan,** in business since 1969 (© **665/654-0040;** www.elmejorpandetecate.com), in the center at Juárez 331.

THE VALLE DE GUADALUPE: MEXICO'S WINE COUNTRY ★★★

The secret's out that Baja's wine country is blossoming into something that potentially could be as big as Napa. For now, a visit to the Guadalupe Valley still feels like an off-the-beaten-path exploration.

A 29km (18-mile) drive northeast of Ensenada along Hwy. 3 toward Tecate will bring you to the Valle de Guadalupe (Guadalupe Valley), the heart of Mexico's small but expanding wine industry. Although more traditional connoisseurs may have been dismissive of Mexico's wine efforts in the past, in recent years the production and quality have made quantum leaps, and several Mexican vintages have earned international acclaim.

Spanish missionaries first introduced wine to Baja California in 1701, when a Jesuit priest, Father Juan de Ugarte, planted the peninsula's first grape vines. In 1791, the first vineyards were established in these fertile valleys at Misión Santo Tomás. In 1888, the Santa Tomás winery was established, giving birth to Baja's wine country.

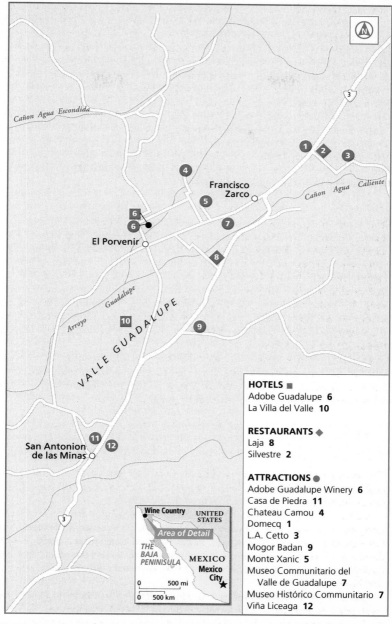

HOTELS ■
Adobe Guadalupe **6**
La Villa del Valle **10**

RESTAURANTS ◆
Laja **8**
Silvestre **2**

ATTRACTIONS ●
Adobe Guadalupe Winery **6**
Casa de Piedra **11**
Chateau Camou **4**
Domecq **1**
L.A. Cetto **3**
Mogor Badan **9**
Monte Xanic **5**
Museo Communitario del
  Valle de Guadalupe **7**
Museo Histórico Communitario **7**
Viña Liceaga **12**

It wasn't until the 1970s that commercial wineries entered the area, with the establishment of the Domecq and L.A. Cetto operations—two of Mexico's largest wine producers, which until recently specialized in inexpensive, mass-produced wines. It was the opening of the boutique winery **Monte Xanic** in the late 1980s that brought the culture of fine wines to the area.

The Valle de Guadalupe is in the "world wine strip," a zone of lands with the climate and porous soil that result in ideal conditions for grape growing—similar to those found in Northern California, France, Spain, and Italy. Northern Baja's dry, hot summers and cool, humid winters added to a stream of cool ocean breezes make the conditions in Guadalupe Valley especially conducive to grape-growing, similar to what you would find in the Mediterranean. The most common wines produced here include chenin blanc, Colombard, sauvignon blanc, and chardonnay among the whites, and cabernet sauvignon, merlot, Barbera, Nebbiolo, and zinfandel among the reds. However, the region's limited rainfall and water supply will likely limit its growth, meaning it is likely to remain the picturesque place it is today rather than growing into a tourist-oriented Napa Valley south.

In 1905, the Mexican government granted political asylum to 100 families from Russia, who arrived in the Guadalupe Valley to cultivate wheat. They soon realized they could earn more for their small colony producing wine and thus became the pioneers of grape cultivation in the area. Although many of the families emigrated to Russian communities throughout the United States during the Cold War, many of the present-day residents are still their descendants. The lovingly maintained **Museo Comunitario del Valle de Guadalupe,** on Francisco Zarco (© **646/155-2069**), has displays and artifacts from this curious time of cultural conversion. Although the information is all in Spanish, museum administrator Alex Gallardo currently is developing English-language materials as well. The museum has a small adjoining restaurant that serves traditional Russian food, and a wine tasting is included with the $2 donation to the museum (the wine and food are not recommended). Just across the street is the **Museo Histórico Comunitario,** affiliated with Mexico's INAH (National Institute of Anthropology and History). Although small in scale, it has informative displays of the indigenous Kumiai culture of the region, and more about the influence of the Russian immigrants in the Valley of Guadalupe. The museum is open Tuesday through Sunday from 10am to 5pm (© **646/178-2531**).

The best time to visit the Valle de Guadalupe is in late August, during Las Fiestas de la Vendimia (Harvest Festivals). Various vineyards schedule a multitude of activities during the festivals, including tastings, classical music concerts, and Masses celebrating the harvest.

 First Crush: The Annual Harvest Festival

The **Fiesta de la Vendimia (Harvest Festival) is held each year in late August or early September. Set among the endless vineyards of the fertile Valle de Guadalupe, the day's events include the traditional blessing of the grapes, wine tastings, live music and dancing, riding exhibitions, and a country-style Mexican meal. L.A. Cetto offers a group excursion from Tijuana (about an hour's drive); San Diego's **Baja California Tours** (© **800/336-5454** or 858/454-7166 in the U.S.) also organizes a day-long trip from San Diego.

Note that most of the roads in the Valle de Guadalupe are dirt-surfaced, so you'll do well to explore in an SUV. The area's only fully paved road is Hwy. 3 (to Tecate), which cuts through the valley. Most of the wineries and attractions are just off this scenic road, which is lined with vineyards and olive orchards.

Winery Tours

Winery tours are available at most of the region's wineries, with some having more structure than others. Especially if you visit the smaller wineries, you'll find you may be the only visitor, meaning you'll enjoy personal attention. But before you snap up cases of the vintages you taste, keep in mind that U.S. Customs limits you to taking only three bottles back across the border.

Daylong winery tours are offered by San Diego–based **Five Star Tours** (© **619/232-5040** in the U.S.; www.sdsuntours.com). Reservations-only tours include visits to several wineries, a historical overview of the valley, transportation from the border, and lunch.

THE WINERIES The area is home to almost 20 wineries, but the following are some of our favorites.

o **Bodegas de Santo Tomás** is Baja's oldest winery. They offer daily tours and hourly wine tastings from 9am to 5pm Monday through Saturday and from 10am to 4pm Sunday for $5. They are in Ensenada, at Av. Miramar 666 (© **646/174-0836** or 174-0829; www.santo-tomas.com).

o **Casa de Piedra** offers free tours and wine tastings through its small but celebrated vineyard by appointment only. It's in Valle de Guadalupe, at Km 93.5, Hwy. 3 to Tecate (© **646/155-3097;** www.vinoscasadepiedra.com).

o **Chateau Camou** offers three different wine-tasting tours, all of which include a souvenir glass, Monday through Saturday from 8am to 3pm and Sunday from 9am to 2pm. The Claret is a 30-minute tour, which includes four wines for $5. The 30-minute Bordeaux tour ends with a tasting of six wines and costs $10. We recommend the Magnum, a $40 reservations-required tour and comprehensive tasting led by the winemaker and capped off with lunch and a glass of wine. This winery has beautiful gardens and panoramic views of the valley. It's in Francisco Zarco, Valle de Guadalupe, just off Hwy. 3 to Tecate (© **646/177-2221;** www. chateau-camou.com.mx).

o **Domecq** hosts free tours and wine tastings for $2.50 Monday through Friday 9:30am to 5pm and Saturday from 10am to 1pm. They have a gift shop and picnic areas on premises. Domecq is in Valle de Guadalupe at Km 73.5, on Hwy. 3 to Tecate (© **646/155-2249;** www.vinosdomecq.com.mx).

o **L.A. Cetto,** one of the largest and most commercial wineries in the region, offers free wine tastings and tours daily from 9am to 4pm. There are also a gift shop, gardens, and picnic areas on-site in Valle de Guadalupe at Km 73.5 on Hwy. 3 to Tecate (© **646/155-2264;** www.lacetto.com).

o **Mogor Badan,** a boutique winery that produces one red and one white that are sold in fine-dining restaurants throughout the world, offers tours and wine tastings by advance appointment. E-mail is the best way to reach Mogor Badan, which is in Valle de Guadalupe, Rancho El Mogor, Km 86.5 on Hwy. 3 to Tecate (©/fax **646/177-1484;** abadan@cicese.mx).

o **Monte Xanic** is a true jewel of a winery to visit, although they change their hours on a whim and can be difficult to reach. Wine tastings (40 pesos for four wines, either red or white, or 80 pesos for all eight) are available Monday through Thursday from 10am to 4pm and Friday through Sunday from 10am to 5pm. These are considered by many to be Mexico's finest wines. Reserve at least 2 days in advance for a free tour. The winery is in Francisco Zarco, Valle de Guadalupe, just off Hwy. 3 to Tecate (© **646/174-6769** or 174-6155; www.montexanic.com).

○ **Viña Liceaga** has by-appointment wine and grappa tastings and tours available daily 11am to 5pm. Don't miss their award-winning merlot. They're in Valle de Guadalupe, at Km 93.5 on Hwy. 3 to Tecate (© **646/155-3281;** www.vinos liceaga.com).

Where to Stay

Adobe Guadalupe   At Adobe Guadalupe, the owners see to it that you don't forget it's a winery first and a hotel second—don't expect a red carpet. Six basic bedrooms, a stunning interior courtyard, and picturesque stables comprise this lovely mission-style structure situated on 26 hectares (65 acres) of vineyard, started in 1998. The cabernet sauvignon, merlot, Nebbiolo, cabernet Franc, Tempranillo, Shiraz, and Viognier grapes are combined to create five blends named after archangels. The guest rooms here pale in comparison to the well-appointed kitchen, living room, and dining room, but they make for a clean, comfortable place to rest after a day of horseback riding, traipsing through vineyards with the hotel's five Weimaraners, sampling wines, or lounging by the pool. Rates include a magnificent made-to-order Mexican breakfast and wine tasting. Dinner is at 7pm and costs $70 for a four-course meal served with Adobe Guadalupe wines. The wine is good and the food is hit-and-miss, but if you plan to have wine with dinner, it's worth it to stay on property and avoid the narrow, shoulder-less highway between Ensenada and the Guadalupe Valley after dark.

Hwy. 1-D, Km 77.5, Guadalupe Valley. (Mailing address: Paracela A-1 s/n Col. Rusa de Guadalupe Valle de Guadalupe, Municipio de Ensenada, B.C. México C.P. 22750) www.adobeguadalupe.com.© **649/631-3098** in the U.S., or 646/155-2094. 6 units. $190 double. Rate includes breakfast and wine tasting. AE, MC, V. Once you've arrived in the town of Guadalupe along Hwy. 3, turn left just past the river into the town of Francisco Zarco. The pavement will soon end, but continue for about 5.6km (3½ miles), past the Monte Xanic and Chateau Camou wineries. At the stop sign (adjacent to the Unidad Médica Familiar building), turn right and continue .8km (a half-mile) more. Adobe Guadalupe will be on your right. **Amenities:** Dining room; concierge; horseback rides; Jacuzzi; massage services; picnic area; heated outdoor pool; tours to other wineries. *In room:* A/C, ceiling fan, TV, no phone.

La Villa del Valle ★★★ 🍸   For the most exquisite take on wine-country accommodations, La Villa del Valle is a delightful sanctuary on 28 hectares (70 acres) of lavender-studded hills in the Guadalupe Valley. No one said living off the land had to mean roughing it—Villa del Valle incorporates the natural Mediterranean-style landscape to create a retreat of organic luxury: flowering herb gardens frequented by the hotel chef, homemade lavender-infused bath products, walls painted with natural minerals, handmade sinks, fresh olive oil made from on-property olive harvests, and river-rock showers, for starters. A vegetable garden with produce ranging from artichokes to lemon grass supplies the restaurant with the freshest four-course dinners ($45 per person); and 14-inch thick beds paired with panoramic valley views make for heavenly rooms.

Rancho Ejido San Marcos Toros Pintos, Francisco Zarco, Ensenada, B.C. www.lavilladelvalle.com. © **646/183-9249.** 6 units. Weekdays $175 double; weekends $195 double; during harvest festival and holidays Mon–Thurs $225, weekends $295. Rates include breakfast and evening glass of wine and appetizers. AE, MC, V. Just past Km 89 on Hwy. 3 toward Tecate, turn left onto the dirt-road exit for Ej.

Porvenir, Delegación, and Rancho Sicomoro. Follow signs to La Villa del Valle, which is about 3.2km (2 miles) down the dirt road. **Amenities:** Restaurant; concierge; Jacuzzi; heated outdoor pool; massage and facial services; meditation labyrinth; yoga studio. *In room:* A/C, no phone, Wi-Fi.

Where to Eat

Laja ★★★ 🍴 CONTEMPORARY MEXICAN This extraordinary gem of a gourmet restaurant, which has won accolades from the major Southern California publications, is reason enough to visit the region. Set in a lovely adobe-and-stone building with picture windows overlooking the valley, Laja, with its own herb garden and small vineyard, serves a daily fixed menu of four to eight courses of local organic produce and wines, unusual seafood, and re-imaginings of such country favorites as head cheese and tripe, as well as a to-die-for apple tart. The concept is all about sustainability, and the place exists as much to promote and support local producers and products as for its own glory—to eat here is to know the Valle de Guadalupe.

On Hwy. 3 Km 83, Francisco Zarco, Valle de Guadalupe. ⓒ 646/155-2556. www.lajamexico.com. Reservations required. Menu 550 pesos; tasting menu 720 pesos. MC, V. Wed 1–3:30pm; Thurs–Sat 1–8:30pm. Closed Dec.

Silvestre ★ 🍴 CONTEMPORARY MEXICAN The country cousin to Ensenada's Manzanilla is, essentially, a very, very upscale picnic without the basket. The cuisine is as complex and exciting as the gourmet temples in town, but it's all prepared outside over a mesquite grill, and eaten at picnic tables on a covered porch that overlooks the vineyards.

On Hwy. 3 Km 73, Valle de Guadalupe. ⓒ **646/175-7073** in Manzanilla. Main courses 150–290 pesos. No credit cards. June–Sept Sat–Sun 1–6pm.

SAN FELIPE: QUIET BEACH VILLAGE ★

407km (253 miles) S of San Diego; 382km (237 miles) S of Tijuana

Unless you happen upon San Felipe during spring break, when thousands of college kids flee south to party at **El Rockodile** on the *malecón* (ⓒ **686/577-1219**), or during Semana Santa—the week before Easter when Mexicans from throughout Baja make a break for the beach with tents and extended family in tow—nothing much happens in this teensy little beach town. And that's just what makes it so special.

Beyond the first impression of tranquillity in this popular camping destination, San Felipe seems to hold a special place in the hearts of the West Coast travelers who've known about it for decades. A survey of So-Cal adults elicits childhood stories of family vacations spent camping on the beach in San Felipe, and the destination still retains an air of nostalgia. Although residential and resort development is winding its way through the surrounding area, those who haven't been back since elementary school will be happy to know not much has changed in the center of town, at least.

Ask anyone what there is to do in San Felipe, and they'll probably say, "not much." If you're expecting anything more than a banana-boat ride ($5 per person, flag down the boat driver on the beach), a sportfishing excursion (call **Tony Reyes Tours** at ⓒ **714/538-8010** or make a deal with the captains on the beach), some fish taco-and-*cerveza* indulgence, or perhaps a few sunny highlights in your hair, San Felipe may not be for you. San Felipe is as low-key as Baja gets, and that makes it an important stopover for those seeking insight into the "old Baja" of yore.

Where to Stay & Eat

Promises of luxurious resorts and residential developments line the highway in the form of billboards, but for now, expect bare-bones accommodations and simple cuisine during your stay.

Stay at **La Hacienda de la Langosta Roja,** Calzada Chetumal 125 (www.sanfelipelodging.com; © **686/577-0483**). It's right in the center of town, a block from the *malecón,* so the location can't be beat. The spare rooms are tidy as can be, the running water is hot, the cable TV and air-conditioning work, and the first-floor restaurant is the closest thing to fine dining you can find in San Felipe. In fact, apart from great Italian food, it serves some of the best ceviche anywhere in Baja, and the wine list has a decent selection of regional and international wines. Rooms go for $49 weekday, $59 weekends, and $79 holidays.

Some may prefer more classic San Felipe accommodations—the ubiquitous campground. For RV and tent campers alike, it doesn't get any better than **Pete's Camp** (www.petescamp.com/principal.html; © **951/694-6704** in the U.S., no local phone), on the north beach of San Felipe. The lovely Navarro family owns and operates the 79-space campsite, which is open to families, RVs, and pets (on leashes), and the on-site restaurant serves Mexican and American favorites. Nightly rates are $15 per vehicle per site. Any vehicles more than 4.5m (15 ft.) in length must take two sites, at a rate of $30 per night.

For seafood, fish tacos, and margaritas that will rock your world, plan to spend a festive afternoon at **Bajamar** (© **686/577-2648**) on the *malecón.* The shrimp tacos ($6) are fried to perfection and the salsa extra fresh.

PLANNING YOUR TRIP TO LOS CABOS & BAJA

GETTING THERE

By Plane

Baja California has four international airports, three in the southern half of the peninsula and one, Tijuana, in the less-populated north. **Los Cabos International (SJD),** by far the busiest Baja airport, is well-connected to most U.S. and Canadian airline hubs. You can connect to Los Cabos, **La Paz (LAP),** and **Tijuana (TIJ)** from major destinations in Mexico as well. Traveling to the south, you'll find the best fares to Los Cabos. Those traveling to Tijuana and the north may find their best flight connections and prices are an hour north of the border in **San Diego (SAN),** served by most major U.S. airlines (to get from San Diego to Tijuana, see "Getting There: By Bus" and "Getting There: By Train & Trolley," below). To find out which airlines travel to Los Cabos and Baja, see "Airline Websites," p. 198; for connections through these major airports to smaller Baja airports, see "Getting Around: By Plane," p. 185.

ARRIVING AT THE AIRPORT

Before landing, you'll be asked to fill out a tourist card. You disembark the plane—often directly onto the tarmac—and enter the line for immigration. Present your passport and tourist card, and immigration officials will stamp your passport with a tourist visa and give you back half of your tourist card. Keep this slip of paper with you; you'll turn it in to your airline when you depart the country. You will then pass to baggage claim, pick up your luggage, and pass through customs. You'll be asked to put all your luggage through a scanner, and then to push a button. If it lights up green, you are free to pass through; if red, you may have your luggage searched. All in all, expect about 20 minutes from landing to leaving.

GETTING INTO TOWN FROM THE AIRPORT

Los Cabos and La Paz airports offer inexpensive shuttle services (p. 49 and 90, respectively); buy your tickets from booths inside the terminal as you exit. Otherwise, taxis at all airports meet arriving flights; most drivers speak English. In Los Cabos and Loreto, watch out for sneaky timeshare sales reps who may pretend to be taxi drivers! Taxis are clearly marked cars outside at the curb, not guys with clipboards waiting for you in the terminal; mix them up and you may find yourself on a timeshare tour.

By Car

Depending on where you're coming from, driving can be an economical way to get to Baja, and once you're there, it's a convenient way to travel the region. But driving the peninsula from north to south is a haul—27 hours for the 1,220km (758 miles) from Tijuana to Los Cabos—and, while travelers to Baja don't need to jump through the import hoops they would driving to other parts of Mexico, it's important to have your papers in order before you go (see "Mexican Auto Insurance [*Seguros de Auto*]" below). Rental cars in Mexico generally are clean and well maintained, although they are often smaller than rentals in the U.S., may have manual rather than automatic transmission, and can be comparatively expensive due to pricey mandatory insurance. Discounts are often available for rentals of a week or longer, especially when you make arrangements in advance online or from the United States. Be careful about estimated online rates, which usually fail to include the price of the mandatory insurance. (See "Getting Around: By Car," p. 182, for more details.)

To check on road conditions or to get help with any travel emergency while in Mexico, call © **800/482-9832** in the United States or 55/5089-7500 in Mexico City. English-speaking operators staff both numbers. The **Discover Baja Travel Club** is a long-standing favorite among Baja road warriors for insurance, travel tips, permits, and more (www.discoverbaja.com). If you're ready for a Baja road trip in your own car, read on.

BORDER CROSSINGS

Baja borders the United States along its entire northern border, with main crossings at Tijuana, Tecate, and Mexicali. Entering Mexico by car, you'll need to fill out the same FMM tourist card travelers by plane do, with the difference that if you're staying in Mexico longer than 8 days, you'll have to pay 262 pesos for yours at a bank at some point before you leave the country. (If you're staying in Mexico for fewer than 8 days, it's free).

Southbound, Tijuana is more convenient for further Baja travel, but northbound lines to reenter the U.S. by car are much longer—allow at least 2 hours from Tijuana, 1 hour from Mexicali, and expect to wait longer on weekends. A more laid-back option is the crossing at Tecate, 48km (30 miles) east of Tijuana, which locals say is a breeze. For wait times at the border, call the U.S. numbers © **619/690-8999** for Tijuana/San Ysidro, © **760/768-2383** for Mexicali/Calexico, © **619/938-8300** for Tecate, or check the U.S. Customs and Border Patrol's website at apps.cbp.gov/bwt for real-time updates.

CAR DOCUMENTS

As long as you stay in Baja, you don't need any special papers for your car other than Mexican auto insurance (see below). If your tour takes you into other states, even for the day, you'll need a **temporary car-importation permit,** available through some Mexican consulates in the U.S.; in CIITEV offices operated by Banco del Ejército (Banjercito) in the Mexican customs offices at land borders; or online at www.banjercito.com.mx, no more than 180 and no fewer than 7 days before you intend to cross the border to allow time to mail you the permit. The permit costs between $40 and $52, depending on where it's issued, and if you pay cash, you'll need to post a cash bond you get back when you check your car out. Another good reason to stay in Baja!

Important reminder: Someone else may drive, but the person (or relative of the person) whose name appears on the car-importation permit must *always* be in the car. (If stopped by police, a nonregistered family member driving without the registered

You can get point-to-point driving directions in English for anywhere in Mexico from the website of the Secretary of Communication and Transport. The site will also calculate tolls, distance, and travel time. Go to http://aplicaciones4.sct.gob.mx/sibuac_internet and click on "Rutas punto a punto" in the left-hand column. Then select the English version.

driver must be prepared to prove familial relationship to the registered driver—no joke.) Violation of this rule subjects the car to impoundment and the driver to imprisonment, a fine, or both. You can drive a car with foreign license plates only if you have a foreign (non-Mexican) driver's license.

MEXICAN AUTO INSURANCE (SEGUROS DE AUTO)

Personal liability auto insurance is legally required in Mexico. U.S. insurance is invalid; to be insured in Mexico, you must purchase Mexican insurance, and you must have proof of U.S. insurance to acquire it. Any party involved in an accident who has no insurance may be sent to jail and have his or her car impounded until all claims are settled. This is true even if you just drive across the border to spend the day. U.S. companies that broker Mexican insurance are commonly found at border crossings, and several quote daily rates.

Discover Baja Travel Club, 3264 Governor Dr., San Diego, CA 92122, is a friendly place to start (© 800/727-2252; www.discoverbaja.com). You can also buy car insurance through **Sanborn's Mexico Insurance** (© 800/222-0158; www.sanbornsinsurance.com). The company has offices at all U.S. border crossings. Its policies cost the same as the competition's do, but you get legal coverage (attorney and bail bonds if needed) and a detailed mile-by-mile guide for your proposed route. Most of Sanborn's border offices are open Monday through Friday, and a few are staffed on Saturday and Sunday. **AAA** auto club also sells insurance.

RETURNING TO THE UNITED STATES WITH YOUR CAR

If you have a temporary car import permit because you were traveling outside of Baja, you *must* return the car papers you obtained when you entered Mexico when you cross back with your car, or at some point within 180 days. (You can cross as many times as you wish within the 180 days.) If the documents aren't returned, heavy fines are imposed ($250 for each 15 days late), and your car may be impounded and confiscated or you may be jailed if you return to Mexico. You can only return the car documents to a Banjercito official on duty at the Mexican Customs building before you cross back into the United States. Again, if you were only traveling within Baja, this doesn't apply to you.

For information on car rentals and gasoline (petrol) in Los Cabos and Baja, see "Getting Around: By Car," below.

By Bus

Greyhound Bus Lines (© **800/231-2222** in the U.S.; www.greyhound.com) offers service nearly 24 hours daily for $13 one-way between San Diego and Tijuana via the San Ysidro border crossing, stopping at Tijuana's Rodriguez airport (TIJ) and ending up at Tijuana's Central de Autobuses, where you can connect to Mexican bus lines for destinations farther down Baja (see "Getting Around: By Bus," p. 185). **Mexicoach** (© 619/428-9517 in the U.S., or 664/685-1470) runs a similar service (hourly, 5am–10pm) between San Ysidro and Tijuana for $4 one-way/$6 round-trip, and for $13 one-way/$20 round-trip it will take you as far as Rosarito. Mexican discount airliner **Volaris** also runs a shuttle between San Diego's Santa Fe train station and Tijuana airport for passengers; cost is $15.

By Train & Trolley

Baja has no trains, but the blue line of San Diego's **Tijuana Trolley** (© 619/595-4949; www.sdmts.com) connects downtown San Diego with the San Ysidro/Tijuana border crossing daily from before 5am to after midnight. The fare is $2.50; the trip takes about an hour from San Diego's Old Town. From points in the U.S., ride **Amtrak** (© 800/USA-RAIL [872-7245]; www.amtrak.com) to San Diego and transfer to the Trolley at Old Town or Santa Fe stations, both downtown and a few minutes' taxi ride from San Diego's international airport. From Tijuana, walk through the border crossing; the Trolley stop is right outside as you exit.

By Boat

Cabo San Lucas is a popular port of call for West Coast cruise ships on their way to Puerto Vallarta and points south. Ships dock at the purpose-built cruise ship port on Bulevar Marina downtown, the staging ground for snorkel and boat tours and a stone's throw from Cabo's touristy downtown. Three-day cruises go from Long Beach, California, to Ensenada and dock a 20-minute walk or a $3 taxi ride from downtown's bars and shopping.

GETTING AROUND

By Car

If you're planning to stick to the town you fly to, it's possible to visit Los Cabos and Baja without a car. That said, driving is by far the best way to see the region, combining maximum flexibility and off-the-beaten path mobility with the road-trip spirit that's been a part of Baja traveling since the peninsula's highway was built. For information on traveling with your own car from the United States, see "Getting There: By Car," above.

NAVIGATING BAJA Finding your way up and down the peninsula is easy. For the most part, Baja has one highway: the Transpeninsular Highway, or Route 1, which connects almost all major destinations from top to bottom. In the south, Hwy. 19 connects Cabo San Lucas with the West Cape, Todos Santos and La Paz, while in the north, Hwy. 3 and Hwy. 5 are useful for getting around San Felipe, Tecate, and Ensenada. Speed limits range between 90kmph (55 mph) on wide, straight highways to 60kmph (37 mph) on more challenging roads. Road signs are helpful and up-to-date throughout the peninsula, making it easy—if you stay on the highways—not to get lost on the many dirt roads that snake through the desert.

Finding your way in Baja's cities and towns, however, is more of a challenge. Streets tend to be poorly marked, if at all, with tiny street signs intended for pedestrians, not drivers. Fortunately, most towns are laid out in a grid system, so if you miss your turn, you can take the next one and double back. Watch out for *topes,* irregular speed bumps, and their treacherous opposites, *vados,* narrow ditches across the road, meant to encourage drivers to slow, giving them a jolt if they don't. Both can be difficult to see at night; look for painted stripes, signs announcing TOPE or VADO, and sometimes piles of stones on the sides of the road.

While roads throughout the peninsula are steadily improving, most are still not as wide, smooth, or well maintained as their counterparts in the rest of North America. Dirt or gravel roads are common, and potholes after an infrequent rain can take awhile to repair. Drive with caution on twisty mountain roads, and avoid driving on country roads or highways at night—poor lighting, unmarked hazards and road damage, and surprise visits of wildlife and pedestrians make nighttime driving one of Baja's few real dangers.

Mexican driving customs have developed in response to Mexican roads, as when a truck driver flips on his left turn signal when there's not a crossroad for miles. He's probably telling you the road's clear ahead for you to pass—give him a wave to say thanks. Flashing hazard lights on oncoming vehicles or the cars in front of you means there's something going on up ahead (animals in or near the road, a car accident, a slow-moving vehicle, and so forth) and to proceed with caution. Most important of all is local practice for left turns. If you stop in the middle of a highway with your left signal on, there's a real chance you'll get mowed down by traffic behind you. Instead, pull onto the right shoulder, wait for traffic to clear, and then proceed across the road.

If you do much driving in Baja, you'll probably run into a military checkpoint or two. Although the stern uniformed teenagers with M-16s may look threatening, there's nothing to fear: Checkpoints are standard procedure in Mexico, so smile, let the soldiers inspect your car for drugs or agricultural products if requested, and then be on your merry way.

BUYING GAS   It's easy to find a gas station in Mexico; there's just one company, national oil company PEMEX, whose green signs dot highways and roads up and down Baja. Gas is slightly cheaper than in the U.S. and Canada; at time of research, the going rate was about 10 pesos per liter for Magna, or regular, gas—roughly $3.75 a gallon. Prices are posted in pesos per liter, and include tax. Many gas stations accept cash only.

CAR RENTALS   Major international car-rental agencies are well represented in Los Cabos and Baja, as well as some worthy local companies, providing mostly the same new, clean, car models for rent—the deciding factor will probably be price, and if you shop around and book ahead, you can get deals for as low as US$100 a week before taxes.

Insurance   It's important to note that in Mexico, drivers are required to carry **personal liability insurance** (PLI), covering any damage in an accident to other persons or property, which is not covered by your home-country car insurance policy. Online bookings, even those promising guaranteed all-inclusive pricing, generally do not include or even offer this insurance, which can lead to an unpleasant surprise when you're slapped with a standard $14/day mandatory charge at the rental counter. And car rental phone representatives in your home country are often not well informed about it. At time of research, the only major rental company in Los Cabos and Baja including PLI in its standard pricing was Hertz.

Non-mandatory insurance is offered in two parts: **Collision and damage** insurance covers your car and others if the accident is your fault, and **personal accident** insurance covers you and anyone in your car. Read the fine print on the back of your rental agreement and note that insurance may be invalid if you have an accident while driving on an unpaved road. Be sure you understand your deductible; some are as high as $3,000, which comes out of your pocket immediately in case of damage. Finally, speak with your credit card company before you leave home. Many credit cards already include car rental collision and damage insurance as a membership benefit, but won't cover you if you purchase insurance from the rental company as well.

Damage   Inspect your car carefully and note every damaged or missing item, no matter how minute, on your rental agreement, or you may be charged. And if you'll be driving in cities, watch out for screw-in radio antennae, which are easy for a vandal to take off the car and expensive to replace.

BREAKDOWNS   If your car breaks down on the road, help might already be on the way. Radio-equipped green repair trucks operated by uniformed English-speaking officers patrol major highways from 8am to 6pm, 365 days a year. These **Green Angels** (© 078) perform minor repairs and adjustments free, but you pay for parts and materials.

Your best guide to repair shops in Baja is a friend who knows. However, the Yellow Pages can work in a pinch. For repairs, look under "Automóviles y Camiones: Talleres de Reparación y Servicio"; auto-parts stores are under "Refacciones y Accesorios para Automóviles." To find a mechanic on the road, ask a local (because Baja is so rough on cars, most locals know a mechanic) or look for a sign that says TALLER MECANICO.

Places called *vulcanizadora* or *llantera* repair flat tires, and it is common to find them open 24 hours a day on the most traveled highways.

MINOR ACCIDENTS   When possible, many Mexicans drive away from minor accidents or try to make an immediate settlement, to avoid involving the police. If the police arrive while the involved persons are still at the scene, everyone may be locked in jail until blame is assessed—this is why you need proof of liability insurance! In any case, you have to settle up immediately, which may take days. Foreigners without fluent Spanish are at a distinct disadvantage. If you're involved in an accident, don't panic. If you're driving your own car, notify your Mexican insurance company, whose job it is to intervene on your behalf. If you're driving a rental, notify the rental company immediately and follow their instructions. When the police arrive, show them your proof of liability insurance. Finally, if all else fails, ask to contact the nearest Green Angel, who may be able to explain your case to officials.

TAXIS   For those who prefer not to drive, taxis are a convenient and economical way to get around in almost all of Baja's resort areas. (The exception to this is Los Cabos, where distances are long and taxis are very expensive: the 35-min. one-way trip between Cabo San Lucas and San José del Cabo, for example, averages $50.) But otherwise, short trips within towns are inexpensive compared to the U.S. Fixed rates between set destinations are usually set by the local taxi union; drivers will often have a written table of prices they can show you. For longer trips or excursions to nearby cities, taxis can generally be hired for around $15 to $20 per hour, or for a negotiated daily rate, although you may find a tour operator offering the same price, but including a guide, water, and snacks. If you're traveling from point to point, a negotiated one-way price may be cheaper than a rental car, and much faster than the bus. Many taxi drivers speak English, especially in Los Cabos and Northern Baja, but your hotel can help arrange a taxi if you prefer.

By Bus

Bus service is not as well developed in the Baja peninsula as in other parts of the country, although it is available between principal points. Travel class is generally labeled *segunda* (second), *primera* (first), and *ejecutiva* (deluxe). **Autotransportes de Baja California** (© 800/025-0222; www.transportes-abc.com) and the affiliated **Autotransportes Aguila** (© 800/824-8452; www.autotransportesaguila.net) have routes between most cities. The deluxe buses usually have fewer seats than regular buses, show movies en route, are air-conditioned, have bathrooms, and make few stops; some have complimentary refreshments. Many run express from origin to the final destination. They are well worth the few dollars more that you'll pay.

By Plane

It's a long drive from north to south, and reluctant road warriors may find the easiest way to travel the length of the peninsula is by plane. Mexican discount carrier **Volaris** (© 866/988-3527 in the U.S., or 01-800/122-8000; www.volaris.com.mx) flies daily between Los Cabos or La Paz and Tijuana. Turboprop carrier **Aereo Calafia** (© 01-800/560-3949; www.aereocalafia.com.mx) flies between Cabo San Lucas (CSL)—not Los Cabos International, but the small general aviation airport outside of Cabo—up the peninsula to Loreto, La Paz, and the small airports of Santa Rosalía, Ciudad Constitución, and Guerrero Negro on an ever-changing schedule. The similar **Aereo Servicios Guerrero** (© 01-800/823-3153; www.aereoserviciosguerrero. com.mx) connects Guerrero Negro and Ensenada.

TIPS ON ACCOMMODATIONS

From resorts to ranchos, mansions to pensions, Los Cabos and Baja have it all—but they don't come cheap. Average accommodations prices here are at least 50% higher than in comparable properties and destinations on the Mexican mainland, and in some cases, much more. If you're looking for a luxury getaway, look no further: Los Cabos's top resorts, for example, are consistently ranked the very best in Mexico and Latin America. Budget travelers, however, will have to do some creative planning. (We've made an effort to include budget properties in the destination chapters as well.) As a general rule, accommodations in Los Cabos are the most expensive in Baja, and prices fall as you move up the peninsula and away from major tourist routes. Note that prices here are usually listed in U.S. dollars, and despite Mexican law to the contrary, often do not include 11% VAT and 3% hotel tax; some hotels also tack on a mandatory daily service charge.

Hotel Cost Category System, in U.S. Dollars

STANDARD DOUBLE PRICE PER NIGHT BEFORE TAX	
Very Expensive	$300 and up
Expensive	$150–$300
Moderate	$80–$150
Inexpensive	below $80

One way to keep your costs down is to consider traveling out of season. In Los Cabos and Baja, this isn't as limiting as it sounds: most hotels list high-season prices only for Christmas and New Year's holidays, and drop to mid-season prices for the rest of the winter and spring. Summer stays are discounted up to 50%, and carry the advantage of swimmable warm water in Baja's two seas. And with the ongoing Mexican tourism crisis, driven by bad press and the economic downturn, there are deals to be had. Keep an eye out for air-hotel package deals, and don't be shy about asking hotel reservations reps if they can offer a discount—many small properties will. Also pay attention to whether breakfast is included in your rate; a la carte breakfast in swish Baja resorts can add $10 to $30 per person per day to your bill, and on resort properties, there's often no alternative.

Vacation rental properties and home swaps are available in nearly every destination. These offer the advantage of space, privacy, and the opportunity to cook your own meals, at a wide range of prices. Local real-estate agencies offer extensive listings; start with **Cabo Property Management** (www.cabopropertymanagement.net) for Los Cabos, **Wolf Property Management** (www.wolf-pm-rentals.com) for Los Barriles and East Cape, **Baraka En Todos** (www.barakaentodos.com) for Todos Santos and the Pacific Side, **Rentals Loreto** (www.rentalsloreto.com) in Loreto, **My San Felipe Vacation** (www.mysanfelipevacation.com) for San Felipe, and **Ensenada Real Estate** (www.ensenadarealestate.com) for Ensenada. **Vacation Rentals By Owner** (www.vrbo.com) and **Home Away** (www.homeaway.com) are excellent international portals for vacation rentals that cut out the middleman. Many rental properties also list directly on their own Web pages and can be found on your friendly local search engine. And with a vacation house swap, of course, there's no rental at all; find out how to trade your home for one in Baja at **www.homeexchange.com**.

Since the early days of road-tripping surfers, Baja travelers have enjoyed sleeping under the stars. Although we don't cover each **campground** in this book, you'll find a campground of some kind in most every Baja coastal town, and where you don't, you'll find plenty of free spirits parking their RVs on remote beaches all winter long. The exception is the northern Pacific beaches between Ensenada and the U.S. border, where crimes targeting campers in recent years have made this a spot where you're better off with a roof over your head. Although many campgrounds cater mostly to RVs, most will show you a spot to pitch a tent for under $10. Campers without their own gear can rough it for a night or two with a hiking, kayaking, or whale-watching tour or go "glamping" at one of the Sea of Cortez's luxury camps. Be aware that Baja's desert nights are chilly, and firewood is hard to come by.

[FastFACTS] LOS CABOS & BAJA

Area Codes Tijuana, 664; Rosarito Beach, 661; Ensenada, 646; Mulegé and Santa Rosalía, 615; Loreto, 613; La Paz, Todos Santos, and West Cape, 612; Los Cabos and East Cape, 624.

Business Hours In general, businesses in larger cities are open between 9am and 7pm; in smaller towns many close between 2 and 4pm. Most close on Sunday. In resort areas it is common to find stores open at least in the mornings on Sunday, and for shops to stay open late, often until 8pm or even 10pm. Bank hours are Monday through Friday from 9 or 9:30am to anywhere between 3 and 7pm. Increasingly, banks open on Saturday for at least a half-day.

Car Rental See "Getting There: By Car," earlier in this chapter.

Cellphones See "Mobile Phones," later in this section.

Crime See "Safety," later in this section.

Customs   Gone are the bad old days of shady inspections and bribes; nowadays, *la Aduana* (Mexican Customs, www.aduanas.sat.gob.mx and click on "English" in the upper right corner) moves like clockwork. When you arrive by air, you'll be asked to put your bags through a scanner and press a button—red means you'll be inspected, green means you're good to go. When you arrive by car, you'll be randomly assigned a green or red light. Be aware that while there are few restrictions on what travelers can bring with them into the country, you're only allowed two cameras and one computer per traveler—any more and you'll have to pay value-added-tax.

Disabled Travelers   Mexico may seem like one giant obstacle course to travelers in wheelchairs or on crutches—and Baja California is no exception. Where curb cuts can be found, they are most often not up to standards, and cities like Loreto and San José del Cabo have difficult-to-navigate cobblestone streets. That being said, most high-end hotels have accessible rooms, including Las Ventanas al Paraíso (p. 63), Guaycura (p. 106), and the Rosarito Beach Hotel (p. 159).

Disabled travelers can opt for a fishing excursion with **Los Cabos Adventures** (© 624/141-0790; www.bajaenterprises.com), a sportfishing tour operator that offers a wheelchair-accessible sportfishing yacht. Owner Larry Cooper, a wheelchair user himself, designed his sportfishing boat to be wheelchair accessible; he even offers free fishing tours to disabled kids and American veterans. Cooper also owns the **Villa Tranquillo** (© 624/141-0790; www.bajaenterprises.com/stay) in Los Barriles, a wheelchair-accessible villa; rates are $200 to $300 per night for accessible suites and casitas, with a 3-night minimum. He also rents out wheelchair-accessible vans and ATVs. In addition, most of the streets in the community of Los Barriles are well paved, allowing travelers the freedom to explore.

For ground transportation in Los Cabos, **Transcabo** (© 624/163-7373; www.transcabo.com) offers wheelchair-accessible vans. They can arrange for transportation to and from the airport and around the region. In Northern Baja **Mexicoach** (© 664/685-1470; www.mexicoach.com), offers first-class wheelchair-accessible buses and shuttles that take passengers from San Ysidro into Tijuana and Rosarito.

At the region's airports, you may encounter steep stairs before finding a well-hidden elevator or escalator—if one exists—and wheelchair ramps sometimes look more like alpine ski runs. Airlines will often arrange wheelchair assistance to the baggage area. Porters are generally available to help with luggage at airports and large bus stations, once you've cleared baggage claim.

The airports in Baja are relatively small compared to those in larger cities and none involve traveling through labyrinthine hallways. It's common in Baja to board from a remote position, meaning you either descend stairs to a bus that ferries you to the plane, which you board by climbing stairs, or you walk across the tarmac to your plane and ascend the stairs. Deplaning presents the same problem in reverse.

Doctors   Any English-speaking consulate staff in Mexico can provide a list of area doctors who speak English. If you get sick in Mexico, consider asking your hotel concierge to recommend a local doctor—even his or her own. You can also try the emergency room at a local hospital or urgent care facility. Many hospitals also have walk-in clinics for emergency cases that are not life threatening; you may not get immediate attention, but you won't pay emergency room prices.

Most resorts have a doctor on staff, and **Amerimed** (**www.amerimed.com.mx**), runs 24-hour, American–standards clinics with bilingual physicians and emergency air-evacuation services in San José del Cabo (© **624/105-8550**), Cabo San Lucas (© **624/105-8500**), and Los Barriles (© **624/141-0797**); it also accepts major credit cards.

You may have to pay all medical costs upfront and be reimbursed later. Before leaving home, find out what medical services your health insurance covers. To protect yourself, consider buying medical travel insurance.

We list Mexico's primary **emergency number** on p. 188.

Drinking & Drug Laws   The legal age for purchase and consumption of alcoholic beverages is 18. Do not carry open containers of alcohol in your car or any public area that isn't zoned for alcohol consumption. The police can and will fine you on the spot.

In the shadow of a raging drug war, in 2009 Mexico decriminalized possession of small amounts of drugs including marijuana and cocaine. However, buying, selling, importing and exporting drugs remains illegal, and violators face stiff fines and imprisonment in a tangled and backlogged legal system that presumes guilt before innocence.

Driving Rules   As at home, Mexican law requires you to wear a seat belt and not use your cellphone while driving. Driving under the influence of drugs or alcohol is both unwise and illegal. See "Getting Around: By Car," earlier in this chapter.

Electricity   Like the U.S. and Canada, Mexico uses 110–120 volts AC (60 cycles), compared to 220–240 volts AC (50 cycles) in most of Europe, Australia, and New Zealand. Wall outlets are exactly the same as in the United States and Canada.

Embassies & Consulates   They can give you the name of a doctor, tell you how to get married in Mexico, and replace your passport, but sadly, your embassy will not get you out of a Mexican jail or fly you home when you run out of money. Most countries have an embassy in Mexico City, and many have consular offices or representatives in Los Cabos or Tijuana.

The Embassy of the **United States** in Mexico City is at Paseo de la Reforma 305, Col. Polanco, next to the Sheraton at the corner of Río Danubio (📞 **55/5080-2000**); hours are Monday through Friday from 8:30am to 5:30pm. Visit www.usembassy-mexico.gov for information related to U.S. Embassy services. In Baja, there is a U.S. Consulate in Tijuana (Av. Tapachula 96; 📞 **664/622-7400;** http://tijuana.usconsulate.gov) and a consular agency in Cabo San Lucas (Bl. Marina C-4 in Plaza Nautica; 📞 **624/143-3566**).

The Embassy of **Australia** in Mexico City is at Rubén Darío 55, Col. Polanco (📞 **55/ 1101-2200;** www.mexico.embassy.gov.au). It's open Monday through Thursday from 9:30am to 1pm.

The Embassy of **Canada** in Mexico City is at Schiller 529, Col. Polanco (📞 **55/5724-7900,** or for emergencies 01-800/706-2900); it's open Monday through Friday from 9am to 1pm and 2 to 5pm. In Baja, there is a Canadian consulate in Tijuana (German Gedovius 10411-101; 📞 **664/684-0461**) and a consular agency in San José del Cabo (Plaza José Green, Bl. Mijares; 📞 **624/142-4333**).

The Embassy of **New Zealand** in Mexico City is at Jaime Balmes 8, 4th Floor, Col. Los Morales, Polanco (📞 **55/5283-9460;** www.nzembassy.com/mexico). It's open Monday through Thursday from 8:30am to 2pm and 3 to 5:30pm, and Friday from 8:30am to 2pm.

The Embassy of the **United Kingdom** in Mexico City is at Río Lerma 71, Col. Cuauhtémoc (📞 **55/5207-2089** or 5242-8500; http://ukinmexico.fco.gov.uk). It's open Monday through Thursday from 8am to 4pm and Friday from 8am to 1:30pm. There's a British Honorary Consulate in Tijuana (Bl. Salinas 1800, Fracc. Aviación; 📞 **664/686-5320**) and Cabo San Lucas (Bl. Paseo de la Marina Lote 7a; 📞 **624/173-9500**).

The Embassy of **Ireland** in Mexico City is at Cda. Bl. Manuel Avila Camacho 76, 3rd Floor, Col. Lomas de Chapultepec (📞 **55/5520-5803;** http://irishembassy.com.mx). It's open Monday through Friday from 9am to 5pm.

Emergencies   In case of emergency, dial 📞 **066** from any phone within Mexico; for medical emergencies 📞 **065** works as well. For local police emergency numbers, turn to the "Fast Facts" sections in each of the individual chapters. You should also contact the closest consular office in case of an emergency. If you break down on the highway, call the Green Angels at ✆ **078** for free English-language repairs and towing.

Family Travel   Mexicans love children, and Baja Sur is a great place to introduce children to the exciting adventure of exploring a different culture. For kids about 8 and up, there's lots to do, from learning new sports to exploring nature. Visiting mother and baby whales in Pacific lagoons, in particular, is a must for families. However, finding restaurant food that kids will eat can be a challenge, and many hotels and guesthouses in the peninsula, especially those with swimming pools, don't accept children younger than 12 or 13. We've made an effort here to list hotels that are kid-friendly; those that are will sometimes offer kids' clubs, special daytime activity programs, or private babysitters, especially in Los Cabos's moderate to expensive resorts.

Before leaving, ask your doctor for advice on medications to take along. Disposable diapers cost about the same in Mexico as in the rest of North America, but are of poorer quality. You can get Huggies and Pampers identical to the ones sold in the United States, but at a higher price. Many stores sell Gerber's baby foods. Dry cereals, powdered formulas, baby bottles, and purified water are all easily available in midsize and large cities or resorts.

Rollaway beds are often available for children staying in the room with parents. (Cribs, however, may present a problem—only the largest and most luxurious hotels provide them.) Child seats or highchairs at restaurants are common, and most restaurants will go out of their way to accommodate your child.

Because many travelers to Baja will rent a car, it is advisable to bring your car seat. Leasing agencies in Mexico do not rent car seats.

Every country's regulations differ, but in general children traveling abroad should have plenty of documentation on hand, particularly if they're traveling with someone other than their own parents (in which case a notarized form letter from a parent is often required). For details on entry requirements for children traveling abroad, contact your embassy in Mexico (p. 188).

To locate accommodations, restaurants, and attractions that are particularly kid-friendly, refer to the "Kids" icon throughout this guide.

Gasoline   See "Getting There: By Car," earlier in this chapter.

Health   Baja has come a long way toward eliminating the water and food contamination that causes traveler's diarrhea and more serious ailments like typhoid and salmonella. The digestive troubles plaguing travelers in mainland Mexico are virtually unheard of here. You can ensure your good health by washing your hands frequently, drinking only purified water, and steering clear of mobile food vendors, whose offerings may not have been prepared in sanitary conditions and in any case can suffer in the heat. Avoid salads and raw vegetables you haven't washed yourself; if you buy produce in a grocery store, soak it for a half-hour in a solution 1 liter water to ten drops microdyne (available at most grocers) before eating it. And when it comes to ceviche, follow your gut.

Should you be unlucky, you can stop the diarrhea with Imodium and rehydrate with Gatorade, Pedialyte, or a solution of salt, sugar, and purified water. If you have a fever or if illness persists more than a day, see a doctor.

Prescription medicine is broadly available at Mexican pharmacies. In Tijuana you may need a doctor's prescription for things sold over-the-counter farther south.

Dietary Choices   Baja can be a challenge for vegans, vegetarians, or anyone who observes any kind of strict dietary regimen. Although it's possible to find vegetarian options on restaurant menus, it's not always guaranteed; the beans on your plate of scrambled eggs probably contain pork. For a list of vegetarian restaurants in Los Cabos, see "Going Green in Los Cabos," p. 59.

Mexican pharmacies carry a limited selection of common over-the-counter cold, sinus, and allergy remedies, similar to what you'll find at home but often with different names. A pharmacist at a major pharmacy can usually look up the U.S. or Canadian drug name and find a Mexican equivalent. Be aware that while many drugs for which you'd need a prescription in the U.S. are sold over-the-counter in Mexico, as of 2011 you'll need a prescription for antibiotics. But they're still much less expensive than at home.

Mexico has no official certification body for organic foods sold inside the country, but many fruit and vegetable growers in Northern and Southern Baja use organic methods and sell their produce as such. (Mid-Baja has little in the way of agriculture at all.) Ask around at farmers' markets for more sources. You can pretty much forget about finding organically raised free-range meat or eggs, but some restaurants source from local farmers who purport to use more natural methods to raise animals.

Also, of note, salsas generally pack more heat in Mexico than in the U.S., so if you're sensitive to chiles, take it slow on your first taste.

Bites & Stings   Mosquitoes and gnats are thankfully less common in Baja than in more humid parts of Mexico, but it can still get buggy on some parts of the coast. If you're prone to bites, bring along a repellent that contains the active ingredient DEET, or ask at a pharmacy for *repelente contra insectos.* In the U.S. and Mexico you'll also find non-chemical, citronella-based formulas that work just as well, but need more frequent application. If all else fails, antihistamine cream will control itching.

Baja's desert areas are full of **scorpions** *(alacránes),* and although very few are deadly you'll want to watch out for them. Shake out clothes, towels, sheets, and shoes before using them, and if you are stung, go immediately to a doctor. If you're planning to camp in remote areas, it's not a bad idea to bring along a scorpion toxin antidote, available at drugstores for about $25.

Watch out for **rattlesnakes** while hiking; they'll only bite as a last resort and will warn you beforehand! Should the unthinkable happen, do not cut open the wound or try to suck out venom. Keep the victim still and calm, elevate the affected area, and get to a doctor right away.

The most common name for the tiny **jellyfish** stings you may feel while swimming is *agua mala* (bad water). While irritating, these stings are far less painful than those from Portuguese man-of-war, common enough in summer that some people swim with a Lycra skin for protection. If you do get stung, don't rub the wound. Most boat captains have vinegar on hand to pour over the affected area and ease the pain.

You're unlikely to encounter **stingrays** in the shallows of Baja's beaches. But you're even less likely if you shuffle your feet in the sand as you go into the water, warning away any who may be dozing in the sand. If you are stung, get medical help as soon as possible; very hot water or, in a pinch, heating the wound on hot rocks or sand is said to ease the pain.

Sun Exposure   The injury you're most likely to suffer in Baja is sunburn. It's easy to prevent: wear sunscreen, a hat, and long sleeves, and stay out of the sun at midday. Remember that you get more sun on boats than you do on the beach.

Insurance   For information on traveler's insurance, trip cancellation insurance, and medical insurance while traveling, visit www.frommers.com/planning.

Internet & Wi-Fi Internet access, usually Wi-Fi, is widely available in Los Cabos and Baja, offered by nearly all hotels and many restaurants and cafes for free. It's usually offered through national telephone provider Telmex—you'll see signs with the logo "infinitum"—and is generally of a speed and bandwidth comparable to the United States. Some U.S. mobile Internet customers can roam for free on Telmex networks; check with your provider for details. If not, you can buy daily access by following instructions as you would in the U.S.

Language As is the rest of Mexico, Los Cabos and Baja are Spanish-speaking. However, English is widely spoken by people who work in the tourism industry and nearly everyone in Los Cabos and Tijuana.

Legal Aid If you behave yourself, the most legal trouble you're likely to get into is a flashing light in the rearview mirror. Pull over as you would at home, hand over your license, and pay your fine at the police station. Police officers may hint at making a deal, but keep in mind that bribing public officials, no matter how willing, is a crime. **Sanborn's Car Insurance** (see "Getting There: By Car," p. 180) includes legal help if you're involved in an auto accident; for rental cars, contact your rental company.

The Mexican legal system is a mess, to put it mildly, and if you get into serious trouble, you'll need a lawyer. Contact your consulate for a list of local ones.

LGBT Travelers Mexico is a largely conservative country, with deeply rooted Catholic religious traditions that are prevalent in many communities. Public displays of same-sex affection are rare and still considered shocking for men, especially outside of urban or resort areas; however, gay and lesbian travelers are generally treated with respect and should not experience any harassment, assuming they pay the appropriate regard to local culture and customs. Los Cabos and La Paz are both very gay-friendly resort destinations, with a few gay bars each, although for serious clubbing you'll have to go to Tijuana. **Purple Roofs** (www.purpleroofs.com) lists many gay-friendly and gay-owned hotel and rental properties in Los Cabos and Baja. **Alyson Adventures** (© **800/825-9766;** www.alysonadventures.com) offers gay and lesbian adventure-travel tours, including a Baja-specific kayaking tour from La Paz to Loreto.

Mail Mexican postal service is reliable, if sometimes a bit slow. Postcards and letters cost 11.50 pesos to the U.S. and Canada, 13.50 pesos to the U.K., and 15 pesos to Australia and New Zealand. Post offices have an unmistakable shocking pink-and-green logo over the storefront, and post boxes are bulky and red, with slots for local and foreign mail. Send packages registered mail for a small surcharge; the tracking number is added security the package will arrive. For valuables or anything urgent, use an international shipping service like **FedEx** (© **800/900-1100**) or **DHL** (© **55/5345-7000**).

Mobile Phones Mobile service in Los Cabos and Baja is spotty; there's essentially one provider, Mexican Telcel, and little coverage outside of towns and resort areas, which means if you break down on the highway, you may not be able to make calls. (Mexico's other provider, Movistar, has limited coverage.) Telcel uses 1900 Mhz GSM and 800 Mhz for 3G. Because Mexico has recently imposed heavy restrictions on pay-as-you-go mobile SIM cards, buying a throwaway phone number to use here is no longer an option. At present, there's no one renting cellphones in Baja, so that leaves your home mobile phone. T-Mobile, AT&T, and Vodafone have roaming agreements with Telcel, and so their coverage is best; you may be able to use your Verizon phone in resort areas. Check for coverage from other carriers at www.telcel.com. Make sure to activate your international service before you leave home.

If you're going to be traveling in remote areas or spending nights on the water and need to keep in touch, you may want to consider bringing a satellite phone. You can rent them before your trip from **Telestial** (© **213/337-5560** in the U.S.; www.telestial.com).

Money & Costs   Los Cabos and Baja are expensive in comparison to mainland Mexico, but still relatively cheap compared to the rest of North America. The farther away from Los Cabos you go, the lower the prices; a meal that might cost you 400 pesos in Cabo might cost you 350 in La Paz and 300 in Loreto. So-called "gringo" establishments—owned by, run by, or catering to Americans and Canadians—are fairly uniform in their (dollar-denominated) prices up and down the peninsula, while so-called "local" places are not only cheaper, but more dependent on location and thus what their markets can bear.

The currency in Mexico is the **peso.** Paper currency comes in denominations of 20, 50, 100, 200, and 500 pesos, color-coded to make it easy to tell one from the other; for most bills, a slightly different old and new design are still in circulation, but the colors remain the same. Coins come in denominations of 1, 2, 5, and 10 pesos, two-tone coins of different sizes, and 20 and 50 **centavos** (100 centavos = 1 peso) which are either gold-colored and ridged or silver-colored, tiny, and very light. (It's not uncommon for Mexicans to round nearly worthless centavos up or down when charging you or giving you change). The current exchange rate for the U.S. dollar, and the one used in this book, is 12 pesos; at that rate, an item that costs 12 pesos would be equivalent to $1.

Although many businesses in Los Cabos and Baja will accept U.S. dollars—indeed, many list their prices in dollars—in most cases, you're better off using pesos. You'll pay less, because in Baja, dollar prices are usually calculated at 10 pesos to the dollar despite a currently higher exchange rate. In just one example, a $6 Los Cabos taxi ride paid in pesos was 60 pesos, or $5. And it's a sign of respect to Mexicans and their country to use their local currency, just as it is to speak whatever Spanish you can muster. It's easy to withdraw pesos at widely available ATMs for a small fee, or buy them at your home bank for the going rate. If you must use U.S. dollars, make sure to have bills smaller than a $20 that are clean and not overly worn—it is up to the discretion of local businesses whether to accept your foreign bills or not! You can also change non-Mexican currency at a *casa de cambio;* however, the exchange rate you'll find at an ATM is generally more favorable. Most machines offer Spanish/English menus and dispense pesos, but some offer the option of withdrawing dollars. **Note:** Most ATMs in Mexico accept four-digit PINs only, so if you have a five- or six-digit number, check with your bank to see if you can get a temporary four-digit number for your trip.

Note: Establishments that quote their prices primarily in U.S. dollars are listed in this guide with U.S. dollars. Prices in this book are listed in the currency advertised by the establishment.

Visa and MasterCard **credit and debit cards** are widely accepted by higher-end Baja hotels and restaurants, supermarkets, retail stores, and tour operators; American Express and other cards are not. At smaller hotels, restaurants, and retailers, expect to pay cash.

THE VALUE OF MEXICAN PESOS VS. OTHER POPULAR CURRENCIES

MXN	A$	C$	€	NZ$	£	US$
1.00	0.08	0.08	0.06	0.11	0.05	0.08

Frommer's lists exact prices in the local currency. The currency conversions quoted above were correct at press time. However, rates fluctuate, so before departing consult a currency exchange website such as www.oanda.com/currency/converter to check up-to-the-minute rates. For help with currency conversions, tip calculations, and more, download Frommer's convenient Travel Tools app for your mobile device. Go to www.frommers.com/go/mobile and click on the Travel Tools icon.

Taxi from the airport to downtown Cabo San Lucas	700.00
Double room, moderate	1,000.00–1,800.00
Double room, inexpensive	600.00–800.00
Three-course dinner for one without wine, moderate	280.00
Bottle of beer	30.00–45.00
Cup of coffee	15.00–25.00
1 liter of premium gas	9.87
Half-day boat tour	300.00–500.00
Admission to most national parks	30.00–50.00

Beware of hidden credit card fees while traveling. Check with your credit or debit card issuer to see what fees, if any, will be charged for overseas transactions. Recent reform legislation in the U.S., for example, has curbed some exploitative lending practices. But many banks have responded by increasing fees in other areas, including fees for customers who use credit and debit cards while out of the country—even if those charges were made in U.S. dollars. Fees can amount to 3% or more of the purchase price. Check with your bank before departing to avoid any surprise charges on your statement. Also be aware that even if prices are listed in dollars, your credit card will often be charged in pesos, which your bank will then convert back to your home currency, almost certainly at a higher cost than the dollar price you thought you were paying. **Traveler's checks** are not widely accepted in Los Cabos and Baja, and with rare exceptions, **personal checks** on a foreign bank account won't be accepted at all.

Newspapers & Magazines   In Los Cabos, a number of local English-language papers are available at newsstands and cafes in places tourists frequent, including the monthly *Los Cabos Magazine* (www.loscabosguide.com), *Los Cabos News, Destino Los Cabos,* and the irreverent, entertaining biweekly *Gringo Gazette* (www.gringogazette. com) for Southern Baja. In Northern Baja, try the northern edition *Gringo Gazette North* (www.gringogazettenorth.com) and the venerable biweekly *Baja Times* (www.bajatimes. com). *El Calendario* (elcalendariodetodossantos.com) is a good monthly source for local events in Todos Santos, and the biweekly *Baja Citizen* (www.bajacitizen.com) covers local news and politics in La Paz. Los Cabos luxury resorts also frequently offer the *New York Times* to guests, either in a complete edition or a digest.

Packing   Baja looks like a tropical paradise, but there's more variation in the climate than many people imagine. You'll do well to pack a light jacket or sweater for evenings, especially in the winter, and a windproof jacket and long pants for boat trips. Dress is casual everywhere with the exception of Los Cabos's very finest restaurants, and even there you'll fit right in with stylish resort wear. Men will almost never need a tie. Hikers should make sure to have good sturdy boots to protect against rocks and reptiles, and indeed anyone who ventures into the inland deserts should plan on wearing long pants and sleeves to protect against sun and cacti.

For more helpful information on packing for your trip, download our convenient Travel Tools app for your mobile device. Go to www.frommers.com/go/mobile and click on the Travel Tools icon.

Passports All visitors to Mexico need a valid passport, upon presentation of which entering the country you'll be granted a tourist visa valid 180 days. To obtain a passport, contact one of the following passport offices:

- **Australia** Australian Passport Information Service (☏ **131-232;** www.passports. gov.au).
- **Canada** **Passport Office,** Department of Foreign Affairs and International Trade, Ottawa, ON K1A 0G3 (☏ **800/567-6868;** www.ppt.gc.ca).
- **Ireland** **Passport Office,** Setanta Centre, Molesworth Street, Dublin 2 (☏ **01/671-1633;** www.foreignaffairs.gov.ie).
- **New Zealand** **Passports Office,** Department of Internal Affairs, 47 Boulcott St., Wellington, 6011 (☏ **0800/225-050** in New Zealand or 04/474-8100; www.passports.govt.nz).
- **United Kingdom** Visit your nearest passport office, major post office, or travel agency or contact the **Identity and Passport Service (IPS),** 89 Eccleston Sq., London, SW1V 1PN (☏ **0300/222-0000;** www.ips.gov.uk).
- **United States** To find your regional passport office, check the U.S. State Department website (travel.state.gov/passport) or call the **National Passport Information Center** (☏ **877/487-2778**) for automated information.

Petrol Please see "Getting Around: By Car," earlier in this chapter.

Police In case of emergency, dial ☏ **066** from any phone within Mexico. To report a non-emergency crime, dial ☏ **089,** or from the U.S. and Canada, ☏ **866/201-5060** for English-speaking operators who can coordinate help. For local police emergency numbers, turn to "Fast Facts" in the individual chapters.

Safety If ever a country had an image problem, it's Mexico. From the drug war along the northern border to the 2009 flu scare to the nicknaming of its capital city "The Monster," a potential visitor could be forgiven for thinking twice. It's not all sensationalism; the war against and, more pertinently, between Mexico's powerful drug cartels has killed more than 30,000 people since 2006, and the violence continues.

The good news is, you won't encounter anything remotely resembling a drug war in Los Cabos and Baja. Southern Baja has one of Mexico's lowest crime rates; U.S. and Canadian expatriates living in places like Loreto and La Paz even leave their doors unlocked. The only exception to this happy rule is Tijuana, which as the world's busiest border crossing, the principal point of transit between Mexico and the U.S., and Mexico's fifth-largest city remains a juicy prize for the bad guys. While the murder rate in TJ remains high (as high as Detroit, although lower than New Orleans), the numbers don't reflect the victims—nearly all of whom are Mexicans, and most of whom appear to be connected to the drug war. But even in Tijuana, tourists are very rarely victims of violent crime; no tourists have ever been killed in the drug war in Baja. The U.S. State Department (travel.state.gov) issued a Travel Warning in April 2011 that begins with the following paragraph:

"Millions of U.S. citizens safely visit Mexico each year, including more than 150,000 who cross the border every day for study, tourism or business and at least one million U.S. citizens who live in Mexico. The Mexican government makes a considerable effort to protect U.S. citizens and other visitors to major tourist destinations. Resort areas and tourist destinations in Mexico generally do not see the levels of drug-related violence and crime reported in the border region and in areas along major trafficking routes. Nevertheless, crime and violence are serious problems and can occur anywhere. While most victims of violence are Mexican citizens associated with criminal activity, the security situation poses serious risks for U.S. citizens as well." Nearly all of the document's specific warnings have to do with non-Baja border areas and Mexico City; the U.S. Embassy in Mexico's Security Updates for 2010 to 2011 mention only a few incidents in Baja involving U.S. citizens—one mugging in Cabo San Lucas in October 2010, and an increase in robberies at gunpoint in Tijuana, Rosarito, and on the Mexican side of both Tijuana border crossings. The State Department's "Spring Break–Know Before You Go" publication (under the "International Travel" heading at http://travel.state.gov) warns Baja travelers not of crime, but of riptides on Pacific beaches and buying illegal prescription drugs in Tijuana.

What all this means is that there's no reason to be scared of Los Cabos and Baja. But there's reason to be smart about your travel, especially around Tijuana south to Ensenada. It's not a good idea to wear lots of flashy jewelry or expensive watches, to walk alone on empty streets late at night, to appear visibly intoxicated or, on the coast between Tijuana and Ensenada, to camp outside of guarded campgrounds. Watch yourself at night around the Tijuana/San Ysidro and Otay Mesa border crossings. And although incidents of road crime are rare, it's just that little bit safer to take the *cuota* toll highway to Ensenada than the *libre* freeway. Take the same precautions you would in any U.S. city, and you'll be fine. Should you fall victim to crime, the Ministry of Tourism has set up toll-free numbers to call from the U.S. and Canada (© **866/201-5060**) and Mexico (© **078**), staffed 24 hours daily with English-speaking operators who can coordinate help from the police.

Women traveling alone don't have to take any precautions that men traveling alone wouldn't, but they should expect a certain amount of unsolicited attention that may at times feel threatening. To minimize it, take the lead of the many Mexican women you'll see on their own in Los Cabos and Baja: Dress conservatively, behave responsibly, and greet unwanted advances with a polite "no."

Where you really should watch out, though, is driving. Baja's roads are lined with crosses remembering people who didn't. See "Getting Around: By Car," p. 182.

For what's legal and what's not, see "Drinking & Drug Laws," p. 188, and "Legal Aid," p. 191.

Senior Travel   Mexico is a popular country for retirees. For decades, North Americans have been living indefinitely in Mexico by returning to the border and recrossing with a new tourist permit every 6 months. Mexican immigration officials have caught on, and now limit the maximum time in the country to 6 months within any year. This is to encourage even partial residents to acquire proper documentation.

AIM-Adventures in Mexico, Apdo. Postal 31–70, 45050 Guadalajara, Jal., is a well-written, informative newsletter for prospective retirees. Subscriptions are $29 to the United States.

Sanborn Tours, 2015 S. 10th St., PO Box 936, McAllen, TX 78505-0519 (© **800/395-8482;** www.sanborns.com), offers a "Retire in Mexico" orientation tour.

Smoking   Smoking is banned in all public buildings in Mexico. It's common and tolerated for smokers to puff away in patio areas of restaurants.

Taxes   There's a 15% IVA (Impuesto al Valor Agregado, or value-added tax, pronounced "ee-bah") on goods and services in most of Mexico, and although it's supposed to be included in the posted price, most hotels and restaurants in Los Cabos and Baja add it on top, in keeping with U.S. customs. You may find that upper-end properties quote prices without IVA included, while lower-priced hotels include IVA. Always ask to see a printed price sheet, and always ask if the tax is included. This tax is 10% in Los Cabos; as a port of entry, the towns receive a break on taxes. There is a 5% tax on food and drinks consumed in restaurants that sell alcoholic beverages with an alcohol content of more than 10%; this tax applies whether you drink alcohol or not. Tequila is subject to a 25% tax. Hotels charge the usual 15% IVA, plus a locally administered bed tax of 2% or 3% (in many but not all areas), for a total of 17% or 18%. In Los Cabos, hotels charge the 10% IVA plus 2% room tax.

You'll pay 15% VAT while shopping, but the good news is, you can get it back (minus a processing fee), if you shop at one of the high-end retailers participating in Mexico's TAX-BACK program (www.taxback.com.mx) and fly out of Los Cabos. Keep purchases and receipts separate from the rest of your packed luggage, and present them with your passport and tourist card at the Taxback office at the airport before leaving.

Mexico imposes an exit tax, which usually is applied to your ticket at purchase, on every foreigner leaving the country.

Telephones Mexico's telephone system is slowly but surely catching up with modern times. Every city and town that has telephone access has a three-digit area code (everywhere except for Mexico City, Monterrey, and Guadalajara, whose area codes are two digits). Local numbers have seven digits (except for in Mexico City, Monterrey, and Guadalajara, where local numbers have eight digits). To place a local call, you do not need to dial the area code. Mexico's area codes (*claves*) are listed in the front of telephone directories, as well as in "Area Codes," p. 186. Area codes are listed before all phone numbers in this book; when an establishment has two phone numbers with the same area code, we will only list the area code once.

To call long distance within Mexico, the cheapest way is by using the Ladatel phone booths, into which you insert prepaid cards—available at most pharmacies and convenience stores. Steer clear of calling home from your hotel room, which can cost as much as $10 per minute. Instead, insert a Ladatel card (available in increments of $5, $10, $20, and $50—the $10 card is plenty for two 10-min. calls home) and dial as explained below. For long-distance dialing, you will often see the term "LADA," which is the automatic long-distance service offered by Telmex, Mexico's former telephone monopoly and its largest phone company.

To make a person-to-person or collect call inside Mexico, dial ✆ **020.** You can also call 020 to request the correct area codes for the number and place you are calling.

Many fax numbers are also regular telephone numbers; ask whoever answers for the fax tone *("me da tono de fax, por favor?").* Cellular phones are widely used as an alternative to land lines for small businesses in resort areas and all businesses in smaller communities; they have the same local area codes as their registered users and consist of seven or eight digits just as land lines do. For dialing instructions, read on.

The **country code** for Mexico is **52.**

To call the Baja peninsula from outside Mexico:

1. Dial the international access code: 011 from the U.S.; 00 from the U.K., Ireland, or New Zealand; or 0011 from Australia.
2. Dial the country code 52.
3. Dial the two- or three-digit city code and then the seven-digit number. For example, if you wanted to call the U.S. consulate in Tijuana, the entire number would be 011-52-664-622-7400.

To call the Baja peninsula from inside Mexico: For local calls, dial only the seven-digit number. For long-distance calls within Mexico, dial 01 before dialing the area code and number.

Cellular phone calls: To call a cell number inside the same area code, dial 044 and then the full 10-digit number, including the city code. To dial a cellphone from outside its local area code, dial 045, then the three-digit area code and the seven- or eight-digit number. To dial a Mexican cellphone from the U.S., dial 011-52-1, then the three-digit area code and the seven- or eight-digit number.

To make international calls: To make international calls from Baja, first dial 00 and then the country code (U.S. or Canada 1, U.K. 44, Ireland 353, Australia 61, New Zealand 64). Next you dial the area code and number. For example, if you wanted to call the British Embassy in Washington, D.C., you would dial 00-1-202-588-7800.

For directory assistance: Dial 040 if you're looking for a number inside Mexico, and dial 090 for numbers to all other countries.

For operator assistance: If you need operator assistance in making a call, dial 090 if you're trying to make an international call and 020 if you want to call a number in Mexico.

Toll-free numbers: Numbers beginning with 01-800 within Mexico are toll-free, but calling a 1-800 number in the States or Canada from Mexico is not. It costs the same as any other overseas call. Replace 800 with 877 and it should work.

Time   The state of Baja California Norte—from Tijuana to Guerrero Negro—is on Pacific Standard Time, and Baja California Sur—from south of Guerrero Negro to Los Cabos—is on Mountain Standard Time. Mexico observes daylight saving time. The rest of Mexico observes Central Standard Time.

For help with time translations, and more, download our convenient Travel Tools app for your mobile device. Go to www.frommers.com/go/mobile and click on the Travel Tools icon.

Tipping   Most service employees in Mexico count on tips to make up the majority of their income—especially bellboys and waiters. Tip bellboys the equivalent of $1 per bag; waiters 10% to 15% of the bill, depending on the level of service. In Mexico, it is not customary to tip taxi drivers, unless they are hired by the hour or provide touring or other special services.

For help with tip calculations, currency conversions, and more, download our convenient Travel Tools app for your mobile device. Go to www.frommers.com/go/mobile and click on the Travel Tools icon.

Toilets   You won't find public toilets or "restrooms" on the streets in Los Cabos and Baja, but they can be found in bars, restaurants, bus stations, and service stations. They're usually quite clean and well kept, although it's not uncommon for them to lack seats. A basket next to the bowl is your indication to throw paper and such there and not in the water; to avoid clogging pipes, do as the locals do.

VAT   See "Taxes," above.

Visas   Visitors from the U.S., Canada, Europe, Australia, and New Zealand don't need visas for tourist stays of less than 180 days. Other nationalities should check with the **Instituto Nacional de Migración** online at www.inm.gob.mx. There's a helpful online flow chart (in easily decipherable Spanish) of who needs what.

Visitor Information   The **Mexico Tourism Board** (℅ **800/446-3942;** www.visit mexico.com) is an excellent source for general information; you can request brochures and get answers to the most common questions from the well-trained, knowledgeable staff. The tourism boards of **Baja California** (℅ **664/682-3367;** www.discoverbaja california.com) and **Baja California Sur** (℅ **612/124-0100;** www.explorebajasur.com) have more Baja-specific information.

In addition to city-specific information included in the earlier chapters of this book, the following websites are useful: www.allaboutcabo.com, www.bajaquest.com, www.baja insider.com, and www.rozinlapaz.com.

Water   While water in Los Cabos and Baja is generally cleaner and safer than in other destinations in Mexico, locals don't drink the tap water and you shouldn't, either. Purified water is cheap and readily available in any supermarket, convenience store, or gas station. Any water or ice you're served in hotels or restaurants will be purified, but if you have any doubts, ask *"es agua purificada?"* See "Health," p. 189.

Wi-Fi   See "Internet & Wi-Fi," earlier in this section.

Women Travelers   See "Safety," above.

AIRLINE WEBSITES

MAJOR AIRLINES

Aereo Calafia
www.aereocalafia.com

Aereo Servicios Guerrero
www.aereoserviciosguerrero.com.mx

Aeroméxico
www.aeromexico.com

Air Canada
www.aircanada.com

Alaska Airlines
www.alaskaair.com

Allegiant Air
www.allegiantair.com

American Airlines
www.aa.com

British Airways
www.britishairways.com

Continental
www.continental.com

Delta
www.delta.com

Frontier
www.frontierairlines.com

Hawaiian Airlines
www.hawaiianair.com

Sun Country Airlines
www.suncountry.com

United Airlines
www.united.com

US Airways
www.usairways.com

Virgin America
www.virginamerica.com

BUDGET AIRLINES

Interjet
www.interjet.com.mx

JetBlue Airways
www.jetblue.com

Southwest Airlines
www.southwest.com

VivaAerobus.com
www.vivaaerobus.com

Volaris
www.volaris.com

WestJet
www.westjet.com

SURVIVAL SPANISH

BASIC VOCABULARY

Most Mexicans are very patient with foreigners who try to speak their language; it helps a lot to know a few basic phrases. We've included simple phrases for expressing basic needs, followed by some common menu items.

English-Spanish Phrases

BASIC PHRASES

English	Spanish	Pronunciation
Good day	**Buen día**	bwehn *dee*-ah
Good morning	**Buenos días**	*bweh*-nohss *dee*-ahss
How are you?	**¿Cómo está?**	*koh*-moh ehss-*tah?*
Very well	**Muy bien**	mwee byehn
Thank you	**Gracias**	*grah*-syahss
You're welcome	**De nada**	deh *nah*-dah
Goodbye	**Adiós**	ah-*dyohss*
Please	**Por favor**	pohr fah-*vohr*
Yes	**Sí**	see
No	**No**	noh
Excuse me	**Perdóneme**	pehr-*doh*-neh-meh
Give me	**Déme**	*deh*-meh
Where is . . .?	**¿Dónde está . . .?**	*dohn*-deh ehss-*tah?*
the station?	**la estación?**	lah ehss-tah-*syohn*
a hotel?	**un hotel?**	oon oh-*tehl*
a gas station?	**una gasolinera?**	*oo*-nah gah-soh-lee-*neh*-rah
a restaurant?	**un restaurante?**	oon res-tow-*rahn*-teh
the bathroom?	**el baño?**	el *bah*-nyoh
a good doctor?	**un buen medico?**	oon bwehn *meh*-dee-coh
the road to . . .?	**el camino a/hacia . . .?**	el cah-*mee*-noh ah/*ah*-syah
To the right	**A la derecha**	ah lah deh-*reh*-chah
To the left	**A la izquierda**	ah lah ees-*kyehr*-dah
Straight ahead	**Derecho**	deh-*reh*-choh
I would like . . .	**Quisiera . . .**	key-*syeh*-rah

English	Spanish	Pronunciation
I want . . .	**Quiero . . .**	*kyeh*-roh
to eat.	**comer.**	koh-*mehr*
a room.	**una habitación.**	oo-nah ah-bee-tah-*syohn*
Do you have . . .?	**¿Tiene usted . . .?**	tyeh-neh oo-*sted*?
a book?	**un libro?**	oon *lee*-broh
a dictionary?	**un diccionario?**	oon deek-syow-*nah*-ryo
a pen?	**una pluma?**	oon ah *ploo*-mah
How much is it?	**¿Cuánto cuesta?**	*kwahn*-toh *kwehss*-tah?
When?	**¿Cuándo?**	*kwahn*-doh?
What?	**¿Qué?**	keh?
There is (Is there . . .?)	**(¿)Hay (. . .?)**	eye?
What is there?	**¿Qué hay?**	keh eye?
Yesterday	**Ayer**	ah-*yer*
Today	**Hoy**	oy
Tomorrow	**Mañana**	mah-*nyah*-nah
Good	**Bueno**	*bweh*-noh
Bad	**Malo**	*mah*-loh
Better (best)	**(Lo) Mejor**	(loh) meh-*hohr*
More	**Más**	mahs
Less	**Menos**	*meh*-nohss
Enough	**Bastante**	bahs-*tahn*-tay
No smoking	**Se prohibe fumar**	seh proh-ee-beh foo-*mahr*
Postcard	**Tarjeta postal**	tar-*heh*-ta pohs-*tahl*
Insect repellent	**Repelente contra insectos**	reh-peh-*lehn*-te *cohn*-trah een-*sehk*-tos

MORE USEFUL PHRASES

English	Spanish	Pronunciation
Do you speak English?	**¿Habla usted inglés?**	*ah*-blah oo-*sted* een-*glehs*?
Is there anyone here who speaks English?	**¿Hay alguien aquí que hable inglés?**	eye *ahl*-gyehn ah-*kee* keh *ah*-bleh een-*glehs*?
I speak a little Spanish.	**Hablo un poco de español.**	*ah*-bloh oon *poh*-koh deh ehss-pah-*nyohl*
I don't understand Spanish very well.	**No (lo) entiendo muy bien el español.**	noh (loh) ehn-*tyehn*-doh mwee byehn el ehss-pah-*nyohl*
The meal is good.	**La comida está buena.**	lah koh-*mee*-dah eh-stah *bweh*-nah
What time is it?	**¿Qué hora es?**	keh *oh*-rah ehss?
May I see your menu?	**¿Puedo ver el menú (la carta)?**	*pueh*-do vehr el meh-*noo* (lah *car*-tah)?
The check, please.	**La cuenta, por favor.**	lah *quehn*-tah pohr fa-*vorh*

English	Spanish	Pronunciation
What do I owe you?	**¿Cuánto le debo?**	*kwahn*-toh leh *deh*-boh?
What did you say?	**¿Mande?** (formal)	*mahn*-deh?
	¿Cómo? (informal)	*koh*-moh?
I want (to see) . . .	**Quiero (ver) . . .**	*kyeh*-roh (vehr)
a room . . .	**un cuarto** or **una habitación . . .**	oon *kwar*-toh, *oo*-nah ah-bee-tah-*syohn*
for two persons.	**para dos personas.**	*pah*-rah dohss pehr-*soh*-nahs
with (without) bathroom.	**con (sin) baño.**	kohn (seen) *bah*-nyoh
We are staying here only . . .	**Nos quedamos aquí solamente . . .**	nohs keh-*dah*-mohss ah-*kee* soh-lah-*mehn*-teh
1 night.	**una noche.**	*oo*-nah *noh*-cheh
1 week.	**una semana.**	*oo*-nah seh-*mah*-nah
We are leaving . . .	**Partimos (Salimos) . . .**	pahr-*tee*-mohss (sah-*lee*-mohss)
tomorrow.	**mañana.**	mah-*nya*-nah
Do you accept . . .?	**¿Acepta usted . . .?**	ah-*sehp*-tah oo-*sted*
traveler's checks?	**cheques de viajero?**	*cheh*-kehss deh byah-*heh*-roh?
Is there a laundromat . . .?	**¿Hay una lavandería . . .?**	eye *oo*-nah lah-*vahn*-deh-*ree*-ah
near here?	**cerca de aquí?**	*sehr*-kah deh ah-*kee*
Please send these clothes to the laundry.	**Hágame el favor de mandar esta ropa a la lavandería.**	ah-*gah*-meh el fah-*vohr* deh mahn-*dahr* ehss-tah roh-pah a lah lah-*vahn*-deh-*ree*-ah

NUMBERS

English	Spanish
one	**uno** (*oo*-noh)
two	**dos** (dohss)
three	**tres** (trehss)
four	**cuatro** (*kwah*-troh)
five	**cinco** (*seen*-koh)
six	**seis** (sayss)
seven	**siete** (*syeh*-teh)
eight	**ocho** (*oh*-choh)
nine	**nueve** (*nweh*-beh)
ten	**diez** (dyess)
eleven	**once** (*ohn*-seh)
twelve	**doce** (*doh*-seh)
thirteen	**trece** (*treh*-seh)
fourteen	**catorce** (kah-*tohr*-seh)
fifteen	**quince** (*keen*-seh)
sixteen	**dieciseis** (dyess-ee-*sayss*)

English	Spanish
seventeen	**diecisiete** (dyess-ee-*syeh*-teh)
eighteen	**dieciocho** (dyess-ee-*oh*-choh)
nineteen	**diecinueve** (dyess-ee-*nweh*-beh)
twenty	**veinte** (*bayn*-teh)
thirty	**treinta** (*trayn*-tah)
forty	**cuarenta** (kwah-*ren*-tah)
fifty	**cincuenta** (seen-*kwen*-tah)
sixty	**sesenta** (seh-*sehn*-tah)
seventy	**setenta** (seh-*tehn*-tah)
eighty	**ochenta** (oh-*chehn*-tah)
ninety	**noventa** (noh-*behn*-tah)
one hundred	**cien** (syehn)
two hundred	**doscientos** (do-*syehn*-tohs)
five hundred	**quinientos** (kee-*nyehn*-tohs)
one thousand	**mil** (meel)

TRANSPORTATION TERMS

English	Spanish	Pronunciation
Airport	**Aeropuerto**	ah-eh-roh-*pwehr*-toh
Flight	**Vuelo**	*bweh*-loh
Car Rental	**Arrendadora de autos**	ah-rehn-da-*doh*-rah deh *ow*-tohs
Bus	**Autobús**	ow-toh-*boos*
Bus or truck	**Camión**	ka-*myohn*
Lane	**Carril**	kah-*reel*
Direct	**Directo**	dee-*rehk*-toh
Baggage (claim area)	**Equipajes**	eh-kee-*pah*-hehss
Intercity	**Foraneo**	foh-rah-*neh*-oh
Luggage storage area	**Guarda equipaje**	*gwar*-dah eh-kee-*pah*-heh
Arrival gates	**Llegadas**	yeh-*gah*-dahss
Originates at this station	**Local**	loh-*kahl*
Originates elsewhere	**De paso**	deh *pah*-soh
Stops if seats available	**Para si hay lugares**	*pah*-rah see eye loo-*gah*-rehs
First class	**Clase primera**	*klah*-seh pree-*meh*-rah
Second class	**Segunda clase**	seh-*goon*-dah *klah*-seh
Nonstop	**Sin escala**	seen ess-*kah*-lah
Baggage claim area	**Reclamo de equipajes**	*reh*-klah-moh deh eh-kee-*pah*-hehs
Waiting room	**Sala de espera**	*sah*-lah deh ehss-*peh*-rah
Toilets	**Sanitarios**	sah-nee-*tah*-ryohss
Ticket window	**Taquilla**	tah-*kee*-yah

SURVIVAL SPANISH | Basic Vocabulary

MEXICAN CUISINE

For more on Baja's unique cuisine, see "Eating & Drinking in Los Cabos & Baja," in chapter 2.

Mealtimes

MORNING The morning meal, known as *el desayuno,* runs the gamut from coffee and sweet bread to a substantial home run of eggs, beans, tortillas, bread, fruit, juice, and maybe even *pozole* soup or tacos. It can be eaten early or late and is always a sure bet in Mexico. In Baja, U.S.-style pancakes are widely available, served with butter and sugar syrup or honey. Don't miss out on succulent, ripe tropical fruit, and of course you can't go wrong with Mexican egg dishes.

MIDAFTERNOON The main meal of the day, known as *la comida* (or *almuerzo*), is eaten between 2 and 4pm. Some stores and businesses still close for the meal so people can eat at home with their families, but in places like Los Cabos, where tourists are king, the traditional *comida* may be cut short. The first course is the *sopa,* which can be either soup (*caldo*) or rice (*sopa de arroz*) or both; then comes the main course, usually a meat or fish dish prepared in some kind of sauce and served with beans; at the end comes a token, small dessert.

EVENING Between 8 and 10pm, most Mexicans have a light meal, *la cena.* If eaten at home, it is something like a sandwich, bread and jam, or perhaps a couple of tacos made from some of the day's leftovers. At restaurants, the most common thing to eat is *antojitos* (literally, "little cravings"), a general label for light fare. *Antojitos* include tostadas, tamales, tacos, and simple enchiladas, and are big hits with travelers. Large restaurants offer complete meals as well. In Baja, popular *antojitos* include *menudo* (a thick soup of cows' feet and stomachs, seasoned with chiles, oregano, and chopped onion), *huaraches* (a flat, thick oval-shaped tortilla, topped with fried meat and chiles), and *chalupas* (a crisp whole tortilla, topped with beans, meat, and other toppings).

Dining Out

At a sit-down restaurant, it's considered polite service to clear plates, glasses, and bottles from the table the very instant you're finished with them, and sometimes before. Waiters will ask "*puedo retirar?*;" a polite "*todavia no*" will send them packing.

In Mexico, you need to ask for your check; it is generally considered inhospitable to present a check to someone who hasn't requested it. If you're in a hurry to get somewhere, ask for the check when your food arrives. To summon the waiter, wave or raise your hand, but don't motion with your index finger, which is a demeaning gesture that may even cause the waiter to ignore you. Or if it's the check you want, you can motion to the waiter from across the room using the universal pretend-you're-rewriting gesture.

Tip 10% to 15% in restaurants, not at all in *taquerías.* Many restaurants in Baja include a service charge or automatic tip—check your bill.

Dining Terminology

MEALS
desayuno Breakfast.
comida Main meal of the day, taken in the afternoon.
cena Supper.

COURSES

botana A small serving of food that accompanies a beer or drink, usually served free of charge.

entrada Appetizer.

sopa Soup course. (Not necessarily a soup—it can be a dish of rice or noodles, called *sopa seca* [dry soup].)

ensalada Salad.

plato fuerte Main course.

postre Dessert.

comida corrida Inexpensive daily special usually consisting of three courses.

menú del día Same as *comida corrida.*

DEGREE OF DONENESS

término un cuarto Rare, literally means one-fourth.

término medio Medium rare, one-half.

término tres cuartos Medium, three-fourths.

bien cocido Well-done.

Note: Keep in mind, when ordering a steak, that *medio* does not mean "medium."

MISCELLANEOUS RESTAURANT TERMINOLOGY

cucharra Spoon.

cuchillo Knife.

la cuenta The bill.

plato Plate.

plato hondo Bowl.

propina Tip.

servilleta Napkin.

tenedor Fork.

vaso Glass.

IVA Value-added tax.

fonda Strictly speaking, a food stall in the market or street, but now used in a loose or nostalgic sense to designate an informal restaurant.

Menu Vocabulary

achiote Small red seed of the *annatto* tree.

achiote preparado A Yucatecan-prepared paste made of ground *achiote,* wheat and corn flour, cumin, cinnamon, salt, onion, garlic, and oregano.

agua fresca Fruit-flavored water, usually watermelon, cantaloupe, chia seed with lemon, hibiscus flower, rice, or ground melon-seed mixture.

ajillo Garlic sauce, often served with fish in Baja; a variety is *mojo de ajo.*

antojito Typical Mexican supper foods usually made with *masa* or tortillas and having a filling or topping such as sausage, cheese, beans, and onions; includes such things as tacos, tostadas, *sopes,* and *garnachas.* Often served as appetizers or snacks.

atole A thick, lightly sweet, hot drink made with finely ground corn and usually flavored with vanilla, pecan, strawberry, pineapple, lemon, or chocolate.

botana An appetizer.

buñuelos Round, thin, deep-fried crispy fritters dipped in sugar.

burrito A rolled flour tortilla filled with beans and sometimes meat or eggs, served with table salsas, onion, and chiles. Much smaller than its U.S. counterpart!

callos   Scallops, sometimes found alongside *almejas* and *ceviche* at Baja mariscos stands.

camarones   Shrimp, served in tacos or by themselves.

carnitas   Pork deep-cooked (not fried) in lard and then simmered and served with corn tortillas for tacos.

ceviche   Fresh raw seafood marinated in fresh lime juice and garnished with chopped tomatoes, onions, chiles, and sometimes cilantro. Often served with tortilla chips (*totopos*).

chayote   A vegetable pear or mirliton, a type of spiny squash boiled and served as an accompaniment to meat dishes or to flavor soups and broths.

chilaquiles   A favorite Mexican breakfast dish of tortilla chips cooked in *salsa verde* or *salsa roja*, topped with sour cream and accompanied by chicken, beef, or eggs, and a side of beans.

chiles en nogada   Poblano peppers stuffed with a mixture of ground pork and beef, spices, fruit, raisins, and almonds. They're traditionally served cool or at room temperature, covered in walnut-cream sauce, and sprinkled with pomegranate seeds. Because this dish highlights the colors of the Mexican flag—red, white, and green—chiles en nogada are Mexico's official Independence Day dish.

chiles rellenos   Usually poblano peppers stuffed with cheese, potatoes, or spicy ground meat with raisins, rolled in a batter, and fried.

churro   Tube-shaped, breadlike fritter, dipped in sugar and sometimes filled with *cajeta* (goat-milk-based caramel) or chocolate.

cochinita pibil   Pork wrapped in banana leaves, pit-baked in a *pibil* sauce of *achiote,* sour orange, and spices; most common in the Yucatán.

damiana   The small yellow flower, indigenous to Baja, known for its aphrodisiacal, fertility-enhancing properties. Liqueur of the same name, made from the blossoms, is served on ice after dinner or as a secret ingredient in margaritas.

enchilada   A lightly fried tortilla dipped in sauce, usually filled with chicken or white cheese, sometimes topped with mole (*enchiladas rojas* or *de mole*); tomato sauce and sour cream (*enchiladas suizas*—Swiss enchiladas); covered in a green sauce (*enchiladas verdes*); or topped with onions, sour cream, and guacamole (*enchiladas potosinas*).

empanadas   Fried or baked dough packets stuffed with a variety of fillings, from fish or meat to chocolate.

frijoles refritos   Boiled pinto beans, mashed and cooked with lard.

garnachas   A thickish small circle of fried *masa* with pinched sides, topped with pork or chicken, onions, and avocado, or sometimes chopped potatoes and tomatoes.

gorditas   Thick, fried corn tortillas, slit and stuffed with choice of cheese, beans, beef, or chicken, with or without lettuce, tomato, and onion garnish.

horchata   Refreshing lightly sweetened drink made of ground rice or melon seeds, ground almonds, and cinnamon.

huachinango   Red snapper, often served whole, head-on, and accompanied by rice and vegetables.

huevos mexicanos   Scrambled eggs with chopped onions, hot green peppers, and tomatoes.

huitlacoche   Sometimes spelled "cuitlacoche." A mushroom-flavored black fungus that appears on corn in the rainy season; considered a delicacy.

langosta   Pacific spiny lobster, served in Puerto Nuevo with beans and tortillas.

limonada   Refreshing made-to-order drink of bottled water and lime juice; its cousin *naranjada*, with orange juice, is also widely available.

machaca   Dried, spiced, shredded beef, often served in tacos or burritos. Very popular in Baja.

manchamantel   Translated, means "tablecloth stainer." It's a stew of chicken or pork with chiles, tomatoes, pineapple, bananas, and jicama.

masa   Ground corn soaked in lime, it's the basis for tamales, corn tortillas, and soups.

mojarra   Tilapia, usually served as a filet in sauces including *ajillo* and *Veracruzana*, baked with tomatoes and onions.

pan de muerto   Sweet bread made around the Days of the Dead (Nov 1–2) in the form of mummies or dolls, or round with bone designs.

pan dulce   Lightly sweetened bread in many configurations, usually served at breakfast or bought in any bakery.

papadzules   Tortillas stuffed with hard-boiled eggs and seeds (pumpkin or sunflower) in a tomato sauce.

pibil   Pit-baked pork or chicken in a sauce of tomato, onion, mild red pepper, cilantro, and vinegar.

pipián   A sauce made with ground pumpkinseeds, nuts, and mild peppers.

pozole   A pre-Columbian-era soup made of hominy, meat, chile, and other seasonings. Often served for breakfast with garnishes ranging from cilantro to radishes.

pulque   A drink made of fermented juice of the maguey plant.

pulpo   Octopus, often served in a stew.

quesadilla   Corn or flour tortillas stuffed with melted white cheese and lightly fried.

queso relleno   Translated as "stuffed cheese," this dish consists of a mild yellow cheese stuffed with minced meat and spices; it's a Yucatecan specialty.

rompope   Delicious Mexican eggnog, invented in Puebla, made with eggs, vanilla, sugar, and rum.

salsa verde   An uncooked sauce using the green tomatillo puréed with spicy or mild hot peppers, onions, garlic, and cilantro.

sopa de flor de calabaza   A soup made of chopped squash or pumpkin blossoms.

sopa de lima   A tangy soup made with chicken broth and accented with fresh lime.

sopa de tortilla   A traditional chicken broth–based soup, seasoned with chiles, tomatoes, onion, and garlic, served with crispy fried strips of corn tortillas. Also called *sopa azteca*.

sope   Pronounced "*soh*-peh." An *antojito* similar to a *garnacha* but spread with refried beans and topped with crumbled cheese and onions.

tacos al pastor   Thin slices of flavored pork roasted on a revolving cylinder dripping with onion slices and the juice of fresh pineapple slices. Served in small corn tortillas, it's topped with chopped onion and cilantro.

tamal   Often incorrectly called a tamale (*tamal* is singular; *tamales* is plural), this dish consists of a meat or sweet filling rolled with fresh *masa* wrapped in a corn husk or banana leaf and steamed.

tequila   Distilled alcohol produced from the *A. tequilana* species of agave (known as Blue Weber agave) in and around the area of Tequila, in the state of Jalisco. Mezcal, by contrast, comes from various parts of Mexico and from different varieties of agave and is considered less sophisticated than tequila (and more easily detected on the drinker's breath).

tomatillo Small, tart green tomatoes that come wrapped in delicate, sticky husks. The base for most green salsas, and also used fresh in some salads.

torta A sandwich, usually on *bolillo* bread, typically with sliced avocado, onions, tomatoes, and a choice of meat and often cheese.

tostada Large, crispy flavored corn tortilla topped with chopped seafood, tomatoes, and avocado.

totopos Fried tortilla chips.

Index

See also Accommodations and
Restaurant indexes, below.

General Index